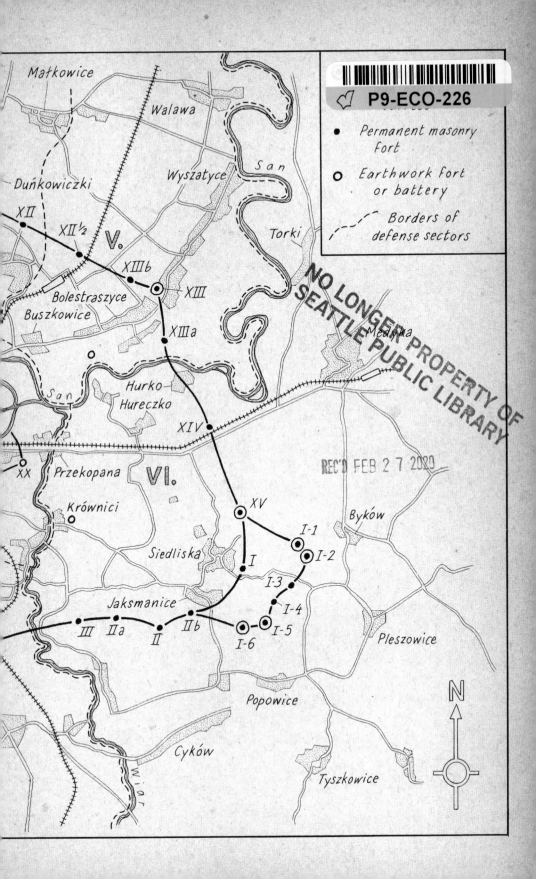

Małkowice

Walawa

Duńkowiczki

Wyszatyce

San

Torki

XII

XII½

V.

XIIIb

XIII

XIIIa

Bolestraszyce

Buszkowice

San

Hurko

Hureczko

Medyka

XIV

XX

Przekopana

VI.

Krównici

XV

Byków

Siedliska

I-1

I-2

I

I-3

Jaksmanice

I-4

III   IIa   II   IIb

I-6   I-5

Pleszowice

Popowice

Cyków

Tyszkowice

• Permanent masonry fort

○ Earthwork fort or battery

- - - Borders of defense sectors

N

PRAISE FOR *THE FORTRESS*

"*The Fortress* is based on extraordinarily impressive research, yet is also vivid, imaginative, and humane. It recaptures one of the most terrible episodes in a terrible war, which—as Watson rightly argues—presaged even greater horrors to come."

 —David Stevenson, London School of Economics and Political Science

"There is a great deal more to this book than an account of the longest siege of the Great War, one that stalled the Russian advance and saved the Central Powers from defeat in 1914. It reveals, in microcosm, every-thing that was mad, bad, and dangerous about the Austro-Hungarian Empire in its final stages. . . . This is a hugely enjoyable book that anyone seeking to make sense of the dark side of twentieth-century Europe would do well to read."

 —Adam Zamoyski, *Literary Review*

"Przemyśl, Habsurg Austria's easternmost fortress, lay in Galicia, a flat borderland between the turbulent German, Austrian, and Russian em-pires. Watson reconstructs the Russian siege in engrossing detail, and also proves that the eastern 'bloodlands' later ravaged by the Nazis and Soviets had already been desolated once before—during World War I and its chaotic aftermath, when the Russians and Austro-Hungarians, desperate to hold Galicia, taught Hitler and Stalin how to weaken and destroy unwanted peoples like the Jews or Ukrainians."

 —Geoffrey Wawro, author of *The Austro-Prussian War* and
  *A Mad Catastrophe: The Outbreak of World War I and the
  Collapse of the Habsburg Empire*

"Przemyśl is best known for its challenges to orthography and pronunciation. But Watson contextualizes the history of this remote Habsburg fortress-city from its beginnings as a strategic pivot to its development as a focal point for overlapping imperial and nationalist aspirations. The defining event was the great siege of 1914, whose everyday routines and long-term consequences Watson presents with a verve and clarity making this a must read for students of the Great War in the east."

    —Dennis Showalter, professor emeritus, Colorado College

"[*The Fortress*] is excellent history, a marvelously readable, though tragic, story of its time and of how the clock can be made to turn backwards under siege conditions; and in its account of the Habsburg commanders' unshakable vanity, philandering, and cockiness it has plenty of modern resonances as a parable of arrogant exceptionalism, imperial conceit, and perilous isolationism."

    —Julian Evans, *Daily Telegraph* (UK)

THE
FORTRESS

ALSO BY ALEXANDER WATSON

Ring of Steel: Germany and Austria-Hungary in World War I

*Enduring the Great War: Combat, Morale and
Collapse in the German and British Armies, 1914–1918*

THE
FORTRESS

THE SIEGE OF PRZEMYŚL AND THE
MAKING OF EUROPE'S BLOODLANDS

ALEXANDER WATSON

BASIC BOOKS

New York

Basic Books
Hachette Book Group
1290 Avenue of the Americas, New York, NY 10104
www.basicbooks.com

Printed in the United States of America

First Edition: February 2020

Published by Basic Books, an imprint of Perseus Books, LLC, a subsidiary of Hachette Book Group, Inc. The Basic Books name and logo is a trademark of the Hachette Book Group.

The Hachette Speakers Bureau provides a wide range of authors for speaking events. To find out more, go to www.hachettespeakersbureau.com or call (866) 376-6591.

The publisher is not responsible for websites (or their content) that are not owned by the publisher.

Print book interior design by Trish Wilkinson.

Library of Congress Cataloging-in-Publication Data has been applied for.

ISBNs: 978-1-5416-9730-0 (hardcover), 978-15416-9732-4 (ebook)

LSC-C

10 9 8 7 6 5 4 3 2 1

For Tim

CONTENTS

CONTENTS

INSERT ILLUSTRATIONS

1. General Franz Conrad von Hötzendorf, chief of the Habsburg General Staff.
2. General Hermann Kusmanek von Burgneustädten, commander of the Fortress of Przemyśl.
3. The eighteenth-century clock tower of Przemyśl, with "Plac na Bramie" (Place of the City Gate) below it.
4. The Old Synagogue in Przemyśl's Jewish Quarter.
5. View over Przemyśl looking northeast onto the railway bridge and up the San River.
6. The main marketplace of Przemyśl.
7. "Russophiles" under arrest in Przemyśl.
8. The village of Żurawica, lying 5 kilometers (about 3 miles) north of Przemyśl, on fire.
9. A Ruthenian Greek Catholic pastor hanged by Habsburg soldiers.
10. The Habsburg Army retreats through Przemyśl in mid-September 1914.
11. Destitute villagers in the rural district of Przemyśl.
12. The "heroes" of Przemyśl defending the Fortress.
13. The interval lines closing the gaps between the forts.

14. Russian attackers storm the Fortress of Przemyśl, October 5–8, 1914.

15. The ghastly ditch in front of Fort I/1 early on the morning of October 7, 1914.

16. Heir to the Austro-Hungarian throne, Archduke Karl, tours Przemyśl's fortifications with Kusmanek on November 1, 1914.

17. A "flyer postcard" flown out of the besieged Fortress.

18. Bomb damage inflicted on a Przemyśl house by Russian aircraft, 1914/1915.

19. Fortress observation balloon.

20. Fortress airman.

21. Military concert during the second siege of Przemyśl.

22. Newspaper boys and girls during the second siege of Przemyśl.

23. Soup kitchen for civilians during the second siege of Przemyśl.

24. Slaughterhouse full of horse carcasses.

25. The destruction of the forts in the early hours of March 22, 1915.

26. The 3rd May Road Bridge, with one end lying in the River San after being mined on March 22, 1915.

27. A Cossack riding up Przemyśl's Mickiewicz Street on March 23, 1915.

28. The expulsion of Przemyśl's Jews at the end of April or early May 1915.

29. The Tsar and Grand Duke Nikolai Nikolaevich visit Fort I/1 on April 24, 1915.

30. Victorious German troops parade through Przemyśl, June 6, 1915.

TEXT ILLUSTRATIONS

MAPS

1. Eastern Front, August 1914.
2. The home bases of Fortress Przemyśl's garrison throughout Austria-Hungary.
3. The Galician Bloodlands.
4. The Fortress of Przemyśl, 1914.

ACKNOWLEDGMENTS

This book has been—though much of the material is extremely dark—a great joy to write. My first thanks are to my editors, Lara Heimert at Basic Books and Simon Winder at Penguin Books, for knowing that, though a place may have more consonants in its name than many people feel right or sensible, it can still be extremely important and possess a fascinating story. I am immensely grateful to them for going over my manuscript so painstakingly, for all their suggestions and improvements, and for their huge enthusiasm throughout the project. This book is all the better for it.

I owe great thanks, too, to a number of people in or at least with very close connections to the city of Przemyśl. Dr. Tomasz Pudłocki, the chief editor of the *Rocznik Przemyski*—the scholarly journal dedicated to the city—became a good friend during the project. I am grateful for his generosity in sharing his contacts with me and in sending literature and giving advice. I am also extremely grateful to Tomasz Idzikowski, who has written the definitive works on the construction and technical organization of the Habsburg Fortress. I benefited hugely from his deep knowledge, relayed both in his many publications and through our long email exchanges. The vivid drawings of Przemyśl's forts as they would have looked in 1914 and the ground plans that appear in this book are all accurate, and are all his painstaking work. I owe him special thanks for his permission to republish them here.

The Muzeum Narodowe Ziemi Przemyskiej (National Museum of Przemyśl Land) in the city was especially helpful in my research. I would particularly like to thank the former director of its Historical Section, Dr. Grzegorz Szopa, for allowing me access to the invaluable papers of Lieutenant-Colonel Elek Molnár, commander of Honvéd Infantry Regiment 8. At the end of Przemyśl's siege in March 1915, Molnár defied orders to burn all documentation and instead hid military notes, orders, a diary, and some unique Habsburg trench newspapers with jokes and cartoons under the floorboards of his billet, where they were eventually discovered in 1966. I also want to acknowledge Dr. Szopa's particular kindness in sharing with me a section of his own grandfather's memoir recounting the siege of Przemyśl. In addition, I am very grateful to the Historical Section's current director, Dr. Lucjan Fac, for his generosity in seeking out and sending me photographs from the museum's collection. Some of these appear with the museum's permission in this book. Lastly, my thanks to Karol Kicman, who as a guide for the Przemyśl branch of the Polskie Towarzystwo Turystyczno-Krajoznawcze (the Polish Tourist and Sightseeing Society), along with his father-in-law, took me on a fantastic tour around the ruins of Przemyśl's forts. I learned a lot and caught their enthusiasm for the place's history.

One of the privileges of working in academia is membership of an international community full of knowledgeable people eager to help. I have racked up several debts. Above all, I thank Dr. John E. Fahey of the United States Military Academy at West Point for generously sharing his excellent doctoral thesis on imperial and local government in Przemyśl, Galicia, 1867–1939. I learned much and am looking forward to seeing the final manuscript in print. I am grateful to Dr. Anton Holzer in Vienna for his assistance in locating the photograph of the hanging priest, which was first published in his book *Das Lächeln der Henker* (Primus, 2008). Professor Serhy Yekelchyk at the University of Victoria was extraordinarily kind in devoting time and resources to help locate photographs from Przemyśl's Russian occupation. I received valuable feedback from seminar audiences at Oxford University, Sandhurst, University College Dublin, the Centre for Urban History of East Central Europe in Lviv, and the Imre Kertész Kolleg in Jena. I am especially grateful to my department at Goldsmiths, University of London. I am extremely lucky to have such excellent and supportive colleagues.

Historical research would be impossible without dedicated archivists and librarians. This book is based on research in ten archives—the Archiwum Główne Akt Dawnych in Warsaw, the Archiwum Państwowe in Przemyśl, the archive of the Muzeum Narodowe Ziemi Przemyskiej, the Archiwum Narodowe in Cracow, the Hadtörténelmi Levéltár in Budapest, the Kriegsarchiv and Allgemeines Verwaltungsarchiv in Vienna, the Central Archives for the History of Jewish People in Jerusalem, the Tsentral'nyi derzhavnyi istorychnyi arkhiv Ukrainy u L'vovi in Lviv, and the National Archives in London—as well as in the Biblioteka Narodowa in Warsaw, the Biblioteka Jagiellońska in Cracow, the British Library in London, and the University Library in Cambridge. I am enormously grateful to them all. I also received much help from collections remotely. In particular, I should mention Director Josef Žikeš and Viera Žižková of the Central Military Archives–Military Historical Archives in Prague (Vojenský ústřední archive–Vojenský historický archiv Praha), and Marek Król in Przemyśl. My thanks to both for permitting me to use their photographs. Special thanks also to the staff of the Kriegsarchiv in Vienna and the Archiwum Państwowe in Przemyśl, both for all the assistance I received while researching there and for the speed and efficiency with which they provided images from Przemyśl's siege. Again, I am grateful for permission to publish.

Many others also contributed to the making of this book. I owe special gratitude to two outstanding scholars for their sterling assistance with the research: Dr. Tamás Révész helped me with Hungarian sources, and Eugene Polyakov with Ukrainian- and

Russian-language material. I am extremely grateful to the teams at Penguin and Basic Books, particularly Kelly Lenkevich, who oversaw the production process, Anna Hervé, and Katie Lambright. I thank Kathy Streckfus, Roger Labrie, and David Watson for their painstaking copyediting and Neil Gower for drawing the beautiful map of Przemyśl and its ring of forts. Penguin has been extremely generous in permitting me to publish this and the book's other excellent maps here. Throughout the writing and production, it has been hugely helpful to have my agent, Clare Alexander, as a source of advice and support.

My final, most heartfelt thanks are to my family. My father-in-law, Alfred, and I had the idea for this book during a walk in an Upper Silesian forest, and I am grateful to him for the inspiration. My own father, Henry, whom I miss every day, and my mother, Susan, have always been models to follow and pillars of strength, wisdom, and love. To them and to all around us, especially to Jana, and to Peter, Wiesia, Alfred, Judy, Tim, Lesley, John, Julia, Sean, Andrew, Erin, Caley, Lindsey, Finlay, Dawn, Marysia, Wojtek, Meng, Anna, Duncan, James, and Emma, thank you for your love. To my wife, Ania, and to my daughter, Maria, and my son, Henry, I love you more than I can say. Thank you for making me smile and for watching out for me and supporting me in bad times and in good.

This book is dedicated to my wonderful brother, Tim, in deep admiration, and with all my love.

Map 1. Eastern Front, August 1914.

N

Fortress Artillery
FstAR 1 – Vienna
FstAR 3 – Leitmeritz and Lwów
FstAR 6 – Pozsony (today Bratislava)
FstAB 3 – Pozsony (today Bratislava)
FstAB 9 – Cracow
FstAB 10 – Graz

111th Landsturm Infantry Brigade
LstIR 17 – Rzeszów
LstIR 18 – Przemyśl
III/Lst IR 18 – Czerteż
LstIR 33 – Stryj
LstIR 34 – Jarosław
Res. Squadron Uhlan Rgt. 11 – Leitmeritz (today Litoměřice)

108th Landsturm Infantry Brigade
LstIR 21 – St Pölten
LstIR II – Bozen
2 Squadron, Mounted Tyrolean Rifles – Innsbruck

Leitmeritz   Jungbunzlau
Prague   SILESIA
BOHEMIA   Opava
MORAVIA
Brno
LOWER
UPPER   St Pölten   Vienna
AUSTRIA   Linz   AUSTRIA   Poszony
Salzburg
VORARLBERG
Bregenz   SALZBURG   STYRIA
Innsbruck   Graz
TYROL   CARINTHIA
Bozen   Klagenfurt
Ljubljana
CARNIOLA   Zagreb
Trieste   CROATIA
ISTRIA

HIR = Honvéd Infantry Regiment
LdwIR = Landwehr Infantry Regiment
LdstIR = Landsturm Infantry Regiment
FstAR = Fortress Artillery Regiment
FstAB = Fortress Artillery Battalion
Underlined places are the home bases / concentration points for Fortress garrison units

BOSNIA
HERZEGOVINA
Sarajevo
DALMATIA
Split

The Home Bases of Fortress Przemyśl's Garrison throughout Austria-Hungary

Map 2. The home bases of Fortress Przemyśl's garrison throughout Austria-Hungary.

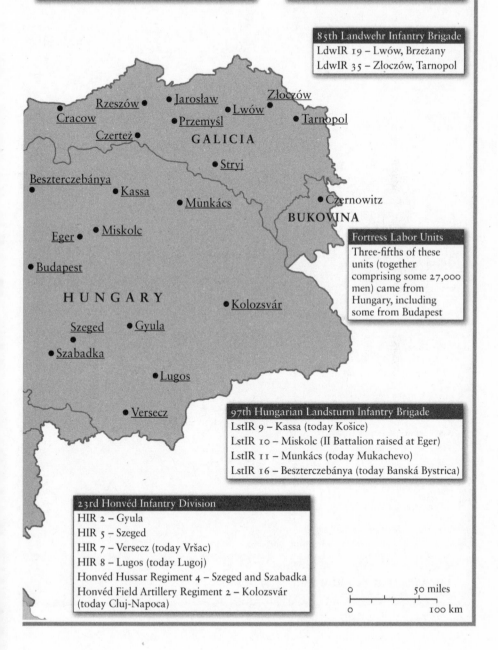

93rd Landsturm Infantry Brigade
LstIR 10 – Jungbunzlau (today Mladá Boleslav)
LstIR 35 – Złoczów

Nickl Group (4 battalions)
These units came from eastern Galicia, probably mainly Lwów (today L'viv)

85th Landwehr Infantry Brigade
LdwIR 19 – Lwów, Brzeżany
LdwIR 35 – Złoczów, Tarnopol

Rzeszów
Cracow
Czerteż
Jarosław
Przemyśl
Lwów
Złoczów
Tarnopol
GALICIA
Stryj

Beszterczebánya
Kassa
Munkács
Czernowitz
BUKOVINA

Eger
Miskolc
Budapest

HUNGARY
Kolozsvár

Szeged
Gyula
Szabadka

Lugos

Versecz

Fortress Labor Units
Three-fifths of these units (together comprising some 27,000 men) came from Hungary, including some from Budapest

97th Hungarian Landsturm Infantry Brigade
LstIR 9 – Kassa (today Košice)
LstIR 10 – Miskolc (II Battalion raised at Eger)
LstIR 11 – Munkács (today Mukachevo)
LstIR 16 – Beszterczebánya (today Banská Bystrica)

23rd Honvéd Infantry Division
HIR 2 – Gyula
HIR 5 – Szeged
HIR 7 – Versecz (today Vršac)
HIR 8 – Lugos (today Lugoj)
Honvéd Hussar Regiment 4 – Szeged and Szabadka
Honvéd Field Artillery Regiment 2 – Kolozsvár
(today Cluj-Napoca)

0   50 miles

0   100 km

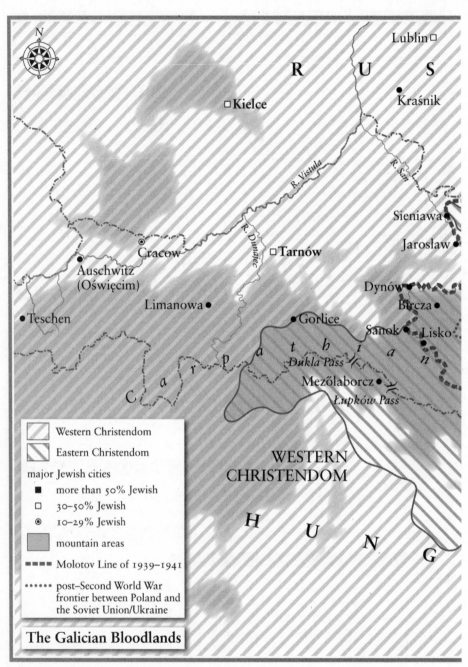

Map 3. The Galician Bloodlands.

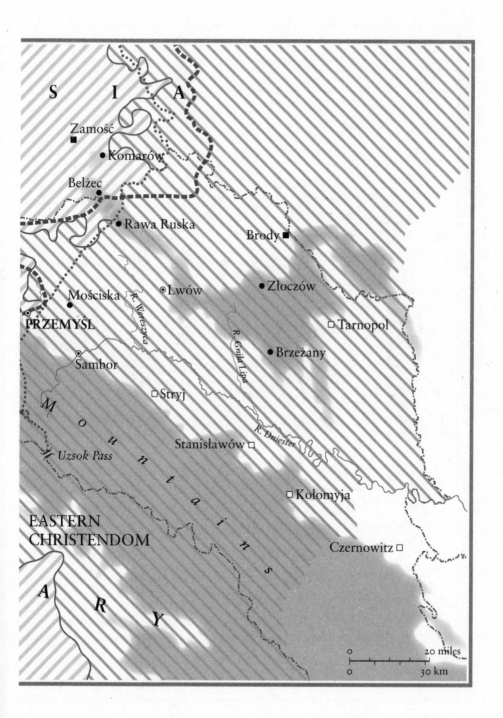

S I A

Zamość

● Komarów

Bełżec ●

● Rawa Ruska

Brody ■

Mościska ●

◉ Lwów

● Złoczów

R. Wereszyca

PRZEMYŚL

□ Tarnopol

● Brzeżany

R. Gnila Lipa

◉ Sambor

□ Stryj

M o u n t a i n s

Stanisławów □

R. Dniester

Uzsok Pass

□ Kołomyja

EASTERN
CHRISTENDOM

Czernowitz □

A   R   Y

0   20 miles

0   30 km

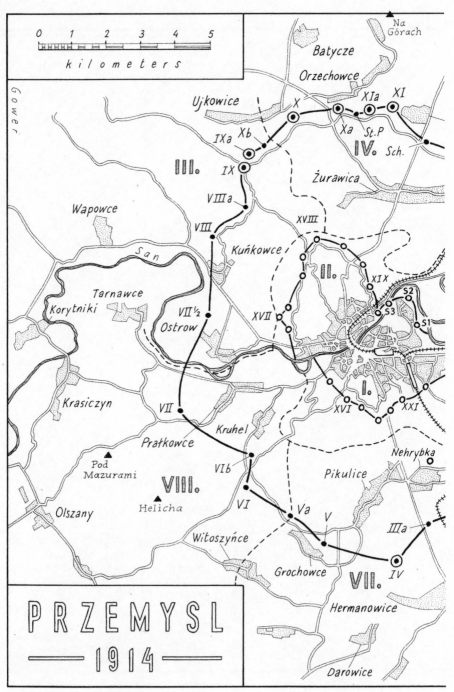

Map 4. The Fortress of Przemyśl, 1914.

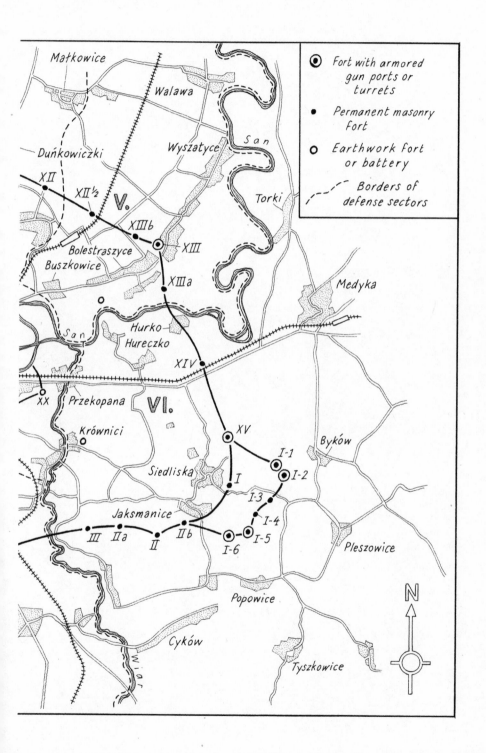

INTRODUCTION

S ometimes, things we assume to be certain, that we take as solid, stable, and lasting, can collapse with shocking suddenness. In the summer of 1914, war broke out all over Europe. Everybody had seen the storm clouds gather. Barely anyone, however, had truly believed that the cataclysm of Great Power conflict could happen. "Progress" was the buzzword of the age. The last truly great war was a hundred years past. Though armies prepared assiduously, some experts declared that in the present age—richer, freer, better educated and more technologically advanced than ever before—war was impossible. Europe's states had become too interdependent, and modern weaponry too destructive. Any conflict, the experts warned, would be "ruinous for conqueror and for conquered" alike, and would end "in general anarchy, or reduce the people to the most lamentable condition." In the continent's towns and villages, people lived as if Armageddon would never come. They worked, built careers and businesses, fell in love, raised children. Yet in 1914, all would be swept up in the maelstrom. The old civilization would be ripped apart, dreams destroyed and lives cut short.[1]

This book tells the story of one fortress-city that was pitched into the calamity and on which, for a few months early in the First World War, the fate of all Eastern and Central Europe rested. The city was called Przemyśl. Today, it lies in Poland's sleepy southeastern corner on the modern border with Ukraine. At the start of the twentieth century, however, it belonged to the Habsburg Empire, a sprawling dynastic state which for centuries had ruled over an amazingly diverse and colorful population in the center of Europe. Fortified, multiethnic Przemyśl, home to 46,000 Polish, Ukrainian, and Jewish citizens and a large garrison, was the empire's most important defensive bulwark in the east.[2]

In September 1914, suddenly Przemyśl stood at the flashpoint of a military disaster. Though war had raged barely a month, already a huge Russian force had invaded the Habsburg Empire and routed its army. Broken troops, defeated, diseased, and out of control, flooded through the city. The Russians followed close behind, determined to seal their victory. The Tsar wished to impose his rule on the surrounding region and subjugate a Slavic population whom he regarded as "little Russians." Only the Fortress of Przemyśl barred his force's way. Its ragtag garrison was composed of middle-aged reservists from every corner of Central Europe—Austrian Germans, Hungarians, Romanians, Serbs, Slovaks, Czechs, Italians, Poles, and Ukrainians. In the service of a military famous for incompetence, armed with obsolete weaponry and scarcely able to communicate among themselves, these vintage soldiers entered a desperate struggle to halt the world's most powerful army.

The siege of Przemyśl in 1914–1915 changed the entire course of the First World War. In the autumn of 1914, when in east and west the alliance of Austria-Hungary and Germany suffered severe defeats, the fortress-city and its 130,000-strong garrison played a crucial role in preventing a Russian invasion of Central Europe. During the pivotal months of September and October, the Fortress blocked the Russians' path, denying them use of the main rail and road connections into the heart of the Habsburg Empire. The steadfast defense saved the empire and its army by decisively slowing the enemy advance. The time won by the Fortress was critical in permitting the broken Habsburg army to regenerate and return to the battle. Though the Russians would renew the siege in November, they had lost their best chance of an early victory.

Przemyśl's subsequent bitter resistance through the winter of 1914–1915—its siege was the longest of the First World War—although ending in defeat, was no less momentous. As the Hungarian war correspondent Ferenc Molnár observed acutely, "Przemyśl was a symbolic point for the monarchy. Nearly all the nationalities of Austria and Hungary defended it." The eventual capitulation of the Fortress in March 1915 inflicted a hammer blow to the prestige of the Habsburg Empire, damaging it in the eyes of its peoples and emboldening neutral powers to join its enemies. Vain and bloody offensives to relieve the fortress-city had hollowed out the Habsburg army. Some 800,000 soldiers were lost. In the aftermath of Przemyśl's fall, the monarchy's German ally concluded that both its army and state were thoroughly "rotten and decayed." "This land," warned the German army's plenipotentiary at Habsburg military headquarters, "can no longer be helped."[3]

Przemyśl's story also has a wider significance, stretching beyond the First World War. The city was a weathervane for the harsh winds of the twentieth century. The lands to which it belonged—the province of Galicia and, more broadly, East-Central Europe—were always a crossroad of cultures. In the modern era, they also became a place of conflict: the point at which rival nationalist and imperial projects collided. Habsburgs and Romanovs, Poles, Ukrainians, and Russian nationalists all laid claim to the land. After 1918, these territories—"shatterzones," as some historians have called them—would be wracked first by vicious local ethnic violence and then by the murderous actions of totalitarian states. Two decades after the First World War, Nazi Germany and the Soviet Union (two entities completely unimaginable in 1914) would together transform the region into an immense battlefield, a site of ethnic cleansing and a center of genocide.[4]

To some historians, the barbarity that changed the face of East-Central Europe, that annihilated its Jews and prised apart Poles, Ukrainians, and other peoples with horrifying bloodshed, is a tale of evil and interlocked totalitarian projects that started with Stalin and Hitler. Others have cast back further, to 1917–1923 and the revolutionary struggles in collapsing empires. Przemyśl points to earlier roots, however. There and all around, the outbreak of the First World War unleashed radical violence with stunning immediacy. Brutal combat, lethal epidemics, aerial bombing, strategies of starvation, and vicious persecutions motivated by racial prejudice were all integral to the fortress-city's early war experience. Most ominously, around and later in the city, the Russian army perpetrated the first ambitious program of ethnic cleansing to befall East-Central Europe. Przemyśl is important because it reveals in microcosm a forgotten prehistory to the later, better-remembered totalitarian horrors. To understand what went wrong in the twentieth century's most ravaged region, it is not enough to start in 1928 or 1933, with the rise of the dictators, or even with the First World War's revolutionary aftermath. As Przemyśl's ordeal disturbingly shows, the story of East-Central Europe's "Bloodlands" rightly begins in 1914.[5]

PRZEMYŚL HAD ALWAYS been a fortress. The very first reference to the town, by the chronicler-monk Nestor (1050–1116), are words of war: "In the year 981 AD Vladimir [of Kiev] marched against the Lyakhs and took their strongholds Peremÿshl, Cherven and others." The following turbulent centuries saw an assortment of exotic rulers lord over the town. For more than 300 years until 1340, Przemyśl lay under Kievan Rus' and its successor Ruthenian principalities. It passed briefly to King Lajos of Hungary and Poland, and subsequently, in 1387, was firmly taken into the Polish Kingdom. Even after this date, violence was never far off. From the fifteenth to the seventeenth centuries, terrifying enemies arrived with frightening regularity from all points of the compass. Tartars, Transylvanians,

Vlachs, Hungarians, Cossacks, and Swedes all laid siege and at times ravaged Przemyśl.[6]

The town was a place where east met west. An important Christian center, it was the seat of two bishoprics. The Eastern Church, which looked to Constantinople for leadership, established its bishop first, in 1218. A Roman Catholic bishop was nominated in 1340. A new wave of religious building was sponsored by the seventeenth-century Counter-Reformation, and by the end of the century Przemyśl's skyline was dominated by seventeen Roman and Greek Catholic churches and no fewer than ten monasteries, as well as strong city walls, a Renaissance town hall, and, on a hill above, a castle. Polish- and Ukrainian-speakers and German artisans all mixed in the medieval town. So, too, from the second half of the fourteenth century, did Jews. Attracted by booming trade, a consequence of the town's position as an intersection linking Hungary and the Baltic with the main commercial route between the Black Sea and Western Europe, a Jewish community grew up in the northeast of the old city. By 1600, Jews made up one-twelfth of Przemyśl's citizens. A stone synagogue signified that they were there to stay.[7]

Przemyśl's modern history, and the tale of how it became the Fortress—the Habsburg Empire's bulwark in the east—begins in 1772. In that year, during the First Partition of Poland, the Habsburgs annexed Galicia, and with it the city. The new province was enormous, covering 68,000 square kilometers (26,000 square miles), and extremely difficult to defend. Its long frontier with Russia lacked natural obstacles. Exacerbating the challenge, the only route suitable for military use from the Austrian interior into Galicia at this time ran from west to east. The Carpathian Mountains blocked the way north from the Habsburgs' Hungarian territories. Tasked with finding a solution, shortly after 1800 the empire's top soldiers began to consider Przemyśl as a promising site for fortification. The city was defensible, situated as it was in the foothills of the Carpathians, and it was a key crossing point over the broad San River. Its position right at the center of the province was also seen as an advantage. The soldiers agreed that Galicia could never be defended at its borders. The only viable strategy, were the province threatened, was to concentrate troops at a safe, fortified base and then launch an offensive.[8]

For decades nothing was done. Przemyśl was not the only site under consideration by the army. Defensive schemes involving other towns, namely Jasło, Stryj, Lwów, and, later, Jarosław—the San River crossing north of Przemyśl—were all put forward. The state's coffers were empty. Furthermore, big expensive fortifications in the middle of Galicia made little sense without control of Cracow. This Free City, 206 kilometers (128 miles) to Przemyśl's west, was a main crossing over the Vistula River. Until it was annexed by the Habsburg Empire in 1846, an invader could attack here and instantly cut the main supply route into Galicia. Thus, only in midcentury was work on the Fortress briefly begun. The immediate impulse was the Crimean War. The Habsburg Emperor, Franz Joseph, supported, with rather more than benevolent neutrality, the Anglo-French-Ottoman coalition arrayed against Russia. The Habsburg army was sent to the Galician frontier to pin Tsarist troops there and stop them from being transferred to Crimea. Though fortified Cracow was at this time regarded as the mainstay of Galicia's defense, in 1854–1855, barracks and fortifications, the latter mostly of earth and only half completed, were hastily built in and around Przemyśl.

Only in 1871 was the final decision reached to turn Przemyśl into a first-rate fortress. Relations with Russia had warmed after the Crimean War, making Galician defense less urgent, and conflicts at the end of the 1850s in Italy, and in the mid-1860s with Denmark and Prussia, distracted attention away. However, in 1868, an Imperial Fortification Commission looked again at Galicia. Most of its members favored fortifying Przemyśl, though some preferred Jarosław as a cheaper but less defensible alternative. The Emperor himself adjudicated, ruling on Przemyśl as the priority. The city was selected because of its strategic position. First, it stood on the last high ground before the border with Russia, 70 kilometers (around 45 miles) to the north. Second, it blocked the approaches over the

Carpathian Mountains to Habsburg Hungary, the Łupków and Dukla Passes. Both had been developed by this point so as to be suitable for military traffic. Lastly, and crucially, Przemyśl had become a major rail hub. The main line from Vienna reached Przemyśl in 1859, and two years later the line ran through it all the way to the provincial capital of Lwów, 90 kilometers (56 miles) farther east. Another railway running over the Łupków Pass from Hungary was completed in 1872, ending at Przemyśl. The city thus controlled both Galicia's rail link to the south and its main east-west transportation route.[9]

The fortification work began intensively in 1878. The main factor influencing progress was, as earlier, the relationship with Russia. This was still cordial in the early 1870s; indeed, an alliance between the Habsburgs, Germany, and Russia, known as the Three Emperors' League, was signed in 1873. Przemyśl's fortification was therefore still not seen as pressing. Hungarian politicians' objections to the high costs impeded the works. There were also manifold technical challenges—most oddly, the introduction into the empire in 1872 of the metric system, which necessitated the redrafting of all existing plans. Nevertheless, relations with the great eastern neighbor soon soured, the result of a foreboding imperial competition in the Balkans. First Russia's successful war with the Ottoman Empire in 1877–1878, and then the Habsburg occupation of Bosnia-Herzegovina in 1878, raised tensions. The Habsburgs drew closer to Germany, sealing a defensive alliance against Russia in 1879 that was still in force in 1914. The military works around Przemyśl were also taken up again, ending a three-year hiatus. This time, there would be no hesitation. Through the 1880s and 1890s, Przemyśl was transformed into a modern fortress.[10]

The Fortress of Przemyśl was an immense, complex military organism. The strong outer perimeter of permanent forts was its most visually impressive element. In 1914, after three decades of building and many revisions to the original plans, the Fortress comprised a chain of seventeen main and eighteen subsidiary forts arranged in a rough ellipse 48 kilometers (30 miles) in circumference around the city. Behind the fortified perimeter, along with a much weaker inner defensive line, was an equally intricate and important network of support services and logistical and communications links all essential for sustaining the forts. Roads were laid and telephone lines installed. The city itself became a military base. By 1910, in and around it were seven barracks, a military railyard, warehouses, artillery parks, munitions and food magazines, and a garrison hospital. This infrastructure was intended not only to serve the defensive garrison, whose wartime strength was set at 85,000 soldiers and 3,700 horses. Przemyśl always had an offensive mission. From the very beginning, the Fortress was designed to support the Habsburg field army, providing it with a secure storage area and a safe concentration zone from which it could launch operations against Russia.[11]

Great thought, careful planning, and much imagination were all invested into the Fortress. A huge quantity of money was invested as well: by 1914, the Habsburg state had spent a grand total of 32 million crowns (208 million US dollars in today's money) on Przemyśl's forts and barracks. Despite all this, the Fortress's designers were unlucky. The last two decades of the nineteenth century saw a revolution in artillery technology. From the end of the 1880s, the introduction of smokeless propellants, steel shells, and high-explosive bursting charges made artillery projectiles swifter, heavier, and effective at longer ranges. From around 1900, the universal adoption of recoilless artillery—guns that did not have to be repositioned and aimed after each shot—increased rates of fire to hitherto unimaginable levels. These innovations quickly rendered all existing fortifications obsolete. A simulated attack conducted at Przemyśl in 1896 against one of the forts built a decade earlier alarmingly exposed the problem. When the fort was placed under live fire during the exercise, parts of it threatened to collapse. Adjudicators agreed that had any gun crews been in the fort's open rooftop emplacements they would have been wiped out to a man.[12]

The Fortress's architects and engineers tried to keep pace. The forts of the 1890s featured new designs with more stone and concrete.

Revolving armored gun cupolas were mounted. Some older forts were upgraded. Yet the technology moved so fast it was impossible to keep up. The defensive concepts on which the Fortress had been laid out were already outmoded by the turn of the century. The obsolescence was exacerbated by neglect in the last decade before the First World War. Unlike his long-serving predecessor, Friedrich Count Beck-Rzikowsky, who had held the powerful position for a quarter of a century, the chief of the Habsburg general staff appointed in 1906, General Franz Conrad von Hötzendorf, saw little use for the two Galician fortresses, Cracow and Przemyśl. The funds he requested for fortification from the cash-strapped Habsburg state went to defenses on the mountainous border with Italy. Conrad's strategy for the defense of the empire's flatter northeastern frontier rested on maneuver. In his view, Przemyśl was an enormous concrete white elephant, useful only as a glorified warehouse for the field army. Modernization works were halted. When the First World War broke out in 1914, it found the Fortress unprepared and antiquated.[13]

THE HABSBURG MILITARY's decision to construct the Fortress transformed the city of Przemyśl. In 1870, it had been a fairly small provincial town of 15,185 people. Over the following decades, as workers and tradesmen poured in to meet military demand for labor—and also because the city became the permanent base of the Habsburg army's X Corps in 1889—Przemyśl's population exploded. By 1890, it already numbered 35,209. On the eve of the First World War, more than 54,000 people lived in Przemyśl, including a peacetime garrison of some 8,500 soldiers. The city was extremely ethnically diverse. At that time, Poles formed no absolute majority. According to the 1910 census, Roman Catholics, the majority of whom would have been Polish-speakers, totaled 25,306, forming 46.8 percent of the city's population. There were 12,018 Greek Catholics (22.2 percent of the populace), the faith associated most strongly with the city's Ukrainian-speakers. Jews numbered 16,062, making up 29.7 percent of Przemyśl's citizens.[14]

To wander through Przemyśl on the eve of the cataclysm was to find a place transitioning rapidly into the modern world. Of course, the medieval past was still prominent. At the top of the hill to the southwest, the castle built by the Polish king Kazimierz the Great loomed over the old city. Below it, but still on high ground, towered the sixteenth-century Roman Catholic cathedral and, only a little to the east, the seventeenth-century domed Greek cathedral. Churches, monasteries, and seminaries of both faiths dotted Przemyśl. As two centuries earlier, spires and domes, and behind them hills, dominated the city skyline.

If one walked down from the Roman Catholic cathedral and through the marketplace, with its rather nondescript contemporary town hall, between the market and the broad River San one quickly came to Przemyśl's old Jewish quarter. Here, it could feel as if one actually had stepped back into the Middle Ages. Ilka Künigl-Ehrenburg, an inquisitive Styrian countess who served through the siege of 1914–1915 as an auxiliary nurse, was fascinated by this poorest part of the town, with its gloomy narrow alleys and old, high wooden houses. From out of the shops in their vaulted basements, she observed, "pale Jewish faces shine otherworldly." Usually, a courtyard lay behind, with an open staircase giving access to the upper floors. From the balconies here, the residents threw down their slop and waste. This was a place one smelled and heard before one saw. In the day, a ceaseless, lively, noisy trade roared. Christian peasant women scrutinized the wares for sale, criticized and bargained, "and the Jew," wrote the countess excitedly, "praises his goods, quibbles and haggles with all the tenacity and virtuosity of which only a Jew is capable."[15]

Nevertheless, from other angles Przemyśl was quite obviously a modern imperial city of some importance. The Habsburg military had made its mark. There were more than sixty army facilities in and around the city, from barracks and powder magazines to a swimming school and a fine officers' club. The most significant, the X

Corps Headquarters, the Fortress Command, and the Fortress Engineering Directorate, were situated on a splendid thoroughfare in the city's east, Mickiewicz Street. The main post office and a branch of the Austro-Hungarian state bank stood here as well. Schönbrunn yellow, the color of imperial officialdom, was also to be found on other buildings, for Przemyśl hosted several civil state offices, including a district office, a tax office, and regional and district courthouses. The elegant main state railway station, renovated and refaced in a Neo-Baroque style in 1895, and, behind it, the iron lattice railway bridge across the San, offered everyday reminders to residents of their literal connections to one of Europe's greatest empires.[16]

The Przemyśl municipal authorities were keen to emphasize the Polish credentials of their city. This too was a mark of modernity, for nationalism was the new, exciting, and inspirational ideology of the late nineteenth century, promising the renewal of real and imagined past glories and a better, more efficient future. The reforms of the 1860s had placed Galicia in the hands of Polish conservatives and granted considerable powers of self-government to Austria's municipalities. As in other Galician cities, Polish Democrats—more liberal and elite than their name might today imply—ran Przemyśl in the decades before 1914. Under mayors Aleksander Dworski (1882–1901) and Franciszek Doliński (1901–1914), the expanding city not only improved its infrastructure—building wells and drains, a municipal slaughterhouse, a hospital, and an electrical power station—but also asserted the Polishness of its public spaces. The most impressive new or rebuilt main streets were named after the most revered Polish poets, Adam Mickiewicz, Juliusz Słowacki, and Zygmunt Krasiński, or landmark events in Poland's history, such as the May 3, 1791, constitution, or the medieval victory of Grunwald over the Teutonic Knights. Statues of Mickiewicz and the Polish warrior-king Jan Sobiecki III, funded by popular subscription, were raised by the old Market Square.[17]

Przemyśl's other ethnic groups were also caught by the new spirit of the late nineteenth century. The Greek Catholic minority generally had little opportunity to make much mark on the city in brick or stone beyond its historic churches. There was, however, one important exception: schools. Language issues, and the right to teach children in one's mother tongue, were becoming central to identity and to political disputes across the Habsburg Empire, and Ukrainian-speakers—or Ruthenes, as they were known in this period—were no exceptions. In the late nineteenth century, elite boys' and girls' secondary schools teaching in Ukrainian were founded, augmenting existing primary provision and attracting pupils from far beyond the city limits. Ruthenes were deeply divided in their identity, and the fractures were reflected in their associations and in the press. "Ukrainian" at this time denoted a political stance: a conviction that Ukrainian-speakers were a distinct nation. The majority of the small clerical and intellectual elite adhered to this view. A lesser group, the so-called Russophiles, disagreed, regarding themselves culturally, and sometimes also politically, as a branch of the Russian nation. Though difficult to enumerate, a fairly large section of lower-class Ruthenes was mostly indifferent to the novel idea of the nation, and persisted in prioritizing the Greek Catholic faith as the foundation of their identity.[18]

Przemyśl's Jewish community displayed some similar divisions. Orthodox Jewry had long predominated, and though this was still true in the early twentieth century, the modern era had brought schism and change. There were four synagogues in Przemyśl by 1914. The oldest, situated in the Jewish quarter, and eight other smaller prayer houses were frequented by the traditionalist, Yiddish-speaking Hasidic Jews who so fascinated Ilka Künigl-Ehrenburg. They were instantly recognizable, especially the men, with their curly sidelocks, beards, black hats, and black kaftans. To attend synagogue with them was a profoundly spiritual experience. Künigl-Ehrenburg ducked under the low doorway of the Old Synagogue one Sabbath and climbed up to the women's gallery to watch. The faithful filled every inch of space. Some sat, others stood, all pressed tightly together. From above, a stream of light pierced the darkness and shone onto the silver-edged Torah scroll displayed by the altar. Wrapped in their gray-and-white striped prayer shawls, the believers rocked back and forth murmuring their sacred devotions. To the Styrian countess, it was strange—"oriental"—but very moving. "Everything was full of atmosphere, harmonious," she wrote.[19]

Times were shifting, however. Beginning in 1901, the *kehilah*, Przemyśl's Jewish communal council, dropped Yiddish and instead conducted its meetings in Polish. The city's three other synagogues had all been built since the 1880s and catered to wealthy, educated Jews. Jews—some of them—had particularly prospered from Przemyśl's rapid expansion, a fact that had not gone unnoticed by their Christian neighbors. The town's credit institutions were nearly all in Jewish hands. The majority of new manufacturing concerns and almost all trading and services were as well. The most intense civic development in the final thirty years of peace had taken place to the east of the old town and in the suburb of Zasanie, north of the San River. In these districts, the housing stock had more than doubled, and it was to there that well-off Jews had moved. They had bought up property on the smartest strips; it was a mild irony that on Mickiewicz Street, named for Poland's national poet, no fewer than 74 of the 139 buildings were Jewish-owned. The synagogues serving these communities, like the people who attended them, took inspiration from modern liberalism and nationalism. The "Tempel" in the old city was home to Jewish progressives keen to integrate into Polish culture. Faced with red brick, like synagogues in the west of the empire, it celebrated Polish holidays and had sermons and prayers in the Polish language. The Zasanie synagogue was popular with Zionist youth.[20]

By 1914, Przemyśl was the third-largest city in Galicia, and around the twentieth most populous in the Habsburg Empire. It was significant enough to warrant an entry in the travelers' bible, *The Baedeker Guide*. A visitor from snooty Vienna could be, if not impressed, then at least satisfied and comfortable. The city offered five upmarket hotels. Hotel City, the most expensive, boasted central heating, warm and cold water in every room, electric lighting, and—that preeminent mark of rising European civilization—an elevator. Of course, there were eastern peculiarities. The absence of a modern waterworks—the city had placed orders for pumps and begun building a plant only in 1914—meant that hygiene could be rather primitive. If one arrived on a Friday evening or a Saturday, one would have to carry one's own luggage to the hotel, because the horse-drawn cabs that waited at the rail station were driven by Jews, who all observed the Sabbath.[21]

Nevertheless, once the visitor was settled there was plenty to see and do. A pleasant way to spend a sunny morning was to stroll through the old town, visit the historic churches and Polish monuments, and then climb up to the pretty landscaped castle park, which offered an excellent panorama over the city and across to the green hills around it. For the less energetic, a leisurely riverside walk along the Franz Joseph Embankment might be just the ticket, with a pause to watch the bathers splashing at the shallow edges of the San. From there one could cross for lunch to Zasanie over the 3rd May Bridge. Three city bridges, one rail and two road, spanned the San, but for residents this one was the most important. Renewed just twenty years earlier and of modern iron girder construction, the 3rd May Bridge was Przemyśl's artery joining the old town to its most important suburb. For sightseers, it was well worth lingering on it to enjoy fine views of the city.[22]

After an early lunch, one might visit another famous local landmark, the Tartar's Barrow. To do so, the visitor would cross the river again and ramble south down modern Słowacki Street, passing the new Scheinbach synagogue and the garrison hospital, and then along unsurfaced roads winding up to the barrow, a mound on a hill with an altitude of 350 meters (1,150 feet). One legend claimed the barrow was the resting place of the city's mythic seventh-century warrior-founder, Prince Przemysław. Others said it had been built for a Tartar khan who had been slaughtered in one of Przemyśl's medieval sieges. To a visitor gazing over the peaceful early twentieth-century landscape, that past violence must have seemed very, very remote.[23]

There was lots to do in the evenings, too. For a tourist feeling homesick, a walk along the main streets of the recently built districts Lwowskie or Zasanie would have been a cure, for, with their two- or three-story Neo-Baroque buildings, they could have belonged to almost any city in any part of the Habsburg Empire. Thanks to the army, a modern entertainment industry had grown up in Przemyśl. The best restaurants and Viennese-style cafés were clustered around Mickiewicz Street, by the rail station and the fortress and corps commands. Here, officers from the garrison, resplendent in blue, gray, or chocolate brown, could be seen relaxing or in earnest debate about some military matter. The very best establishment, Grand Café Stieber, offered live music. Naturally, the waiters all spoke German. Visitors willing to test their Polish might attend one of the summer theatrical performances held up at the castle. Three cinemas entertained the city. For Przemyśl's apprentices and for the thousands of soldiers in the garrison, mostly men from the surrounding region undertaking their obligatory two years of peacetime training, there was beer, beer, beer. Half of Przemyśl's municipal budget was funded by alcohol taxation.[24]

For sure, Przemyśl had its problems, conflicts, and jealousies. The nationality struggles that dominated the politics of the late Habsburg Empire were ever present. The empire had undergone a fundamental political restructuring in 1867. Emperor (or, as he became known in Hungary, King) Franz Joseph still presided over the realm and retained an imperial foreign minister, war minister, and finance minister, but Hungary had been separated from Austria, and each had been granted its own government and parliament with substantial powers in state affairs. In the following years, within Austria, Galicia had also attained autonomy. Although significant constitutional freedoms had been granted to all Franz Joseph's subjects, including equality of rights of languages in schools, administration, and public life, among the nationalities there had been winners and losers, and Ruthenes clearly fell into the latter group.[25]

Ruthenes complained justly that the Polish elites who ran Galicia's administration had disenfranchised them and were deliberately underfunding their education. In Przemyśl, tensions peaked in April 1908, when in Lwów a former pupil at Przemyśl's Ukrainian-language secondary school, Miroslav Sichynsky, sensationally shot dead Galicia's governor, Count Andrzej Potocki. Arrests of young Ruthenian radicals in the city immediately followed. Endemic anti-Semitism was also a problem. In May 1898, a time of anti-Semitic disturbances right across the west of Galicia, there had been a riot and looting of Jewish-owned shops. Smaller-scale disorder had followed in 1903, and in later years some Polish clergy and Ruthenian newspapers had called for boycotts of Jewish traders.[26]

Nevertheless, before the First World War the horrors that would ravage Przemyśl in coming decades were scarcely imaginable. For sure, the boundaries between citizens were becoming institutionalized. Poles, Ruthenes, and Jews each had their own libraries, theater groups, even sports clubs. Yet Christians of different churches still frequently intermarried. Citizens of all faiths and tongues could cooperate. In the 1907 election, the first held on the basis of equal male suffrage, Ruthenes, Jews, and Polish apprentices united to reject a nationalist Pole and voted a Polish-speaking Jewish socialist into the city's seat in the Austrian parliament. It was a reminder that, even in a city without industry like Przemyśl, modern categories of class, as well as older loyalties to church and Emperor, could compete with nation in shaping people's identities and allegiances.[27]

The real threat to Przemyśl was never internal but international conflict. For decades, the empire enjoyed peace. Its army's last conflict before 1914 had been a counterinsurgency campaign in far-off Bosnia in 1878–1882. However, the risk of a Habsburg clash with Russia mounted rapidly from 1908 as a result of Balkan quarrels. Russian belligerence grew. In Galicia, the Habsburg army feared and suspected, with some evidence, that the Tsar's secret service was recruiting Ruthenian Russophiles to spy on its defenses, and above all, on the Fortress. Convictions for espionage increased from four in 1908 to fifty-one in 1913. In the autumn of 1912, during the First Balkan War, the powers teetered on the brink. The Russian army conducted a "trial" mobilization just across the border to pressure the Habsburg government to accept Serb victories. In reply, Franz Joseph's forces in Galicia also arrayed. Przemyśl's X Corps was one of the formations brought to full strength and held at readiness until March 1913. Although conflict was averted, the respite proved temporary. In the summer of 1914, the infamous assassination of the Habsburg heir in Sarajevo would spark war, placing Przemyśl, and all of East-Central Europe, on a new and terrible path.[28]

THE MEMORY OF the First World War is dominated by youth. In the aftermath of the conflict, the sacrifices of soldiers who had just come of age in 1914 were immediately invested with deep but rival political meanings. For fascists, the heroism and hardiness displayed by young men on the battlefields of 1914–1918 were tangible proof of the nation's virility and of its ability to resurrect itself after disappointment and defeat. In competition was another, ultimately more lasting narrative of the "lost generation," in which these same young men symbolized a future promise squandered in the bloodbath. No one articulated more eloquently or with greater pathos the special victimhood of this generation of youth than Erich Maria Remarque (born 1898), author of the war's defining novel, *All Quiet on the Western Front*. "The war swept us away," sadly muses the young middle-class German soldier, Paul, who narrates Remarque's story. "Things are particularly confused for us twenty-year-olds, for Kropp, Müller, Leer, and me, the ones Kantorek [our teacher] called young men of iron. The older men still have firm ties to their earlier lives— they have property, wives, children, jobs and interests, and these bonds are so strong that the war can't break them."[29]

The story of Przemyśl offers a different, and in some ways even more chilling, parable of the horrors of war. The 130,000 Habsburg soldiers who defended Przemyśl in 1914–1915 were mostly not of

Remarque's youthful generation. The backbone of the Fortress's wartime garrison was formed by distinctly unglamorous "Landsturm" (territorial) regiments, filled with men between thirty-seven and forty-two years old. The middle-aged, too, were drafted into this terrible war, and although their casualty rates were far lower than those of younger soldiers, their sacrifice was not insignificant: one in every eight Habsburg military fatalities was over thirty-five years of age. For these men, the war was an especial disaster, for they were far more deeply invested than youth in the world before 1914. Worse, their emotional and material bonds proved much more fragile than Remarque's young Paul naively believed. Above all, in East-Central Europe, where armies ranged widely, violence swept over communities, and borders shifted, the war possessed an awesome power. All that was most precious, all on which these men had built their identities—property, jobs, wives and children, even the very societies in which they lived—could be blown away. Though the middle-aged had a greater chance of physical survival, the war destroyed them nonetheless. They were the real "lost generation"— not absent but adrift in a brutal postwar world.[30]

A glance at the lives of a few middle-aged individuals who appear in the pages of this book illustrates this truth. Jan Vit (born 1879), a Czech hailing from the small town of Dobřichovice near Prague, was just one of many men thrown by war onto an unimaginable odyssey. In peacetime, he was an engineer working for a firm that specialized in bridge-building. In 1907, he had married his wife, Maria. They had three children, a boy and two little girls. When Vit was called up at the outbreak of hostilities to serve as an army lieutenant 700 kilometers (430 miles) away in the Fortress of Przemyśl, his eldest was seven and the youngest just one year old. He had not wanted to leave them. The war's opening, he later reflected, "turned out to be fatal for my peaceful family life."[31]

Vit served through the siege of Przemyśl, surviving its violence and hardships. After the Fortress fell, he was incarcerated first on the Volga; after the Russian Revolution broke out, he ended up in a camp near the Siberian city of Omsk, some 4,300 kilometers (2,700 miles) from Dobřichovice. There, in 1918, Vit enlisted in the Czechoslovak Legion; he traveled with it to the Pacific port of Vladivostok and on June 8, 1920, left on a ship bound for Canada. He and his comrades crossed the North American continent, then boarded another vessel that took them over the Atlantic and through the Mediterranean to the now former Habsburg port of Trieste, which Italy had just annexed. Having circumnavigated the globe, Vit arrived back in Dobřichovice to children he had not seen for more than six years. His wife, Maria, was no longer alive. She had died of tuberculosis, a disease that ravaged the starving cities of the Habsburg Empire in the second half of the war, at the beginning of 1917.[32]

The personal stories of two Galicians, Dr. Jan Jakub Stock (born 1881) and Stanisław Marceli Gayczak (born 1874), tell similarly of bourgeois lives broken by the cataclysm. Stock was born in Dobromil (today Dobromyl in Ukraine), just 25 kilometers (15 miles) south of Przemyśl, and was educated at the city's Polish-language secondary school. Before the war, he had a position in the Physics Department of Lwów University, where he specialized in electrical and hydrodynamic research. He was married with two children. In August 1914, he was drafted as a private to the Fortress's garrison. Given his expertise, he expected to be posted to the fortress radio station; the army, however, decided he could best be put to use as a supplies clerk. Trapped in Przemyśl, he probably had no knowledge that his wife was pregnant with their third child. The boy was born on March 28, 1915, six days after the Fortress's fall. Years of captivity in Kazakhstan and Uzbekistan were hard on Stock. Worse, when he returned home to Dobromil in the autumn of 1918, he was immediately forced to flee, for the Habsburg Empire was collapsing and violence between Poles and Ukrainians had broken out. Weakened by his war service and his captivity, Stock died in Cracow in 1925 at the age of forty-four, leaving his young family behind.[33]

Stanisław Marceli Gayczak was a quintessential Habsburg man, for he had studied at the universities in both Vienna and Cracow and found lasting love with a German from Moravia. Together, they had four children. In peacetime, Gayczak was a secondary school teacher, the erudite author of several Latin, Greek, and German textbooks, and a member of the Provincial School Council in Lwów. After activation as a Landsturm officer on the outbreak of war, he caught a last glimpse of his family on September 2, 1914, when his unit evacuated through his home city of Lwów to escape the advancing Russians. Six days later, Gayczak was in Przemyśl as a member of the fortress garrison. Once the siege ended, the Russians imprisoned him nearly 2,000 kilometers (1,200 miles) to the east in a camp at Saratov, on the Volga. Returning to Lwów before the war finished, he was more fortunate than Jan Vit in finding all his family still alive, despite a long Russian occupation and severe food shortages in the city. Nevertheless, the certainties that Remarque imagined such men had enjoyed had dissolved. Gayczak was quickly embroiled in the vicious ethnic conflict that swept the collapsing Austro-Hungarian Empire. When Ukrainian nationalist troops seized his city in November 1918, the scholar turned soldier once again, joining, at the age of forty-four, the Polish Citizens' Militia. As a district chief, he fought off the insurgents and helped to bring the city under Polish control.[34]

For men and women in the middle years of their lives, the war was a traumatic rupture. The certainties of the pre-1914 world gave way to displacement and cruelty. The life of Ilka Künigl-Ehrenburg (born 1881), the curious Styrian countess who so vividly described the Jews of Przemyśl, offers a disturbing illustration. She was born in Marburg, in Styria (today, Maribor in Slovenia), as the daughter of a secondary school teacher. After marrying Count Emil Künigl-Ehrenburg, she lived in Vienna. She was thirty-two when she arrived in the Fortress, and her memoir of the siege of Przemyśl, published at the end of 1915, set her on a new path as author and songwriter. However, the postwar years were difficult. Her husband's ancestral lands in south Tyrol were annexed by Italy at the war's end, and although the couple at first tried to stay, in 1926 they emigrated to

Graz, in the rump Austrian state. In the 1930s her health rapidly deteriorated, and in 1937 she was admitted to a psychiatric hospital just outside Innsbruck. There, under the Nazis' T4 Euthanasia Program for the mentally and physically disabled, she was scheduled for extermination. Before she could be murdered, however, on September 18, 1940, she died.[35]

Dr. Bruno Prochaska, born in Moravia in 1879, trod a different road. This talented author found his professional way in the war's aftermath, but lost his moral compass. Prochaska was a well-educated man, completing a doctorate in law at the University of Vienna in 1903. In peacetime, he had a mundane existence as an official in the Austrian Tobacco Monopoly. In his free time, however, he wrote for some of the German-speaking world's best periodicals, most notably the satirical weekly *Simplicissimus*. When war came, he served in Przemyśl with Jan Vit, as a battalion adjutant in Landsturm Infantry Regiment 18, a multinational unit fighting in the defense of a multinational empire. In the post-1918 world, however, this experience counted for little. When the Nazis annexed Austria in March 1938, Prochaska contributed a piece to the *Bekenntnisbuch österreichischer Dichter* (Professions of faith of Austrian writers), a book that became notorious as a pledge to Hitler by the country's literary elite. He joined the Nazi Party in May and wrote regularly for the party's newspaper, the *Völkischer Beobachter*. By 1942, Prochaska was an influential Nazi literary figure, leading the Lower Danube branch of Propaganda Minister Joseph Goebbels' Reich Chamber of Writers.[36]

THE SOLDIERS AND civilians of Przemyśl and the horrible ordeal through which they passed at the start of the First World War lie at the heart of this book. Little in their prior lives had prepared these men and women—neither the townspeople, nor the mass of peasant soldiery, nor their bourgeois officers—for a modern siege. In what had been an age of unmatched personal mobility, to be trapped in the claustrophobic confines of a city surrounded and beleaguered was intensely frightening and shocking. The Fortress was stormed, starved, and severed from the world. Mentalities of war—ruthlessness, racism, endemic suspicion, and a readiness for absolute destruction—seized the opposing armies. The violence they unleashed in 1914 would ultimately come to consume both the Habsburg and Russian Empires.

Most terrifyingly, although the empires disintegrated, that violence persisted, mutated, and further radicalized. There would be no return to the safety and toleration—noisy and disputatious though that was—of the pre-1914 era. The biographies of the generation who fought at Przemyśl scream of this loss of security and the endemic hatred, malice, and bloodshed that took its place. The city itself bears witness. After Russian occupation, in which Przemyśl's Jews were for a time forced out, ethnic tensions within the community spiraled in the later war years, bursting into violence in 1918. Bitter ethnic conflict would tar the city's existence throughout the interwar years in independent Poland.

In 1939, the Nazis and the Soviets marched in. Under the totalitarian dictatorships, Przemyśl ceased to be a crossroad of culture between east and west. Instead, division was cast in concrete. The Molotov Line, the heavily fortified frontier between these two evil empires, sliced right through the city. By 1945, war-torn Przemyśl's population was barely half what it had been thirty-one years earlier. The once thriving Jewish community had been massacred in the Holocaust; its old quarter lay in ruins. A Polish communist government would soon after the war expel all the Ukrainians. The bloody road on which the city, and the wider region, had been set in 1914 reached its end with genocide, deportations, and a new border to the east. What had been lost was staggering.

CHAPTER ONE

A BROKEN ARMY

In the center of Przemyśl's old town stands an eighteenth-century clock tower 40 meters (130 feet) high. On the morning of September 14, 1914, anyone atop this Baroque relic of a more peaceful era had a frightening view. Down the main road from Lwów to the east, a chaotic mass of men and animals stumbled toward the city. Military wagons, driven four abreast, wheel to wheel, filled the wet and muddy road. Between them staggered the remnants of once proud regiments. Their bowed heads, sunken eyes, and dulled gaze told of sleepless weeks and great horrors. The column lurched its way forward. In one place a tired horse would fall, in another a wagon would drop into the roadside ditch and everything behind would jolt to a halt. There would be cursing, the obstacle would be pushed aside, but then the procession would continue painfully on its way. Similar miserable columns, stretching as far as the eye could see, blocked all other routes in the east, north, and south of Przemyśl. Ragged soldiers, who had deserted their units and dumped their kits in their haste to reach safety, also tramped across the countryside. In the wake of this dark mass converging on the city, abandoned in ditches

or under bushes, was a trail of dying and dead, struck down by typhus or cholera. This was Austria-Hungary's broken army.[1]

THE CITIZENS OF Przemyśl, like most people living in the Habsburg
Empire, had not expected the outbreak of European war. Of course,
the assassination of the imperial heir and his wife in Sarajevo at
the end of June had been widely reported. The local press had condemned the "hideous crime" and pondered darkly whether Russia
had a hand in it. However, nobody could imagine that the death
of one man, even a man so important as Archduke Franz Ferdinand, could end nearly half a century of peace. Europe was the home
of reason and humanity. Crises in the half-civilized Balkans were
nothing new. The newspapers had soon turned to other subjects.
Besides, it was summer. The city's intelligentsia were on holiday, en-
joying the warm weather. The peasantry in the surrounding villages
were too busy preparing for the harvest to bother about anything so
abstract as conflict between the Great Powers.[2]

The announcement of general mobilization on July 31 thus "struck
us like a thunderclap," remembered one resident. Large posters appeared on the streets ordering all adult men up to the age of forty-two
to report for duty. The army, always prominent in this fortress-city,
became ubiquitous. Already before August 6, the day the Habsburg
Empire declared hostilities against Russia, schools had been com-
mandeered for use as military hospitals. Przemyśl's lively local press,
full of conflicting opinions in peacetime, closed down. Instead, information came through monolithic, uncontradictable official proclamations. These were numerous. Step by step, they placed the city
on a war footing. Perceptive observers realized the conflict would be
all-embracing. Dr. Jan Stock, a physicist at Lwów University drafted
into the ranks and stationed at Przemyśl, marveled at the preparations: "Every living human is not only taken over by the war, but
takes an active part in it. I wouldn't have believed, had I not watched
with my own eyes, that everything which calls itself life could so

subordinate itself to one will and to war. Telegraph and telephone communications, railway, maritime and road traffic—all of it given over for use in war."[3]

The dynamism of those days caught imaginations. "Movement, shouting, noise" defined Przemyśl's mobilization. The streets were the place to be. Reservists hurried through them to their units. Their wives stood still, queuing outside banks to withdraw the family savings or waiting in front of shops to buy food. Unfortunates, arrested on suspicion of spying or treason, passed anxiously or sullenly by under escort. Soldiers marched and sang. Army transport rumbled. When Przemyśl's own 24th Division departed, the men moved briskly to the music of their regimental brass bands, with flowers and oak leaves— the traditional field sign of the Habsburg army at war—in their caps. It would have looked joyous, noted one watcher, "had they not been accompanied by many lamenting and weeping women."[4]

At the city's main rail station, the bustle was greatest. Here one could also best see that Przemyśl's mobilization was part of a vast imperial war effort. The Habsburg army deployed more than two-thirds of its strength, around 1.2 million men, in Galicia that August. These soldiers were drawn from across the empire, and many passed through Przemyśl. To shouts of "Hoch!" in nasal Viennese came a Slovenian "Živi!" or a Polish "Niech żyje!" Flamboyant Hungarian Honvéd arrived singing, in wagons decorated in their country's colors of red, white, and green. Other troop transports carried chalked caricatures of enemy monarchs and belligerent jokes reflecting the many foes and immense geographical spread of the conflict:

> *Every shot a Russian,*
> *Every punch a Frenchman,*
> *Every kick a Brit*
> *And the Serbs smashed to pieces![5]*

Przemyśl's destiny was bound to this multinational empire. The first Habsburg victory over the Russians, at Kraśnik, 150 kilometers

(90 miles) to the north in Tsarist Poland, on August 25, seemed to underscore this, for local regiments had taken part. The city council put up posters announcing the good news. A celebratory torchlight procession was held.[6]

Then, at the end of August, the news became less good. Masses of wounded arrived. The sight of these trainloads of suffering humanity was intensely shocking: "shot-through lungs and hearts, terrible stomach wounds, blood, vomit, feces. . . . Not a single groan, apathy," was how one local lady serving hot drinks at the main station summarized the misery. Those able to speak told stories of fighting utterly at odds with official pronouncements. The Habsburg artillery had shot up its own infantry. Supposedly camouflage "pike gray" (in fact a shade of light blue) uniforms were too bright and made the troops easy targets. "Victory," it turned out, was really just a euphemism for "heavy losses." The front in the east was moving closer. Treason was everywhere. The soldiers particularly damned the Ukrainian-speaking population for its treachery. Flags, mirrors, and smoke, they bitterly recounted, had all been used to signal their positions to the enemy. In one village, it was believed, civilians had brazenly held a procession praying for Habsburg victory past artillery emplacements, to draw attention to them so that the Russians would know where to aim their shells.[7]

As if to testify to the truth of these tales, on August 30 the dull boom of artillery fire in the east could be heard for the first time in Przemyśl. Preparations to ready the Fortress for action added to residents' unease. At night a ring of fire encircled the city, as the military burned down the villages in front of the forts. Definitive confirmation of looming disaster came in the form of choked-full evacuation trains from Lwów. So desperate were people to get out, they were riding on the carriage roofs. There, the capital of Galicia just 90 kilometers (56 miles) east of Przemyśl, ruled a chaos not seen since the invasions of the Tartars in the sixteenth century. The city's mayor, the provincial authorities, and the bank officials had all fled. Both the rule of law and the food supply had collapsed. Traumatized refugees told of streams of Habsburg wounded retreating through the streets, of overflowing hospitals, of soldiers left injured and dying in the city parks.[8]

Przemyśl's residents listened to these accounts with horror. Yet it was worse when, after September 1, the refugee trains stopped arriving. Word went around that Przemyśl was now the end of the line. Lwów had fallen. This unofficial news opened what citizens later called "the times of panic." Anyone with money or connections beyond the city scrambled to get out. The Fortress Command announced a compulsory evacuation for September 4. Six thousand people, most of them Ruthenes and Jews, were ordered to depart, along with anybody who did not possess three months of food. The military had counted on around 20,000 people leaving. However, repeated admonitions to the population since the start of August to stockpile food or be ready to get out within twenty-four hours had been heeded. Even the poor had hoarded supplies and, with nowhere to go, refused to board the evacuation trains. On September 11, another proclamation was therefore issued publicizing more free trains over the next two days. This was couched in far harsher language: "Whosoever does not voluntarily obey this call," it warned, "will be exiled by the army applying coercive measures with the utmost ruthlessness."[9]

By the time the field army started to retreat in force through the Fortress on September 13 and 14, the military could report that 18,000 civilians remained in Przemyśl. In actuality, considerably more had stayed and were simply not counted in the general confusion. What these residents saw was a broken army. For some, it was the scale of the retreat that made the most impression, the seemingly "endless chain" of wagons rattling over the city's main square. Most distressing for others was the total exhaustion of the soldiers, the rags they wore, and the "sadness on all faces." Disturbing though these sights were, even more anxiety provoking was the thought of what lay behind, crawling toward Przemyśl. Residents had already caught some hints. Days earlier, a train carrying Russian prisoners had rolled slowly through the city station. One prisoner, a Pole in the Tsar's service, had stuck his head through the bars of his wagon and shrieked out to onlookers: "Oh! You poor, poor people. A great power is coming toward you. They will murder you."[10]

THE MAN WHO bore the most blame for the disaster was the Habsburg army's general staff chief, Franz Conrad von Hötzendorf. He had served in this position, as the army's lead operational planner and trainer, since November 1906. Conrad was that most dangerous of men, a romantic who believes himself a realist. He embraced a Social Darwinist conviction in the inevitability of struggle and was not optimistic about Austria-Hungary's prospects. The political compromises that kept the empire alive were, he felt, contemptible. He had watched with horror as in the last decades of peace the empire's international standing fell and its military power ossified while prospective enemies grew ever stronger. Only immediate, violent, decisive action could, Conrad believed, reverse the decline, force internal reform, and guarantee the empire's survival as a Great Power. The sixty-one-year-old general also had more personal reasons for favoring a war policy. For the best part of a decade, he had become disastrously obsessed with a married woman little more than half his age, the beautiful Gina von Reininghaus. Even as the European emergency spiraled out of control, he spent a startling amount of his time writing her long and effusive letters. Conrad came to believe that by romantically returning as a war hero he might have a slim chance of overcoming Austria's inflexible divorce law—and Gina's own hesitancy—to marry the object of his desire.[11]

The challenges Conrad faced in preparing Emperor Franz Joseph's army for war were unquestionably formidable, and not of his own making. The general himself, and for decades afterward his apologists, intoned that blame for the empire's defeat lay with its politicians, who had refused in peacetime to grant the army sufficient funding or manpower. There was truth in this argument. In 1912, the empire's military budget amounted to little more than a third of what Russia was spending, and around two-thirds of the funds France allocated to its army. The annual draft remained stuck at a level set in 1889. Whereas Germany trained 0.49 percent of its citizens every year, and Russia, which, thanks to its colossal population of 170 million souls, had no need to be thorough, conscripted 0.35 percent, the Habsburg Empire, with 51 million inhabitants, annually took just 0.27 percent into military service. The Hungarian parliament, filled with Magyar gentry demanding their own national army, blocked any increase until two years before the war. Consequently, the empire's defenses remained unmodernized, much of its artillery old-fashioned and its field army small. On mobilization in 1914, against 3,400,000 Russian troops and 250,000 Serbs, the Habsburg army could field only 1,687,000 men.[12]

In the powder keg that was Europe in the years before 1914, a wise man might have looked at these numbers and counseled caution in opening any hostilities. Conrad had acted with extreme belligerence. The general staff chief made repeated rabid demands for the empire to launch preemptive war. These had brought him into conflict with the Emperor's foreign minister, Alois Lexa Count Aehrenthal, and had eventually led to his dismissal in November 1911. He was brought back just over a year later as crisis overtook the Balkans. Conrad's ire focused particularly on two opponents who harbored irredentist ambitions for Habsburg territory; indeed, he believed conflict with them to be inevitable. Italy, though a Habsburg ally, was the first of his bugbears, and he channeled scarce resources to strengthening fortifications on the southwestern border and procuring new mountain artillery to fight it. Within months of his appointment in 1906, the general staff chief had advocated a surprise attack on the ally. He still favored the irrational idea five years later in spite of disapproval from both diplomats and the Emperor. His year-long dismissal had been triggered when he tried to demand a strike on Italy for the spring of 1912.[13]

Fatefully, Conrad's other obsession was Serbia. Although he at first regarded it as a lesser threat than the Habsburg "hereditary enemy" Italy, the general staff chief became increasingly obsessed with the small country. As early as 1907, he imagined forcibly incorporating it into the empire. In 1908, the Habsburg annexation of Bosnia-Herzegovina significantly worsened the countries' already poor relations, and Conrad started to think seriously about the implications of a clash. Serbia enjoyed close relations with Russia, and tension risked unleashing a much wider conflict inconceivable without backing from Austria-Hungary's close and much more powerful ally, Germany. Talks between Conrad and the Prussian general staff chief, Helmuth von Moltke, brought an assurance that if Russia intervened, Germany would regard this as cause for war. In 1912–1913, Serbia's military success and expansion south during the two Balkan Wars presented a real threat to Habsburg regional interests. From January 1, 1913, to January 1, 1914, Conrad pushed to open hostilities no fewer than twenty-five times. Half a year later, after the Sarajevo regicide, his entirely predictable advice was "War! War! War!"[14]

Conrad not only recklessly advocated war, but also failed to prepare the imperial army for the coming confrontation. For sure, Hungarian nationalists had squeezed the army's resources, but the general staff chief did not make the best use of those that were available. His mobilization plans betrayed a fundamental misunderstanding of Austria-Hungary's strategic needs. Conrad prized flexibility in his preparations. He had plans for war with Italy, Serbia, and Russia, as well as for combinations of these powers. While notionally sensible, flexibility sacrificed speed, which would be crucial if an existential conflict broke out with Russia. This was a huge mistake, for as Russia recovered from a lost war with Japan in 1904–1905 and focused attention on the Balkans, the probability of it intervening if Austria-Hungary attacked Serbia increased. The Tsar's provocative trial mobilization on the Galician border over the winter of 1912–1913, intended to intimidate Austro-Hungarian leaders into accepting Serbia's gains at Ottoman expense in the First Balkan War, signaled a new assertiveness.

To meet all eventualities during a mobilization, Conrad divided his army into three echelons. The largest, A-Echelon, was allocated twenty-seven of the army's forty-eight divisions and tasked with defending Galicia. Each division had around 18,000 men. A smaller "Balkan Minimal Group" with nine divisions would protect the empire's southern frontier from Serbia and Montenegro. The third group, B-Echelon, was a swing group of twelve divisions. In a war against Serbia and Russia, it was intended to bolster the Galician defense. Against Serbia alone, it would be sent south as an offensive force. This organization delayed deployment against Russia because, to maintain strategic flexibility, B-Echelon was held still while the other two groups were transported to their fronts. Had speed been the priority, then B-Echelon's divisions, stationed far from Galicia but near good railways, would have been loaded first. Compounding the error, Habsburg military transports moved at a snail's pace, just 18 kilometers (11 miles) per hour. The consequences were serious: although Russian intelligence predicted Habsburg deployment would end within fifteen days, it actually took twenty-four. Even before hostilities opened, any chance of achieving an early local superiority and dealing a blow to the large but slow-mobilizing Tsarist army was squandered.[15]

Breathtaking incompetence exacerbated these flaws in planning when the war Conrad had long demanded finally began in the summer of 1914. Through hesitancy and reluctance to confront the realities of a two-front war, Conrad left the empire's northeastern frontier frighteningly exposed to Russian attack. His first grave mistake was to order deployment only against Serbia—the country he wanted to fight—and, with characteristic wishful thinking, to persist in this course even after Russia's intention to intervene became undeniable. The alarmed Emperor prevailed upon Conrad at the end of July to redirect B-Echelon to Galicia, but the military rail technicians then insisted it was already too late. Farcically, the troops were permitted to continue south and sent on a 1,000-kilometer

(600-mile) diversion through the Balkans. Three divisions remained there to face the Serbs, two others were further delayed, and even the remainder, arriving "punctually" (by the schedule of the tardy general mobilization), detrained in eastern Galicia in time only to participate in the rout of the inadequate force that had been left to guard the region.

Conrad also botched the deployment of A-Echelon, the majority of his army, in Galicia. In the decade before the war, the Habsburg army had been riddled with Russian espionage. Top-secret documents had been stolen. A 1:42,000-scale plan of the defensive perimeter of the Fortress of Przemyśl and detailed technical descriptions of its individual forts were among them. So, too, was the 1912/1913 offensive deployment plan for war against Russia: a betrayal all the more chilling and humiliating as it was perpetrated by the former deputy chief of the Habsburg military intelligence service, Colonel Alfred Redl. Only after Redl's unmasking and suicide in May 1913 had this loss been discovered. Conrad had duly altered A-Echelon's deployment, opting, in case of war with Russia, to deploy the troops defensively deep inside Galicia behind the San and Dniester Rivers. This was a relatively strong position, but it meant abandoning at the outset a third of the province, including its capital, Lwów, to the invader.[16]

In mid-July 1914, as conflict with Serbia loomed, Conrad had confirmed these dispositions with his rail staff. Probably he hoped that maintaining a defensive position deep in Galicia would, even if Russia intervened, buy time for a lightning victory against the smaller Balkan enemy. On the evening of July 31, however, when it became impossible to ignore the menace of Russia's military mobilization, and pressure from the Emperor prompted him to switch B-Echelon units north, Conrad also decided to revert to an offensive stance in Galicia, and deploy along the province's border. As the military rail technicians insisted that their schedules were now unalterable, Habsburg units could not be carried by train to these new concentration points. Instead, more madness ensued: the troops were unloaded, as per the abandoned defensive scheme, in the middle of the province, and then they marched. Many had very long distances to cover. As part of the Second Army guarding the east of Galicia, III Corps offers a good example. The corps' units left their bases around Graz and entrained on August 10, taking a week to travel around 900 kilometers (560 miles) to the town of Stryj, behind the Dniester. There, they were unloaded from their rail wagons and ordered to march with all haste another 80 kilometers (50 miles) to jump-off positions just east of Lwów, the largest rail terminus in Galicia.[17]

The consequence of Conrad's unrealistic thinking and fumbling was a campaign lost before it had begun. By the end of August, a huge Russian force of fifty-three divisions stood against just thirty-four Habsburg divisions on the eastern front. Had the Habsburg general staff chief followed his original plan, the Galician defense would have had thirty-nine divisions, but the decision to send B-Echelon south had removed three permanently and delayed others from coming into action. His misconceived mobilization planning had already squandered any chance the army had of achieving a temporary local superiority in Galicia through rapid deployment, but the mess in detraining A-Echelon units far from their final jump-off positions caused further delay, and the long marches exhausted the troops before they had fired a shot. Despite his later exculpations, Conrad knew he had blundered. When the campaign started to go badly wrong, he would ruefully remark that if the former heir to the throne, Franz Ferdinand, were still alive, "he would have me shot." The punishment would have been richly deserved.[18]

THE HABSBURG ARMY High Command (AOK) arrived in Przemyśl, ready to direct operations, late on the afternoon of August 17. The commander-in-chief was a Habsburg, Archduke Friedrich, whose three qualifications for his important position were that he was a grandson of the general who had beaten Napoleon at Aspern in 1809;

that, thanks to a stocky frame and mutton chops, he looked suitably bluff and soldier-like; and that he lacked the confidence and competence to question Conrad's decisions. Stepping off the train with him were the new imperial heir, twenty-seven-year-old Archduke Karl, who was tagging along to learn how a war was fought, and, of course, general staff chief Conrad himself, who was to be the real director of the imminent campaign. The company set up their headquarters in vacated barracks in the city's Zasanie district north of the river. In the operations room, a large 1:400,000-scale map was spread out on a table. Red- and blue-painted lead counters were placed on top, marking the positions of the opposing forces. The game was afoot.[19]

The defense of Galicia posed a considerable challenge. To both the north and the east lay Russia, and the border, running 750 kilometers (460 miles), was huge. Conrad's solution was to create four armies. The First and Fourth Armies, positioned in the west and center of the province, were envisaged as a strike force. With a combined strength of seven corps, they were to attack to the northeast, into Russian territory. The Third Army, a small force of two corps stationed in the province's east, was to protect their right flank. The Second Army, whose four corps were supposed to be assisting farther south, was temporarily missing. Its staff and half of its troops were still stuck in the Balkans. In its place was a weaker formation of two corps named "Army Group Kövess," for its commander General Hermann von Kövess. While these forces arrayed, Conrad sent his ten cavalry divisions on a disaster-strewn reconnaissance mission 100 kilometers (60 miles) inside Russian territory. A new saddle, designed to keep soldiers sitting erect on parade, turned out to rub the skin off the horses' backs. Many riders had to dismount. Others were easily shot down when they collided with Russian infantry. Negligible information about enemy dispositions was gained, but the exertion broke the famous Habsburg cavalry, once the pride of the empire.[20]

The northeastern strike Conrad planned was strategic nonsense. Years before the war, Conrad and Moltke had tentatively discussed a joint concentric offensive from Galicia and East Prussia to encircle the Russians. On August 3, 1914, with the bulk of the German army deploying against Belgium and France, Moltke ruled it out. Without German cooperation, Conrad's attack was a push into the ether. The lack of any operational objective was betrayed by orders he issued on August 22, which, as the commander of the Fourth Army, General Moritz von Auffenberg, noted, "contained very detailed march tables, but no description . . . of what we were expected to *do*." Even so, initially both the First and Fourth Armies enjoyed some success as they advanced toward Lublin and Zamość. The strength of the opposing forces on this battlefield was roughly equal, and the first major clash, at Kraśnik on August 24, involving the First Army, went the Austrians' way, although with very heavy casualties. Two days later, the Fourth Army smashed into the Russian Fifth Army's flank, and an encirclement battle at Komarów, about 30 kilometers (19 miles) north of the border, began. The Russians escaped the trap, but lost 20,000 prisoners and 100 guns.[21]

In the east of Galicia, Habsburg forces were stretched thin and extremely vulnerable. The Russian Third and Eighth Armies opposing them had around 350,000 men—more than twice the defenders' strength. The victories in the north were of no help. Indeed, in trying to seal Auffenberg's partial success at Komerów, Conrad temporarily detached for him one of the Third Army's two corps. The Third Army was also not at all psychologically prepared for the ordeal it was about to face. General Rudolf von Brudermann, who had taken command on August 11, had no experience of a modern war. In this he was no different from all the other senior Habsburg commanders. Several of their Russian opponents, in contrast, had served in senior positions against Japan in 1905. Nevertheless, Brudermann had sought to cultivate an entirely misplaced bravado. What purported to be intelligence assessments were circulated claiming that Russian officers had no initiative, that their artillery had "so far hit nothing," and that their troops were afraid to attack. Fatuous advice was issued. Officers were urged to stand firm if they could not advance and, if troops shot off all their ammunition, to attack with the bayonet. Ominously, they were ordered "to acknowledge no limit on the infantry's sacrifice."[22]

On August 24, the Third Army, strengthened by the addition of III Corps from Army Group Kövess, was set marching. Conrad envisaged the army standing on heights behind the Gniła Lipa, a tributary of the Dniester River 40 kilometers (25 miles) east of Lwów. This was a strong position. The valley below was marshy, and bringing heavy military transport and guns across on the few large bridges would pose a challenge for any attacker. Brudermann, however, had other ideas. Full of bluster, and utterly ignorant of the strength of the enemy before him, he was keen to attack immediately. He hurled his troops forward over the tributary and advanced toward the town of Złoczów. On the sunny morning of August 26, they ran headlong into the advancing Russian Third Army.[23]

Colonel Jan Romer, a tough professional in command of the 30th Lwów Field Artillery Regiment, described this baptism of fire. His regiment had moved off at four o'clock in the morning, and six hours later it arrived at the village of Busko, in the north of the battlefield, where it went into action. Intelligence passed down by higher commanders suggested that in front lay only scattered enemy infantry and some Cossack squadrons. That this was a spectacular underestimation became obvious as soon as well-concealed Russian artillery opened up. Romer estimated there must have been thirty or forty guns firing, smothering his position in smoke and shrapnel. His own field guns, sixteen pieces in all, were drawn up in close support behind the infantry line.

To the colonel's great satisfaction, his gun crews did not waver. Like Romer himself, they were local men, defending hearth and home. Most were either active troops or recently released reservists, and so their training was fresh. "The bringing up of ammunition happened automatically during the fiercest fire, without the least need to force the men," he remembered. Indeed, so rapidly was salvo after salvo fired in support of the Habsburg infantry charging forward that Romer only feared his supply of shells would run low. The regiment suffered very heavily in this first action. After three hours, a fifth of the men were casualties. Romer himself was struck in the chest by a spent bullet and wounded in the knee, but after allowing himself to be bandaged, he returned to the battle.[24]

The Habsburg army displayed almost superhuman courage in this early fighting, but it was outnumbered and, crucially, heavily outgunned. Russian divisions fielded sixty guns to the Habsburg divisions' forty-eight. Their artillerymen were more skilled, too. The Tsarist force had absorbed many lessons from humiliating defeat at the hands of the Japanese in the war of 1904–1905, among them the importance of combined arms operations. Its field regulations stressed the dominance of firepower in combat, and its artillery was expected to work closely with forward infantry to support any advance. By contrast, as Romer frankly confessed, cooperation between the Habsburg artillery and infantry was weak. The gunners chose their own targets, often with only vague knowledge of enemy positions. Much ammunition was wasted. The obvious superiority of the Russian gunners, who seemed everywhere capable of putting down accurate and heavy bombardments, was debilitating. As one staff officer of the 11th Division, fighting on the Third Army's right, observed, the enemy's shellfire "instantly caused a feeling of defenselessness, which grew from one battle to the next."[25]

The Habsburg army's tactical doctrine exacerbated the problem. In peacetime, Conrad had enjoyed a reputation as a tactical genius, although his ideas about how to balance fire and movement, the most important military debate of the period, had barely developed since 1890, when he had first put them in print. Conrad, like most commanders of the day, was a firm advocate of the offensive, but he stood out for his uncompromising belief in the ability of sheer willpower to conquer the fire-swept battlefield. In Conrad's conception, artillery was not needed to clear a way forward. His 1911 regulations asserted that physically tough, determined, and aggressive infantry could alone "decide the battle." Within the professional officer corps, his subordinates thoroughly imbibed this mentality. Manic admonitions to act "ruthlessly" or "with utmost energy" were virtually obligatory in any order. At the outset, heavy casualties were not seen so much as a problem as proof of troops' "outstanding feats of arms."[26]

This toxic combination of inadequate fire support and a tactical doctrine encouraging impetuous rushes directly at the enemy brought horrendous loss of life when it was tested on the battlefield in the autumn of 1914. Officers suffered catastrophic casualties, for they led from the front, pulling their peasant soldiers forward through their own exemplary courage. The professionals, in particular, were determined to display no fear; as critics scathingly observed, they behaved as though accurate, long-range rifles were never invented and refused to use cover. Russian snipers, ordered to take down anyone wearing officers' distinctive yellow gaiters, reaped a grim harvest. The same mentality fostered a disdain for lifesaving digging. Regiments were quickly obliterated. On the first day of battle, August 26, units of the III "Iron" Corps, operating farther south from where Romer was fighting, lost between a quarter and a third of their men. Infantry Regiment 47, a mainly Austrian German unit, had 48 officers and 1,287 other ranks killed, wounded, or missing that day. Infantry Regiment 87, filled mostly with Slovenes, suffered 350 killed and 1,050 wounded in clumsy and fruitless attacks.[27]

The Third Army and, below it, Kövess's small force were stopped dead and then, on the 28th, knocked back. Brudermann ordered a retreat behind the Gniła Lipa, but his regiments had already taken such punishment that the Russians came irresistibly onward. On August 29, there were breakthroughs in the south of the Third Army's front. Lwów, the Galician capital, was threatened. There, confusion ruled. The city had been declared a fortress, although, unlike Przemyśl, and, farther west, Cracow, it had no permanent fortifications. Brudermann, in despair, could not see how his disintegrating army could defend it. He commanded the guns and garrison to be evacuated on August 30. The following day, as the evacuation was underway, the order was countermanded; Conrad had intervened. The fortress commander had to rush to the railway station and personally stop the departures. Heavy guns were unloaded and hastily returned to their positions outside the city. Lwów was now "to be held at all costs."[28]

"A STRATEGIST WITH an unusually fertile mind," was how Germany's General Erich Ludendorff once described Conrad: a backhanded compliment at best. As disaster loomed, the Habsburg general staff chief thought he spied opportunity. If the Fourth Army, which at this time was operating to the north in the Habsburg-Russian border area, could be turned about quickly, it might advance southeast and smash the flank of the Tsarist armies invading eastern Galicia. Conrad hurried to put this ambitious new scheme into action. Brudermann was told to hold on a shorter line just outside and south of Lwów. The Second Army, which at last was being completed with divisions that had been delayed in Serbia, was to defend farther south. The Fourth Army was still embroiled in the Battle of Komarów, but by the evening of September 1 it had routed its opponents. From the AOK, a command was dispatched directing General Auffenberg, the Fourth Army's commander, to shift as much strength as he could from the north, and from September 3 attack toward Lwów.[29]

While, in the safety of Przemyśl, Conrad choreographed elaborate maneuvers, Brudermann's headquarters in Lwów had all but ceased to function. The retreat from the Gniła Lipa had been badly mishandled. General Hermann von Kövess, on the right of the Third Army, believed its commander and staff had lost their grip. On August 30, he had been assured that his Transylvanian XII Corps' southern flank was covered, when in reality the units that were supposed to be protecting it were in full flight. The Russians had advanced into the gap and attacked, spreading chaos and forcing the corps into a disorderly retreat. Kövess found himself in the midst of the debacle.

Artillery fire had caught him in the open, knocking down his horse. Bruised and disheveled, but otherwise unhurt, he had picked himself up only to be surrounded by panicking Hussars galloping to the rear. The members of his staff who were with him scattered. With presence of mind, the general had seized a riderless cavalry mount and headed back to try to rally his troops. A week later, he wrote to Conrad to complain. What was needed, he fumed, was for real men to be put in command. "The old women and neurasthenics in uniform are killing us."[30]

Brudermann's days were numbered. Though on September 1 the AOK had reiterated its order to hold Lwów, the Third Army was by now so fatigued and frightened that resistance was fading. The disastrous collapse of two Hungarian formations, the 97th Landsturm Brigade and the 23rd Honvéd Infantry Division, that night north of Lwów exposed the troops' fragility. Both these formations would go on to serve in the garrison of Fortress Przemyśl. The Landsturm Brigade, which was where the collapse began, had in fact suffered rather less than most of the Third Army's units, for it had been sent up from Przemyśl as reinforcement and had been in action only since August 30. However, it was missing essential armament—above all, machine-guns. Moreover, its men were older and less fit than those of the field army, and they were just getting over a long and exhausting march. They had sustained terrible losses. Landsturm Infantry Regiment 10, one of the brigade's four regiments, had been sent into attack twice on September 1, and by evening it was missing a third of its complement, 26 officers and 1,200 men.[31]

Drained, dirty, and miserable, Landsturm Regiment 10 was directed to the small town of Kulików, 18 kilometers (11 miles) north of Lwów. Here, the dysfunctionality of the Third Army Command was on full display. The town was clogged with soldiers. Artillery and infantry trying to march up to the front collided and crossed with troops returning. Baggage wagons, of which Habsburg units towed an excessive number, blocked the way. There was no room to move. Everyone, wrote Lieutenant Emerich von Laky, one of the

Landsturm regiment's platoon commanders, using a very Central European simile, was rammed together "like herrings in a barrel." In this highly vulnerable situation, the troops were alarmed to hear rifle fire suddenly cracking through the darkness. The hubbub over the regiments ceased as everyone listened. A patrol was sent to investigate. Laky described what happened next:

> After a few minutes a part [of the patrol] appeared in disorganized clusters running at the exit [from the town]. There they halted, turned, and fired frantically but blindly at an invisible enemy. Another group, which did not stop, ran directly at the packed crowd.
>
> As if the Devil himself had run over, a cry of horror rose from a thousand voices:
>
> "Cossacks—Cossacks!"
>
> Everybody now started pushing and shoving to get away. More men began shooting, and the crackle of rifle fire and glint of hastily fixed bayonets in the lantern light added to the panic. Shrieking horses broke away and rampaged and trampled over men who had fallen in the crush. The screams of the wounded shattered the air. Officers who tried to restore order were ignored. Soldiers were driven by a single thought: flee to safety.

Lieutenant Laky thought he would not survive. Bullets were hissing all around. He only just succeeded in throwing himself into a doorway as a mob of panicking soldiers charged past. To escape the crush, other officers climbed walls and fences, peering down from their precarious perches like frightened gargoyles. At last, a bugle call sounded faintly above the chaos: "Cease fire!" At that moment, two other buglers ran past Laky, and he gave chase. Catching them, he grabbed both by the collar and shrieked into their ears "Sound that horn signal or I'll shoot you down!"

Once the signal was taken up by these and other buglers, it was astounding—so Laky observed—how quickly the panic ended. There were no Cossack horsemen. In fact, the nearest enemy was over

20 kilometers (12 miles) away. It had all been fantasy. Slowly, officers collected their men. With no orders, and unsure of where the rest of their regiment was, Laky and his fellow officers marched with two companies back down the road to Lwów in the small hours of the morning. The devastation caused by the panic loomed before them:

> Our hearts cringed at the sight of the rifles thrown away by cowardly and base soldiers. . . . Overturned wagons abandoned by their drivers and escorts, carts with scattered cargoes of sacks, wine, rum, and schnapps barrels, boxes of hard tack, thousands of loaves of bread all lay in piles on the ground, as if thrown haphazardly together by waves after a shipwreck. Between them were many cowhide knapsacks. . . . The corpses of horses and men lay in the ditches to the side of the streets. . . . The birds of prey had not yet detected the feast but human beasts, the defilers, the corpse robbers, were already on the scent, feasting like predators on the loot. In many places we drove off the corpse robbers with swords and bayonets. God be thanked [claimed Laky, a proud Magyar] that among the villainous corpse robbers there was not a single German or Hungarian. All were Polish infantrymen or Ruthenian supply soldiers.[32]

The panic had grave consequences. The flight of the 97th Landsturm Brigade and 23rd Honvéd Infantry Division left Lwów naked against attack from the north. At 7:00 a.m. on September 2, Third Army Command glumly informed the AOK that it must retreat another 25 kilometers (15 miles) westward, behind the Wereszyca River. Galicia's capital would be abandoned. Reluctantly, Conrad agreed. However, his patience with Brudermann was now at an end. The withdrawal from Lwów, which began that day, was executed with the usual incompetence. Thousands of rifles were left behind. Rations were doused with gasoline and burned as troops who desperately needed them marched by. On September 4, the "neurasthenic in uniform," Brudermann, was dismissed. In his place, the Third

Army at last received an effective commander, a grizzled Croat, the battle-tested General Svetozar Boroević.[33]

THE FINAL PHASE of the struggle for eastern Galicia now opened. Conrad's new ambition to encircle the Russians by pinning them to the front using the Second and Third Armies and driving into their flank with Auffenberg's Fourth was always doomed to fail. On his 1:400,000-scale map in Przemyśl his scheme must have looked very fine but, like most of the general staff chief's operational ideas, it was not grounded in reality. As Conrad in fact well knew, the Third Russian Army, into whose flank Auffenberg was supposed to smash, had changed its direction of march farther north. The two forces would instead have a bloody frontal collision. Moreover, after its Komarów offensive, the Habsburg Fourth Army was spent. Auffenberg reckoned that of its initial strength of 300,000 men at least 40,000 had become casualties. There was also a huge shortage of horses to pull the transports and guns. His own staff had no faith in the operation. "Our troops were overstrained, had frightful losses, our nerves were tensed for the worst," remembered Lieutenant-Colonel Theodor von Zeynek, the Fourth Army's chief of intelligence. "The mood was despairing, for we saw that our struggle was in vain."[34]

Even so, Auffenberg obeyed Conrad's orders. The Fourth Army left two of its corps facing northeast, about-turned its other three corps, and advanced. On September 6, battle was joined with the Russian Third Army. Meanwhile, on Auffenberg's right, the Habsburg Third and Second Armies stood on the Wereszyca. The Russian pursuit had been mercifully slow, permitting these troops crucial time to restore a semblance of discipline and establish their defenses. Boroević's appointment had also had a galvanizing effect: the Third Army's new commander castigated his subordinate generals for lackadaisical leadership and took measures to stiffen his soldiers' resolve. The Habsburg Army did not believe in static defense, even behind a strong river line. Instead, the Third Army's mission was to go forward in support of Auffenberg's offensive. To deter his tired troops from wavering in the attack, Boroević stationed 1,600 military police wearing high-visibility white armbands immediately behind them. Cowardice and disobedience would not be tolerated.[35]

The Second Battle of Lemberg (the German name for Lwów), as it was later titled, was the largest Habsburg operation of the First World War. All four of Conrad's armies, with forty and a half divisions fielding 600,000 combat troops, were committed. The memoir of Béla Moldován, a reserve officer of Honvéd Infantry Regiment 31 recruited from around the western Hungarian city of Veszprém, conveys a sense of how ghastly and confused the fighting was in this final, desperate struggle to retain eastern Galicia. Moldován served in the regiment's 4th March Battalion, one of the scratch-built units that Conrad's army rushed forward to seal gaps in its line. These lacked the veterans who in established units taught new recruits the fieldcraft they needed to survive; cohesion in their ranks was weak because the men had only recently been thrown together, and equipment was scant. The march battalions' combat performance was thus poor, and their casualties were atrociously heavy.[36]

The 4th March Battalion arrived at Rawa Ruska, a flashpoint of the battle, on September 7. The town's burned-out rail station with its dislodged name sign marked the threshold to a new and terrifying world. The houses were all shot up and the place was eerily deserted. Everybody had fled. Even the birds had gone.[37]

The sudden rumble of guns caused the virgin soldiers to freeze. "Artillery! Sounds like we're getting near the thick of it," opined someone. "Or it's getting near us," was the dark reply. The "big push" was underway: that much the men of the Fourth knew. What their role would be, no one had yet told them. They were ordered to post lookouts and get some sleep. The weather had turned. It was cold and damp now. Fires were forbidden for fear of alerting the enemy, and the soldiers had been issued only with light summer capes. Fog blanketed them, and by dawn all were soaked and shivering.

That next day, the march battalion set off for the front line, weapons at the ready. As they reached open ground, the earth immediately erupted. Shells threw up fountains of soil. Men were blown into the air. "Into the woods, on the double, and take cover!" officers shouted, and the men sprinted for safety. From the northeast, small-arms fire opened up. Bullets hammered into the trees. Branches fell. Moldován, a painter in private life, observed with almost detached fascination as the soldiers of his platoon cringed, curled up behind trees, or tried to use each other for cover. "Fantastic, what fear can drive us to," he later wrote.

It was not long before the battalion was called from this reserve position into the firing line. The soldiers formed into skirmish waves and moved off, trying to creep silently through the undergrowth. Soon, signs of battle started to multiply. The trees became more pockmarked and splintered. Abandoned equipment was strewn across the forest floor. The soldiers stumbled over their first dead, men of another Honvéd unit. Most striking were the hundreds of discarded Mannlicher rifles lying on the ground. The sandy soil that covered the battlefield had jammed their firing mechanisms, rendering them useless. "What has happened here?" wondered Moldován nervously. "It looks as if we've been sent to plug the gap left by some enormous rout."

Once the battalion reached the front line, some answers began to emerge. There was no good news. The day before, the first of the battle, the Russians had thrown back another Hungarian unit from the area. The enemy had strong positions, up on hills overlooking the 4th March Battalion's forest. The Russians' artillery outnumbered the brigade's by three to one, and it had the range of the battalion's line. A major action was expected for the following day.

The men spent an uneasy night at the front. When a reddish moon rose over them, some panicked that it was a Russian signal to attack, so stretched were their nerves. Word had circulated that their colonel, a "peacetime hero," had forbidden the digging of foxholes, as it "leads to cowardice and undermines discipline." Moldován wisely disobeyed and urged his platoon to use what time they had to dig in. He had not been issued with a spade, and so spent the small hours using the lid of a tin to scrape a shallow hole for himself. It would serve equally well as a makeshift firing position, or as a grave.

The first disaster happened before light. Somewhere in front voices speaking a Slavic language could be heard. The men of the Fourth had received strict orders to fire only on command, but they were nervous. One soldier, perhaps by accident, possibly because he could endure the tension no longer, loosed off a shot. Another followed. Then the entire line came alive as scared soldiers blazed away blindly into the darkness. It soon became clear that they had shot men of their own army. A detachment from the 34th Kassas, a regiment from northern Hungary filled with Slovaks, had fallen victim.[38]

Around dawn at five o'clock, the Russian bombardment began. "A flash of light straight ahead," recorded Moldován. "A howling noise above our heads, then the curtain of heaven is rent apart. Shrapnel shells!" The barrage at first fell to the rear and then slowly shifted forward toward the 4th March Battalion's positions—"so that no one can escape," Moldován realized. The precepts of peacetime training were exposed as false. Officers were supposed to command and inspire their soldiers, but under the hail of bullets and shrapnel balls Moldován found it impossible to move, much less direct his platoon, which was spread out along a 50-meter (164-foot) line. His shouted orders were drowned out by explosions and shooting. He could barely hear himself.

The brigade's artillery offered the beleaguered Hungarian infantry some sporadic support, but it was outmatched by the Russian guns. After a couple of hours, it ceased fire. Moldován and his men were pinned down. Though not yet hit, Moldován felt completely impotent. "The continuous deafening explosions, the howling of the flying shell fragments have practically stupefied me," he wrote. One shell landed so close that he was showered in soil, choking for air and scrabbling in panicked self-preservation. The rest of the battalion pulled back at midday, but he and his men, stationed out on the left flank and tasked with covering any retreat, did not get the message. As the day closed, he had no idea who of his platoon was still alive or who had fled. He was stunned and apathetic.

The appearance of a noncommissioned officer (NCO) by his side shook Moldován from his torpor. "Sir, I can see movement up ahead," the man warned. "Don't you think we should pull back? Those are Russians. If they find us here they'll beat us to death." After a slug of *pálinka*—strong Hungarian liquor—Moldován summoned the will to order a retreat. He jumped up and turned to flee the hell. Survivors from his decimated platoon followed. Past the debris of battle they ran, past piles of cartridge cases, past discarded equipment, past dead men. The Russians shot after them.

The Second Battle of Lemberg was another disaster for the Habsburg army: the bloody culmination of a campaign run on complacency and incompetence. Conrad talked up his attempt to encircle Russian forces invading eastern Galicia as a "very audacious plan." "Everything is, so to say, bet on a single card," he explained to his political adviser at the AOK on September 9. "If one army fails, then a total debacle is possible." The problem was that the Habsburg army's numerical weakness and Conrad's dispositions invited such failure. Through shifting the bulk of the Fourth Army and the belated completion of the Second Army, Conrad achieved what proved to be a rough parity of forces in eastern Galicia. From Rawa Ruska in the north to the Dniester River in the south, 454 understrength Habsburg infantry battalions, backed by 124 cavalry squadrons and 1,232 guns, faced off the Russian Third and Eighth Armies' 352 battalions, 267 squadrons, and 1,262 guns. Yet the penalty for this parity was the denudation of the northern frontier. There, the Habsburg First Army and the two corps which the Fourth Army had left behind as a rearguard quickly came under unbearable pressure.[39]

The defeat began with the Habsburg general Viktor Dankl's First Army. After victory at Kraśnik, the First Army had marched on Lublin. The Russians had raced in reinforcements to stop the city from falling, and at the start of September, two Tsarist armies and parts of a third—in all, 22 divisions supported by 900 guns—counterattacked Dankl's 13 divisions. The Russian Fourth Army went forward in the center, while a new Ninth Army attempted to turn Dankl's left flank. Most dangerously, on the right, the Russian Fifth Army, which Auffenberg had supposedly destroyed at Komarów, returned to action. The departure of most of Auffenberg's Fourth Army southeast had opened a 40-kilometer (25-mile) gap between the two corps it had retained in the north and Dankl's force, and into this the Russian Fifth Army charged. By the evening of September 9, Dankl was short on ammunition and unable to hold his position. He ordered his troops into a 15-kilometer (9-mile) retreat, wiring the AOK for permission to take them back a full 60 kilometers (40 miles), behind the San River.[40]

The advance of the Russian Fifth Army was not just dangerous for the Habsburg First Army but posed a lethal threat to the rest of Conrad's force. The gap into which the Russians were advancing widened as Dankl retreated, exposing the rear of the other Habsburg armies, fighting in the east, to attack. The two corps left by Auffenberg in the north were themselves threatened with encirclement and helpless to intervene, and the rest of the Fourth Army, the three corps directed southeast to outflank the Russians, was pinned around Rawa Ruska and unable to advance. Far from encircling the enemy, as Conrad had intended, the Habsburg army was in peril of having its own lines of communication severed. With his "very audacious plan" fast unraveling, the AOK debated whether the operation should be halted. The general staff chief himself was sharply opposed to that. The reason why offers a disturbing insight into Conrad's extraordinary self-obsession. What preyed on his mind was not so much the blow to his field army, and still less the loss of eastern Galicia, with all the attendant suffering, as the disaster that such a defeat would spell for his plans with Gina. "If I fail," Conrad confided, "then I shall also lose this woman; an appalling thought for me, for then I would have to withdraw into solitariness for the rest of my life."[41]

There was also a straw for Conrad to grasp in order to legitimize the continuation of the operation. Though the Fourth Army's corps facing the eastern invader were stuck, farther south, on September 8, the Habsburg Second and Third Armies had gone forward over the Wereszyca River. Astoundingly, given what they had already passed through, the troops fought ferociously. The fairly fresh IV Corps, recently arrived from the Balkans, achieved particular success on the Second Army's right wing, fueling hope that perhaps the Russians could be taken in the southern flank. On the 10th, Conrad hurried to Boroević's headquarters and then on to the battlefield to stiffen resolve, the first of only three visits he would make to the front during the entire war. On return to base at Przemyśl, the general staff chief fired off a characteristic order urging his armies onward in "irresistible, energetic, ruthless advance."[42]

In the end, it was all in vain. On September 10, the attacks in front of the Wereszyca bogged down. Worse, on the morning of the 11th, the Habsburg Army's radio intelligence section at Przemyśl intercepted a message, helpfully transmitted *en clair*, revealing that the Russian Fifth Army had ordered two corps to advance that day through the gap behind Auffenberg's Fourth Army as far as Cieszanów and Brusno. If the Russians reached these objectives, they would cut off the Fourth Army's supplies and its line of retreat. No forces were available to stop them. After eighteen consecutive days of battle, Auffenberg's rearguard, the two corps he had left in the north, had lost four-fifths of their strength and numbered just 10,000 men. This proved decisive. Though Conrad procrastinated, Auffenberg wisely disengaged his army to escape the trap. If the Fourth Army withdrew, then the Third and Second Armies below had to follow. That afternoon, Conrad reluctantly accepted that eastern Galicia was lost. At 5:30 p.m., the order went out to all armies for a general retreat to the San River.[43]

THE ARMY THAT fell back the tens of kilometers to Przemyśl was a shadow of the force that had concentrated in Galicia less than a month previously. From an initial strength of around 900,000 combat troops, 250,000 had been killed or wounded and another 100,000 languished in Russian captivity. The survivors felt hardly human. One company commander, Captain Rudolf Fleischer of the Bohemian Landwehr Regiment 30, an infantry unit in Auffenberg's Fourth Army, might stand to illustrate the wretchedness. Two weeks in action had cost his regiment 92 percent of its officers and 68 percent of the men in the ranks. The captain, a lucky survivor, had lost two batmen killed, and with them his greatcoat and kit. He was filthy, bearded, and wearing the same clothes he had put on at the start of the campaign. Like most of the men in the army, he was weak from stomach cramps and explosive diarrhea. The order to retreat, he remembered, after so much adversity and bloodshed, had left him "speechless and badly shaken."[44]

The retreat itself was a nightmare. The heavens opened and it rained and rained. The roads were churned to glutinous mud by the tramping of a hundred thousand feet and the wheels of heavy transport and artillery, all struggling westward. Stoppages were frequent, as troop columns crossed each other and stuck supply wagons blocked the way. There was no time for rest or food, however; orders from above and the feeling that the enemy might be just behind drove the hungry, dazed men onward. For Captain Fleischer, it was not the sights but the sounds of those desperate days and nights of marching that seared his consciousness:

> The crunching of the wheels in the sand, the snorting of horses and the bellowing of the cattle, the shouts and cries of the wagoneers and supply soldiers, the crack of whips and the cursing and scolding of the column commanders and men, the raucous quarrelling of the agitated, colliding people all wanting to reach safety, together generated an undefinable noise, a din and muffled roar, which . . . spread over the whole land. This was the breath, the voice of retreat.[45]

A defeated army is a dangerous thing. Propelled by fear, discipline fraying, humiliated, its officers and ranks search for scapegoats. In eastern Galicia, Ukrainian-speakers bore the brunt of the troops' rage. From the outset of the campaign these Ruthenes had been objects of suspicion. Senior commanders knew that a minority of the local intelligentsia regarded itself as Russian and had painful memories from peacetime of embarrassing conversions to the Russian Orthodox Church and spy scandals in Galicia. Though there was little hard evidence of treason, and later official investigation would conclude that most Ruthenes were either ardent Habsburg loyalists or, among the ill-educated peasantry, at least indifferent, self-exculpating commanders credulously seized upon and circulated tawdry fantasies of civilian betrayal. Before any major battle, army orders warned of local Russophile civilians ambushing Austro-Hungarian troops or signaling their positions to the enemy. Draconian countermeasures, justified with reference to the army's *Kriegsnotwehrrecht* (a law on the "right of self-defense in wartime"), were immediately instituted. Conrad was well aware of the ensuing brutality and approved of it. "We fight on our own territory as in a hostile land," he declared. "Everywhere Ruthenes are being executed under martial law."[46]

The full extent of the Habsburg army's assault on the Ukrainian-speaking population it was supposed to protect will likely never be known. The Russian army estimated that Conrad's men executed 1,500 people under martial law. Figures provided by local Ukrainian politicians were far higher, reaching over 30,000 shot or hanged. Drumhead courts and punitive massacres left a trail of blood and anguish, but little paper, which accounts for the uncertainty. What is sure, however, is that defeat and retreat stoked the violence. Every unit had its own tale of betrayal and revenge. Columns of Ruthenian prisoners, arrested on suspicion of spying, signaling, or digging trenches for the enemy, or simply because Russian soldiers had been found in their villages, were marched among withdrawing Habsburg troops and fleeing Jews and exposed to vicious reprisals. Landsturm

Infantry Regiment 10, which had panicked outside Lwów, hanged sixty-one civilians alone on the night of September 8–9. A soldier of Landsturm Infantry Regiment 21, another unit that would join the Przemyśl garrison, witnessed an entire Ruthenian village community being herded westward. The column halted so that the mayor, a man of "Herculean build," could be put against a wall and shot. Others were strung up. Corpses on the roadside trees, bobbing in the wind, marked the path of the retreating Habsburg army.[47]

The broken army converged on Fortress Przemyśl. The Second Army was supposed to pass by to the south. The Third and Fourth Armies were meant to cross the San River at and to the north of the Fortress. So mixed up were their supply units and so numerous were stragglers and deserters, however, that men of both these formations ended up in and around the city. The garrison's officers had been instructed about where to direct displaced troops and how to keep order, but none of them were really mentally prepared for the scenes of chaos they encountered as the flood of defeated troops and transport poured over the Fortress's outer defenses. "Even today, horror grips me," commented one fortress engineering officer fifty years later as he remembered the sights and sounds of that moment. What confronted the garrison on September 13 and 14 was no longer a military force, but a mob of frightened men and horses. Discipline was gone. So, too, was hope. Seeking a way of understanding the disaster, some yardstick by which to measure it, the officer settled on a historical analogy—the greatest military catastrophe of the modern age: "I saw the scenes which portray Napoleon's retreat from Russia rise up again incarnate before my eyes."[48]

THE FIELD ARMY did not linger in Przemyśl. Already on the evening of September 14, as Boroević's troops limped past the city's outer defenses, Conrad had decided to take them back another 140 kilometers (around 90 miles) to the Biała and Dunajec Rivers. Within the safety of the Fortress's walls, the soldiers were given rest and food, and then, on the 17th, set marching westward again. To the northwest, the Russians were already pushing on the outer flank of the First Army. Though moving cautiously, they were also following the retreat from eastern Galicia in overwhelming force. To remain on the San would invite encirclement by a vastly superior enemy.[49]

The Habsburg army was irreparably damaged through the debacle of Conrad's opening campaign. Although losses were horrendous, the ranks could be refilled; at this early stage of the war there was no shortage of cannon fodder. Impossible to replace, however, were the officers who had been trained in peacetime. Nearly half of them had become casualties by the year's end, and one in every fifteen lay dead on the battlefield. Moreover, the army was mentally scarred by the trauma of defeat and retreat. Years later, according to its official history, the cry "Cossacks are coming" could still trigger panic in some units. The same was true of its commander. For Conrad, defeat in eastern Galicia in the autumn of 1914 was not only a professional humiliation, but also a personal tragedy. His youngest and favorite son, Herbert, a second lieutenant in the 15th Dragoons, perished near Rawa Ruska on September 8. He was slaughtered in one of the vain assaults embodying the élan his father had once seen as the key to victory.[50]

In mid-September 1914, survival hung by a thread for the imperial army and the Habsburg Empire. If Conrad could take the troops back unimpeded to the Biała-Dunajec line, there was still a good chance of regenerating his crumbling force. Drafts could be brought up, ammunition replenished, veterans rested. The Germans, fresh from victories against Tsarist armies farther north, were promising to redeploy above Cracow, enabling a joint counteroffensive. For this to become reality, though, time was desperately needed. Somehow, the Russian pursuit had to be slowed. The city-fortress of Przemyśl, which controlled the main logistical arteries through to the west, suddenly and wholly unexpectedly became the pivot on which rested the fate of an empire. Conrad had never before had much faith in static fortifications, seeing them as cumbersome distractions from the maneuver warfare which alone could be decisive. Now, however, he reinforced the garrison, gritted his teeth, and hoped for the best. On September 16, as the field army prepared its final departure, the general staff chief issued Order No. 2096: "The Fortress Przemyśl will, for the moment, stand on its own and is to hold at all costs."[51]

CHAPTER TWO

"THE HEROES"

The Fortress of Przemyśl, the last hope of the Austro-Hungarian Empire in the autumn of 1914, was at least outwardly an imposing defensive complex. Seventeen main forts, eighteen smaller intermediate or forward forts, and two lines of trenches were positioned around its 48-kilometer (30-mile) outer perimeter. The forts were mostly obsolete designs, a lack of funds had limited upgrade, and nearly a third of their artillery dated from 1861, but their squat frontages, steep escarpments, and wide ditches still exuded menace. The same could not be said of the fortress garrison. Four Landsturm (territorial) brigades from western Austria, northern Hungary, and Galicia formed the backbone of the defense. No career officer with any self-respect or prospects would dream of serving in these units. Instead, they were led by academics, businessmen, and middling state officials with reserve commissions; or, as one bluntly described his comrades, "well-past-their-prime fatties." Their soldiers were an ethnographer's dream, though to most observers they were an undifferentiable, ill-educated peasant mass. All were in their thirties or forties, at the outer limits of military eligibility. The Austrian press would praise them to the skies during the siege, but the troops knew they were no good. With irony, they embraced the journalists' high-flown rhetoric and dubbed themselves "the Heroes."[1]

THE FIRST UNITS of the wartime garrison, belonging to the 111th Central Galician and 97th Hungarian Landsturm Infantry Brigades, had arrived at the Fortress on August 13. The Hungarians, who had several hundred kilometers to cover, journeyed by train. The Galicians, who lived closer and were less lucky, had marched. The regiments, all of older men, wore a mix of uniforms. Some had been issued with modern pike gray; others had made good shortages by distributing clothing in more conspicuous, obsolete dark blue. All their soldiers were very heavily laden. A cowhide knapsack, blanket, spare underwear, rolled-up greatcoat, leather equipment with sheathed bayonet, bread bag and water bottle, 120 rounds of ammunition, and a Mannlicher bolt-action rifle all weighed in at around 30 kilograms (around 66 pounds). It was a lot to carry for middle-aged conscripts who had been civilians just a fortnight earlier, and who had had no chance to prepare for the intense physical demands of wartime active service.[2]

Among the units sweating on Galicia's dusty roads that scorching August was the 3rd Battalion, Landsturm Infantry Regiment 18. Formed in the village of Czerteż, around 80 kilometers (50 miles) southwest of Przemyśl, it set out early on the morning of August 11 and arrived at the Fortress after a three-day march. This Landsturm battalion embodied most of the eccentricities common to these least martial of military units. Its single professional officer was its commander, Major Vinzenz Zipser. Like most professionals, he was a fanatical Habsburg loyalist. His subordinates joked that his blood ran "black-gold," the colors of the imperial standard. He had drawn a short straw with this posting, but was determined to meld the unpromising human material at his disposal into a fearsome fighting force. To his multinational officers, he stated firmly but ineffectually that the language of military service was German, and that he expected this to be their exclusive mode of communication, even in private conversation. He terrorized the men, too, stalking the ranks in search of dress misdemeanors. Wherever a tunic button was missing or a belt buckle tarnished he would punish the miscreant zealously, seeing in such sloppiness a mortal threat to the Habsburg war effort.[3]

This rigid command style did not sit well with the other officers, reservists from another world. Their military training was a decade in the past. The most exalted and exotic among them was the Polish nobleman Count Jerzy Wodzicki, the vice president of the Lwów City Council. There was also a university professor from the city of Brno, two judges, two architects, and a geometrician. Two others owned factories, and another a furniture warehouse. The remaining reserve officers, fifteen in total, were of irreproachably middle-class stock, mostly professionals, administrators, or officials. As a guest list for a gentlemen's club dinner, the officers' roll of III/Landsturm Infantry Regiment 18 would have promised a fascinating evening. However, as a warrior fraternity, a band of brothers sworn to defend to their dying breath the realms of a venerable emperor, these officers were unlikely to strike fear into many enemy hearts. In this terrible war, their ranks began to thin immediately. The first casualty was Dr. Wolf, the librarian of the Museum of the Czech Kingdom in Prague. This hero was, as a comrade remembered, "a very fat gentleman": "After the exhausting march to Przemyśl he fell ill and after a stay of a few hours in hospital departed on leave to Prague. I never saw him again."[4]

Beyond the almost complete absence of military qualities, what is also striking is how entirely alien the officers of the regiment were to the men they led. Of course, class distinctions between officers and their soldiers were virtually universal among the armies of 1914, and they even had advantages: the self-confidence, self-control, and education associated with an elite upbringing were, commanders insisted throughout the war, the best foundation for military leadership. However, the officers of the battalion were also geographically remote. Most lived 500–600 kilometers (310–375 miles) from Czerteż. Eight came from Vienna, five from Brno, and nine from other parts of Moravia or Bohemia. Only two, one Pole and one Ukrainian (this last a cadet rather than a full officer), were from Galicia. The cultural gulf between these officers—bourgeois big city slickers from the most economically advanced western regions of the Habsburg Empire— and the Central Galician battalion's rank and file was immense. In the eyes of the pious middle-aged peasants they led, the officers might as well have landed from Mars.[5]

The regional divide between III/Landsturm Infantry Regiment 18's officers and other ranks raised practical problems of language. All the battalion's officers, with the exception of the two from Galicia, had as their mother tongue Czech or German. Their men, by contrast, spoke Polish or Ukrainian. Occasionally, one came across a Yiddish-speaking Jew. Theoretically, this posed no great difficulty, for the Habsburg army had long experience of managing polyglot units. The army recognized three different types of languages. The "language of service," which was German in most of the army, and Hungarian in Honvéd and Hungarian Landsturm units, was used for all communication above the company level. (The Magyar term for Landsturm was *Népfelkelő*.) More important for interaction between the officers and the men was the "language of command," which was a list of eighty basic military words and phrases in either German or Hungarian, such as "March!," "At Ease!," and "Fire!" To cultivate deeper relations between ranks, all units also had one or more "regimental languages." Any tongue spoken by at least one-fifth of the regiment's personnel was so designated, and officers were obligated to learn every one of them in order to engage with their subordinates, bond with them, and exert influence over them.[6]

In III/Landsturm Infantry Regiment 18, as in most wartime formations, such intricate arrangements were pipe dreams. For officers, a decent grasp of the German language was essential, as it was the medium for communication with the various levels of the Fortress Command and with other units. Within the battalion's mess, German was also widely spoken, although, to annoy Major Zipser, the Czech officers made a special point of speaking their mother tongue to each other. Communication with the men was, kindly put, a challenge. Some officers may have gotten by with "Army Slavic," a most peculiar military Esperanto blending Slavic grammar with German military terminology. Thus, for example, the battalion's Poles could be ordered to *antretować* (from the German *antreten*—to form up) on parade, and would then *narugować* (*nachrücken*—to move up) to the front, before forming a *szwarmlinia* (*Schwarmlinie*—firing line). Others who spoke only German relied on the battalion's few Jews to act as intermediaries. Still, even with goodwill, careful listening, and much imagination on all sides, frontline command of Landsturm troops was difficult, as the battalion's adjutant, Second Lieutenant Bruno Prochaska, remembered:

> It is not easy to lead a Landsturm patrol. The men are good-natured, willing, and brave but slow, clumsy, and untaught. . . . None of them understands a word of German. Only the noncommissioned officer has mastered a little Austrian military German. The few nuggets of Polish that the officer knows fail when a man comes running up in haste and splutters rushed words in his Złoczów farmer's dialect. If the NCO is not immediately available, the officer must himself hurry over and see what it's about, even though it is perhaps nothing of consequence.[7]

The single but most defining shared characteristic of the officers and men in III/Landsturm Infantry Regiment 18 was age. Landsturm units were filled with the last class of the Habsburg conscription system, men between the ages of thirty-seven and forty-two. Their officers could be slightly, but not much, less ancient (in a military context): Prochaska, for example, was thirty-five. Their physical fitness was generally poor. The units had been allocated as a static fortress garrison because they would not have survived the hectic maneuvering of field service. With age came another distinctive quality:

risk aversion. The Landsturm were, quite literally, a dad's army, and men with familial responsibilities are rarely prone to vain heroics. The coming siege would show they could be courageous. It would reveal other attributes, too, above all an extraordinary capacity to endure great suffering. Nevertheless, these were soldiers more likely to be found in prayer at the bottom of a trench than charging over the top. A satirical "Saga of Heroism" penned unofficially during the siege for the garrison's amusement captured their mentality with gentle wit. These men who "in Landsturm Regiment their service gave (which everyone knows is very brave)," whenever in the forward line, would hope and pray to God divine "the enemy would not appear, on their horizon far or near."[8]

THE COMMANDER OF the Fortress, Lieutenant-General Hermann Kusmanek von Burgneustädten, was wisely chosen. Running a complex fortress-city like Przemyśl in war required a breadth of expertise in command and administration, and Kusmanek had proven credentials. His military career had begun in 1879, he had quickly qualified for a place on the General Staff, and he had honed his skills as a leader of men, rising to divisional command before his transfer to Przemyśl in May 1914. No less relevant, before 1908 Kusmanek had managed the Habsburg War Ministry's chief office for a decade. The experience of bureaucratic routine and dealing with civilians made him almost uniquely suitable for the challenges of commanding a fortress-city.[9]

This was as well, for Kusmanek faced immense responsibility at the outbreak of war. Przemyśl needed immediate protection from any Russian surprise assault, internal order had to be maintained and espionage combatted, and the Fortress had to be armed for battle. The AOK's designation of Przemyśl as its headquarters, and its arrival on August 17, added to the pressure. The Fortress's armament program was initiated on August 2, and was scheduled to take forty-two days to complete. Underinvestment in peacetime, and the military's erroneous expectation that a major conflict would be preceded by a period of tension in which neglected preparations could be made, meant there was a mind-boggling amount to do. Between August 14 and 18, a huge force of 27,000 military laborers joined 2,200 specialist technical troops and 300 officers in Przemyśl to carry out the works.[10]

A flurry of building began. Barracks, field kitchens, stables, and munitions and food magazines were quickly erected to accommodate the expanding garrison. To improve Przemyśl's defensibility, labor units laid roads and flung two new bridges across the San River. Most of the effort, though, was invested in readying the fortifications. When, in mid-August, news arrived that German infantry had captured the Belgian fortress-city of Liège by infiltrating between its forts, much of Przemyśl's labor force was hastily redirected to digging a continuous ring of trenches around the Fortress's outer perimeter. The men then strung about a million meters of wire in front of these positions. They sowed minefields and constructed some 200 artillery battery emplacements. After six weeks of toil, the fortress-city possessed three defensive belts. A circle of batteries and strongpoints guarded the inner core, the *Noyau*. Farther out lay some scattered intermediate provisional artillery emplacements, grandly known as the second line. By far the strongest position, and the only one that would matter if the enemy laid siege, was the 48-kilometer (30-mile) outer perimeter. This mostly lay 6–7 kilometers (around 4 miles) from the city center—though at its greatest extent in the southeast it was 11 kilometers (7 miles) away—and contained Przemyśl's permanent forts.[11]

The nerve center of the defense was the Fortress Command. It was located at 24 Mickiewicz Street, a handsome three-story corner house on one of the city's main thoroughfares. The Engineering Directorate and the main engineering and artillery depots, with access to the railway, were situated farther up the same road. From Mickiewicz Street, Kusmanek and his staff were connected by telephone to subordinate headquarters. The Fortress was divided into eight defense sectors, each with its own commander, artillery, and engineering specialist. Sectors I and II, south and north of the River San, together covered the inner defensive core. The other six sectors, numbered III to VIII, radiated out from this core like a spoked wheel, with each sector defending a section of the perimeter. Their commanders, and the subsector chiefs below them, had responsibility for the combat readiness of all the installations and troops in their sectors. Supply, maintenance, training, and hygiene all fell in their remit. In case of attack, these officers were to coordinate defensive operations.[12]

The keystones of Przemyśl's defensive system were the forts. Since the early 1880s, when the first of them had been built, artillery technology had advanced with staggering speed, leaving fortress designers struggling to catch up. The eight main perimeter forts constructed before 1887 were all high-standing trapezoid platforms with artillery positioned in open rooftop emplacements; these were intended to suppress enemy batteries at a distance and to withstand assault by infantry. As early as 1890, however, they were rendered obsolete by the development of the high-explosive shell and mortar shrapnel charge. Designers responded to these advances in a second wave of building in the next decade. The new "unit forts" were similar to the old forts in layout but incorporated thicker concrete and mounted armored gun turrets. At the turn of the century, the long-range capabilities of the latest artillery forced fortress designers into a radical tactical rethink. With enemy guns now able to bombard from positions far beyond their observers' sight, forts could patently no longer win long-distance artillery duels. Instead, as most clearly seen in forward works built around 1900 in Przemyśl's southeastern sector, the focus switched to dominating forward terrain through networks of fortifications built for mutual fire support.[13]

A tour of Fort I, "Salis-Soglio," offers a good sense of how these defensive installations looked and functioned.[14] Fort I was located on a dominating hill outside the village of Siedliska, 9 kilometers (5.5 miles) from the city center, and was a subsector headquarters

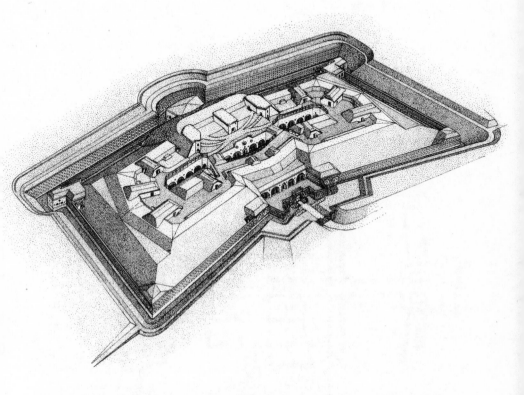

Fort I, "Salis-Soglio" (built in 1882–1886): Fort I was a tall, trapezoid "artillery fort" designed for independent long-range defense. In common with other forts of this decade, it was constructed of brick, concrete, and earth, with open rooftop gun emplacements.

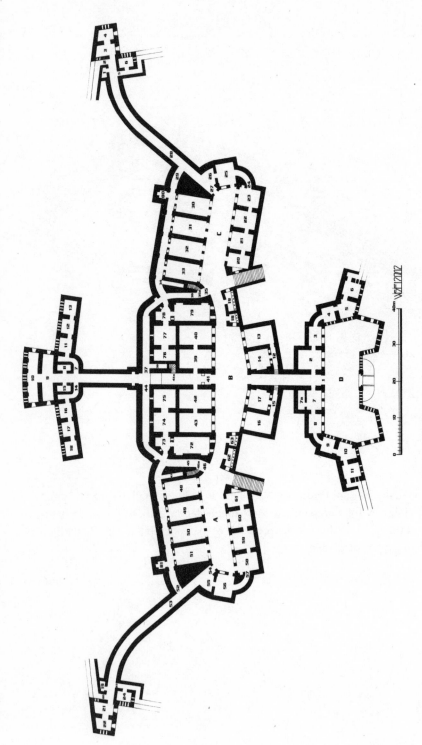

Fort I, "Salis-Soglio": ground plan.

Fort I, "Salis-Soglio" (Built 1882–1886)

Garrison: 1 commander, 7 other officers, a doctor and 400 soldiers

MAIN BUILDING

1—Entrance

2—Sleeping quarters for 11 soldiers

3, 8—Sleeping quarters for 5 soldiers

4–6, 9–11—Loop-holed rifle positions

7—Guard-room

7a—Cell

12, 15—Corridors to officers' sleeping quarters

13, 14, 16—Sleeping quarters for 4-5 officers

17—Fort commander's quarters

18, 63—Officers' latrines (6 in total)

19, 62—Soldiers' latrines (12 in total)

20—Telephone and telegraph center

21–23 and 58—Food magazines

24, 27, 29, 35–37, 46, 53, 54, 57—Corridors

25, 56—Kitchens

26, 55—Wells with pumps

28, 53—Tunnels to ditch corner caponiers

30–33, 39, 40, 42, 43, 48–51—Sleeping quarters for 19–22 soldiers

34, 47—Fuel and tool stores

35a, 38, 41a, 46a—Staircase

41—Central tunnel and shelter for 32 soldiers

59–61—Sickbay (with a total of 28 beds)

72–79—Artillery munitions magazines

80, 81—Munitions lifts

A, B, C, D—Open courtyards

DITCH CAPONIERS

1, 8, 15, 19—Munitions magazines

2, 5, 7, 14, 20, 23—Corridors

3, 4, 9, 10, 21, 22—15 cm M59 light cannon casemates

6, 11–13, 16–18, 24—Loop-holed rifle positions

in VI Defense Sector (in the southeast). The fort had been named in honor of General Daniel Salis-Soglio, the military engineer who had initiated the building of Przemyśl's defenses, but among the troops it was irreverently known as "Aunt Sally." Salis-Soglio had designed Fort I himself; construction had begun in 1882 and ended in 1886. Like other artillery forts built at this time, it was approximately trapezoid in shape, with a rear entrance and circumferential wall and ditch. The original plan had looked forward to the forts of the 1890s, though, insofar as it had incorporated two enormous armored cupolas, each carrying two 12 cm cannon. Budgetary constraints had forced their cancellation, but the center-front of the finished building still had a distinctive raised artillery platform where the cupolas should have been mounted, giving it a very high profile. Officers who served in "Aunt Sally" in 1914 considered it totally outmoded. The fort, wrote one cynic, was an ideal match for the Landsturm men who garrisoned it: for both, their "function mainly appears to be to draw enemy fire onto themselves."[15]

A visitor to Fort I would first arrive at a metal grille gate placed between high earthen embankments. The fort's main entrance—a high and heavy iron double door set into a red brick gatehouse and guarded by loopholes and a ditch—was directly ahead. It would have been natural to feel some unease as one crossed the short bridge over the ditch and passed through that door, and the sight of Fort I's rear courtyard must have accentuated the sense of threat. Here, the fort's grass-covered angular bulk loomed over the visitor. To either side were walls with more loopholes, behind which stood invisible sentries ready to blast away any intruder. To the front were brick and concrete casemates with sandbagged windows and, in the middle, a strong wooden door.

That sturdy door opened to reveal the interior of the fort. In summer months, men found it hard to suppress a shiver due to the abrupt drop in temperature as one crossed that threshold. Our visitor would enter a sloping passage. On the left was a guardroom with an adjacent windowless cell for any soldier who broke discipline.

The Habsburg army, in common with other contemporary militaries, sanctioned a wide range of punishments, but one unique to it was clapping men in irons, a holdover from the eighteenth century permitted only in war. In all likelihood, the fort possessed its own set of manacles, and it was to this cell that delinquents would be brought, to be cuffed in stress positions for several hours. On the other side of the passage were two small dormitories and, farther on, up some stairs to the left and right, officers' accommodation. Only the commander had his own quarters. The fort's other seven officers and doctor slept two or three to a room. These were thick-walled, vaulted chambers designed to survive impact from above. Each was equipped with a furnace and windows overlooking the central of the fort's three small inner courtyards.[16]

The fort's garrison consisted of its commander, three infantry officers, three artillery officers, an engineering officer, a doctor, and 400 NCOs and soldiers. From the passage, the visitor would emerge into the central courtyard. This, and the two other inner courtyards to the left and right, were fronted by and gave light to the twelve dormitories designated for the other ranks. Conditions here were extremely cramped. Although barely larger than the officers' rooms, each was equipped to sleep twenty to twenty-two soldiers. Worse, the 2.52 square meters (27 square feet) of personal space that army norms dictated were a soldier's entitlement were not really his own. As a third of the garrison was always on duty, the fort provided beds for only 266 men, and so a shift system operated. Toilet provision was even worse, though revealing of a nineteenth-century army's priorities. Officers, whose dignity needed to be maintained, had their own two blocks, each with three medieval-style privies. Theoretically, thanks to this generous provision, nearly the entire officer complement of the fort could defecate simultaneously. By contrast, the 400 other ranks were allocated just twelve toilets.

Fort I was supposed to be capable of sustained, independent resistance under siege. Two weeks of rations were therefore stockpiled in magazines opposite the men's barracks in the left- and right-hand courtyards. There were also two kitchens and freshwater wells. In the left-hand yard was a sickbay with twenty-eight beds, and in the right, a very important facility: the telephone center for the entire VI Defense Sector. If the garrison had trouble sleeping, this was not solely due to its cramped conditions; it was also because the fort's munitions magazines perilously surrounded the dormitories beyond the central courtyard. These held more than 10,000 explosive, shrapnel, and canister shells. Each of the fort's cannon had a quota of 500 shots stockpiled. According to the regulations, 100 for each gun had to be fused and ready for immediate use. For the fort's infantry, 269,000 rifle rounds were kept in storage.[17]

Standing in the central courtyard, our visitor had two choices. The first was to climb one of five staircases to the rooftop artillery platforms. From the grassy emplacements, gunners enjoyed excellent views over the surrounding countryside. At the front of the fort, where most of the guns were positioned, six lifts hoisted munitions from the magazine to an intermediate level, where they stayed in safety until needed. Concrete bunkers built between the emplacements had stairs to this level which gunners would use when carrying shells the rest of the way to the firing platform. This elaborate system would have been excellent had Fort I possessed any artillery worth firing. Nothing in the fort's armory could match the range of the modern Russian field artillery. Apart from four retrofitted but still mediocre 9 cm M75/96 field guns, the main armament comprised four 15 cm and six 12 cm Model 1861 cannon. These fifty-year-old pieces were dismally slow, as recoil meant they had to be repositioned after each shot, and their range, about 3 kilometers (less than 2 miles), was half that of the opposing artillery. Every time one was fired, its shell's old black powder propellant produced a plume of dense smoke, betraying the gun's position—though, as the fort itself was a huge sitting duck, this mattered little. The explosion when the shell reached the end of its flight path was disappointingly puny. Many were duds.[18]

The obsolescence of Fort I's artillery made its infantry positions all the more important. Our visitor's second option was to walk forward from the central courtyard down a steep tunnel known as the *Poterne*. The air here was musty, the walls damp. The tunnel ran through the middle of the fort to a "caponier," a bunker with gun ports, bisecting a frontal ditch that was 17 meters wide and 3.5 meters deep (about 56 feet by 11 feet). Two smaller caponiers, also reached by tunnels, were located at the fort's front corners. The main position for most of the garrison's 273 infantrymen was an exposed fire step running along the forward lip of the fort ditch. In front of this was a belt of wire 12 meters (about 40 feet) thick. If this infantry position fell, then the caponiers were the last line of defense. Inside, soldiers armed with rifles and light cannon could shoot down the length of the front and flanking ditches. Any enemy who jumped down into the caponiers' field of fire had little hope of climbing out alive.[19]

During those first hectic weeks of preparation, the greatest difficulty Kusmanek and his engineers encountered was how to clear the terrain in front of the forts. There were two problems: trees and people. Around much of the perimeter, forest offered an approaching enemy cover from observation and defensive fire. In the warm, dry weeks of August, the trees could easily have been burned down, but by the time labor units arrived in the middle of the month, other urgent tasks took priority. When, in September, the Fortress Engineering Directorate at last turned its attention to the forests, the weather had changed to rain and the opportunity was lost. Instead, soldiers were sent out to chop the trees down. One Defense Sector ended up deploying a quarter of its workforce on this task, with consequent neglect of other crucial building works. In the end, although the men tackled around 1,000 hectares of wood, the trees were totally cleared only on the southern perimeter, around Fort IV, "Optyń." Even there, the stumps promised attacking Russian infantry useful cover.[20]

The eviction of people living in front of the perimeter appeared at first, by contrast, straightforward. The Fortress Command was keen to do this, both to clear fields of fire and because it suspected the Ruthenian communities there of Russian sympathies and regarded them as security threats. No fewer than fourteen villages were blown up or burned down. Another fourteen were punished with demolition in the second half of September, when reports arrived that their inhabitants, likely under some duress, had assisted Russian troops with transportation services.[21]

The ruthlessness with which these actions were executed and the disregard for innocent people was chilling. Hungarian units cemented an evil reputation for brutality during these operations. Galician troops, who in some cases were throwing their own kin out of their homes, were horrified, but obeyed. Villagers were given very little warning, often just a few hours. Gendarmes would appear and announce that all the houses must be immediately evacuated. The victims had no chance to help themselves. Young men were already conscripted, and those left were women, children, and the infirm and elderly. If they argued, as they generally did, the army would be called. Menaced with bayonets, villagers packed what they could and left. Farm carts loaded high with possessions and carrying infants and the sick were flanked by overburdened adults, weeping children, and livestock, heading sadly westward.[22]

The Habsburg Empire and its army, having ejected and dispossessed these people, did little to help them. Some found their way to the bigger cities of Galicia, where they were placed on evacuation trains and joined the flood of 600,000 displaced people heading for the interior. Many spent the following years rotting in shoddily built refugee camps, where over the winter epidemics raged and killed up to a third of inmates. To the great concern of the Fortress Command, however, not all of them departed. Hundreds of families, on being turned away by nearby communities that had problems enough without taking in impoverished refugees, returned to their ruined homes. Stopped by troops on the defensive perimeter from seeking sanctuary in Przemyśl, these poor souls would endure a purgatory trapped between the besieging army and the Fortress. Desperate, knowledgeable about local topography, and sometimes furnished by the more humanitarian-minded officers with nearby minefields' locations, they posed exactly what the Fortress Command had initially feared: a worrying security risk.[23]

KUSMANEK'S FIRST TWO tasks at the war's start were to protect the Fortress from surprise attack and to prepare it for siege. The third, however, was inward-looking: to maintain internal order. Kusmanek possessed formidable powers to fulfill this objective. Galicia fell within the extensive "Area of the Army in the Field" declared on July 31, 1914, in which military commanders were placed above the civilian administration. On August 2, repressive martial law was imposed throughout this area. Unrest or rebellion, high treason, espionage, *lèse majesté*, and a host of other offenses detrimental to smooth mobilization were henceforth to be tried in military courts. Through the Fortress Command court, over which Kusmanek presided, passed a stream of civilian cases from the surrounding region.[24]

The Fortress Command, like other military and civilian authorities in Galicia, acted preemptively to smash all possible resistance. Lists of potential traitors had been drawn up by district officials in peacetime, and across the province, over 4,000 people were arrested in the first days of war. The Russophile intelligentsia was the primary target, but through paranoia, denunciations, and the cynical exploitation of the emergency by some Polish officials to rid themselves of troublesome local opponents, many Ukrainian nationalists, for whom rule by the Tsar would be a catastrophe, were also taken into a Kafkaesque "preventive detention." The Greek Catholic Church, to which most Ruthenes adhered, suffered particularly grievously. The similarity of its eastern rites to those of the Russian Orthodox Church, and the fact that a small minority of its priests were Russophile, all fueled suspicion. Its churches around Przemyśl had been built with Russian funds, went one rumor, as landmarks to help orientate an invading army. In the Przemyśl diocese, where 873 clergy had their ministries, more than a third of the priests, 314 altogether, were interned.[25]

Father Mykhailo Zubrytsky, the Greek Catholic priest of the village of Berehy Dolne, around 60 kilometers (around 40 miles) south of Przemyśl, was one of the many innocents caught up in these arrests. Zubrytsky, as a Ukrainian patriot, was an enemy of the Russophiles, but he also abhorred the Polish conservatives who ran Galicia. This did not, however, make him a traitor to the Habsburgs. On September 7, he was arrested by the local Polish gendarme. Zubrytsky had to ask what crime he was accused of, and was informed there was a rumor that he had publicly said, "The Russians are coming here, and it will be better for us." Awkwardly, the single alleged witness denied he had heard any such statement, but the gendarme nevertheless saw fit to place Zubrytsky in custody. Two days later, the priest found himself shut in a goods wagon traveling to Przemyśl. He and his fellow prisoners knew from others' experiences what awaited them when their train reached the city: "We heard on the way that those led under guard were inhumanely harassed: sand was thrown in their eyes, they were punched in the face and beaten around the head, were spat on. . . . The soldiers and gendarmes were on the side of the people and 'saw nothing.'"[26]

To Kusmanek, it must have seemed that treason and disloyalty were everywhere. Through Przemyśl passed columns of internees destined for the interior of the empire. Most of the alleged Russophiles, including Zubrytsky, ended up in Thalerhof camp near Graz, a name that would soon inspire dread. Already in mid-September, 3,267 people were incarcerated there, the majority without trial. Later, that number would double. Public executions, arbitrary violence, and lethally primitive conditions stamped this place, and 1,767 people would perish there.[27]

Denunciations brought many others accused of treasonous actions to the Fortress Court. Kusmanek scrupulously reviewed every single case. There were alleged Russophiles, such as Father Julian Połoszynowicz, who, according to the arresting gendarme (though no one would confirm it), had told his flock, "We have nothing to fear from the Russians, for we belong to them and they are marching only against the Poles and Jews." There were also people angered by the witch hunt, such as Katarzyna Ilków of Sanok, who thought "it would be better if Russia came here and held the government to account for the arrest of the politically suspicious." In these paranoid times, even the rude and ridiculous could stand before military judges if the insult was against the monarch. Agnieszka Szczęsna, from the village of Bolestraszyce in the northeast of the Fortress's defensive perimeter, found herself in this tragic position after she burst out: "Your Emperor can kiss my arse." Penalties were savage. Already in mid-August, the cowed citizens of Przemyśl were counting "ever more frequent executions." A diarist wrote, "They no longer shoot, but are now hanging."[28]

In later years, the story would circulate among Ukrainians that Kusmanek had declared, "If even a single Ruthene remains in Przemyśl, I cannot guarantee the Fortress!" Whether he said it or not, as the field army suffered defeat after defeat, stories of endemic treason circulated wildly, and the fortress commander embraced the paranoia, implementing one of the first ethnic cleansings of the Great War. On September 4, two days after Lwów's fall, he ordered that "*all persons of Ruthenian ethnicity* and *every person of other ethnicities whose political reliability is not absolutely certain* must be removed from the fortress area." Przemyśl's police and civilian authorities were co-opted to participate in this action, which covered the entire city and the surrounding villages. In military documentation, there was a revealing shift in language. Correspondence organizing trains to evacuate 6,000 "Ruthenian" workers eligible for military duty from Przemyśl in the middle of the month, for example, quickly came to refer instead to "Russophile" workers. Political loyalty was being equated with ethnicity, and in army administrators' minds, "Ruthenian" and "Russophile" had merged; indeed, they had become interchangeable.[29]

Beyond the city limits, this dangerous conceptual confusion, paired with a military legal system sanctioning instant and extreme punishment, generated extraordinary violence. Habsburg troops on operations could invoke the *Kriegsnotwehrrecht*—the law on the right of self-defense in wartime—to justify hostage-taking, summary executions, and the punitive destruction of habitations. Kusmanek repeatedly urged his garrison to make full use of this right. "It is the *duty* of all commanders to proceed as harshly as possible," he admonished on September 9. Two weeks later, while the Russians encircled Przemyśl, he warned again that "only the utmost ruthlessness and severity, most especially against the more influential persons, will have a chance of nipping in the bud the current highly treasonous movement within the population." As the siege started, the practice of dispatching suspected spies to the Fortress Court ceased, and what passed as justice was instead dispensed summarily by the defense sector commanders. Trials were condemned as unnecessarily slow and bureaucratic. Much better, as one sector commander explained, to execute such people on the spot than to make unnecessary arrests and fill the Fortress with "useless eaters."[30]

The sector commanders and their officers followed Kusmanek's orders assiduously. Troops who had been temporarily withdrawn from the garrison to support the field army farther east, or who joined it only after the army's retreat, already had experience of mass repression. The II/Landsturm Infantry Regiment 10, a Hungarian unit, had strung up tens of Ruthenes on the retreat to Przemyśl, and now applied its skills to Ruthenian settlements lying between the city and the surrounding ring of forts. As Lieutenant Emerich von Laky, one of its platoon commanders, reminisced, "there were some villages [here] in which the entire population had to be hanged, because they pulled out Russian rifles and cartridges from their hiding places and fired salvos at us." Sector commanders reinforced such fearful fantasies and further radicalized the violence against civilians. Colonel August Martinek of VII Sector in the south, for example, who was also commander of the 108th Landsturm Infantry Brigade, granted his men a license to murder: "All those inhabitants who remain between the opposing forward positions are—as has often been ascertained—traitors," he claimed sweepingly at the start of

October. "These, wherever they are met and even if momentarily no blame can be attached to them, are to be killed immediately without scruple or mercy."[31]

The racism, endemic fear, and contempt for civilians' lives among the officers, and the lifting of all limits on violence both around and beyond the fortress perimeter, undermined the garrison's discipline and brought bloodshed into the heart of the city. On September 15, Przemyśl became the scene of a massacre. That afternoon, a sorry column of prisoners followed the well-worn road from the Bakończyce rail station, which served Przemyśl's southeast, to police headquarters in the center of town. The forty-six Ruthenes were from the nearby district of Dobromil. Some, at least, had no idea why they had been arrested. One man, according to his widow, was on leave from the army and had thought when the gendarme arrived at his home that he was being called back. Only when the train drew into Przemyśl was it explained to the prisoners that they were accused of spreading Russophile propaganda. Most were peasants, though better-educated people, including railway workers, were also among them. There were two women. Mariya Ignatyevna Mokhnatskaya, the daughter of a parish priest, was just seventeen years old, still a schoolgirl.[32]

These were acutely anxious times in Przemyśl. The Habsburg field army's retreat through the fortress area had begun two days before. The mob that habitually met internees as they came off the trains was in a particularly vicious, retributive mood. The scene that confronted the prisoners must have been terrifying. A sea of faces contorted with rage and hate howled, shrieked, and screamed at them. A cry went up: "Traitors, hang them!" The prisoners were jostled and spat on. They were pushed and punched. Stones were thrown. A Landsturm corporal and five soldiers—their escort—forced their way forward and led the column down the long Dworski Street, which ran to the center of the city.[33]

The walk to police headquarters should have taken only a quarter of an hour, but it turned into a march to Golgotha. Harassed all the way, the prisoners were herded down the road, passing the city's Landwehr barracks. They had covered less than half the distance when, at the corner of Siemiradzki Street—named for a luminary of the Polish art world—the column encountered a group of Habsburg soldiers. One Hungarian stepped forward and asked where the prisoners were headed. The escort's reply was a gesture—most probably head tipped to one side, tongue stuck out, and a hand grasping an imaginary rope—that indicated the gallows.

Other soldiers surveyed the column in hostile silence. Most were dragoons, veterans of the retreat from eastern Galicia. Suddenly one of these "heroes" shouted. He recognized some of these prisoners. They were peasants who had ambushed a cavalry patrol and killed two of his comrades. In point of fact, Dobromil had not been touched by fighting, but fact had played no part in bringing these Ruthenes their misery, and it would not save them now. As the soldiers closed in menacingly, Mariya, the priest's daughter, dropped to her knees and cried out to the Mother of God to save the helpless people. A Honvéd felled her with a blow to the head from the blunt butt of his revolver. He then aimed between the girl's eyes and fired.[34]

The frenzy of bloodshed lasted half an hour. The soldiers slashed and stabbed with their sabers or ripped out planks and posts from an adjacent fence and used these to beat the prisoners to a pulp. Eyewitnesses spoke of victims being literally "torn to death." Anybody who tried to run was shot. The Landsturm escort stood back, unwilling or simply not brave enough to intervene. Then, as suddenly as the massacre began, it ended. The killers dispersed. The streets emptied. When a policeman belatedly arrived on the scene, there remained only "quivering, steaming hunks of meat" strewn around the road and the blood- and brain-spattered walls of surrounding houses. Miraculously, two male prisoners survived. One, severely wounded, was taken to the hospital. The other was brought to the police cells. He was later conscripted into the Austro-Hungarian army. After a most perfunctory investigation, the case was closed. No perpetrator was identified and no charges ever laid for this atrocity.[35]

As the Russian army approached Przemyśl, the fortress garrison swelled to 131,000 men and 21,000 horses. This was strength far beyond anything planned in peacetime, when 85,000 men and just 3,700 horses had been thought an adequate defense. The vastly inflated numbers marked how critical the Fortress had suddenly become, for with the field army in full flight, General Franz Conrad von Hötzendorf desperately needed Przemyśl to stall the enemy and win time for recovery and reorganization. The numbers also reflected the deficiencies of prewar preparation, for included in the total were the nearly 30,000 military laborers who, together with many horses, stayed to continue upgrading the defenses. At midday on September 12, in pouring rain, the AOK slipped away, relocating 180 kilometers (110 miles) west to the town of Nowy Sącz. Four days later, as the field army also prepared to withdraw, Kusmanek received the inevitable but unhappy news that he and his garrison were now on their own and must "hold at all costs." It was his fifty-fourth birthday.[36]

The garrison had been expanded with units retreating through Przemyśl under the Third Army. At the height of the crisis in the east, only the 111th Galician Landsturm Brigade had remained to secure the Fortress. Now, after a fortnight on operations with the field army, the 97th Hungarian Landsturm Brigade returned and the 108th western Austrian and 93rd eastern Galician Landsturm Brigades were also transferred to Kusmanek's command. These units were not only poorly equipped, without machine-guns, and filled with older men, but had been devastated by the heavy fighting. Most were at half or two-thirds strength and utterly demoralized. Commanders used contorted logic to raise their mood and spin recent defeats positively. The field army, these troops were assured, had won a stunning success by denying the enemy decisive victory. The flight from eastern Galicia was an obvious act of inspired leadership: "As the army would have exhausted its strength in any further advance, an operational pause was necessary," explained the 108th Landsturm Brigade's Commander dubiously. Therefore the army has been pulled back, despite its triumphant progress.[37]

The enlarged garrison's elite formation was the 23rd Honvéd Infantry Division. Its commander, Lieutenant-General Árpád Tamásy von Fogaras, who had been in the post for less than two weeks, became Kusmanek's deputy in the Fortress. The formation came from southern Hungary, and while two of its regiments had been raised in predominantly Magyar areas, the other two, the 7th Versecz and 8th Lugos Infantry Regiments, contained Romanians, Serbs, and Germans as well as Hungarian-speakers. Whereas the Landsturm Brigades, backed by regular fortress artillery, served as the mainstay of the defense, the 23rd Division's younger, better-armed, and more recently trained personnel provided the Fortress with an offensive capability, opening the opportunity for spoiling operations beyond the forts. Even so, the division's combat record was mixed. At the start of September, its discipline had dissolved in a night panic outside Lwów. The troops had fired on each other and then fled helter-skelter into the city, where the divisional commander (Tamásy's predecessor) and his two brigadiers had checked themselves into a hotel and refused to be roused from bed.[38]

How dedicatedly these troops, some with homes a thousand kilometers away, would fight in Przemyśl's defense was an open question. Over half of the 40½ Landsturm battalions in the garrison were recruited in Galicia, and it might be supposed that these local men would most strongly resist Russian invasion. This was not the view of the Fortress Command, however. Kusmanek's paranoid gaze had widened to embrace the entire garrison, and by mid-September he feared for the loyalty of the 19½ battalions containing substantial numbers of Ruthenes. The defense was urgently reorganized to stop perimeter forts from being manned solely by these troops. Trusted Hungarians were stationed in their stead in key defensive installations. One eastern Galician unit, Landsturm Infantry Regiment 19, was even hysterically condemned as "dangerous for the Fortress" and sent away to join the field army.[39]

The shoddy treatment of Landsturm Regiment 19 underlines how ethnic prejudice influenced senior Habsburg officers' handling

of their troops. Distrust of the regiment was inflamed by its commander, who complained that, in fighting farther east, the men had
"left officers in the lurch and fled," discarding arms and equipment in
their haste to escape. In the chaos and defeats of the early autumn of
1914, however, such behavior was hardly unique. The 23rd Honvéd
Division's inglorious night panic offers just one telling example. Yet
whereas the Hungarian formation's dissolution was firmly blamed
on lackadaisical leadership, in judging Landsturm Regiment 19 senior officers fixated on the ethnic composition and loyalty of the
unit's rank and file. Around one-third of the men in the regiment
were Polish; the other two-thirds were Ruthenes from the district
of Brzeżany, southeast of Lwów. The commanders insisted this was
a "Russophile area" and castigated the men as "socialists and Russophiles." In reality, as the initial regimental report conceded, the
unit was deplorably unprepared for battle. There was a shortage of
officers, and those present were unfit; moreover, the soldiers were
"too old" and their rifle training was "equal to zero."[40]

The senior commanders held a firm trust in formations from the
Austrian heartlands and Hungary, and this trust rested on similarly
ingrained, but positive, ethnic and regional stereotypes. The 108th
Landsturm Brigade drew men from Saint Pölten, near Vienna, and
from Tyrol and Vorarlberg, a mountainous border region facing Italy
with a long and romantic martial tradition and a reputation for piety
and dynastic loyalty. For Habsburg professional officers, these traits
were the gold-standard guarantees of dependability. Even so, the
troops were deployed very far from home. Their commander, Colonel Martinek, spoke of a "holy duty" and reminded his men they
had sworn before God "to assist *wheresoever* His Majesty wishes in
the defense of the Realm." This did not halt growing discontent in
the ranks. As the soldiers well knew, the Landsturm was primarily
intended for local defense, and rumors flourished that their transfer
to the Galician front was illegal.[41]

This disgruntlement had real consequences for the brigade's combat motivation. March discipline on the way to battle in eastern

Galicia was appalling. Of course, the hot weather and a lack of training did not help, and some officers, ever sensitive to perceived minority disloyalty, saw in the mass straggling evidence of dissension among the formation's Italian-speaking contingent. However, dissatisfaction was clearly far more widespread. Belying the stereotype of stolid, unquestioningly monarchist peasantry, one German-speaking *Vorarlberger* wrote to his province's chief official to relay his comrades' resentment, asking whether the provincial authorities had really sanctioned the use of these family men in lethal fighting so far from home. He was hauled before a court-martial. Incorporation into the Przemyśl garrison, and with it immediate reduction to fortress rations, which were lower than those for troops on field service, did nothing to improve morale. One educated Pole who served alongside these soldiers described them as "depressed." "All are old men aged 37–42 with wrinkled faces and furrowed brows," he wrote. "They haven't looked death in the eyes; they've stayed in the family home. And now they're bid here to defend a land that is totally foreign to them! How could they be enthusiastic?"[42]

The Hungarians, and above all their officers, were far more positive about service at Przemyśl. They considered themselves the backbone of the defense, though everyone else thought they were thugs who hogged the medals, terrorized civilians, plundered worse than the Russians, and forced "defenseless women to give them everything that pleases them." The Magyar gentry, who provided the Honvéd's leadership, nurtured a fond sense of themselves as an ancient warrior nation. For centuries their people had been the first bastion of European civilization against eastern barbarism, and Przemyśl would add another heroic chapter to this glorious history. Sadly, as the 23rd Honvéd Division's panic outside Lwów testified, reality did not always match this exalted self-image. Such rhetoric also ignored the great ethnic diversity of many "Hungarian" units. Serb and Romanian conscripts subjected to the particularly harsh discriminatory and assimilationist policies of the past decade were unlikely to have welcomed this compulsory opportunity to contribute to the glory of the Hungarian nation.[43]

Even so, for true Magyars there were good reasons to fight. Hungary, or at least the members of its ruling class, the nobility, had benefited greatly from the 1867 "Compromise" with the Habsburgs. They had gained a decisive voice in the workings of a venerable empire and complete autonomy in their own historic Lands of St. Stephen, stretching from Croatia to the Carpathian Mountains. There were plenty of Magyars who despised the Habsburgs, taking inspiration from the thwarted War of Independence in 1848–1849. Franz Ferdinand, the assassinated heir, had been widely reviled for his plans to reduce Hungarian influence. Yet the monarch's call to arms had moved even independentists, and although, as one Hussar officer put it, the heir "was not our friend," honor demanded avenging the murder at Sarajevo. The Hungarian government articulated the sentiment stirringly when, at the outset, it had called on its people to disabuse "those who in their brazen presumption believed that we could be insulted without consequence. . . . For our threatened interests and for our honor we shall bring to bear the tested strength of our nation and our glorious army."[44]

Revulsion against the Russians was also widespread in Hungary, and not just because they were blamed for escalating the small Habsburg "punishment expedition" against Serbia into a European conflagration. Much of the Magyar elite had neither forgotten nor forgiven the Tsarist army's brutal intervention in 1849 and its decisive defeat of Magyar rebels fighting for freedom. A more universal motivation, though, resonating among all classes, was fear of what the Russians might do if they invaded Hungary a second time. Better to fight at Przemyśl than in Pest. In the editorial of its very first issue on October 4, the Fortress's Hungarian newspaper, the *Tábori Újság* (Field News), expressed this guiding thought ringingly: "We all feel that we are standing at the gates of Hungary. In this exposed place we are defending our homeland, our families, our loved ones, our little children, our present happiness and our future hope. If we do not hold, the way is open for the Russians to Hungary."[45]

COSSACK HORSEMEN APPEARED to the north of Przemyśl on September 17. These field-stained warriors, mounted on small, tough steppe horses and brandishing lances, were harbingers of a powerful force just behind them. The Russian Third Army was closing in, and on the next day, the fortified bridgehead across the San River at Jarosław, 30 kilometers (19 miles) downstream from Przemyśl, came under attack. Kusmanek sent reinforcements, but the defense held for only three days. The San, its waters swollen by the autumn rains, had presented a formidable obstacle to the Russian advance, but with the bridgehead's fall the Russian XI Corps was able, on September 22, to push across advance troops and begin the blockade of the north side of the Fortress. Two other formations, the IX and X Corps, invested the east and southeast of the Fortress perimeter. A huge cavalry force, numbering four divisions, some 16,000 riders, was dispatched to complete the encirclement.[46]

In the Fortress, there was final frenetic activity. Labor units were kept very busy. The Habsburg Third Army had departed Przemyśl on September 17 and 18, leaving behind an almighty mess to clean up. The field units' other gift to the Fortress was dysentery and cholera, which doctors feared would spread out of control. The garrison's own hygiene was dubious. Daily orders complained of unburied human and horse excrement and putrid kitchen waste strewn around the main training ground at Wilcza, northeast of Przemyśl. In the city itself, the filthy public toilets were condemned as "*great dangers.*" Troops had to be vigorously reminded not to clog latrines with rubbish and not to relieve themselves in the open. Disinfectant was in short supply. Strict disciplinary measures and the terror that cholera inspired among the soldiers forced improvement. The waterborne epidemic killed one in four of everyone it touched in an exceptionally ghastly manner. Vomiting and an uncontrollable diarrhea, with a characteristic yellowy rice-water stool, caused severe dehydration and a collapse in blood pressure with consequent kidney damage. In the worst cases, death might take just four gruesome hours.[47]

A mass of supplies rolled into the city at this eleventh hour. The Fortress's food stocks were, according to its armament plan, supposed to suffice for a three-month siege. Despite the larger-than-expected garrison and the necessity to surrender a vast quantity of flour—equivalent to around one and a half months' rations for the expanded garrison—to the field army, this was nearly achieved. At the siege's opening, the Fortress magazines held enough vegetables to feed the troops for 95 days, 89 days of flour rations, and preserved meat and live cattle for 74 days. The horses were slightly less well-provisioned, with 69 days of oats. Much of this food came into the Fortress by rail until the bridges on the last working connection, running south from Przemyśl, were blown on September 19. Some was also collected by the Fortress Command. The Fortress had 4,000 wagons to bring in fodder and grain from the surrounding countryside. Around 1,400 were also sent to the Jarosław bridgehead before it fell to evacuate supplies. This wagon column was an imposing 18 kilometers (11 miles) long, but through incompetence, only the first 800 wagons received an armed escort. The other 600 traveled unprotected, and on their return journey were intercepted by roving Russian cavalry. Nearly half were lost.[48]

The Fortress's stock of other essentials for the siege was disappointing. For its 988 artillery pieces there were 475,000 shells. The scarce modern pieces in its armory, twenty-four 8 cm M05 field guns and four huge and powerful 30.5 cm M11 mortars, had, respectively, 500 and just 75 shells per weapon. The infantry was better supplied, with 4.6 million rounds of small-arms ammunition. Stores of clothing were patently inadequate. The depots held just 42,500 shirts and 15,300 pairs of shoes, not nearly enough to replace items damaged on service. Indeed, many labor units wore their own civilian clothing for lack of uniforms. Most dramatically, disaster was only narrowly avoided when the Fortress's entire supply of gasoline was accidently evacuated by rail. Frantic telegraphing to stations along the line achieved a promise that the seven tankers would be returned, and the Habsburg army rear command dispatched another twenty-two, without being sure if they would still make it through to Przemyśl. Fortunately, both trains rolled into the city station before lunchtime on the 19th, only hours before the Niżankowice bridge to the south was destroyed, severing the last rail link.[49]

While this prime example of what the empire's German ally would wearily call *Habsburger Schlamperei*—"Habsburg sloppiness"—was underway, Kusmanek made an important last-minute alteration to the fortress perimeter. The forts in the southwestern sector had been built close to the city, and a line of hills lay ahead. The commander fretted that if the Russians occupied those hills, 6–7 kilometers (around 4 miles) from Przemyśl's center, they would be able to bring the major bridges across the San under artillery fire. Movement between the north and south of the Fortress would become impossible, and the fortress headquarters itself would be a target. To forestall such a catastrophe, Kusmanek ordered that trenches, strongpoints, and battery positions be dug on these hills. From September 22 to 26, the long-suffering labor units hurriedly carried out the works under the eyes of the enemy. The new "Pod Mazurami–Helicha" advance line required four extra infantry battalions, some 4,000 men, but thanks to the reinforcements that had just joined the fortress garrison, this proved no great problem.[50]

The garrison nervously watched as the ring tightened around them. The last road to the west was cut on September 23; a convoy sent from the Fortress to fetch ammunition in Dynów, 45 kilometers (28 miles) away, reached its destination but found the way blocked by the enemy when it tried to return. The day before, shells fell on the perimeter. All the time, Russian troops were pushing and probing, testing the defenders. Advance posts on the Fortress's eastern and southeastern fronts were forced back. Kusmanek tried to resist. On the 25th, a sortie with five battalions (some 5,000 men) went forward to retake lost positions in the east. Two days later, the 23rd Honvéd Divion's commander, Tamásy, with a formation more than double that size, struck in the south. Tamásy's Hungarians punched through the enemy sentry chain and advanced 7 kilometers (more than 4 miles) before retreating that same evening. To the soldiers, the exertion must have appeared pointless, but it did briefly distract the Russians, prompting them to divert reinforcements to contain the threat.[51]

The fortress commander attempted to steel his men for the coming ordeal. The reinforcements were put through a crash course in garrison procedures. However, there was much confusion. The decision to intermix units from various parts of the empire in the defense sectors, intended to hedge against Ruthenian treason, had served to create less a bulwark than a Babel. Whatever language they used, the troops were anxious. Soothing orders explained how thoroughly the Fortress had been prepared. The men were issued with painstaking instructions on how to react to attack, and reassured from "past experience" that Russian artillery tended more to "make a din than inflict casualties." Nobody, and especially not those regiments whose ranks had already been ravaged by shellfire in open ground, believed it. To the Fortress Command's alarm, subaltern officers in charge of the forts appeared less interested in strengthening their defenses than in ascertaining under what conditions they would be permitted to evacuate. After the rumor circulated that bombardment by heavy calibers would justify abandoning the forts, Kusmanek intervened. The fort garrisons "are not permitted in battle to leave alive," he warned. Anyone who fled would be shot down by troops positioned to the rear.[52]

Kusmanek's counterattack to the east on September 25 offered a taste of how his multinational garrison would perform in battle. The III/Landsturm Infantry Regiment 18 took part, along with other

Galician and Hungarian Landsturm. The start of the operation was not without problems. One Magyar battalion commander had a heart attack and fell off his horse as he led his men to their jump-off positions. In III/Regiment 18, so worried were officers about morale after three sleepless nights exposed in forward positions that they decided not to forewarn their soldiers about the coming assault: "The poor things went into combat without being aware of it," remembered one lieutenant, guiltily. Nevertheless, once the operation began, training kicked in and the unit quickly spread out into loose order. Commanders were impressed: it was "just like on the parade ground," with a line of reserves to the rear and, in front, a well-spaced-out skirmisher line. The men moved rapidly in order to present a difficult target for enemy artillery.[53]

The afternoon's big success was won by I/Landsturm Infantry Regiment 17, fighting on the left flank around the village of Medyka. The unit, raised from around Rzeszów in central Galicia, was predominantly Polish but with a small Ruthenian contingent. It was one of the units Kusmanek distrusted. Its objective was Russian positions just to Medyka's southeast, on Hill 251, and this was to be its baptism of fire. Wisely, the battalion's officers eschewed a frontal assault. Instead, they had their companies cooperate to take the position in the flank. Not all went well. One of the companies retreated as soon as the first shrapnel burst over it, and another panicked and fled when it was caught in a crossfire. However, proving Poles and Ruthenes could fight, the 4th Company stormed the hill, captured the Russian artillery observation post on the summit, and took five prisoners. As a bonus, at least in the eyes of its officers, the battalion also burned down half of Medyka.[54]

Elsewhere the battle went badly. The right wing of the operation was aimed at expelling Russians from the woods northeast of the village of Byków, around 3 kilometers (2 miles) from the perimeter. The III/Landsturm Regiment 18, for which this was also the first major engagement, went bravely forward through artillery fire but then ran into a classic problem of twentieth-century combat:

the enemy was invisible. The Russian infantry, more than a match for their opponents, had entrenched just inside the wood. The regiment's officers searched in vain for the clear target their army's regulations had taught them to expect. The neighboring Hungarian battalion had the same problem, and was pinned in the open. Bullets zipped around them, filling the air with noise. Some droned, others cracked or flashed past. Those that flew high whistled and sang. The frightened men clawed into the sodden ground. Soon, cries of wounded added to the cacophony.[55]

When, on that bitterly cold and depressing night, the Landsturm withdrew inside the Fortress, Kusmanek and the "heroes" had much to mull over. The Russians were clearly formidable opponents. For Habsburg commanders, the operation had displayed ominous shortcomings. Cooperation between battalions of different nationalities had been nonexistent. The day's problems and panics had exposed their old soldiers' fragility in the face of modern battle. In the ranks, unease was felt at leaders' willingness to sacrifice lives for positions that could neither be taken nor held. Even so, there were bright spots. The Galicians had performed creditably, and at their best had even surpassed the trusted Hungarians. Discipline had mostly held. Moreover, if the Russians attacked the Fortress, then it would be they who would have to cross open ground, and the perimeter defenses were far stronger than those that had stopped the Landsturm. The forts and interval trenches were ready. Perhaps there was hope.

ON THE MORNING of October 2, a small party of Russians strolled down the Jarosław Road north of the fortress perimeter. The four men—a bugler, an NCO, and two officers—walked under a white flag. The leader, a lieutenant-colonel, carried a letter from the commander of the Third Army, General Radko Dimitriev. The Russians knew Przemyśl's forts were antique, and they had not been impressed by what they had seen of the Habsburg garrison's fighting capabilities. They wanted a quick surrender.[56]

The Russians' intention was to intimidate. General Dimitriev, a short, stocky Bulgarian in the Tsar's service whose admirers optimistically claimed was blessed with "a profile reminiscent of Napoleon," was not charged with taking Przemyśl. His army had encircled the city, but he and his men had already been ordered to advance on Cracow, and a new blockading force was in formation. However, Dimitriev's name inspired some awe. He had won fame during the First Balkan War two years earlier, when he led Bulgarian troops to the gates of the Ottoman capital, Constantinople.[57]

The Russian party was allowed into the Habsburg forward positions, and the commander of nearby Fort XI, "Duńkowiczki," telegraphed to the Fortress Command for instructions. The answer received was to hold the lieutenant-colonel blindfolded but to send back his companions. A car would come. Three hours passed.

While the envoy waited, Kusmanek and his staff hatched a plan, and 24 Mickiewicz Street underwent a little light redecoration. When at last the Russian was collected and brought to the Fortress Command, he was received by Tamásy, a big man who, resplendent in his lieutenant-general's uniform, could not fail to impress. The Hungarian introduced himself as the Fortress's general staff chief, accepted the envoy's letter, and exited through a door on which was prominently displayed a freshly painted sign: "Army Commander." The fortress staff were trying a deception of their own. Tamásy's introduction and the sign both implied the Fortress had double the strength and far higher-quality troops than were in fact present.

Kusmanek was livid when he, Tamásy, and the Fortress's real staff chief, the much lower-ranked Lieutenant-Colonel Ottokar Hubert, read Dimitriev's letter:

Fortune has abandoned the Austrian Army. Our troops' most recent successful battles have given me the opportunity to encircle the Fortress Przemyśl entrusted to Your Excellency. I regard any help for you from outside as impossible. To avoid needless bloodshed, I believe now is the time to propose that Your Excellency surrender the Fortress. Should this be done, it would be possible to request from the High Command honorable conditions for you and your garrison.

The commander of the army blockading Przemyśl
General Radko Dimitriev

The company laughed loudly and scornfully for the benefit of the envoy in the adjacent room, and then a note was returned. Kusmanek's celebrated reply was curt: "I find it beneath my dignity to grant a substantive answer to your insulting suggestion." If the Russians wanted the Fortress, they were going to have to fight.

CHAPTER THREE

STORM

Hermann Kusmanek von Burgneustädten must have felt himself the loneliest man in the world. The fortress he commanded was stranded deep in enemy territory; the nearest friendly troops were 70 kilometers (around 45 miles) distant. His defenses were obsolete, his garrison mostly unfit, and he had just insulted an emissary from the most powerful army on the planet. He had one sliver of hope. On October 1, an Albatros biplane had made a bumpy landing on the fortress airstrip. Its passenger, Captain Franz von Raabl of the General Staff, brought a promise so secret that the AOK had decided it must be delivered in person: an Austro-Hungarian offensive was imminent.[1]

In the following days, uncertainty ruled at the Fortress Command. Would the Russians attack? On October 3, enemy troops were seen leaving the vicinity north of the Fortress. An operation was launched early the next morning to try to disrupt their departure. Otherwise, the front was mostly quiet. Yet any illusion that Przemyśl might escape assault was shattered on the night of October 4–5, when the Fortress's northwestern front signaled an enemy approach. Soon similar reports followed from the north, and then from the southeastern and southern fronts. Kusmanek was under intense pressure. If the Fortress was going to survive long enough to be rescued, he would have to divine correctly where, on its 48-kilometer (30-mile) circumference, the Russians would direct their main thrust, and then quickly dispatch reinforcements. Worse, and pivotal in the coming battle, was a matter he could do little about. Defeat or victory hung on the resilience of the garrison's old soldiers in the eye of the storm.[2]

GENERAL ALEKSEI ALEKSEEVICH Brusilov, the commander of the Russian army group around Przemyśl, was a real warrior. In stark contrast to Kusmanek—whose father had been a policeman—he was scion of a noble military family which through generations had made its name in the Tsars' service. Alone among Imperial Russia's generals, he would emerge from the First World War with an enhanced reputation, thanks to his famous victory over the Habsburg army in 1916. Already in 1914, he had star quality. With his slender frame and intelligent eyes, Brusilov stood out from the majority of thick-set Russian general staff officers, and he differed from them too by eschewing their tactical conservatism. He was a risk-taker, a cavalryman with "a heart for every adventure," yet also savvy, with broad experience and a reputation as a thorough trainer of men. Although in the post only since October 1, he immediately made it his mission to conquer the Fortress.[3]

The capture of Przemyśl, Brusilov realized, would open the way for an invasion of Central Europe. At the very least, taking it would secure Russian gains in eastern Galicia. Yet much more could be expected. Stavka, the Russian high command, was at this time transferring forces north for a huge war-winning offensive from the Vistula River to bring about "a deep penetration into Germany." Seizing the important transportation hub of Przemyśl would let Brusilov put the main east-west railway traversing Galicia into service. Together with the release for field operations of the 90,000 men currently blockading the Fortress, it would also offer the possibility to, as he put it, "develop and extend" the main campaign in the north with an advance on Cracow. There was no time to lose. Signs were mounting of the Austro-Hungarian field army's coming counterattack, and preparations had not yet begun to take Przemyśl by storm.[4]

Brusilov had command of three armies. The Third and Eighth Armies formed the Galician front, while a separate, improvised blockade army surrounded Przemyśl. Believing an attack on the Fortress to be too risky, Stavka had wanted it merely screened, and so the blockade army comprised just five fairly low-grade reserve infantry divisions and a cavalry division. Brusilov now strengthened the force considerably. Its commander, Lieutenant-General Dmitry Grigorevich Shcherbachev, was told on October 2 to prepare an immediate assault. From the Eighth Army, the 12th and 19th Divisions, peacetime-raised "active" formations with substantial artillery support and troops trained in modern tactics; the 3rd Rifle Brigade, another "active" formation filled with young, fit soldiers; and a reserve division were transferred to his command. He also received reinforcements of heavy artillery.[5]

Even with a total of 483 guns, 117 infantry battalions, and 24 squadrons of cavalry, Shcherbachev's task was difficult. Artillery was his big weakness. In the years before the war, some states had developed fortress-busting ordnance. The Habsburg army's Škoda 30.5 cm siege howitzers, 8 of which it had loaned out to its ally, and Germany's own Krupp 42 cm monsters had leveled Belgium's forts at Liège and Namur—both of more modern construction than Przemyśl—in a few days in August 1914. However, the Russian army had neglected the development of siege artillery. The heaviest modern weapon it fielded in 1914, of which Shcherbachev had 23, was the much smaller, French-designed Schneider-Creusot 15.2 cm howitzer. Even with 36 12.2 cm howitzers and 4 highly accurate 10.7 cm guns, of every 8 artillery pieces in Shcherbachev's army only 1 was a heavy piece. Worse, as the Russians would soon discover, none of this ordnance was sufficiently powerful to crack the Przemyśl forts' stone and concrete casemates.[6]

Brusilov did not consider the blockade army's lack of siege artillery as a major problem. He believed that Przemyśl could be taken with only minimal bombardment, and so Shcherbachev pressed ahead with planning. The blockade army would storm the Fortress simultaneously from three sides. In the north, a subordinate group of 168 guns and 43 infantry battalions was placed under Lieutenant-General Leonid Lesh to launch a diversionary attack, designed to distract and draw in the Fortress's mobile reserve. Meanwhile, over on the south side, 7 rifle battalions backed by 24 guns would go forward to guard the flank of the main assault in the southeast. Thirty-nine heavy artillery pieces, among them all of the 15.2 cm howitzers, along with 232 field guns, would support 65 battalions concentrated to the northeast of and around the village of Siedliska on this decisive front.[7]

Shcherbachev had good reasons to select the southeastern sector as the focus of his assault. Defenses on the west side of the Fortress were weak, but too far removed from transport links to supply an attack force. The Fortress's northern sector was its strongest, while any Russian victory in the south would not be decisive, because behind this sector's forts ran a line of hills, on which the defenders could rapidly organize effective emergency resistance. By contrast, conquering the southeastern sector, and above all its center around Siedliska, where the elevated terrain dominated both flanks and the rear, promised to crack open the Fortress's entire defensive perimeter. Observation over the sector's thirteen permanent forts was excellent, nearby hills offered good cover for the attackers' artillery, and the proximity of the Lwów–Mościska railway line meant that supply would be easy. The defenses in the crucial Siedliska subsector were vulnerable to bombardment by Russian guns positioned both to the east and the south.[8]

The attack would be no walkover. At Siedliska, Fort I, "Salis-Soglio," may have been outmoded, but in front of it was a crescent of six smaller forward forts, four of which had been built at the turn of the century and were equipped with armored gun turrets. Yet for an assault force lacking heavy firepower, choosing the Siedliska area as the focal point of the storm made particular sense. Unlike elsewhere in the southeastern sector, here woods, gullies, and ruined villages offered assaulting infantry a good, covered approach to within 1–2 kilometers (around a mile) of the forward forts. Shcherbachev deployed his best unit, the 19th Division, against the crescent's northern defenses, Forts I/1, I/2, and I/3. To help it and its southerly neighbor, the 69th Reserve Division, break through quickly, he issued wire cutters, extra shovels, and even—a novelty in 1914—scarce supplies of hand grenades. As compensation for the artillery's impotence against the fort casemates, sappers carrying guncotton charges would accompany the infantry to blow holes in the fort walls. Everything depended on closing with the defenders.[9]

The attackers' preparations were necessarily hasty. Brusilov's Third and Eighth Armies would be unable to hold when the reinvigorated Habsburg field army counterattacked from the west. Shcherbachev's first order to his army on October 3 was to deploy to jump-off positions 2–4 kilometers (1–2.5 miles) from the Fortress by the next morning; as reinforcements had long distances to cover, however, this proved impossible. On the northern and southern fronts, units were still 6–8 kilometers (4–5 miles) from Przemyśl's defensive perimeter in the evening. The 19th Division, designated for the primary assault in the southeast, hurried through mud and pouring rain all night on the 3rd, arriving exhausted some 7 kilometers (a little more than 4 miles) away from the Fortress on the following day. There was no time to begin an artillery bombardment or for the infantry to reconnoiter the front. Nonetheless, Shcherbachev shared his chief's confidence. After all, the Russians had the fortress plans. Their intelligence bluntly judged its installations to "belong to the realm of history." Poor shooting had betrayed the garrison's ancient guns and low level of training, and deserters had, with drama, told of the deep alienation of the Ruthenes and the poor spirits among the men of the Landsturm. There was little doubt: the Fortress must fall.[10]

THE MEN OF the 3rd Battalion, Landsturm Infantry Regiment 18—mostly Poles and Ruthenes—had spent the morning of October 5 training on the Wilcza exercise grounds northeast of the city. It was cold, and rain was coming down in sheets. The instruction had taken on a new urgency though, for word of the Russian emissary's visit had spread quickly. Besides, everyone had seen enemy reconnaissance aircraft circling like birds of prey over the Fortress. Most ominously, since eight o'clock that morning a swelling rumble of shellfire had echoed from the forward forts.[11]

With their training over for the day, the soldiers were glad to return to barracks and dry out their sodden clothing. At three o'clock, as they were busy with fatigues, a bugle call suddenly rang out: Alarm! Men struggled uncomfortably into still damp greatcoats, fumbled with equipment, and grabbed rifles. Their NCOs hustled them into marching order. No one was sure what the alert was about. Officers appeared, orders were issued, and the column set off on the glutinous road to the southeast, toward Siedliska. On the horizon, above the hills in front of them, the soldiers could see columns of smoke erupting. Small white clouds darted across the dark sky. Detonations, never quite synchronous with the clouds, resounded with ever greater force as the column marched onward. It was, felt one officer, "as if an enormous fist [was] raining furious blows on a locked door."[12]

As dusk fell, the battalion at last arrived at Fort I. "Aunt Sally" had taken a beating. The earthen roof was pockmarked by direct hits, and the rear courtyard was strewn with fallen masonry. Russian artillery had now ceased fire for the night, but Austrian guns in the sector continued to blaze away deafeningly. Major Vinzenz Zipser, who headed up the battalion, left his men on the road and went to report to the subsector commander. A password was whispered, and the sentry heaved open the heavy iron door. The major disappeared inside the bowels of the fort.[13]

While the battalion waited, frenetic activity began all around them. Along the road trundled unlit wagons carrying munitions and repair materials. A constant stream of messengers circulated through the fort, and from it also emerged engineering details, sent out to patch shot-up telephone wires. At last Zipser returned with some definite information. Gathering his officers around him, and trying to hide his nervousness, he gravely told them that the Russians were ready to launch their infantry assault. The battalion was to stay near Fort I as the subsector reserve. He personally would take up position inside the fort. Companies were to disperse in the vale between fort and road. Each man should dig a hole as protection for when the enemy bombardment resumed in the morning. Lastly, Zipser admonished his comrades, whatever the danger, officers should keep their heads and remain calm. At that moment, a nearby howitzer let off another shell. Zipser jumped. The aura of manly strength was ruined.

THE STANDING ORDERS of the Przemyśl defense were very clear: "The garrison's mission is to hold the Fortress as long as possible. That, from beginning to end, is the guiding consideration." By the evening of October 5, Kusmanek and his staff had good reason to worry that "as long as possible" would not be very long at all. The Russian infantry had taken all its first-day objectives in the critical southeastern defense sector. Austro-Hungarian advance posts on hills outside the perimeter had quickly fallen. Now, enemy assault troops were only 1–2 kilometers (around a mile) away and preparing to storm the forts themselves.[14]

Virtuoso Russian tactics had been on display since the early morning, when lookouts and artillery observers had seen groups of men in drab green suddenly rise up out of the earth and advance toward the Fortress. With their own light artillery firing over them to keep down defenders' heads, the Russian infantry had dispersed into droplets, trickling forward individually or in small bands, and then digging in. The forts' guns fired ineffectively. The Russians' tactics denied them good targets, and firing the 1861-era ordnance—"slow, inaccurate, and unpredictable"—was, wrote one frustrated artillery-man, like using flintlocks against modern rifles.[15]

Following their training, which had imbued a healthy respect for firepower, the Russians never exposed themselves for long. Once the first assault troops had entrenched, others came forward to join them in cover. Then the procedure would be repeated: run, dig, run, dig, run, dig, rhythmically closing the gap with the defense. At-tacking to the east of Siedliska, the Russian 19th Division lost just 23 men dead and 239 wounded taking the Austrians' advance hill-top positions. By evening, Forts I/1 and I/2 faced its regiments only 1,000 paces away.[16]

To brace the defense, Kusmanek started to dispatch reinforce-ments. Four batteries of modern field guns arrived outside Fort XIV, "Hurko," in the sector's north, that night. Infantry, too, were alerted. Landsturm Regiment 18 was among the first units to be sent, but as the fortress staff became convinced that the southeast was the decisive attack front, more troops were gradually committed. The 23rd Honvéd Infantry Division, the Fortress's best formation, was stationed in reserve, behind Siedliska. By the evening of October 6, the defenders in the sector had doubled, from thirteen to twenty-five battalions.[17]

Though the first day's fighting had gone badly, Kusmanek could take some consolation from the resilience of the forts. So far, these had withstood enemy shellfire. The Russian artillery was difficult to locate and possessed ample ammunition, which it fired extremely accurately, but it lacked the power to wreak major destruction. Even its heaviest shells had failed to penetrate the forts' concrete carapaces. In consequence, the garrison's casualties were extremely low: on the entire southern front during the first day of fighting, there were just four dead and nineteen wounded. To the attackers' surprise, the ar-mored turrets on the upgraded and more modern forts also proved impervious to their fire. Over the following three days they put only a single one out of action, on Fort XV on the southeastern front, and this only because a shell bent the gun barrel protruding from it.

On another occasion, a hardened steel observation cupola was spun around by a direct hit, but the unfortunate observer inside, though doubtless shocked and deafened, remained unharmed.[18]

The major source of worry for Kusmanek and his staff was the all-important human component of the defense. Officers appeared to be disturbingly fragile. Even before the guns had opened up, the commander of Fort IV, "Optyń," the key defensive installation on the southern front, had a sudden nervous collapse. Once the fighting began, more officers immediately reported they were sick. The loss of the Fortress's forward positions so quickly, parts of which had been strongly built and manned, was also highly disconcerting. The Fortress's intelligence officer, Felix Hölzer, put most of the blame on the Ruthenian-Polish Landsturm. These troops were "pretty worthless!" he wrote disgustedly. Their precipitous retreat was not a manifestation of lack of patriotism or monarchical loyalty, however; they simply could not cope with the combat. One Polish artillery officer who had just returned from duty in the advance trenches evinced their shock: "His overcoat had been ripped by shrapnel fragments, he was shivering all over from cold because he was soaked—and from nerves. With wild eyes he told of how they had been smothered with pounds of iron fragments, and that hell couldn't be worse."[19]

If Kusmanek and his staff had little sleep that night, their overwrought troops had none at all. In the forts, gunners frantically fired blindly into the blackness, repelling phantom legions. Powerful searchlights on the roof walls ceaselessly crisscrossed no-man's-land. Sentries strained for any sign of attack. The men of III/Landsturm Regiment 18 shared in the general fear. Lieutenant Jan Vit's 10th Company had moved forward from Siedliska to shelters situated in the gap behind Forts I/4 and I/5, ready at a moment's notice to man the interval trenches. They ate a bite of bread and sausage and lay on the bare floor, tossing and turning. "With apprehension, we waited for what would come next," remembered the lieutenant. Whatever this would be, one thing was for certain: it would be horrible.[20]

An illustration from "A Saga of Heroes" (*Eine Helden Sage: Przemysl*, 1915), p. 8a, a very funny epic poem composed by an anonymous soldier that circulated among the garrison of Przemyśl during the siege. The story follows the travails of two Russian deserters, whose desperate wish to surrender is thwarted at every turn by the fortress defenders' cowardice. This picture shows panicking Austrians in a communications dugout. The Landsturm soldiers at the front have fled before the approaching deserters, assuming them to be the vanguard of an assault force, and sent warning back to the "heroes" pictured here that an overwhelming Russian offensive is underway against the Fortress.

OVER IN RUSSIAN headquarters, the commander of the blockade army, Lieutenant-General Shcherbachev, was a man in a hurry. The evening of October 5 had brought unwelcome reports that the Habsburg field army had started its advance. Little time was left to capture the Fortress. Keen to build on the day's successes and win, in his orders for October 6 Shcherbachev instructed his forces to take the perimeter forts. "We are engaged in a great undertaking," he reminded all his divisional commanders. "For success an unyielding determination is necessary, heroism and skill. No obstacle can be permitted to stop us. The enemy is capable of fighting, but already shaken. God and the prayers of all Russia are with us."[21]

However, Shcherbachev was to be thwarted. His army was not yet ready. On the northern front, Lesh's 78th and 82nd Reserve Divisions and 12th Division were still deploying. The southern and southeastern forces were well positioned, but only the 19th Division, opposite Siedliska, and the 58th Reserve Division, to its north, were close enough to the forts to attempt an immediate storm. The commander of 19th Division, Major-General Ianushevski, whose soldiers were to conduct the main push, categorically rejected Shcherbachev's blithe confidence. His view was that until the artillery knocked out the forts' armored gun turrets and the flanking installations in his attack zone, no assault could succeed. His regimental commanders backed him, warning of "enormous casualties."[22]

These fears were proven wholly correct when, early on the morning of the 6th, the 58th Reserve Division launched an attack along the Przemyśl–Lwów road. In front was Fort XIV, "Hurko," and, farther south, Fort XV, "Borek," this latter a modern fortification with two rotating turrets mounting 8 cm cannon and a two-gun "traditor" battery (a set of guns within a casemate built into the fort's side for flanking fire) covering the road. The attacking division was supported by two batteries of heavy artillery. Like their Austrian and Hungarian opponents, the Russians in this sector had not had much sleep. However, they had used the night well. When dawn broke, alarmed defenders found that storm troops had advanced again under cover of darkness and were dug in just a few hundred meters from Hurko's wire entanglements.[23]

The Russian artillery was learning new tricks. The day before, its observers had noted that whenever the older forts with open rooftop artillery positions were bombarded, their gun crews would cease fire, carefully place their weapons under cover, and retreat into shelter. Accordingly, during assaults, the Russians now laid down a continuous barrage on the fort roofs to neutralize the defensive ordnance and protect their own foot soldiers. On the left of the 58th Reserve Division's attack, this tactic had little success. Fort XV's armored turrets were immune to the shelling and kept up a steady fire. The attackers, reservists less skilled than their comrades farther south in the "active" 19th Division, advanced in thin lines that made excellent targets. They were obliterated.

Against Fort XIV, an older fort without armor, the attackers came farther. Russian shells damaged the fort's rooftop artillery emplacements and smashed its breastworks. That nobody was killed can only be attributed to the speed at which the garrison took cover. With the defensive artillery suppressed, assault troops were able to advance to 500 meters (1,640 feet) from the fort's glacis. The infantry in the fort and interval trenches had been instructed to hold fire until the enemy was only about 300 meters (980 feet) away, but they were so frightened by the sight of Russians running at them that they started shooting. This was enough. Some attackers fell, some fled, and others attempted to take cover in the ditches on either side of the Lwów road, which were enfiladed by the defenders and so death traps. By 10:00 a.m. the assault was over.[24]

October 6 thus became a day of artillery bombardment as the Russians softened up Przemyśl's defenses for a decisive attack. Over the four-day operation, from October 5 to 8, Shcherbachev's artillery threw around 45,000 shrapnel and high-explosive shells into the Fortress. On October 6, probably a quarter of this total was fired off, a fire intensity a third greater than on the previous day. The bulk of the heavy artillery, five 15.2 cm howitzer batteries, was concentrated against the crescent of forts in front of Siedliska. The 19th Division's attack front in the north of this crescent was especially targeted. Beginning in the morning, three of these howitzer batteries bombarded Forts I/1, I/2, and I/3, with the purpose of silencing their guns and those of mobile batteries in the vicinity. Fifty-six field guns under the division's control sprayed both the forts and interval trenches with fire.[25]

By the standards of later war years, especially when set beside the storms of steel that swept the western front in 1916–1918, the Russian bombardment of Przemyśl on the 6th was an explosive drizzle. There were incomparably fewer shells, the ordnance was lighter, the Russian gunners fired only while daylight lasted, and they took a break for an hour at midday for lunch. As an instrument of physical destruction, the bombardment was an utter failure. The guns were no more capable than on the previous day of puncturing armored turrets or shattering concrete casemates. Yet despite all this, the psychological distress and intimidation the shells inflicted on the middle-aged defenders of the Fortress was immense. In all their years of peaceful existence, these men had never imagined anything like it. More than anything, the noise of the October bombardment seared itself into their memories. Survivors of the siege would later claim that "it wasn't possible to endure the roar of the artillery."[26]

The forts themselves amplified the shock. Their thick roofs and walls proved extremely effective at protecting their garrisons from physical harm, but the gloomy subterranean tunnels and crowded low-ceilinged chambers were intensely claustrophobic and underlined the redundancy of the men's instinctual "fight-or-flight" reaction. To shelter there under bombardment, surrounded by echoing noise and impotent to act against the danger, was terrifying. Second Lieutenant Bruno Prochaska, the adjutant of III/Landsturm Infantry Regiment 18, who spent the morning of October 6 in Fort I, described the fear and tension:

First quietly, in the far distance, begins the shrill whistle, which quickly swells to a piercing howl. And then [the shell] thuds like a colossal battering ram furiously against the earth covering of the old fort. . . . The building resounds and shudders down to its foundations. The blast rushes powerfully through the cold, dark corridors. Dust and gasses from the explosion forcing their way in make the air heavy and suffocating. Sand trickles through the old walls. Stones, turf, clods of earth patter down like a thundershower into the courtyard. . . . The impact of the first shot is still reverberating, when already a shrill whistle announces the approach of a second. Involuntarily, each man bows his head, tenses muscles and nerves.

To be in a fort during a bombardment was, concluded Prochaska, "a real hell." It was preferable to be in the trenches outside, he thought: "Death would be easier [to face] in the open air than in that cramped, suffocating box."[27]

The soldiers who manned the interval lines between the forts knew better. The 2nd Battalion, Landsturm Infantry Regiment 10, a Hungarian unit raised in Eger, spent October 6 in trenches on the most contested and heavily bombarded front, the northern section of the Siedliska crescent. This was a far more dangerous posting than any fort, and the men were tested to, and beyond, the limits of their endurance. Their experience illustrates well the strain the attack placed on the defenders' morale. The battalion's commander, Captain Constantin Komadina, described those evil twenty-four hours as "the hardest day of my life."[28]

The day began at 3:00 a.m., when Komadina received the order to move his battalion to positions around Fort I/2. Two companies manned the interval trenches on either side of the fort; a third reinforced Strongpoint Byków a little farther to the south. Whatever Prochaska might claim, these "open-air" earthwork positions were not much less claustrophobic than the forts. They were narrow with winding traverses and fire bays. Zigzag communications trenches led to shallow dugouts in the rear. Unlike trenches on the western front, the fire line was roofed with "shrapnel shields," planks or logs spanning the trenches on which earth was piled. If high explosives burst nearby, these would collapse, braining and burying the trench's occupants. Mostly, however, the Russians threw shrapnel shells at the interval lines, and against their lethal little steel balls the shields generally gave excellent protection. The 2nd Battalion was finally in position at 6:00 a.m. At 6:45 a.m., the Russian guns opened up.[29]

Through the morning Komadina sat perilously in battalion headquarters, a wooden shack just behind the fire line, impotently receiving demands—all urgent, naturally—for reinforcements and extra munitions. The bombardment raged. "Shells and shrapnel flew past so close that we did not know from where they came," he complained. "For officers and men the effect was horrendous." All telegraph wires back to the sector command at Siedliska had been cut by Russian shelling, so the only way to communicate the troops' distress was by sending runners through the hail of fire. One brave Hungarian made the journey six times. Everyone was anxious that the Russians might suddenly attack, and the feeling of vulnerability increased further when fire from the neighboring forts seemed to slacken. Mist and pouring rain veiled the activities of the enemy infantry, who were dug in just beyond the entanglements.[30]

The battalion's situation took a turn for the worse after midday. The first misfortune was a direct hit on its dressing station. Dr. Winkler, the medical officer, had set himself up in a vacant artillery shelter, but casualties from the bombardment soon filled this and spilled over outside. The shell that exploded in their midst eviscerated these waiting wounded and blew the doctor into the mud. Winkler was able to pick himself up, but at the awful sight he broke down in tears and spasms. He was evacuated as a "nerve shock" case.

Shortly afterward, two enormous 30.5 cm Habsburg howitzers opened up somewhere in the rear of Komadina's position. The Russian heavy artillery replied by adding high explosives to the shrapnel raking his trenches. The blasts were so powerful that his officers were convinced they were under fire from real 21 cm caliber siege artillery.

Lieutenant Emerich von Laky, one of Komadina's company commanders, felt at this point that "the value of our lives sunk to zero." The heavy shells landing in their trenches blew pieces of equipment, uniforms, and body parts into the air, setting them down 20–25 meters (65–80 feet) away. "Lacerated human limbs . . . bloody shreds of flesh, intestine and brain parts" hung surreally from the branches of nearby pine trees. An entire platoon was torn away by two shells. The battalion adjutant and two other officers collapsed with nerve shock. When darkness fell, and the Russian guns at last ceased fire, Komadina had just three officers still in the line.[31]

The bombardment produced some distinctly odd stress reactions. One thirty-four-year-old corporal, a veteran of several battles with no history of mental illness, was brought into the garrison hospital's psychiatric unit suffering from what the doctors described as a "confused mania." He shrieked, "Where is the general! Come here! I want to shoot! Bring my uniform! . . . I want to go home! Everyone, let's go. The whole company's going!" He hallucinated that he was in the brigade offices and then took off all his clothes and ripped up his underwear. At one moment he was singing hymns, the next jumping around the ward and attacking the hospital orderlies. He refused all food. The military doctors diagnosed schizophrenia, noting that he likely had a concealed hereditary disposition: comrades from his village had confirmed that both his father and his brother had poor mental health. Although German-speaking psychiatric and neurological professionals accepted that battle trauma might trigger illness, few would concede that it could turn healthy men mad. Psychiatric disorders were almost always perceived as reflections of preexisting constitutional weaknesses or a lack of moral fiber.[32]

At the end of the day, Shcherbachev knew he could wait no longer. Not only was the Habsburg field army approaching, but the Fortress's crucial southeastern sector was strengthening. Thanks to Kusmanek's reinforcements, 350 guns now faced the 279 of the Russians opposite. Russian divisional commanders remained unimpressed with their artillery's work. "Despite the accuracy, no destruction is visible," fretted the 69th Reserve Division's commander. Yet in the Fortress Command, the situation appeared fragile. Even the Fortress's most senior officers and technical experts shared the delusion that they were under fire from 18 or 21 cm caliber siege artillery, shells that were too powerful for most of the forts to withstand. Officers were voicing fears that the Russians would break in and then "make goulash out of the inhabitants." Defeatist rumors among the troops had started to circulate in the city, threatening an outbreak of panic. The Fortress's fate hung in the balance. At 8:45 p.m., Shcherbachev's order went out. At 2:00 a.m., the final storm would commence.[33]

WITH SHCHERBACHEV'S ORDER, the entire blockade army moved in to attack. Even Lesh's group on the northwestern and northern fronts, which to this point had been stuck in preparations, at last went forward. The 1st Brigade of the 9th Cavalry Division, the unit tasked with screening the west side of the Fortress, also saddled up and rode to assist the 3rd Rifle Brigade with its attack on the southern front. Little time was allowed, barely five hours, between the order's release and the opening of the general assault. In a world without friction this would not have mattered, for the command simply supplemented the previous evening's instructions and most of the troops were waiting to advance. However, where communications failed, the late arrival of the order would have disastrous consequences. As the fortress artillery remained operative, a storm under cover of darkness offered the Russian infantry its only chance of closing with the defense.

The three divisions under Lesh on the northwestern and northern fronts, commanded vaguely "to break through," had the farthest to advance. Compounding their problems, the 82nd Reserve Division in the center was surprised by Shcherbachev's order, and could initially get only two batteries—a third of its field artillery—into action. Nevertheless, the force did well. Its 12.2 cm howitzers were unique during the siege in inflicting significant damage on a fort when they smashed one of the caponiers guarding Fort X's frontal ditch. Employing the tactic tried at Fort XIV, "Hurko," the day before, they also efficiently suppressed much of the old fort's artillery, which had only splinter protection, by smothering the roof with fire. The Russian infantry moved off promptly at 2:00 a.m. and under the cover of darkness advanced rapidly. One by one, the garrison's forward positions on the hills in front of the perimeter fell. By midday, the attackers were closing in on the forts themselves. Ultimately, they managed to entrench just 70 meters (230 feet) from Forts XI, "Duńkowiczki," and XIa, "Ziegelofen." There, however, they were held.[34]

The Russians' second subsidiary attack, in the Fortress's south, had no greater success. The 3rd Rifle Brigade had already seen some action the previous day, and so its commander, Major-General Fok, was expecting orders to continue the assault. He had tried to be conscientious. Fort IV, "Optyń," the sector's main defensive installation, had been bombarded by the brigade's light artillery for two hours on the evening of the 6th, and volunteers had been sent to cut the defenders' wire entanglements. Both initiatives were futile. Optyń was large and modern, one of the very few truly fearsome forts on Przemyśl's outer perimeter. It shrugged off 230 hits from the field guns, and its alert garrison used searchlights and flares through the night to keep the Russians away from the wire in front.[35]

Worse, in this sector Shcherbachev's order arrived late, just an hour before the storm was supposed to begin. This threw the brigade into confusion. When Fok arrived at the front at 5:00 a.m. to observe the progress, he found the troops had not moved. Dawn had just broken, and sending his young soldiers in broad daylight against the mighty Optyń, its invincible armored turret guns rotating slowly and menacingly, felt like murder. He had just resolved to delay the attack until evening when the troops launched their assault. Predictably, they quickly ran into trouble. Extra but ineffectual artillery support was ordered. Through skillful use of terrain cover, some

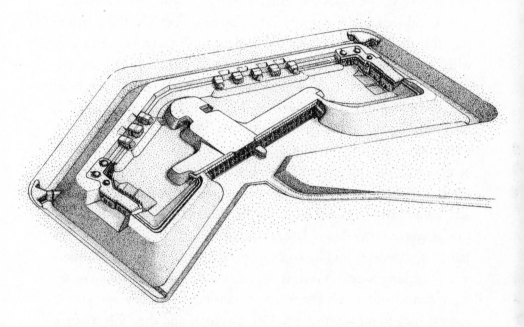

Fort IV, "Optyń" (built in 1897–1900): Fort IV was the strongest defensive position in the south of Przemyśl's perimeter. Its garrison numbered 9 officers and 439 soldiers. It was tougher than the forts of the 1880s, of more modern construction, and had expensive armored components. Two casemates built partly of granite stood at the front corners, each mounting an armored observation cupola and two rotatable hardened steel Škoda turrets with 8 cm field guns. Adjacent, on the fort's left (clearly visible here) and right, were traditor batteries to cover the flanks, each with four 12 cm M96 cannon protected by armor plate. Other artillery pieces stood in open emplacements along the fort's forward wall. Two triangular caponiers armed with machine-guns defended Optyń's ditch.

soldiers managed to close with the fort. They were stopped by intense fire 300 paces short of the glacis.[36]

Shcherbachev's attention was fixed on his main offensive on the southeastern front. Expectations were high. In preparation for a breakthrough, the blockade army's long-range 10.7 cm caliber guns were bombarding targets within the Fortress. Fort XX, the interior-ring fort defending the eastern approach to the city, was hit along with the Fortress's main ration depot and the adjacent garrison hospital. Assaults against the sector's southern and eastern sides piled pressure on the defenders. Between Forts II, "Jaksmanice," and III, "Łuczyce," in the south, the 60th Reserve Division's infantry set off punctually and crept unobserved to the wire entanglements in front of the interval lines only to be pinned by a hail of fire. In the east, damage to the field telephone network delayed the order for a repeat attack on Hurko until 5:45 a.m., so there the 58th Reserve Division's troops started four hours late. A single regiment managed to entrench 100 paces from Hurko, but heavy defensive fire forced others into disorderly retreat. What really mattered, though, was the fighting between these two attacks, at Siedliska. The entire operation's success hinged on whether the 19th Division and the 69th Reserve Division could break the crescent of Forts I/1 to I/6.[37]

The 19th Division and 69th Reserve Division faced quite a challenge. The crescent, in conjunction with Fort XV to the north, comprised a powerful defensive network of mutually supporting fortified installations. The two forts in the crescent's middle were thirty years old and had no armor, but those on the flanks were squat modern designs fitted with steel observation cupolas and gun turrets. Each was built and equipped to provide lethal flanking fire in support of its neighbors, defended by platoons of infantry, and fronted by a deep ditch and obstacles. The equipment issued by the blockade army to assist in their capture was minimal. Each assaulting regiment received eight scaling ladders, eight steel cables, eighteen bridges, each 8 meters (26 feet) long, and sixty-five wire cutters, as well as, laughably, thirty-two hand grenades. With heavy artillery lacking and so little technical assistance, the officers of Infantry Regiment 274 (69th Reserve Division) were less inspirational than brutally accurate when they told their men on the eve of the attack that "the Fortress must this day be taken at the point of the bayonet."[38]

The Tsarist army's infantry tended to be pitied by Habsburg officers as dumb Russian peasants—good-natured, but apathetic and devoid of idealism, unable to do much beyond slavishly follow orders. Those officers were wrong on two counts. First, many of these infantrymen were not Russian. The regiments that attacked Siedliska's forward forts were raised from territories located in what is today Ukraine, which at that time were highly ethnically mixed. The 19th Division's regiments had titles like "Crimea" and "Sevastopol," though in fact their men came from the Podolia Governorate, home to Ukrainians, Jews, Russians, Poles, and Romanians, farther northwest. The 69th Reserve Division was raised in Kharkiv.[39]

Second, as these units' performance in the previous days had demonstrated, their soldiers were neither dumb nor apathetic. The spade tactics used to advance so quickly toward the fortress perimeter had demanded considerable self-discipline and individual initiative, not to mention courage. Interrogation reports of prisoners from these regiments testify to good morale on the eve of the attack. There were complaints about rations, and some men stated that they had attacked unwillingly, but many, especially the NCOs in the 19th Division, expressed strong determination to go forward.[40]

To go into assault, perhaps helping to carry a bridge or ladder, against the Siedliska forts must have been terrifying. The stormers had a good idea of what confronted them, for in the daytime they could see from their foxholes looming just beyond the wire the forts' intimidating silhouettes and cratered earthen glacis. At night, the ground these soldiers had silently to traverse was crossed by searchlight beams and periodically bathed in light from flares. Obstacles would have to be overcome. There was always the risk of tripping a landmine. Why did they brave the peril? For sure, discipline, training, and leadership all counted. This was especially true of the "active" 19th Division. Its officers led from the front. Many of its men would have been close to completing two or three years of conscript service when war broke out. They had been through an overtly nationalist training program: introduced after the 1905 revolution, it had stressed their common belonging to a Russian motherland over love of the increasingly discredited Tsar. Most would have been well integrated into their regiments. They were obedient to military authority but, no less importantly, they knew their NCOs and had trusted comrades alongside them, with whom they had already faced battle.[41]

Of course, fear also propelled men forward. The 69th Reserve Division had a large complement of older reservists. Their prerevolutionary conscript experience was different from that of younger soldiers and more alienating, with little input from officers or combat training. These reluctant warriors were warned by commanders that machine-guns positioned behind them would shoot anybody who retreated. To deter surrender or desertion, gruesome tales of prisoners' maltreatment and mutilation at Austrian hands were circulated. Imaginatively, some soldiers were even told that in order to avoid wasting valuable food on captives, the fortress garrison made them drunk on schnapps and then set them alight. Most of all, though, men went forward because, even for the petrified, there was no other realistic option. Their presence before the Austrian wire was precarious, and to flee individually would be to expose oneself to enemy fire more than if one advanced with one's unit. Horrid to think, but for these assault troops in the small hours of October 7, the only possible way to safety lay straight into the mouths of the fortress guns.[42]

IN THE ANNALS of Habsburg war history, there are few more glorious episodes than the defense of Fort I/1 on that cold, wet October morning. Fort I/1 was situated on the northwesterly end of the Siedliska crescent. The hero of the defense was Lieutenant Janko Švrljuga. Slim and dashing, manly, with piercing eyes and a finely clipped military moustache, he was every inch the ideal professional officer. Under him served a garrison drawn from both halves of the empire. Austrian artillerymen hailing from the imperial capital, Vienna, manned the fort's traditor battery and its two state-of-the-art retractable turret cannons. The infantry on the wall were loyal Hungarian peasantry. This multiethnic, quintessentially imperial force would find itself that day at the crisis point of the fighting, and would stand firm against the very best the Russian army had to throw at it. The battle offered a potent demonstration of what could be achieved when, arrayed under professional military leadership, the empire's diverse peoples united.[43]

That, at least, was the story. The reality was chaotic, confused, and redolent of Habsburg military dysfunctionality, though for this all the more human and heroic. The actual commander of Fort I/1 was not the professional officer Švrljuga but an amateur soldier, Hungarian Landsturm Second Lieutenant Dr. István Bielek. Bielek was thirty-nine years old and had been born in the obscure village of Máriavölgy (today Marianka in Slovakia), located at the unfashionable northwestern end of Hungary. Just a few weeks earlier, before civilization had collapsed, he had been a Budapest lawyer. Like other Landsturm officers, he tried, but had not quite managed, to look the military man. His moustache was a little too bushy, his face too round, and his high forehead hinted less at great intelligence than the early onset of male pattern baldness, an impression confirmed by a rather obvious comb-over. Even so, there was determination in his eyes. This was not a man to give up easily.[44]

Bielek had taken command of Fort I/1 two weeks earlier, bringing with him 112 men from his 2 Company, Landsturm Infantry Regiment 11. They were an eclectic bunch. The unit was recruited from around the town of Munkács in northeastern Hungary, home to Hungarians, Ruthenes, many Orthodox Jews, and the occasional Slovak. Forty-six men from Fortress Artillery Regiment 1 under Second Lieutenant of the Reserve Otto Altmann and Ensign Hans Seiler manned the fort's guns. There were also twelve sappers stationed there. Far from

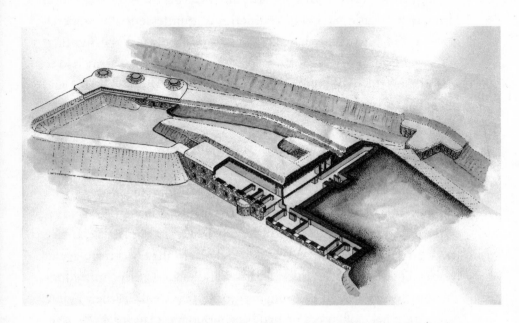

Fort I/1, "Łysiczka" (built in 1897–1903): This reconstruction shows Fort I/1's low two-story main building in cross-section and, over to the left, its heavily armored artillery complex with an observation cupola and four 8 cm guns, two in a traditor position and two in retractable turrets. Unlike earlier forts, Fort I/1 was built as part of a network of fortifications designed to control the forward terrain through mutual fire support. The fort's primary mission was to cover the landscape in front and to the north, between it and Fort XV, "Borek," which is why all its artillery was placed on its left. The infantry positions ran along the rear lip of the earthen "wall," whose front sloped into the protective ditch. Two tunnels, not shown here, linked the main building to the artillery complex and to the T-shaped ditch caponier, defended by machine-guns.

being a model of imperial cooperation, Fort I/1's disparate garrison clearly did not gel. Their provincial background distanced Bielek and his men from their new Viennese brothers-in-arms; so did language, of course. But age was also a factor: Fortress Artillery Regiment 1 was a peacetime standing unit, and therefore made up of reservists and "active" soldiers a good ten or fifteen years younger than the Munkács Landsturm.[45]

That distance was accentuated by Fort I/1's layout. The main complex contained the garrison's dormitories, a kitchen, toilets, and a well. The infantry positions were here, on an earthen wall overlooking the forward terrain and down a long subterranean tunnel running from the center of the fort, in a T-shaped caponier set in the middle of its frontal ditch, with loopholes permitting a clear field of fire along the ditch. The artillerymen had their sleeping quarters in the main building, but their guns and ammunition magazines were in a shoulder complex over on the left, connected to the rest of the fort only by a narrow 20-meter (65-foot) tunnel. They therefore spent their waking and working hours at a remove from the infantry and had no sense of belonging to a unified command. They regarded their own officer, Second Lieutenant Altmann, as the ultimate authority. On the morning of October 7, they would fight a battle largely separate from the Landsturm infantry they were supposed to support.[46]

On the eve of the Russians' assault, Bielek's mood, and that of his garrison, was tense and tired. They had been under bombardment for two days, and Bielek was certain that an enemy storm was imminent. The answer from his superiors to his warnings had not lifted his spirits much. They had sent as reinforcement thirty Romanians of doubtful reliability from the 32nd Honvéd March Battalion and, in his own words, "made me responsible for whatever would happen." Adding to the pressure on Bielek was the arrival of the artillery group commander of the subsector around the Siedliska fort crescent, none other than Lieutenant Janko Švrljuga. Quite what business Švrljuga had in the fort was glossed over in later official accounts. The word was that the command position from which he had been directing the subsector's guns had been destroyed and all his observation posts, located vulnerably in trees, had been shot down. Possibly Švrljuga came to Fort I/1 hoping to find a telephone line that still functioned. A less charitable explanation is that he simply sought refuge from the bombardment.[47]

On the infantry wall that night, sleepy sentries peered into a moonless blackness. The noise of work parties mending barbed-wire entanglements that had been damaged during the day's shellfire wafted faintly back to the fort, but otherwise there was silence. The fort's searchlight had been knocked out earlier that evening and flares were in short supply, but the watchers felt secure in the knowledge that a listening post had been stationed beyond the ditch to warn of any Russian approach.[48]

Shortly after 3:00 a.m., something alarmed the sentries. Accounts differ on the reason: it may have been the noises from the wire continuing long after work parties had been withdrawn. Others said some of the listening-post men had managed to fire off a few warning shots before enemy storm troops silently slit their throats. Bielek was called up onto the wall. He ordered flares to be fired. Their light revealed Russian soldiers already at the bottom of the fort glacis.[49]

At that moment, from Russian trenches to the southeast a powerful searchlight was switched on, cutting through darkness and fog to illuminate the fort. Simultaneously, a bombardment came crashing down. For the Landsturm men on the wall, this sudden sensory assault was overwhelming. Dazzled and deafened, they began firing in the direction of the enemy storm troops, who, losing no time, were now cutting paths through the wire in front of the ditch.[50]

To the Russians' surprise, Fort I/1's artillery remained silent. Bielek sent down repeated requests for support to Švrljuga, as the senior artillery officer, and was perplexed by the absence of any reaction. "It was my impression," he observed scathingly, that Švrljuga had "lost not only his self-control, but also his ability to command and influence his men. Without his direct orders no other artillery officer was brave enough to take charge." Other Hungarians were harsher. A rumor, never acknowledged in any official history, later circulated among the battle's survivors that at this moment of crisis the fort's only professional officer suffered a nervous breakdown. "He had hidden himself inside the fort, was crossing himself over and over again and moaning 'Oh my God . . . Oh my God . . .' All appeals, pleading, and threats were in vain. Švrljuga did not move."[51]

On the rooftop wall, István Bielek bravely led Fort I/1's defense. He and Altmann prepared for the worst by ordering that sandbags and thick wooden beams be readied for barricading the fort's doors and shuttered windows. Trying to conserve his manpower under the bombardment, Bielek sent some soldiers back into the safety of the fort. They soon had to be recalled, as the defenders' casualties mounted. One of the two rooftop machine-guns was put out of action, its crew killed. Over the next two hours, the two battalions of Crimean Infantry Regiment 73—around 2,000 men—tasked with taking the fort drew steadily closer. So near did they come that Slovaks and Ruthenes among the defenders could understand the assault troops' officers commanding them to the right and left across the barbed wire.[52]

As 5:00 a.m. approached, the Russian infantry launched a final storm, laying a bridge over the ditch and breaking through opposite the fort's right shoulder. With catastrophe threatening, Ensign Hans Seiler damned the rank hierarchy. He at last fired the turret guns, spraying short-range canister shot over the ground to the front, and even, as the storm troops climbed up to the fort's infantry positions, across the wall. Shot from his guns also most likely dislodged the Russians' bridge, sending it crashing down. Those soldiers who had been on it, and others who jumped into the 3-meter-deep ditch, with the hope of climbing out the other side, were massacred by the caponier machine-guns. Later, 151 enemy dead and 70 heavily wounded were found in this open grave.[53]

Seiler's fire won time for Bielek and the Munkács Landsturm on the wall, but only a little: 250 men of the Crimean Regiment had crossed over and were scaling the fort. Shellfire was still falling, and only forty defenders remained standing. As the first assault troops climbed over the parapet and vicious hand-to-hand fighting commenced, the lawyer from Budapest decided, a little belatedly, that he had to get his surviving men back into the fort. As he shouted the command, shrapnel burst overhead, severely wounding him. The heavy iron door that gave access to the interior from the fighting platform had already been shut, but his men carried him there and hammered on it. Briefly, it was opened again. Bielek was taken through. Those of his soldiers who could disengage followed. Then the door was bolted.[54]

There now developed a curious standoff. The Russians had braved the killing zone. They had stormed over fire-swept ground, surmounted barbed-wire obstacles, avoided mines, and crossed the death-trap ditch. The hard work was done: they were in complete control of Fort I/1's exterior, occupying its courtyard and standing on its roof. Yet they had no way of getting inside. They dropped their guncotton explosives down the fort's chimneys, but no blast followed. The detonators were damp.[55]

Oblivious to the problems of the Russians above, the garrison barricaded inside the fort was in a state of terror. "Even the toughest," wrote Bielek, "felt that the desperate defense could not last very long." There was no way of calling for help, for shellfire had cut the fort's telephone connection. Every moment felt as if it could be the last. Unnerving bangs and thumps came from within the walls as the attackers dropped things down chimneys and fired into ventilation shafts. The cries of the wounded, which echoed through the fort's stuffy, oppressive chambers and dim corridors, acted as a constant, frightening reminder of the fate that awaited if the enemy broke in. When the Russians' explosives failed to blow, their attention turned to the fort's main rear entrance and the rooftop iron door. For two suspenseful hours, a few soldiers shooting from loopholes at these two critical access points kept the attackers at bay. Franz Suchy, a thirty-one-year-old roofer from Vienna who defended the main door, afterward claimed, to a press ardent for desperate glory, to have shot more than forty Russians.[56]

At last, at around 7:30 a.m., help arrived. From two sides, Honvéd infantry of the fortress reserve, the best troops in the garrison, approached Fort I/1. The Russians, who had been expecting the relief, knew they were trapped. Seiler's guns kept up a steady fire to the front, preventing either further reinforcement or retreat. Explosives and assaults had failed to unlock the fort. As dawn broke, the Russians, in despair, had bandaged the Landsturm men lying wounded on the roof while interrogating them about other ways inside, but in vain. Their commanders, three officers and an ensign, had positioned a machine-gun on the roof covering the back areas. Their exhausted troops, flagging after the night's exertions, built barricades in the fort's courtyard and set them alight. The besiegers had become the besieged.[57]

The final act of Fort I/1's drama now began. The fresh Honvéd men advancing from the right made short work of the Russians' machine-gun, killing its crew and then turning the weapon on its erstwhile owners. Meanwhile, their comrades on the fort's left also attacked, and together the two groups picked off the enemy on the roof and then charged the barricades. At this decisive point both the Russian and Habsburg artillery unhelpfully opened fire on the fort, the former trying to hold back the relief, the latter mistakenly believing the fort to be in Russian hands. Two of the Russian officers, realizing the end had come, shot themselves. Their men panicked.[58]

Faced with mutual annihilation by the big guns, both Honvéd and Tsarist infantrymen dropped their fighting and rushed to the fort's rear entrance. Desperate men in blue and green beat on the iron door, demanding sanctuary. The garrison, unable to hear much through the thick walls over the noise of the bombardment, and with its vision limited to what could be seen out of narrow embrasures, had little idea of what was going on and was not taking any chances. Only after considerable time and much swearing from outside were the thick wooden beams removed, the door unbolted, and the Hon-véd rescuers, with their 149 Russian prisoners, allowed entry. It was a messy relief, but Fort I/1 was at long last out of danger.[59]

From this bloody farce, with its dysfunctional fort garrison, dozy sentries, dud explosives, and friendly fire, the Habsburg army quickly built a heroic legend. The gorgeous Švrljuga was made the public face of the defense, receiving a promotion to captain and the highly prestigious Order of the Iron Crown, 3rd Class. When gullible jour-nalists arrived on the scene a week later, he was on hand to guide them, spouting all sorts of nonsense—eagerly repeated—about his inspirational leadership in telephoning for relief and dispatching men to request a bombardment on the fort. In reality, the telephone cables had been cut by shellfire before the attack began, and men could never have made it through the impenetrable encirclement. As the only professional officer present, Švrljuga was inevitably going to hog the glory, irrespective of his actual comportment in the battle. Altmann, the other artillery officer, was a reservist—and worse, a Jew—and so obviously unsuitable to be credited with any major role. As for István Bielek, the one officer in Fort I/1 who did have a claim to the name "hero," by the time the press arrived he had long been evacuated to hospital. He and his middle-aged Munkács Landsturm men who had stood at the fort wall that night, faced the Russians, and paid the blood sacrifice would instantly be forgotten.[60]

IN FAILING TO take Fort I/1, the Russians blew their best chance of defeating the Fortress before the arrival of the Habsburg field army. No other attack on the Siedliska fort crescent came nearly so close to success. The Russian artillery's shelling was twice as intense as on the previous day, and the assaults started in the dark, but the crescent's interlocking defenses worked as they had been designed. The forts' guns were supported by the artillery of the mobile reserve that Kusmanek had deployed by Fort XIV, "Hurko," to the north. Throughout October 7, these guns placed waves of attackers under devastating concentric fire. Nowhere else in the sector did the storm troops even reach the defenders' main positions.[61]

In the north, below Fort I/1, the 19th Division's infantry advanced no farther than Fort I/3's glacis. The main threat came from the Russian artillery. A heavy bombardment triggered panic at the intermediate earthwork position, Strongpoint Byków. Captain Constantin Komadina's II/Landsturm Infantry Regiment 10 was stationed in this part of the line, and he found himself trying to halt a stampede. "Alone, with revolver in hand, I stopped half of the soldiers from my 7th Company," he related with shock. Romanians in the ranks were blamed, though their Hungarian officers also fled. Komadina led them back to their positions and stayed there until a fresh company could be brought up. The strongpoint had been abandoned for two hours. Fortunately, the attackers' attention was fixed to either side on Forts I/2 and I/3, and this gaping hole in the defensive line was neither noticed nor exploited.[62]

In the south of the crescent, the 69th Reserve Division's attacks also failed. Lieutenant Vit's 10th Company, III/Landsturm Infantry Regiment 18, missed the first assaults, but at 7:00 a.m. it relieved troops in front of Fort I/4. Just as the company arrived, the Russians stormed its trenches. The defenders' fire stopped them dead. The day was spent wallowing in mud and rain. Vit's company was fortunate in that most of the shellfire was aimed at the fort 200 paces to the rear, and so went over its positions. Instead, the prime danger came from enemy snipers dug in just 50 paces from the wire. "It was enough for one of us to raise his head, and immediately we heard the hiss of a bullet," Vit recounted. Several men were shot in the face. Later in the day, an attack was launched on the left, marked by "a sudden 'hurrah,' a sound of shots, the beating of machine-guns, rapid artillery fire." Ahead, however, only small groups of the enemy attempted to advance. "One by one, the [Russians] ran from cover," Vit said. "If they were shot at, they often feigned dead, fell to the ground, slid seemingly inert down the hill, but a moment later jumped up and again ran on."[63]

The greatest drama unfolded not at the front but from behind, at Siedliska. At the Southeastern Sector Command, officers and the units stationed around the village became dismayed at reports coming from the crescent that morning. Rumors that a fort had fallen were particularly alarming. When lookouts saw Russians on the road behind the defensive perimeter, order briefly collapsed. These Russians were in fact prisoners, survivors of the failed assault on Fort I/1 being escorted to the rear. However, officers and men of the garrison lost their heads and assumed the enemy had broken through. Infantrymen going up to support the battle line now rushed back in panic. Artillerymen also fled, clutching the breech-blocks of their abandoned guns so that the enemy could not turn these against them. By one, possibly once libelous account, even the sector commander, Major-General Alfred Weber, was drawn into the general dissolution. Embarrassingly, he was halted by a company of Landsturm Infantry Regiment 18, which he had positioned to the rear with strict orders to shoot anybody who retreated.[64]

Faced with such an enemy, Shcherbachev's decision that night to terminate the assault on the Fortress might appear premature. However, the Russians were out of time. The Habsburg field army was approaching, and Brusilov's staff predicted that it would smash into his Third Army on the following day. The fortress defenses remained unbroken. The forts had proven invulnerable against Russian artillery fire, and the Landsturm soldiers were, though shaken, capable of further tough resistance. Over October 8, the blockade army's assault units carefully disengaged, and that night those on the main southeastern front withdrew completely. When the sun rose the next morning, euphoric defenders found the enemy gone: "Victory! Victory! Gloria in excelsis Deo! Hurrah!"[65]

THE FIRST CAVALRY patrol from the Habsburg field army trotted up to the Sanok Road Barrier in the west of the Fortress at midday on October 9. A few days later, infantry and artillery from the main force arrived. The Fortress Command had been telegraphed in advance to have ready enough loaves for 88,000 men—around 61,600 kilograms (136,000 pounds) of bread. Though the field army came to Przemyśl's relief, it was in fact the Fortress's garrison that had saved Austria-Hungary's military and wider war effort.[66]

Most crucially, the Fortress's resistance had won time. The need to lap around and encircle the Fortress had significantly slowed the advance of the Russian Third and Eighth Armies in the second half of September, taking pressure off the retreating, broken Habsburg army. Shcherbachev's blockade army, once it was reinforced with assault divisions and artillery, comprised well over 100,000 men who otherwise would have been beating their way westward. Most important, the Fortress had posed a constant, active threat to the rear of the Russian army and had denied it control of all major transport arteries. Without possession of the vital east-west railway running through Przemyśl, Russian offensive ambitions were stymied. The Habsburg field army used this necessary respite to rest, reconstitute itself, and await assistance from its German ally. Recovery was far from complete, but sufficient for the force to return to the offensive. Those who witnessed field units marching through Przemyśl in mid-October were struck by their lack of officers. Lieutenants, once in charge of sixty-man platoons, now often commanded 1,000-strong battalions.[67]

The resolution of the fortress garrison also handed the Habsburg war machine an invaluable propaganda victory. Though there was no shortage of valor in Austrian newspapers in 1914, readers were starved for news of actual success. Przemyśl showed at last that the Russian steamroller could be stopped. Brusilov had suffered a humiliating reverse, and was reproached by Stavka. The defenders were celebrated as "the Heroes of Przemyśl." Journalists rhapsodized about these "simple men . . . taken from civilian life in order to fulfill their duties as soldiers," who with "devotion," "courage," and "resolve" had "accomplished such a glorious success and averted such a grave peril." The initial reports claimed bloodthirstily that the garrison had inflicted over 40,000 casualties. Later, there was talk of 70,000 Russian losses. In fact, the blockade army squandered around 10,000 men, one-third of whom were killed. The spearhead of the attack, the 19th Division, lost a quarter of its personnel, some 44 officers and 2,975 men.[68]

The mortal cost of the victory to the Fortress's "heroes" was very light. Thanks to effective protection from forts and roofed trenches, the garrison suffered just 1,885 casualties, among them 313 deaths and 290 missing. Nevertheless, the shock of this brutal confrontation was felt very deeply by these middle-aged soldiers. In II/Landsturm Infantry Regiment 10, 150 men, around a quarter of the battalion's strength, went sick in the battle's aftermath. Officers, too, seemed stunned at the slaughter. They wandered the abandoned battle-field as in a nightmare, haunted by the sight of hundreds of bloated corpses huddled in foxholes and hanging on wire entanglements: "I shall never forget that view," wrote one commander. What they had witnessed, though, was merely a shadow of the horrors soon to befall East-Central Europe. A new, ideologically radical and total warfare was on its way.[69]

CHAPTER FOUR

BARRIER

They announced themselves as liberators of the Slavic peoples from the German yoke. And then they marched in. They [were] . . . like a vast filthy tidal wave, blown over the land by a heavy wind. And they swept away everything that was in their path. Affluence and order, peace and civilization. Their way was marked by destruction and despoilment, arson and rape.

Anonymous Polish report on the Russian invasion of Galicia, ca. 1915.[1]

The Russian juggernaut's advance jolted to a halt outside Przemyśl. The Austro-Hungarian field army's arrival, along with the garrison's resistance, forced Tsarist troops away from the Fortress's west, south, and north. The garrison celebrated, but the relief was short-lived; within a month, the Russians would reestablish the encirclement. Moreover, it brought no rest, for throughout October the Fortress's east side stood as a strongpoint within the Austro-Hungarian battle line. Artillery was redeployed to support the army, and garrison troops took part in heavy fighting outside the perimeter. At this time Przemyśl continued to be, as one of its defenders proudly observed, "the most important barrier against Russia." Much was at stake. Already in the autumn of 1914, the war in the east was taking on a new, and dangerous, ideological dimension. The Fortress not only blocked the advance of enemy armies but also stood as a haven and barrier against a frighteningly modern and radical program of ethnic reorganization intended to change the face of Eastern Europe.[2]

GRAND DUKE NIKOLAI Nikolaevich, supreme commander of the Russian army, was a Goliath of a man. At six feet, six inches (two meters), he loomed over everyone around him and seemed to embody Russian might. He was the Tsar's cousin and his most trusted confidant, and he returned that trust with absolute devotion. His enemies, of which there were many, feared him. Vladimir Sukhomlinov, the Russian war minister, thought him "cruel and merciless," an "evil genius." To Sergei Witte, the intelligent former prime minister, he was simply "unbalanced." His fearsome temper was legendary. Even within the imperial family, he was known as "the terrible uncle." However, when in August 1914 the armies he commanded crossed the Galician frontier, his face was fixed in a soothing smile. The Tsar's troops, he reassured the population in widely distributed proclamations, were on a mission of liberation. Great Russia stood for "the restoration of right and justice." Austria-Hungary's peoples would at last be granted "freedom." To Poles, especially, he promised a Poland united and reborn "under the scepter of the Russian Tsar . . . free in the preservation of its faith, mother tongue, and autonomy."[3]

These enlightened sentiments jarred coming from a Romanov, son of a family that had ruled Russia with an iron fist for 300 years. Freedom and autonomy had not been very noticeable in their treatment of Russia's subject peoples. Poles knew this better than anyone: the rump Kingdom of Poland established under Russian care in 1815 had lasted barely fifteen years. Polish noble uprisings in 1830–1831 and 1863 had been savagely suppressed. Moreover, in the last decades of the nineteenth century, the Romanovs had embraced Russian nationalism as a prop to their waning legitimacy and embarked on haphazard but aggressive Russification of Poles and other minorities in their empire's western borderlands. In Galicia, it was just conceivable that, as a sop to Poles and to Russia's French and British allies, the annexed west of the province might be joined after a successful war to Russian-ruled territory in a new "Polish" administrative unit with very limited autonomy. However, in the east of the province, in lands that included both Przemyśl and Lwów, ambitions were far more extreme. Here, the Russian army was intent on undertaking the very first of the radical programs of ethnic cleansing to ravage Eastern Europe in the twentieth century.[4]

This plan became apparent immediately. The new military governor general appointed to run occupied Galicia, Count Georgii Bobrinskii, was quite clear when he spoke to assembled Polish dignitaries, intelligentsia, and clergy in the provincial capital of Lwów on September 23. "Eastern Galicia and the Lemkos lands are an eternal part of a single Great Russia," he told his horrified audience. "In these lands, the true population was always Russian; thus the administration of this land should be based on Russian principles. I shall introduce here the Russian language, Russian law, and the [Russian] system." What Bobrinskii proposed was illegal by international law. It was also nonsense. Eastern Galicia had been dominated by Polish-speaking nobility for centuries, and Roman Catholic Poles composed a full quarter of the population. Another 619,000 natives, around one in every eight inhabitants, were Jews. Russian nationalists dismissed the rights of both peoples in the region, however, casting them as political oppressors and economic predators who exploited the 3-million-strong Greek Catholic Ruthenian—or, as the nationalists and army problematically insisted, "Russian"— peasant majority.[5]

From Przemyśl, where the governor general's speech was reported on, residents followed through articles published in the local press Bobrinskii's efforts to turn Lwów into a Russian city. The predominantly Polish city council was, as a strictly temporary measure, permitted to stay; the Tsarist army desired, above all, that calm be maintained. Four Poles, four Jews, four Ukrainian nationalists, and four Russophiles were taken hostage as further insurance. This apparently equitable treatment of Lwów's ethnic groups quickly ceased, however. Instead Ukrainian nationalists became a prime target. For the Tsarist vision of eastern Galicia as an eternally "Russian" land, these people posed an immense problem. Their pride in their own Greek Catholic Church, their rejection of Russian Orthodoxy, and their insistence that Ukrainians were not, as the Tsarist elite termed them, "Little Russians," but instead a separate, proud nation, presented a direct ideological challenge. Worse, their Ukrainian nationalism had taken root in the Ruthenian populace. In 1907, in Austria's first parliamentary elections run on the basis of universal and equal male suffrage, Ukrainian nationalist parties had won twenty seats. The Russophiles, who regarded the people as a branch of the Russian nation, managed a paltry five.[6]

To destroy this ideological threat, and as a first step to refashion Galicia in Russia's own image, Tsarist military occupation authorities adopted a decapitation strategy similar to that utilized in the region by Nazi and Soviet occupiers twenty-five years later. The Tsarist effort was less thorough and certainly far less lethal, but the intention was the same: to eliminate the intelligentsia. Freedom of thought, rival ideological convictions, and the ability to organize made educated people dangerous to these regimes. Archbishop Andrei Sheptits'kyi, the charismatic Greek Catholic Metropolitan, was a special target. In Russian eyes, his great influence as head of the Greek Catholic Church, his staunch resistance against Russian Orthodoxy's expansion in Galicia, and his sympathy for the Ukrainian nationalist cause all made him the most dangerous man in the province. Grand Duke Nikolai's right-hand man, his chief of staff General Nikolai Ianushkevich, had promised to take Sheptits'kyi "dead or alive." When Russian forces entered Lwów at the start of September, the archbishop was immediately placed under house arrest and, in the middle of the month, exiled with his clerical entourage into Russia.[7]

Further repression soon followed. The Russian authorities not only attacked Ukrainian national political organization but also tore down Ukrainian cultural and educational institutions. Throughout eastern Galicia, Ukrainian reading societies and libraries were closed and their books confiscated or burned. Ukrainian-language newspapers—indeed, all Ukrainian-language publications and notices—were banned. The educated, nationally minded people who had led and nurtured this cultural life in peace, whose numbers had already been gravely depleted by the repressive, self-defeating actions of the Austrian civil and military authorities at the start of the war, disappeared. Provisional lists of deportees to Russia drawn up by Galician authorities in the autumn of 1915, shortly after most of the province had been liberated, testified to the damage inflicted on the small Ukrainian intelligentsia. Among more than 100 people identified—probably around half the true total—were senior officers of the Ukrainian mutual insurance organization "Dnister," police, justice and council officials, and, beyond Lwów, village representatives. Lawyers, doctors, priests, academics, and teachers were also prominent among the victims of this Russian purge.[8]

With the Ukrainian intelligentsia intimidated or imprisoned, the way lay open for the grand duke and Governor General Bobrinskii to "return," as they saw it, Galicia's Ukrainians to their "primordial" Russian state. Language and religion were to be reformed, as the Russians believed these were two crucial areas where Polish and Austrian authorities had deliberately cultivated artificial difference between themselves and Galician Ruthenes. The Russians were prepared to play a long game. The eradication of the Ukrainian people would take more than a single generation, and schooling was to be a key weapon. Training courses in the Russian language, with full board provided, were organized in St. Petersburg and in the major Galician cities in the east, and 300 Ruthenian teachers underwent instruction. A former director of primary schooling from the Kiev region of the Russian Empire was brought in to establish a network of Russian-language state schools in Galicia. A few private schools teaching in Polish were to be tolerated in Lwów, provided that they used approved textbooks and taught at least five hours of Russian language weekly. For Ruthenes, however, there was no provision for Ukrainian-language tuition. Their children were to become little Russians.[9]

Even more important was the issue of the faith of the Galician Ruthenes. Though strange to modern sensibilities, at the start of the twentieth century language was a much weaker marker of ethnic identity than religion in Eastern Europe. Russian nationalists grieved deeply that Orthodoxy—the faith of the Tsars—had barely a foothold in Galicia. The Greek Catholic Church dated back to the Union of Brest of 1596, when the Orthodox bishops of the Polish-Lithuanian Commonwealth, to which Galicia and the western borderlands of early twentieth-century Russia had then belonged, submitted to the supremacy of the Pope in Rome but kept their eastern rites. In the Tsarist Empire, Orthodox clergy and officials alike considered the Greek Catholic Church a despicable sham, a ruse by Catholics to tear Ukrainian- and Belorussian-speaking peasants from the true Russian faith. During the nineteenth century, it was abolished in the Tsar's realms. Very considerable force had been used in compulsory mass conversions to Orthodoxy in 1839 and again in 1875. Peasants who rejected Orthodoxy had been beaten by Cossacks and exiled to Siberia.[10]

In Galicia, however, the Greek Catholic Church had prospered under Habsburg rule. Soon after annexing the territory in the 1770s, the Habsburgs had raised its status to be on par with the Roman Catholic Church; in 1914, its upper clergy still felt immense gratitude for the rights and privileges they had been granted, and they were ardent supporters of the dynasty. Moreover, in the nineteenth century the Greek Catholic Church had become a powerful symbol of Ukrainian nationhood. Many of its priests were among the first and most influential leaders of the Ukrainian national movement. For Ruthenes across eastern Galicia, whether living in towns like Przemyśl or part of the peasant masses in the countryside, their Greek Catholic faith was the most important characteristic distinguishing them from Orthodox Russians and their Roman Catholic Polish neighbors. It perfectly embodied their position on the cusp between east and west. It was the defining component of their identity.[11]

The Greek Catholic Church thus posed the most formidable obstacle to Russification, and the occupiers were divided on how to weaken it. For the grand duke, Ianushkevich, and Bobrinskii, once Archbishop Sheptits'kyi had been neutralized caution was the watchword. The Russian army was engaged in heavy fighting throughout the occupation, and until victory was achieved, its leadership had no wish to incite Greek Catholic peasants or cause unrest along its lines of communication. Bobrinskii was willing to prevent Greek Catholic clergy who had fled from returning to their parishes, but he took a very conservative approach to those still in place. He had promised religious tolerance at the outset, and he ruled that only in communities where three-quarters of the parishioners voted by secret ballot to convert should an Orthodox priest be sent; even then, the local church should remain in the hands of the resident Greek Catholic clergyman.[12]

Unfortunately for harmony among the occupation authorities, the Russian Orthodox Church disagreed. Its man in Galicia, dispatched at the end of 1914 with the blessing of the ultra-pious Tsar, was the Catholic-hating Archbishop Evlogii of Volynia and Zhitomir. He had made his reputation a few years earlier as a fanatical opponent of religious toleration, smashing the last remnants of Sheptits'kyi's church in Chełm, across the Russian border. On arrival in Lwów in mid-December, he immediately celebrated the Tsar's Name Day by serving Mass according to the Russian Orthodox rite in two of the city's most important Greek Catholic churches, against the wish of their priests. To add to the provocation, his sermon, "To the Galician-Russian Nation and Clergy," called on his ecclesiastical opponents to drop their resistance, embrace their "Russian spirit," and return to the "faith of your fathers, that faith, in which your sacred ancestors had lived and found salvation." His demand was met with implacable hostility. Even Greek Catholic priests who felt some affinity to Russian culture declared conversion to Orthodoxy sinful. Despite pressure and intimidation, they refused to surrender any of Lwów's churches to Evlogii and his Orthodox interlopers.[13]

Evlogii thus turned his attention instead to the Greek Catholic faithful. He pushed hard, with some success, to persuade Bobrinskii to loosen the rules around conversion. By February 1915, in communities whose Greek Catholic clergymen had fled, a request by a minority of parishioners sufficed for Orthodox replacements to be sent. In the countryside, a campaign of terror was unleashed. Evlogii evicted some Greek Catholic incumbents on his own authority. Others were chased out by his allies in the Galician-Russian Society, an extremist organization containing local Russophiles. Embittered by Austrian persecution, these people were intent on forcing the pace of Russification and had scores to settle. To create vacancies, priests were murdered, or, like Father Harasowski in the village of Balice, just down the road from Przemyśl, arrested, and their Orthodox replacements then commanded the community to convert. Trickery was also used to proselytize. Ruthenian peasants were told that the faiths were the same, a lie made convincing by the similarity of their rituals. Despite all this, Evlogii faced staunch resistance. There were 1,906 Greek Catholic parishes in Galicia. Fewer than a hundred defected to Orthodoxy before most of the province was liberated in the summer of 1915.[14]

Governor General Bobrinskii was deeply uneasy about Evlogii's aggressive missioning and complained bitterly to his superiors. The governor general preferred a more subtle approach to creating a new Russian reality. At his command, the Galician capital, Lwów, gradually took on the appearance of a Russian city. The Russian flag was flown from City Hall. Shopkeepers were ordered to repaint their signs in Cyrillic. Against dogged opposition from the city council,

Russian street signs were screwed over the Polish ones. The only news available to citizens was heavily censored Russian news, and the newspapers appeared only in Russian or Polish. The word "Ruthene" was banned from use. The ruble circulated. Time itself changed. The eastern Julian calendar was introduced, putting the date back by thirteen days. Clocks went forward to St. Petersburg time. Russian public holidays were observed. Here, Bobrinskii's subtlety reached its end. To enforce the correct festive atmosphere for the Tsar's Name Day celebrations in December, the Russian police went from house to house threatening and cajoling residents to hang Russian flags from their windows.[15]

This underlying current of brutality was what really defined the Russian occupation. The Tsarist army's ideological impulse to "return" eastern Galicia to an imagined "primordial" Russian state was malevolent. The attempted cultural extermination of Ukrainians brought much suffering. Exacerbating this for all Galicia's peoples was the arbitrary power of the occupiers. Bobrinskii did not, as he had threatened, introduce Russian law, but he certainly brought Russian "system." Corruption and cruelty ruled.

While Przemyśl's fortifications stood, its citizens were protected. Word was smuggled into the city, however, of the torment undergone in nearby occupied villages. Theft was ubiquitous. No one was safe. "We pray to God incessantly," wrote one Polish woman to her soldier-husband defending the Fortress, "that our troops will at last come again, for already we can no longer cope with these Russians. No peace, either by day or by night. . . . The Russians terrorize us, saying they will slaughter us." Christians of all denominations passed through dark days. Yet there would be no greater victims of this violence, and of the Russians' dystopian plans, than Galicia's Jews.[16]

THE RUSSIAN ARMY's hatred of Jews manifested itself already in the first days of the invasion. The first pogrom took place at Brody, a northeastern border town where more than two-thirds of the 18,000 inhabitants were Jews. Cossacks rode in on August 14. At the sight of the Tsarist horsemen, people raced for shelter. For forty-five minutes there was heavy shooting, and then silence. When the residents emerged cautiously from their cellars, no one was sure what had happened, though the Cossacks later made the spurious claim—as they would in countless other places where they rampaged—that a Jewish girl had fired on them. A few days later, the horsemen returned to punish and plunder. A Jewish drayman who witnessed their assault recounted what happened:

> [The Cossacks] halted at the end of town, dismounted, and, not saying a nasty word, used their spears to toss something through the windows of the houses. The houses then burst into flames. They allowed the residents to leave only with the clothes on their backs and without carrying anything out. And while some Cossacks set fire after fire, others looted the houses. They broke into the shops, stormed into the homes, and grabbed everything they could lay their hands on. They didn't relax until the entire neighborhood was burned down and the town grew silent.

By the end of the day, 162 houses were smoldering ruins. Three men, two women (one of whom was a Christian), and a girl, who had been impaled on a Cossack's lance, were dead.[17]

Like flame following a gunpowder trail, violence blazed toward Przemyśl. Cossack cavalry were especially dangerous and fiercely anti-Semitic. They had a long history of murderous conduct—or, as they glorified it, of righteous slaughter of infidels. In Russia, they were the Tsar's enforcers, and they had been instrumental a decade earlier in harshly suppressing revolution. In Galicia, they lived up to their reputation as wild and merciless. Everywhere, Jews were mugged and shops looted. In some places, worse crimes were perpetrated. Men were beaten or murdered, women raped. Christians were also sometimes attacked, but from the start it was clear that their Jewish neighbors were the invaders' main targets. That the violence might pass them by, many displayed icons of Mary the Mother of God, Jesus, or Saint Nicholas in their windows or on the roofs of their dwellings. Jews, trying to save their property, copied that example. Many fled. By some estimates, nearly half of Galicia's Jewish population, up to 400,000 people, ran for the Austrian interior. Witnesses described an "interminable file of refugees . . . poor wretches who had left everything behind them except a few belongings on their backs." These frightened, fatigued, fleeing Jews "presented a picture of truly piteous misery."[18]

The worst atrocity befell Lwów. There, on September 27, after nearly a month of tense but peaceful occupation, a pogrom flared. News of this pogrom reached Przemyśl in January 1915 through a spy who had been sent out to reconnoiter the zone of occupation. In his account, it was a ploy "in real Russian style" by Tsarist troops to circumvent a ban on plundering. A soldier had fired off a shot from a house on a street in the Jewish quarter, and a cry had then immediately gone up that the Jews were attacking the military. The soldiers were ordered to punish the Jews and given permission to plunder their shops. In its outline, the spy's account was correct. Who fired the shot which sparked the pogrom was never firmly established. The occupation authorities insisted, of course, that it was a Jew. Not in contention, however, was the brutality of the Russian reaction. Cossacks stormed through the streets beating and shooting helpless Jewish civilians. They butchered 47 Jews and arrested 300 Jewish bystanders.[19]

Neither Grand Duke Nikolai nor his subordinate commanders organized or officially sanctioned this ill-disciplined violence. However, the atmosphere of anti-Semitic hatred at Stavka, the Russian High Command, and the toleration of atrocities against Jews at all levels of the army's command structure made it possible. The Russian Empire was Europe's most anti-Semitic Great Power. Religious, economic, and, by the First World War, especially political prejudice, increasingly influenced by the modern ideology of race, stamped the Russian ruling elite's and military's hostility toward

Jews. The abortive 1905 revolution, for which shadowy Jewish financiers and Jewish socialist revolutionaries were conspiratorially blamed, had radicalized their anti-Semitism. There had been terrible mob violence against Jews in these years, and more than 3,000 had lost their lives. While the first pogroms had surprised the Russian state, in the final, most violent stage of the revolution, from October 1905 to January 1906, the soldier that the Tsar had charged with restoring order, General D. F. Trepov, had secretly incited them. In warped anti-Semitic logic, smashing Jewish communities would break revolutionary power.[20]

The Tsarist army thus had a history of tolerating vicious, disorderly violence against Jews. Early, with pseudoscientific fervor, it had also embraced a fixed view of race that was based not primarily on blood but on indelible ethnic characteristics. Officers regarded Jews, especially foreign Jews, as inherently untrustworthy and politically treacherous. Small wonder, then, that in 1914 the Russian army's leadership saw no place for "kikes" (no one at headquarters ever called them "Jews") in the ethnically homogeneous "Russian" land that it hoped to build out of multicultural eastern Galicia. Over morning tea at Stavka, military and civilian officials killed time discussing how to go about "exterminating" the minority. Some speculated that expulsion to Austria might solve the problem. No one condemned the troops' excesses. On the contrary, these neatly dovetailed with other parts of the evolving plan. Looted Jewish property was distributed to the impoverished Ruthenian peasant population to make Russian rule and assimilation more attractive.[21]

The chief of the general staff, General Nikolai Ianushkevich, was a particularly vicious and obsessive anti-Semite, and he sat at the center of the occupation regime's anti-Jewish policy. Urged on by Stavka's Diplomatic Bureau and influential local Russophiles, from late September he started to plan the expropriation of Galician Jews' landholdings. By Ianushkevich's logic, this made sense. The Tsarist army was brutal, but despite idle talk about "extermination," not actually genocidal. In Ianushkevich's fevered imagination, Jews were foremost economic exploiters, whose power lay in their wealth. He had been informed that more than a third of the province's land was in their possession; in fact, the true figure was just 8 percent. Dispossessing them would therefore suffice to break their malign influence and "liberate" the Slavic peasantry. Speed was of the essence. In peacetime, such an arbitrary action would provoke international condemnation and parliamentary opposition. In wartime, these obstacles fell away. To remove Galicia's Jews from the protection of international law, he cynically proposed that all be compulsorily given Russian citizenship. This would "legalize" the robbery, for as Russian subjects in a war zone rather than foreign subjects under occupation, Galicia's Jews would lie entirely within the legal jurisdiction, and at the scant mercy, of the Russian army.[22]

Ianushkevich's scheme met with considerable internal resistance. In Russia, the Tsar's Council of Ministers rejected his proposals as premature. In Lwów, Governor General Bobrinskii, fearing for the peace of the rear areas in his charge, stalled. With the support of Grand Duke Nikolai, Ianushkevich drove forward his plans nonetheless. Over the winter of 1914–1915, a survey of Jewish landholdings in the zone of occupation was undertaken, and in February 1915 the Tsar himself approved a "Liquidation Law" permitting the confiscation of any land belonging to Austro-Hungarian subjects within 160 kilometers (100 miles) of the front line. Other economic assaults were also launched. Particularly harmful for the mass of Galician Jews, who were rarely landowners but very often traders or tinkers, was a ban on Jews moving from Russia to Galicia or between Galicia's districts. The following month, in March 1915, Jews still employed in Galician courts were fired. In some parts of the occupation zone, all Jews working in the civil administration lost their positions. In addition to these central measures, rampant arbitrary confiscations and requisitions by local occupation commanders and military units singled out and destroyed Jews' livelihoods.[23]

The anti-Semitism of the higher Russian military authorities gave carte blanche to lower commanders, troops, and administrators to exploit, brutalize, and demean Galicia's Jewish population. The officials and police dispatched to help run the occupation were the dregs of the Tsarist Empire's bureaucracy: ill-educated, capable of speaking only Russian, and often picked for transfer to Galicia solely because their incompetence, venality, and sloth had made them useless in their previous posts. These people ensured Jews' everyday life was a hell. Corruption and blackmail were endemic. Protection under the law was denied to the minority. Public whippings, arrests, and allocation to compulsory labor details were used to terrorize the Jewish populace. As in future persecutions, there were unspeakable acts of sadism. Sons were made to hang their own fathers before being strung up themselves. One Jew was beaten to death for trying to rescue Torah scrolls from a burning synagogue. Another had a rope placed around his neck and was dragged through the streets until he perished.[24]

The humiliation of the Jews was deliberately made a public spectacle. Lower Tsarist officials and soldiers acted from base prejudice, cruelty, and greed, but their brutality was also intended to signal the rise of a new order. In the Russian land that eastern Galicia would become, there would be no place for Jews except, at best, as a dispossessed and marginalized minority. The economic hold that Jewry was commonly accused of wielding over befuddled and innocent Christian peasants was to be broken. Officials intentionally stirred ethnic resentments, telling these peasants the Tsar would give them the property of the Jews and encouraging them to rob their Jewish neighbors. The old hierarchies were overturned. The traditional courtesy of kissing the hands of landowners was subverted by the Russians, who forced Jewish owners, and their wives and children, to kiss the peasants' backsides.[25]

Throughout the Tsarist army, right to the very top, anti-Semitism underwent further radicalization as the military campaign proceeded. Economic discrimination had seemed sufficient at the outset, for the army stereotyped Jews as materialistic and too cowardly to resist. However, as the Russians failed to break the resistance of the Habsburg forces and casualties mounted, the paranoia of the Russians grew, and officers began scapegoating the Jews as spies. The ban on the movement of Jewish traders between districts was in part intended as a late countermeasure. The Russians' first reaction was to take hostages. Although Jews constituted only 11 percent of Galicia's population, more than half of the 2,130 hostages seized by April 1915 were Jewish, mostly local community worthies. In Przemyśl, word of the practice likely reached Jews sheltering in the city early, shortly after neighboring towns were affected. In Lisko, 60 kilometers (40 miles) southwest of Przemyśl, the town's failure at the end of September to pay a fine of 10,000 crowns as punishment for delivering bread late to the invaders resulted in four hostages being taken, three of whom were Jewish. When the Russians withdrew from Jarosław, just 30 kilometers (19 miles) away, on October 9, they took twenty-eight hostages, mostly Jews, with them.[26]

The totalizing impetus of the war soon made itself felt again. In January 1915, the Tsarist military leadership ordered mass deportations of Jews. There was already precedent for this action: during the autumn and winter of 1914, using its special wartime powers on the maintenance of security, the military had forcibly exiled hundreds of thousands of enemy subjects and ethnic Germans living in Russia's own western borderlands. However, in Galicia, this escalation took place as a consequence of the warring Habsburg and Romanov Empires' racialized fantasies of treason and a vicious cycle of brutal reprisals. The Habsburg army's suppression of both real and imaginary Russophiles had horrified Tsarist commanders. Though unable to grasp its full extent—they were roughly correct in estimating that 10,000 Ruthenes from the province had been interned, but greatly underestimated the number of those executed, at 1,500—they knew it was widespread, and they believed local Jewish populations were playing a decisive role. Ianushkevich complained bitterly that "every adjustment in our lines that leads to a temporary withdrawal . . . is followed by brutal measures by our foe toward the portion of the population that is sympathetic to us and whom the Jews denounce to the [Austrian] Germans."[27]

Grand Duke Nikolai's solution was, as his general staff chief explained, "in order to prevent atrocities against the population which is devoted to us—and [to protect] our forces from espionage, which the Jews pursue along the entire front . . . to drive the Jews after the retreating foe." This command fitted seamlessly with the military leadership's determination to cleanse multiethnic Galicia and remake it as a Russian land. Even so, for frontline units it was scarcely practicable. Any attempt to drive crowds of panicked civilians around busy military rear areas, through entrenchments and over the battlefield, was a recipe for chaos. Many units found it simpler to send Jews eastward. In consequence, by March 1915 there were well over 10,000 displaced people in eastern Galicia. Among those uprooted early that month was the Jewish population of the town of Mościska, situated just east of Przemyśl. Frustrated at the Fortress's long resistance, the Russians accused these Jews of spying and blamed them for the failure to take the Habsburg stronghold. The expulsion operation was ruthless and total. Escorted by Cossacks, the entire community was marched 35 kilometers (just over 20 miles) to Gródek, and, for some unfortunates, double that distance to Lwów. Invalids, the aged, and new mothers were among the expellees, all condemned as dangerous enemy agents on account of their faith.[28]

The expulsions eastward caused unforeseen but entirely predictable and serious disruption for the Russian army. Governor General Bobrinskii, who had opposed Ianushkevich's desire to displace Jews, found himself confronting a humanitarian crisis. In desperation, he contacted the governors of various Russian provinces in order to organize the transfer of the displaced Jews to their areas. The Council of Ministers, now learning of Ianushkevich's deportation order for the first time, categorically forbade Galician Jews, with the exception of hostages, entry into the empire. The army therefore redoubled its efforts to push Jews instead toward enemy lines. In an order of April 1915 to his soldiers, General Radko Dimitriev of the Third Army was frank about the motives: "In view of the fact that we in Russia already have far too many Jews, a further influx of these people—and worse still from Galicia—will not be tolerated. The illustrious supreme commander has therefore ordered that when our troops occupy new territory all Jews are to be gathered and driven forward, toward the enemy troops."[29]

By the time the occupation ended in the summer of 1915 with the Russian army beaten back by German and Habsburg forces, 50,000 Jews had been forced out of Galicia into the Tsarist Empire. A similar number had been herded around the province, often after attempts to push them across the battle lines had failed. Russian aspirations and actions in Galicia were deeply ominous—and not just for fearful citizens watching from behind the Fortress's walls and worrying about their immediate future. Though the Tsarist army lacked the state direction necessary for a genocide, and divisions within its leadership lent its policy a chaotic quality, its occupation served as a forerunner for later totalitarian projects. The vision of a "Russian" land in Galicia was, if less bloody, as utopian as future German and Soviet invaders' racial and class designs. The ambition to perpetrate the cultural extermination of the Ukrainian people, the venomous anti-Semitism, and the deportation of entire communities had roots in the nineteenth century but looked forward to a far more ruthless twentieth. Most momentous was the paranoid and racialized thinking that already ruled on the eastern front in 1914–1915.[30]

IN THE MIDDLE of October 1914, there was still hope Galicia might escape a long Tsarist occupation and the ruinous plans being prepared for its transformation into a Russian land. The relief of Przemyśl had been gratifyingly easy, against little resistance, and the chief of the Habsburg general staff, Franz Conrad von Hötzendorf, was determined to maintain his armies' momentum. With characteristic hubris, he fantasized about returning the AOK headquarters to the Fortress and, from there, directing an immense operation to roll up the Russian army from its southern flank. On October 10, the day after cavalry reached the Fortress, he issued his ambitious orders. The Second and Third Armies, deploying to Przemyśl's southeast and east, would advance another 80 kilometers (50 miles) to the front and north of Lwów. These forces would provide protection for the main thrust northward. The Fourth Army, above them, was to march a similar distance, enabling it either to participate in an assault on Galicia's capital or turn north. The First Army, in cooperation with the German Ninth Army, would execute the war-winning blow up the Vistula River, smashing and chasing the Tsar's fleeing and demoralized troops.[31]

The fate of Conrad's plans, and indeed of Przemyśl's Fortress, was not, however, wholly in his hands. The Galician campaign was becoming just one part of a struggle now spreading all along the eastern front. The early October offensive that had relieved the Fortress was made possible by the partial recovery of the Habsburg field army, but it was also pulled along by German action farther north. The German army, in stark contrast to its ally, stood triumphant in the east. A Russian invasion of East Prussia, Germany's northeasterly province on the Baltic, had been repelled in weeks. Gallingly for the envious Conrad, at the Battle of Tannenberg in the last days of August an entire Tsarist army had been encircled and destroyed: it was just the type of operation the Habsburg general staff chief dreamed of accomplishing himself. By mid-September, a second Russian army had been forced from the province. With East Prussia cleared of the enemy, the victors, General Paul von Hindenburg and his staff chief, the ruthless Erich Ludendorff, had been placed at the head of a new force, the Ninth Army, that was being formed just northwest of Cracow, across the border in Upper Silesia. This 140,000-strong army had orders to assist the Austrians with a new offensive.[32]

On September 28, the Ninth Army had marched forward into Russian-held Poland. The Russians had seen this attack coming and, wishing both to counter it and launch an invasion of Germany, had transferred three armies away from Galicia to Central Poland. This move had hugely benefited Conrad. His Third and Fourth Armies advancing east toward Przemyśl beginning October 3 had met barely any opposition. The Habsburg Second Army, coming from the southwest at the same time over the Carpathian Mountains, had faced a determined defense only around the Uzsok Pass. However, for the German Ninth Army, the powerful Russian force now arraying along the Vistula—comprising 47½ infantry divisions and 11½ cavalry divisions, over a million men—presented a great danger. When the Ninth Army reached the river on October 3, its way was blocked. Dragging the Habsburg First Army behind them, the Germans turned and advanced north toward Russian-ruled Warsaw. The opening of the Tsarist armies' general offensive on the Vistula in mid-October then posed a big dilemma for the Central Powers. The Ninth Army was overextended and vulnerable, but a withdrawal would expose the flank of the Habsburg armies fighting outside Przemyśl and force them into retreat.[33]

Not only was Conrad beholden to his German allies, but he also drastically underestimated the difficulty of advancing into eastern Galicia. The Third, Eleventh (Blockade), and Eighth Russian Armies had withdrawn from Przemyśl in good order and had taken up strong positions on the right bank of the San River. Though the Habsburg armies in central Galicia had 40½ divisions to the Russians' 26, Conrad's men found breaking through over the swollen river impossible. On October 14, the Habsburg Fourth Army began attacking at Jarosław and farther north, but the troops lacked bridging equipment and their efforts withered under heavy shellfire. The Third Army went forward in support just to the south, at Radymno, on the 17th, but also failed. With far smaller forces, the Russians did better. On the night of October 17–18, Radko Dimitriev's Third Army suddenly attacked and succeeded in forcing bridgeheads over the San. On the southern extreme, the Russian Eighth Army, going onto the offensive a few days later, forced the Habsburg Second Army into a short retreat. Far from a victorious march of liberation, Conrad's forces were taking heavy casualties and failing even to hold their ground.[34]

A crisis of supply was the principal reason for the Habsburg army's poor performance; indeed, this factor would later have portentous consequences for the Fortress's continuing resilience. Through their advance to Przemyśl, Conrad's forces had overstretched their supply lines. The Third Army fighting to the east of the city, for example, had its railheads 70 kilometers (around 45 miles) away in Zagórz and Rzeszów. Alone this army's 200,000 men required 800 tons of food daily, as well as fodder for 60,000 horses, not to mention munitions and equipment. All of it had to be conveyed by horse-drawn transport along a single highway that had been destroyed by constant marching and four weeks of pouring rain. To try to carry out Conrad's offensive design and feed its men, the field army helped itself to Przemyśl's siege stocks. Some 22,000 shells were transferred from the fortress magazines to the field batteries, and the fort artillery fired off 10,400 shells in support of the Third Army's operations. Most harmfully, huge quantities of food were taken. By October 19, when further withdrawals were forbidden, the amount of food that had been removed was equivalent to nineteen days of standard fortress rations. If oats to feed the horses, which could in an emergency be diverted for human consumption, are reckoned into the calculation, then the Fortress lost over one month's precious food stocks.[35]

The Fortress's supplies could not be easily replenished. For two and a half weeks after its relief, it remained beyond the reach of rail traffic. The line from the west, which curved over the top of Przemyśl and entered it from the northeast, was in Russian artillery range and so remained unusable. The line from Hungary, which ran into the city's south, had been broken by the demolition of the Niżankowice bridge on September 19, just before the encirclement. The army needed time to rebuild the bridge. At last, on October 28, it was finished, and over the following six days 213 trains were rushed into the Fortress: 128 of them designated for the Fortress's resupply, and the other 85 for the field army. On average, a train arrived at one of the city's stations every forty minutes. This eleventh-hour influx of supplies, supplemented by foraging beyond the perimeter, left the Fortress's garrison of 131,767 men and 21,484 horses with 111 days' worth of flour and biscuits, 139 days' worth of vegetables, enough meat for 72 days, and enough oats for 90. The munitions magazines were half full.[36]

The severe shortage of artillery ammunition—and, to a lesser degree, thanks to the Fortress's stocks, rations—exacerbated a second problem holding back Conrad's armies outside Przemyśl: the morale of his soldiers. There were places where the troops fought well. Third Army units, including the 23rd Honvéd Infantry Division, reattached to the army from the Fortress, achieved a significant local success in capturing the Russian fortifications on the Magiera Heights 20 kilometers (12 miles) southeast of Przemyśl. These formidable hilltop positions put Russian artillery in range of Przemyśl's southern rail lifeline: had they not fallen on October 18, no resupply of the Fortress at the end of the month would have been possible. The national prejudices of the Habsburg army commanders were also gratifyingly challenged by the steadfastness of some of the formations. Przemyśl's own X Corps, full of despised Poles, Jews, and Ruthenes, was singled out for special praise. The XVII Corps' best unit was reportedly the 19th Division, predominantly composed of distrusted Czech troops.[37]

Nonetheless, the Habsburg armies' battlefield performance was mostly lackluster. Conrad was furious, especially when the Russians achieved what his more numerous troops had failed to do and crossed the San, but the reasons were clear. The field army's combat units lacked leadership and training. At the regimental level, professional officers had been wiped out in the opening battles; those who survived were disillusioned with the failed tactical tenets they had been taught in peacetime but unsure how to improve on them. In the ranks, most drafts conscripted to fill the gaping holes had a measly six or eight weeks of instruction. Unsurprisingly, neither veterans who had passed through Conrad's earlier debacles nor these new recruits were burning with martial ardor. Men wounded themselves to escape. "In no phase of the war," wrote the army's official historian, "were there relatively so many 'self-mutilators' as in this." He added, condescendingly, that "they were especially numerous in regiments from lands of backward culture." Losses were horrendous. In the 23rd Honvéd Division, infantry regiments were down to half strength by the end of October. Along with dead, wounded, and missing from battle, which together constituted around two-thirds of the casualties, cholera took a very heavy toll on the formation's soldiers.[38]

The Habsburg armies' struggle on the San was terminated by disaster farther north. Stavka's transfer of armies to Central Poland had concentrated a vastly superior offensive force against the Germans. Though the first attempts by the Russian Fourth Army, positioned in the middle of the front, to cross the Vistula River on October 10 failed, Ludendorff recognized the looming danger and on October 18 ordered a retreat, to begin two days thence. Conrad agreed that the First Army would head north up the Vistula, opposite Ivangorod, to cover the Germans' right flank as they withdrew. He also came up with another war-winning plan. The First Army, together with the retreating Germans, would permit the advancing Russian troops over the Vistula and then counterattack, trapping them with their backs to the river and seizing a stunning victory.[39]

Unsurprisingly, given the troops' condition and their commanders' woeful past record, Conrad's ploy did not go as planned. The Habsburg regiments duly deployed well back from the river, and on October 22 they were ready to throw themselves at the unsuspecting enemy. The first day's fighting appeared to go well, but at midday on the 23rd, officers on the First Army's staff were shocked to learn from an intercepted telegram that the Russians had already pushed between eight and ten divisions over the Vistula. The Austrians had let too many enemy cross. The First Army's own force of seven and a half divisions came under unbearable pressure in the following days as more Tsarist troops poured across the river, tipping the balance of strength more than two to one against it. Early on the afternoon of October 26, after the army's south wing had been thrown back, its commander, General Viktor Dankl, ordered his men into a 90-kilometer (55-mile) retreat. The debacle had cost the army 40,000–50,000 casualties.[40]

The First Army's new positions ran 90 kilometers (55 miles) from the mouth of the San westward to the town of Kielce. It reached them on October 31, after a four-day forced march. There was no real hope that it would be able to hold here. The army lacked the strength to defend such a long front. Its divisions were down to 7,000 or 8,000 men, and it was short on ammunition. Moreover, the Germans were keen to withdraw their Ninth Army, which was needed to cover the First Army's westerly flank, in order to redeploy and attack the advancing Russians farther north. Conrad persuaded his allies to wait and grimly ordered the First Army to stand firm while supplies were rushed into Przemyśl on the newly reopened rail link. Dankl's anguished pleas for permission to retreat were refused until, on the afternoon of November 2, the Russians broke through on the First Army's right wing. Early that evening, Conrad accepted the inevitable and ordered a general retreat. The First Army would immediately march another 50–60 kilometers (30–40 miles) southwest, seeking protection behind the Mierzawa and Nida tributaries. To avoid being taken by the Russians in their flank and rear, the armies on the San were to withdraw more than 150 kilometers (90 miles) west behind the Dunajec River and southwest into the Carpathian Mountains.[41]

The general retreat came at a particularly bad time for Conrad. The Germans had just proposed the establishment of a joint high command on the eastern front, with the Habsburg commander-in-chief, Archduke Friedrich, as the nominal head and Erich Ludendorff as his chief of staff. Conrad would be shunted into an intermediate post and robbed of influence. In Vienna, Emperor Franz Joseph was clearly tempted, for on November 4 he had the chief of his Military Chancery, the geriatric Arthur Baron von Bolfras, write to the AOK with the idea. Only Archduke Friedrich's staunch support saved Conrad. For Przemyśl, the timing was even worse. The Fortress's stores had been ransacked by the field army in its vain efforts to push forward beyond the San. The railway, which had taken more than a fortnight to repair, was in operation for less than a week before, on November 4, its bridges again had to be blown. The fortress commander, Kusmanek, contemplating the departure of the Third Army's rearguard that night, must have been filled with foreboding. "As a result of the three-and-a-half-week presence of the army in the area of Przemyśl," he later ruefully observed, "the difficulties of the Fortress, especially with regard to materiel, had significantly grown."[42]

ONCE CONRAD ACCEPTED the necessity to withdraw the field army from the San, all that remained was to decide what to do with the Fortress. The tough commander of the Third Army, General Svetozar Boroević, and the Fortress's pragmatic chief of staff, Lieutenant-Colonel Ottokar Hubert, both thought it should be abandoned and its garrison evacuated. Przemyśl lacked the supplies for a sustained siege. For both men this was the essential fact, for no rapid relief could be expected. The Germans, whose early autumn offensive had been instrumental in enabling the Habsburg army to return to Przemyśl, remained heavily committed in France. Their new general staff chief, General Erich von Falkenhayn, continued to seek decisive victory there; despite Conrad's pleading, he had few troops to spare for the eastern front. The Habsburg army's past performance offered little confidence that it would be capable of beating a way forward by itself and breaking a second Russian encirclement of the Fortress.[43]

Moreover, this time there was no compelling operational reason to leave such an enormous garrison to the rear of the field army. In mid-September 1914, the Fortress had provided the crucial service of covering a chaotic retreat and winning time for Habsburg forces to reconstitute, restore discipline, partially recover, and return to the attack. At the start of November, the strategic situation was very different. Fighting had extended all along the eastern front, and Central Poland, not Galicia, was now the front's primary theater of operations for the Russians. Przemyśl thus no longer stood in the midst, but rather on the periphery, of the decisive action. Additionally, unlike earlier in the autumn, the Habsburg field army was not retreating in panic. Its withdrawal in November was necessitated by an operational failure to the north. The troops marched away from the San River in good order, ready to resume the battle in defensive positions farther west.[44]

Yet a powerful political and psychological rationale pushed Conrad to retain the Fortress. The general staff chief's position, and with it his reputation and dreams of marrying his lover, Gina, hung by a thread. Relinquishing the Habsburg Empire's key defensive complex in the east would surely result in his dismissal. Accentuating the dilemma was Przemyśl's new prominence as the empire's symbol of resistance. The Fortress's defense in early October had captured imaginations across the Habsburg lands. Kusmanek's defiant reply to the besiegers' demand to capitulate, the epic battle at Fort I/1, the dramatic relief by the field army, and the immense damage reportedly inflicted by the garrison on the Russians had enthralled a public starved of victories. For Conrad, a vain man, the thought of the ridicule and wide censure that abandoning the recently triumphant bastion would provoke must have been unbearable. Doubts about the AOK's competence would grow. Slurs of defeatism would be thrown about. The blow to popular morale would be grievous.[45]

Thus, on November 3, the order was passed around the Fortress's garrison to write farewell letters to their families. Przemyśl's "heroes" were again to face the Russian army on their own. Conrad's instructions, resembling a fig leaf to hide his embarrassment, were to conduct an active defense. The swollen garrison should "draw considerable enemy strength onto itself." The badly depleted 23rd Honvéd Division was returned to the Fortress. So, too, were batteries of heavy guns borrowed by field units. Reinforcements, comprising another infantry brigade and a squadron of aircraft, were left behind. By November 5, these, along with half-empty storehouses and hospitalized casualties too ill to evacuate, were the only reminders of the departed Habsburg field army. The Russians reacted quickly. Within three days, a new encirclement of the Fortress was complete. The Tsar's armies hurried forward, lapping around the Fortress in pursuit of their retreating enemy. Darkness descended over the conquered land.[46]

CHAPTER FIVE

ISOLATION

The news that the field army was, once again, going to retreat from Przemyśl was met with shock in the town and garrison. "Like a thunderclap out of the blue!" exclaimed Lieutenant Stanisław Gayczak in his diary. "Horror!" Posters appeared on November 3 ordering civilians to get out. When police went door to door the following morning, few had packed anything in preparation for leaving. The unfortunates were given time only to throw some clothes in a bag and then herded to the rail station. There, chaos ruled on the platforms. The crowd was far too big for everyone to travel on the last trains out. Gayczak, who had a family of his own stranded in Russian-occupied Lwów, wept openly at the sight of tiny children being bundled into the crammed wagons by desperate parents. Whether because they were designated essential workers, had dodged the police patrols, or had missed the evacuation trains—and were unable to afford the high cost of a place on a cart out of Przemyśl—around 30,000 civilians stayed, together with the 130,000-strong garrison. With rumors predicting anything from a cataclysmic defeat by Russian heavy artillery in a week to a grueling year-long siege, the city newspaper tried to reassure the trapped people. "There is no cause for anxiety or fear, it is not necessary to scare either yourself or anyone else and lower morale," it admonished. "After all, we find ourselves in a powerful and victorious fortress."[1]

THE SECOND ENCIRCLEMENT of Przemyśl opened an attritional struggle presaging the "total war" that Central Europe would face in later years. The Russians, still smarting from their defeat in October, and unwilling to take strength from their main effort farther north, against Germany, had no intention of attempting another storm against Przemyśl. Instead, all the intelligence reaching the garrison commander, the freshly promoted General Kusmanek, indicated the enemy was settling in for a long siege to starve the Fortress out. The blockade force comprised six and a quarter reserve infantry divisions and a cavalry division capable of containing but not conquering Przemyśl. Later in November, some of these second-line units were replaced with even lower-grade militia units filled with older soldiers not very different from those shut inside the Fortress. These mediocre units took up positions well back from the fortress perimeter, outside the range of the defenders' artillery. Cut off from the world, Przemyśl's garrison and citizens were entirely dependent for survival on their own stockpiled supplies, ingenuity, and mental resilience.[2]

The most urgent material requirement of the garrison in the first days of the encirclement was winter clothing. During the relief, the Fortress Command had requested that a huge quantity of clothing be delivered, but by the time the railway connection was severed it had received only 4,300 cloaks and, unhelpfully, 6,000 calf-skin rucksacks. In the second half of November, the temperature plummeted to -17°C (1.4°F), and, with troops still in summer uniforms and wearing worn-out boots, casualties with severe frostbite started coming in from the perimeter trenches. To Kusmanek's and Przemyśl's credit, the shortage had been foreseen and measures to alleviate it were underway. Already at the beginning of October, the Fortress Supply Department had appealed for 100,000 pieces of thick cotton underwear to be manufactured in the city. Municipal authorities responded rapidly by setting up thirty sewing machines in the vacated district court and recruiting 160 women. Some were professional tailors and seamstresses, while others were from the respectable middle classes, such as teachers and secondary school pupils. Within a week or two, they were producing 250 sets of warm underclothes every day. Work continued until mid-February 1915, when the factory ran out of material.[3]

The fortress garrison embraced a spirit of experimentation and self-help. Bright soldiers of the 23rd Honvéd Infantry Division had the idea of turning the surfeit of calf-skin rucksacks into vests, providing each of the division's battalions with sixty of these warm garments. The problem of worn boots was tackled by various means. One simple expedient was to issue wooden soles with straps to bind them tightly to existing footwear. More impressively, a means of hardening raw leather using a chemical process involving chrome was invented, making possible the manufacture of replacement leather soles. The same readiness to innovate was also applied to other shortages. The Fortress's Engineering Directorate improvised weaponry, ranging from mortars made from drainpipes to an armored train. Drawing on the skills and knowledge its citizen-soldiers brought to the army, it ruthlessly converted the sparse material resources available in Przemyśl to war use. Soap and shoe polish were among its products. Most notorious were its 20,000 boxes of "Fortress matches." The boxes were plastered with warnings—"Handle with caution!" and "Treat striking surface with care!"—because their contents were so dangerous. On being struck, the matches would alarmingly "flare up with a small explosion and splutter like rockets."[4]

Przemyśl's civilians had other problems. For them, from the outset of the siege the overriding worry was food. The private stocks gathered painstakingly in the summer were depleted, and anything edible was already eye-wateringly expensive. Before the field army's withdrawal at the beginning of November, municipal authorities had set maximum prices for food and other essentials that were one-third or more above their peacetime cost. Sellers could legally demand 12 heller for a single egg (7 heller was the norm in peacetime), 68 heller for a kilo of flour (earlier 40 heller), 13 heller for a kilo of potatoes (earlier 8 heller), and 2.40 crowns for a kilogram of pork (earlier 1.60 crowns). Once Przemyśl was blockaded no one heeded these regulations, despite the threat of six months in jail and a fine of 2,000 crowns. By the middle of the month, prices had already spiraled to double what they had been before the war. Consumers were lucky if they could find sustenance and if the seller was willing to accept cash. With money rapidly losing value, often the only means of purchase was barter; that, however, only worked if one already had something worth swapping.[5]

City leaders stepped in to avert immediate catastrophe. Przemyśl's first soup kitchen was established in mid-November. The Fortress Command supplied much of the food, and the kitchen was run by nuns, who cooked 650 meals daily. As more and more larders grew bare, other charitable actions were organized. A citizens' committee led by the Roman Catholic bishop Father Józef Pelczar opened two kitchens the following month; by the end of the siege, seven such kitchens were in operation, as well as tea rooms serving hot drinks and lighter meals. Class sensibilities were also catered to. There were bourgeois citizens who would rather starve than suffer the shame of standing in a soup kitchen queue. For them, a dining room was set up in mid-January. The Fortress Supply Department provided raw ingredients at half price and volunteers served up meals costing 30 or 40 hellers. For this token sum, people could keep their dignity and fill their bellies.[6]

The tactic of blockade was as old as siege warfare itself. Far from feeling themselves to be at the dawn of a new era of mass violence, to many incarcerated in Przemyśl it appeared that time itself was in retreat. Muffled riders and ragged soldiers huddling around camp-fires in the snow resembled figures in scenes from the Napoleonic

Wars a hundred years earlier. The demise of money, and the spread of barter, inspired some to cast much further back. "At present we live as if in prehistoric times," observed the town newspaper, comparing Przemyśl's citizens to Eskimos, Siberians, and the "half-wild peoples in Central Africa." Long decades of peace and progress had led citizens to believe the horrors of war had been consigned to the past. Yet twentieth-century barbarity brought deprivation and misery to match that of any earlier conflict, and soon citizens would be jolted by reminders that their suffering was indeed rooted in the modern age. The most startling of these came as a new threat from the skies.[7]

ON THE MORNING of December 1, 1914, a Russian airplane appeared high over Przemyśl. A cacophony began as the city's defenders opened fire, and pink-white bursts of smoke plumed and then melted away in the sky. In the snow-covered streets, crowds of people gathered, watching with interest to see what would happen. Some stared intently. Others joked and laughed about how frightened the pilot must be.

Suddenly, small roundish objects—to some they looked like gray eggs—dropped from the aircraft. Down, down they fell, tossed by the wind until they landed with loud detonations. A shocked cry went up: "The Russians are throwing bombs!" Panic ensued. Everyone began to run. Some people hurried home to take shelter in their cellars. Others fled from their houses into the street, thinking they were safer there than in a building that might collapse at any moment on top of them. A few citizens, knocked to the ground by the snow the explosions had dislodged from roofs, picked themselves up, discovered with surprise they were still alive, and took to their heels.[8]

This was the first of a series of aerial strikes on Przemyśl, and among the earliest to be faced by any civilian urban population in history. Throughout the siege, Russian aircraft dropped 275 bombs on the city and its environs. These caused fairly minimal damage. The local newspaper was not far from the truth when it tried to reassure citizens that the small bombs were "neither so terrible nor so deadly, because either they do not explode at all or . . . do not have great power and so cannot penetrate ceiling[s]." The official line was that the first raid's casualties amounted to a dead horse, a damaged roof, and some shattered windows. However, well-informed locals heard that people, too, had been hurt. One girl had had half her head cleaved off by shrapnel or falling masonry and had been rushed, twitching, to the hospital. Another had been badly wounded in the chest, and a boy had suffered multiple minor injuries.[9]

Przemyśl's civil leaders and the military were quick to react. Within days, posters went up instructing the public not to stop and watch enemy aircraft, but instead to take cover immediately on the lowest floor of their homes. The Fortress Engineering Directorate started work on countermeasures to defeat this novel threat. Eight captured Russian machine-guns were mounted for antiaircraft defense and, thanks to a Landsturm engineer who had worked at a precision mechanics firm before being drafted, a brilliantly simple but effective rangefinder was developed capable of measuring the height and distance of aircraft. Nevertheless, the population was not reassured. The first raid triggered great fear. People glimpsed an apocalyptic future that was indeed to come, but not yet in this war. A rumor circulated that, along with the bombs, the airplane had dropped cards promising that an aerial armada was on its way to obliterate the city.[10]

The Russians' primary targets during these air raids were the bridges over the San and the military installations in and around Przemyśl, such as the Fortress Command and food and munitions magazines. However, terror was the main impact. Although the attackers proved incapable of hitting anything of strategic value, they inflicted a trickle of civilian casualties. In all, perhaps ten or more citizens were killed and around double that number injured. Intense emotions were aroused. The Russians seemed to have reached a new depth of barbarity. Aerial attack meant nowhere was now safe. Among the victims were women and, at least according to popular rumor, many children, too. Moreover, although objectively the danger was slight, the threat from the skies was tremendously unnerving. Dr. Richard von Stenitzer, based in the city center, described the "peculiarly excruciating feeling, when the airplane appears high over one in the air. One gets the impression, as if he is targeting one personally." The winged enemy provoked an almost superstitious dread. Life under the raids reminded the fearful doctor of a fairy tale "where the dragon comes to a habitation at a particular hour and demands his victim."[11]

THE POPULATION OF Przemyśl lived a strange, strained existence under siege. Time had a different tempo. Ilka Künigl-Ehrenburg, the Styrian countess who had followed her medic husband to the Fortress, summed it up best: "From day to day, from week to week, from month to month—waiting—waiting." The encirclement could only be an interlude, before relief (in every sense of that word) or utter disaster. Everyday life in the besieged Fortress was an unnerving mix of monotony and ever-present menace. People craved normality. When city schools were permitted to reopen in January, "I taught gladly," remembered a teacher, Stanisława Baranowicz, "because for a while I could forget about the looming danger." By all accounts, the children were also thankful for the resumption of routine, even one punctuated by the thunder of war. They arrived "with joy" and attended regularly, "despite the crash of bombs and the din of artillery and machine-guns."[12]

The question on everyone's lips, the obsession that permeated every waking hour, was to know when the ordeal would end. For those in search of answers, the place to go was Grand Café Stieber. The café, located on the ground floor of the magnificent Hotel Royal opposite the railway station, just a short stroll from the Fortress Command, was Przemyśl's most celebrated meeting point. In the words of one rather snooty Austrian officer, it was "neither elegant nor handsome, just big . . . with a lot of tables and armchairs, two billiard tables and several large windows." Certainly in the winter of 1914, the café was not at its best. Most of the waiters had evacuated, there was no food or heating, and, unless one could afford its overpriced and very ordinary schnapps, the only drink available was tea sweetened with raspberry juice. Nevertheless, it was here that the officers of the Fortress Command and the Supply Department came to relax and gossip, and so it was the place to visit if one wished to gauge the Fortress's prospects. It was always stuffed with people.[13]

Rumor flourished in the blockaded city. Nobody quite knew how the tales of approaching relief, peace, or catastrophe began, but they spread like wildfire. So outlandish were some claims that at times it appeared Przemyśl's citizens had lost all touch not only with the outside world but also with any grasp of reality. Toward the end of November, for instance, an unconfirmed report that Lwów—90 kilometers (56 miles) to the east—had been freed from Russian control triggered hysterical joy. "This news electrified the whole town," recorded Lieutenant Gayczak. "Soldiers fell into each other's arms, embraced, wept." He himself could not sleep the entire night, for his head was filled with the vision of an imminent return home to his family. Another rumor, which did the rounds in January, asserted that neutral powers led by America were insisting on peace negotiations. The disappointment when these stories were exposed as fantasy was crushing. A bitter cynicism took hold. "We already believe nothing," confided Gayczak miserably to his diary.[14]

These optimistic tales, as well as doom-laden stories of the Russians tunneling under the forts or bringing up Japanese fortress-busting artillery, reflected and refracted the hopes and fears of the besieged. The rumors manifested a blend of boredom and nervous expectation, and under their influence men grew irritable and tempers frayed. Many—by the end of the siege quite probably most—of the soldiers became depressed. The Galician troops were in the worst situation, for not only were they, like the rest of the garrison, separated from their families, but they also usually had no idea what had become of their loved ones after the Russian invasion. Not a day went by when Stanisław Gayczak did not pine for his wife, Lucy, and their four children, whom he had left behind in occupied Lwów. He was tortured by fear of what could have befallen them. Were they starving? Were they dead? He kept their photograph with him, talked to it, and caressed it. He prayed for them and he wept, sometimes for hours. In mid-December, a well-meaning clergyman triggered an episode of collective breakdown that publicly laid bare the feelings of desolation, worry, and loss tormenting Gayczak and the other soldiers of his eastern Galician unit. Writing in his diary, Gayczak reported:

> This morning [December 14] a Polish priest came to the company, gave a short sermon and granted everyone present general absolution should they die. We prayed for the Emperor and then, when he said "and now we shall pray for our wives and children," a howl rose up in the company. I myself wept like a child! And I prayed sincerely, so sincerely for you most beloved Mama and for you, my beloved children, that the Lord God and Mother of God hear my prayer and preserve you in life and health![15]

The city offered some solace in distraction. A stroll around the pretty park and up the castle hill in the southwest of the city could help clear minds, though on windy days the rumble of distant guns was more audible here and one could no longer go right to the top, as in peace, because Russian prisoners of war were locked in the old castle. Theaters were open, offering slapstick comedy as a cure for depression. Most tellingly, Przemyśl's cinema, the "Olympia," did a roaring trade. With Sherlock Holmes thrillers and *A Thousand and One Nights*, its silver screen could, for a precious couple of hours, miraculously transport beleaguered citizens and soldiers over the Fortress's walls and away from Central Europe's misery and bloodshed to romantic lands in the farthest corners of the world. "In this sanctuary of cheap thrills," wrote the city newspaper, gauging the mood perceptively, "we seek comfort from tragic comedies and comic tragedies when facing cholera, Russians, and war."[16]

This being old Austria, the land of Mozart, Liszt, and Strauss, perhaps the greatest morale-raiser was music. Przemyśl's main rail station, lying in disuse, was converted to a concert hall. Taking advantage of the presence of renowned musicians within the garrison, performances were held for the benefit of the Widows' and Orphans' Fund for the Defenders of Przemyśl—a charity established to provide support to the families of those killed defending the Fortress. However, it was the free weekly concerts held at the order of the Fortress Command in Przemyśl's main square that most moved the public. The performances began at the opening of the siege— the first was held on Sunday, November 8—when the unheralded cheerful clang of a regimental brass band, a sound associated with happy holidays in peacetime, both surprised and delighted onlookers. The ever-observant Ilka Künigl-Ehrenburg poignantly captured the moment:

A Honvéd band marches onto the market square. It halts, arranges itself in a circle, and the bandmaster steps into the middle. He raises his baton and the music begins. . . . For months the Fortress has heard no music. No military music has played since the outbreak of war. Now these tones lure the people from all the alleys. Anyone going to the square takes quicker steps. And anyone going in the opposite direction turns around. First amazement, then a flash of joy passes across their faces. This becomes a smile as they go on. It is as if a powerful magnet pulls the people to it from all alleyways. They tumble and hurry in swarms from all the streets leading into the square. And one is amazed that so many are still in the besieged Fortress.[17]

The market concerts were also popular for another reason. They offered a chance to meet members of the opposite sex. Men in pike

A joke concert program for "Csûtak's Grand Variety Show" from an unofficial Hungarian trench newspaper, circa end of 1914 or early 1915, p. 24. The show was supposedly running on Mickiewicz Street—the location of the Fortress Command. The imaginary acts included Louis Chanta de Csutak's "terrific dances with leg-twitch and half-turn"—probably a reference either to shell-shock or death throes—Professor Dr. Weiss with "Bad Bertha"—a German nickname for a siege gun—and "Zsiga the wire-artist" singing his popular number "All Quiet on the Line." "After the show," the mock program advises, "visit the Bohemian District Restaurant, where the most expensive and best horsemeat is served. After that, we shall be in a Czech situation," a Hungarian expression meaning "in a very bad state."

gray mingled with the women still in the city, mostly volunteer nurses and local workers. Künigl-Ehrenburg noticed teenage girls making eyes at the officers. The Fortress was a place of loneliness. It was also a place where peacetime rules and proprieties were eroding. A ubiquitous sense of living through the Last Days of Judgment helped to loosen constrictive Victorian morals and corsets alike. Love and lust, erotica and exploitation, were, at least for much of the officer class and some civilians, also a part of life in the besieged Fortress.

As a garrison city, Przemyśl was no stranger to military-civil romance. In peacetime, no ball or society function was complete without officers resplendent in dress uniforms to waltz the city elite's daughters around the dance floor. These were marriage markets, in which a young lady might hope to meet a dashing dragoon. Lower down the social hierarchy, conscripts from the surrounding region doing their two years of service were eager to impress the young women of the city, sometimes to the point of harassment. Those who failed to form a relationship could always take advantage of a murky underworld of sex. At the turn of the century, municipal authorities had counted around a hundred prostitutes in the city.[18]

In wartime, though, the circumstances were very different. For a start, the garrison, which in peace had made up around one-sixth of the city's population, now outnumbered it fourfold. Officers' peacetime pool of partners, the daughters of the municipal elite, had mostly evacuated. The pent-up frustrations of this overwhelmingly male society were on display in unofficial trench newspapers written by bored junior officers. Their editorials groused with schoolboy humor about "the absence of the female element," and mock advertisements placed in the papers were frankly dirty. "Gentlemen!" announced one. "If you need good and reliable serving-maids . . . call Pál Paja's nurse employment office. Cooks, maids, nurses—tested by his own methods—are available." An "Uncle Göre" (possibly a brother officer's nickname) promised "aid and free consultancy to pregnant women" as well as "hot pork"—a play on the Hungarian word *disznóság*, meaning also "lousy trick" and "behaving like a pig in bed." For German-speaking officers, a "Collection of Erotic Publications for Fortresses" included such useful titles as *How Can I Sleep Snuggly?*, "an essential handbook for the encircled"; *The Little Defiler*, "a practical guide for use in the field"; and—in an apparent reference to homosexuality in the trenches—*The Surrogacy of Love*, "experiences from diverse dugouts."[19]

There were enterprising men in the city who were quick to recognize the financial opportunities awaiting those who could satisfy officers' desires. "Most noble sir," wrote one hotelier to a Polish lieutenant, "please do not refuse my request; come to us. There will be a few pretty young girls for you to amuse yourself with in these difficult times." Sex was sold openly. In the afternoons and evenings, Przemyśl's promenades took on, in the words of one journalist, "a rather 'big city' appearance," thanks to young women in furs and feathers on the game. "They pursue their career with simply fabulous ease," he went on, "especially as the soldiers have no shortage of money." The women came from a variety of backgrounds. Most likely there were local sex workers among them, who had made a living servicing the garrison before the war. As deprivation worsened, though, competition increased. Working-class and, later, some bourgeois women whose food supplies were exhausted were forced onto the street. The newspaperman's jibe about their fantastical earnings was unfair. The going rate for a session in a side street, or, if you were luckier, in a bed, was 30 crowns—an enormous amount of money in peacetime, to be sure, but by the end of the siege not worth much more than a loaf of bread.[20]

More glamorous women were also available—for much higher prices. Blonde Amy was one example, a young woman so stunning that a hush fell over Café Stieber when she walked through the door. She had worked the best hotels of Budapest before the war, and offered her clientele a little exotic thrill by using the pseudonym

Miss Maud and passing herself off as an American—though the only words of English she knew were "all right" and "goodbye." By her own account, she could make 15,000 crowns a week in Przemyśl. Few officers could have afforded Amy. Most were anyway less discriminating. Two aspects of their love lives inflamed particular criticism. First was the eagerness not just of young but also of middle-aged officers with families to participate in "wild orgies." The second complaint focused on the inferior social standing of their partners. The public debauchery of these "men of honor" was disturbing, but worse was that they were openly consorting with, in one critic's scathing words, "tarted-up women, who . . . had until a few days earlier ruled the floor cloth and cooking spoon." Stanisław Gayczak made the same point, fulminating about the presence of a "*common* prostitute in the officers' mess. This is what we have come to! Rabble."[21]

There were, of course, relationships struck up in the besieged city that were, so far as we can know, sincere and loving. The delight of Lieutenant Stanisław Tyro on the "blessed day" that he first "kissed and caressed my gorgeous Walerya, a lady whose beauty has no equal in Przemyśl," is rather touching. Frequently, however, there was something transactional about siege relationships. Access to food, not looks, charm, or wit, was what made a man attractive in a blockaded city. Some young women, who chose wisely, acquired simply staggering quantities of food from their officer lovers. Aniela Wilk, daughter of a retired locomotive fireman, shacked up with a captain who ran the military uniform magazine. He showered her with so much flour, rice, biscuits, and butter that when, in January 1915, city police searched her mother's apartment, they needed two carts to carry away all the illicitly obtained provisions. Twenty-one-year-old Stefanie Haas was not only gifted a month's food for her whole family by her Hungarian fiancé, a cavalry lieutenant, but at Christmas was invited to an exclusive soirée at Fort VII, "Prałkowce," where she was serenaded by a violin and dined on Swiss cheese, sausage, and chocolates. Sentiment which, in the world outside, lovers would

1. THE ARMCHAIR GENERAL.
General Franz Conrad von Hötzendorf, the chief of the Habsburg General Staff, at his desk conceiving an "audacious plan." Conrad knew the battlefield only from maps. In four years of war, he visited the front only three times.

2. THE FORTRESS COMMANDER.
Lieutenant-General Hermann Kusmanek von Burgneustädten, the celebrated "Defender of Przemyśl," looking dapper for the camera.

3. PRZEMYŚL (1). "An ancient town and important fortress on the San" was how the Baedeker Guide described Przemyśl before the war. View southwest from the top of Mickiewicz Street, showing the city's eighteenth-century clock tower.

4. PRZEMYŚL (2). The Old Synagogue, dating from 1594. By 1914, Przemyśl had been home to a thriving Jewish minority community for over half a millennium.

5. PRZEMYŚL (3). View northeast over the city marketplace, showing the town hall (in the bottom left corner), the Old Synagogue (just right of center), the railway bridge, and, beyond it, the wooden road bridge

6. PRZEMYŚL (4). "I'm sending you a postcard from Przemyśl, so you can see where Aunt Alexa does her shopping everyday—but now the market is not so full," wrote the sender of this card on September 5, 1914. Two and a half weeks later, the city would be completely encircled by the Russian army.

7. ATROCITIES (1). Suspected "Russophiles" under arrest in Przemyśl. In the first days of the war, over 4,000 people accused of Russian sympathies or treasonous behavior, often on flimsy or no evidence, were taken into custody in Galicia.

8. ATROCITIES (2). A ring of flame encircled Przemyśl in early September 1914 as the garrison ruthlessly burned to the ground villages obstructing the forts' fields of fire. This village, Żurawica, lay inside Przemyśl's defensive perimeter and was razed only in June 1915, but the sights and smells must have been similar ten months earlier.

9. ATROCITIES (3). A hanged priest of the Greek Catholic Church, with his Hungarian executioners posing proudly. Ukrainian-speaking Ruthenes, and especially their clerics, suffered most from the depredations of the treason-obsessed Habsburg military in the first months of the war.

10. A BROKEN ARMY. Supply wagons and exhausted soldiers of the defeated Habsburg Field Army clog Przemyśl's Mickiewicz Street during the general retreat of mid-September 1914.

FLÜCHTLINGE BEI PRZEMYSL NACH RÜCKKEHR   PHOT BERGER

11. GALICIANS. Destitute villagers in Przemyśl district. Rural communities around the city were forcibly evacuated to the Austrian interior in the autumn of 1914, where they rotted in disease-ridden internment camps. Those who stayed in their ruined homes found themselves trapped between the fortress perimeter and the Russian blockade line in a starving purgatory.

Heldenmütige Verteidigung der Festung Przemysl

12. "THE HEROES." Habsburg propaganda portrayed Przemyśl's middle-aged, multiethnic garrison as a model of imperial cooperation, martial competence, and manly courage. The reality was far less glorious, though the men displayed extraordinary endurance under siege.

13. THE DEFENSES. The Fortress's 48-kilometer (30-mile) perimeter comprised thirty-five forts and, sealing the gaps between them, hastily dug "interval trenches," some of which are shown here. Note the camouflaged "shrapnel shield" over part of the front line, a common protective feature in this theater not seen on the more famous Western Front.

14. STORM (1). Russian troops assault the Fortress during the offensive of October 5–8, 1914. To judge from this French propaganda postcard, even the Russians' closest allies regarded them as barbarian hordes.

15. STORM (2). Fort I/1's ghastly frontal ditch during the most critical clash of the Russian offensive, early on October 7, 1914. Although not accurate in its technical detail—the ditch was defended by a central caponier, not loopholes in the walls—the artist's portrayal does evoke the horror of the fighting. Seventy badly wounded Russians and 151 corpses were pulled from the ditch after the battle.

16. A ROYAL VISIT. The Habsburgs were keen to wring every publicity advantage from the Fortress's victorious defense. The heir to the Austro-Hungarian throne, Archduke Karl (in the center of the photograph), toured the fortifications with Kusmanek (here on Karl's left) on November 1, 1914, just days before the field army abandoned the Fortress and its garrison to a second, fateful siege.

17. AIRMAIL. Przemyśl made history when, in January 1915, it pioneered the world's first-ever postal service to use powered aircraft. Cargo capacity was very limited and censorship tight, so soldiers shared postcards. Eight men sent this one to the village of Petőháza in western Hungary. On the reverse is written: "Dear families, wives, fathers, mothers, relatives, we inform you that we are alive and in good health and we wish you good health as well."

18. DEATH FROM THE SKY. A Przemyśl house hit by a Russian aerial bomb. Note the shock of the onlookers. Russian aircraft dropped 275 bombs on the city and its environs during the second siege, killing around ten citizens. Although damage was slight by later standards, the bombing of civilians inspired intense fear as a new form of barbarity.

19. FLYING DICK. A Parseval-Siegsfeld M98 Observation Balloon. These tethered balloons were 24 meters (79 feet) long, held 750 cubic meters (26,486 cubic feet) of highly flammable hydrogen, and were used for artillery-spotting by the Fortress. Their long, sausage shape and scrotum-like rear stabilizer prompted soldiers to nickname them "dicks." Aptly, the seductress Hella and her officer-lover were rumored to have used one to escape besieged Przemyśl.

20. OVERSEXED AND OVER PRZEMYŚL. A Fortress flyer strikes a pose in front of his machine.

21. LIFE UNDER SIEGE (1). A public concert by a Hungarian regimental brass band. Music had the rare quality of being able to overcome language divides and unite Przemyśl's multiethnic garrison and citizenry. The first of the siege's military concerts was held on November 8, 1914, and thereafter they took place weekly, lifting the spirits of the population.

22. LIFE UNDER SIEGE (2). Newspaper boys and girls holding up copies of the Fortress's Hungarian newssheet, the *Tábori Újság* (Field News). Polish- and German-language editions were also sold to the multiethnic garrison. The multitude of children trapped in the Fortress, and the uses made of them during the siege, is striking.

23. LIFE UNDER SIEGE (3). One of seven soup kitchens set up to help feed Przemyśl's citizens during the siege. Note the elegantly coiffed society lady proprietarily brandishing the ladle, and the Roman Catholic nuns, who played a major role in these charitable initiatives. The bundled-up children gripping empty bags and receptacles testify to the harsh climate and desperate need in the city that winter of 1914–1915.

24. LIFE UNDER SIEGE (4). Horse slaughterhouse. Though citizens and soldiers faced immense hardship, it was far more dangerous being a horse than a human during the siege of Przemyśl. From the 21,000 horses in the Fortress at the start of the siege, 17,000 were eaten by the garrison and nearly all the rest were killed at the Fortress's capitulation.

25. ARMAGEDDON (1). "A magnificent and, at the same time, a terror-inspiring sight. As if from active volcanoes, shafts of red fire exploded all around Przemyśl, lifting huge stones and debris and belching monstrous billows of black smoke" (resident and eyewitness Józefa Prochazka). The destruction of the Fortress by its garrison began at 6:00 a.m. on March 22, 1915. All the forts, the powder magazines, and the city's bridges were blown up.

26. ARMAGEDDON (2). The 3rd May Bridge, Przemyśl's main artery for road traffic and pedestrians between the old town and the northern suburb of Zasanie, resting with its southern end in the San River. The demolitions of March 22, 1915, literally rent apart the city.

27. OCCUPATION. A lone Cossack canters westward up Mickiewicz Street on Przemyśl's second day under Russian rule, March 23, 1915.

28. EXODUS. Przemyśl's Jewish population prepares for exile on the orders of the Russian military, end of April or early May 1915. Some 17,000 Jewish men, women, and children were forced out of the city and surrounding district. Note the mounted Cossacks at the rear surveying the crowd.

29. CONQUERORS (1). Tsar Nikolai II (left) returns the salute of Lieutenant-General Serhij Delwig (right), who served briefly as the Russian commander of the Fortress, at the ruins of Fort I/1 on April 24, 1915. Looming over both is the supreme commander of the Tsar's armies, Grand Duke Nikolai Nikolaevich.

30. CONQUERORS (2). German troops goosestep past the town hall, June 6, 1915. These are men from the 11th Bavarian Infantry Division, which had a central role in the recapture of Przemyśl. The Germans would return and conquer the city again, far more brutally, on September 15, 1939.

show with diamonds or pearls was, in the starving Fortress, said with cigarettes, sardines, and salami.[22]

For all that some women were doted upon and a very few made substantial money, it was men who nearly always held the power in siege relationships. In the hospitals, the army hierarchy placed male doctors above young volunteer nurses, who became objects of excited male fantasy and censure. It was rumored pornographically that they were in position solely to "serve the lust of the officers and . . . doctors. . . . Not one goes around without a fur, though their underwear is filthy!" In reality, to resist advances from predatory superiors in a rigid military medical institution must have been very hard for young women who were alone and far from home. In the city, too, women were always the supplicants, for it was men who had access to food. A glance into the diary of a drone-like field officer of the 23rd Honvéd Infantry Division—his name is lost to us—offers a taste of the exploitation this permitted. There was a girlfriend in Hungary waiting for him, but he liked female company and had plenty of free time to party. He had an on-off Polish girlfriend in Przemyśl, "Mici," whom he treated appallingly. He went with other women and he threw Mici out when she accused him of giving her venereal disease. She was back within a week, though. He kicked her out of bed in the night, too, but again she returned. She disappears from this "hero's" diary, and presumably also from his life, only on February 7, when he told her that he could not feed her. She departed in tears.[23]

There were a few rare women who, through the erotic fantasies that men invested in them, were able to reverse this power relationship. No one did this more successfully than Ella and Hella, the Fortress's "Flyer Princesses." Their real names were Ella Zielińska and Helena Dąbrowska, and they acquired their moniker because they consorted with Przemyśl's pilots and aircrew. They also "partied hard" with officers of the elite 23rd Honvéd Division. A sensual mystique surrounded these women. For one thing, they were pretty. Helena, we are told, "was past the first flush of youth but slim and stylishly dressed. Her subtle perfume, her sunny laugh and her pleasant voice made her very attractive." Yet the Princesses' appeal went beyond their physical appearance. They kept company only with the Fortress's best, and the glamour of the flyers and shock troops rubbed off on them. For everyone else, they were unobtainable, but in fevered male imaginations, for those who were worthy, those who were chosen, they were the ideal lovers. Ella and Hella. The soft vowels of their names oozed femininity, and the delicious way in which the rhyme tripped off the tongue hinted at the possibility of a *ménage à trois*. They were supposed to be dynamite in bed.[24]

A host of stories attached themselves to the Flyer Princesses. Some whispered they were Russian spies, which only accentuated their attraction. The rumors were sufficiently persistent to prompt the Habsburg military to launch a belated investigation into them after the Fortress's fall.[25]

One tale, probably apocryphal but revealing of the awe in which these young women were held, had it that Hella seduced an officer in the Fortress Command. He was a close friend of the flyers and a hero of the October battles, and his superiors trusted him intimately. The couple lived an idyllic existence. The man's duties were light, they ate the best food in the Fortress, and their days were filled with romantic walks and sledding. When, on one of their jaunts, they visited the Fortress's balloon section, its commander was so bewitched by Hella's charm that he took them on a joyride. From the tethered observation balloon high in the sky, they enjoyed magnificent views of the fortress defenses and the snow-blanketed countryside beyond.[26]

All the time, so the story goes, Hella was working to turn her companion. When a vacancy arose in the balloon section, she urged him to join, while still retaining his job at the Fortress Command. Once he was in his new post, she sometimes visited him, keeping the balloon crew sweet and discreet with gifts of sugar and rum. In the middle of December, the garrison made a determined breakout attempt to the southwest, trying to link up with the Habsburg field army, which at last had started to roll toward the Fortress. Hella's officer was hard at work, helping first with the planning at headquarters and then, once the operation was launched, in the basket of the balloon, tirelessly braving turbulent weather to follow the progress of the breakout force. The Fortress Command puzzled over how the Russians seemed able to predict its every move. The operation was a total failure. The Honvéd infantry were thrown back, badly depleted and demoralized.

After the thwarted breakout, his own treason weighed heavily on the conscience of Hella's officer. To his comrades, the man appeared apathetic and distressed. He feared he would be discovered, especially when military police began to arrest others suspected of betraying the Fortress. However, Hella—as listeners of the story would expect—had her lover on a leash. She scared him, soothed him, silenced him, and she hatched a plan of escape.

The first days of February had been foggy. To discover what the Russians were up to, a nighttime balloon flight at full moon had been ordered. Under Hella's thrall, the officer volunteered. The couple burned their papers, and at the appointed time, Hella pulled an army greatcoat over her warm clothing, donned a soldier's cap, and, with a small but heavy case, the two traveled to the balloon section. The ground crew, fond of Hella, understood why a lady might find a flight by moonlight romantic and made no protest.

The couple climbed into the basket, taking their case with them ("new instruments," explained the officer), and the yellow gas-filled balloon was raised. Up, up it went, until it was high in the sky. Then suddenly, the balloon's steel tether tumbled to the ground. The officer had released it, and the balloon was free. Blown by a southwesterly wind, Flyer Princess Hella, her secrets, and her victim floated over the Fortress and disappeared into Russian-held territory.

The veteran who narrated this tale could not vouch for its truth. Doubtless, like all salacious gossip, it came from a "reliable" source, an almost certain sign that someone invented it. Nevertheless, he was able to say something definitive: with his own eyes he had seen

Hella one last time after the fall of the Fortress. She was sitting comfortably in a Russian staff car with a Tsarist officer beside her; they were roaring down the road to Lwów. Perhaps, then, Helena Dąbrowska was a spy. Or perhaps she was simply one of those rare and remarkable individuals who through their own gifts and wits were able to navigate the violent, changeable currents of Central Europe's twentieth century.

THOUGH IT WAS 200 kilometers (125 miles) behind enemy lines in November 1914, Przemyśl was not entirely cut off. Thanks to modern technology, it possessed two fragile channels of communication with the outside world. The first was the Fortress's radio station, which represented the state of the art in early twentieth-century radiotelegraphic equipment. It was located atop the Winna Góra, a hill with an altitude of 238 meters (781 feet) north of the city. An imposing wooden mast 72 meters (236 feet) high mounted the antenna, and below sat the station itself, where the fifteen-man crew worked and slept, and an engine house with a 26-horsepower Fiat gasoline motor and two 23-kilowatt electricity generators.[27]

The radio had been installed only a fortnight before the outbreak of war. Much of the crew had no specialist training and had to learn on the job. The equipment quickly developed teething troubles. The Fiat motor first proved temperamental, and then, during the first siege, broke down irreparably. In the admirable spirit of improvisation that characterized much of the garrison's activity, the crew swapped it for the engine from a caterpillar tractor, and within thirty hours they had the station back in operation. The fortress radio beamed its precious messages to and fro through the ether from that point on until it was hit by Russian artillery fire on March 21, 1915.

The radio station proved to be an excellent investment. During the first siege, it kept the Fortress in touch with the AOK and with the Third Army. All the Russians' attempts to jam its signal failed. In the second siege, General Franz Conrad von Hötzendorf, who was notoriously secretive, was far too fearful of interception to share any detailed plans over the airwaves, but the Third Army used radio communications to keep the Fortress informed of its operations. Coded orders and reports were also transmitted. In quieter moments, the radio crew scanned the frequencies for news of the world beyond the encirclement. These bulletins, along with reports on the progress the Austro-Hungarian army was making toward relieving the Fortress, were—when optimistic—published and distributed in newssheets in German, Hungarian, and Polish.[28]

The Fortress had four newssheets, a number more reflective of the multiethnicity of the readership than the amount of actual news available. The German-language *Kriegsnachrichten* (War News), published also in Polish as the *Wiadomości wojenne*, was a dry affair. The format was always broadly the same: a single sheet with news of the Central Powers' latest victorious operations on the Russian front, something glorious about the destruction of Serbia, and briefer reassurance that the French and British were also losing the war. There was also often a meteorological report and occasionally some ghastly song or poem dedicated to Kusmanek and celebrating the Fortress's resistance, composed by an overzealous member of the garrison who perhaps hoped for promotion. Toward the siege's end, the paper became considerably more exciting, not because of any improvement in its content but because the newsprint ran out, and so packing paper and even tissue paper were used instead. Later numbers appeared in a rainbow of green, yellow, red, and blue.[29]

The Hungarian *Tábori Újság* (Field News) presented much the same information; but, as the Hungarians liked to feel superior to the rest of the garrison, it was three pages long instead of a single sheet. Despite the heavy censorship, eager soldiers and civilians alike daily parted with the 10 heller cover price for these examples of military journalism. "At no time has man been so possessed by hunger for news," marveled Ilka Künigl-Ehrenburg. "From early morning onward, people wait in front of the [newssheet] printers. The whole street is blocked with people. Sad-eyed Jews in Kaftans, officers' batmen sent by their masters, Polish schoolchildren, off-duty officers and nurses and soldiers." This audience became skilled at divining real meaning from the brief and ever-optimistic bulletins. They noted stock phrases—"we are continually gaining ground," "we have attacked there and there and taken 500, 1,000, 2,000 prisoners"—and they saw, too, that the locations did not change. "Regrouping in a new, more favorable position" was understood as defeat. Worst of all was when Galicia disappeared entirely from the news. That was a sure sign something terrible had happened.[30]

The Fortress's fourth paper—the only real newspaper—the Polish-language *Ziemia Przemyska* (Przemyśl Land), was an altogether more impressive publication. Unlike the military newssheets, it dated from before the war and was run by a civilian editor. As the fortress radio station had a monopoly on news from the outside world, the paper could provide no more information on current affairs than its military rivals could. However, its professional journalists proved to be masters in creating copy to fill their news columns. The editorials were engaging, and the paper helped its Polish readership understand their experiences of living under siege. The present turmoil was skillfully put into historical context in articles on Fortress Przemyśl in the time of the old Polish Republic and the Cossack attack on the city in 1648. A long account of the siege of Paris in 1870–1871 reassured readers that their ordeal was also not unique in the modern period.[31]

Ziemia Przemyska also tackled the ongoing ordeal in interesting feature stories. It critically analyzed the Russians' ambitions in Poland and carried reports "from our special correspondent"—probably refugees—about their actions in occupied Galician towns, many of which were homes to members of the garrison. It chronicled life within the Fortress. It gave voice to civilians' frustrations about rocketing food prices, projected an image of communal solidarity by reporting on the numerous charitable efforts, and tried to bring city and garrison together by carrying interviews with soldiers about the fighting on the Fortress's front lines. With a sense of humor absent in the stodgy military newssheets, it was even able to tackle the crucial question on the trapped population's minds, the conundrum "that incessantly torments people" and that the army's publications did not dare address: "When will the war end?" The paper's definitive answer, arrived at through a tongue-in-cheek spiritualist-style formula, was comforting, as convincing as any propaganda, considerably more entertaining than any realistic assessment could be, and had the virtue of being based on logic—of a sort. Taking the Emperor's birth date and year of accession, and the digits from the years of his life and rule, it came up with a complicated equation showing definitively that "on December 12, 1914, the present world conflagration will end": "We offer this information," the paper comfortingly confided, "to stressed and distressed pessimists. Whoever so wishes, let them believe."[32]

NEWS OF THE outside world, of the progress of the war, and of the prospects for relief was important for the mental survival of the besieged population. Yet at least as significant, above all for the men of the garrison, were more personal contacts. Soldiers yearned for their families. The war had raged for three months by the opening of the second siege, and even for men with homes far from any battlefield there was plenty of reason to worry about the well-being and financial security of their loved ones. After relief in October, priority had been given to bringing delayed post into Przemyśl, and first letters and then some 10,000 parcels had arrived. Garrison troops wrote back. Once the field army retreated, however, this correspondence quickly ceased. The last post out of the Fortress was dispatched on November 6. On the following morning, an attempt to bring more letters out was aborted, because 15 kilometers (9 miles) southwest of the city the delivery wagons ran into Russian cavalry.[33]

To keep soldiers in touch with their families, a second, and new, channel of communication was opened during the second siege: the world's very first airmail service. The Fortress Command proudly announced this new capability on January 4, 1915. In reality, officers and even men of other ranks had unofficially been handing post to airmen flying from the fortress airfield situated to the east of the city since the beginning of the second siege. Dr. Jan Stock, the physicist and extraordinarily overqualified private and military clerk of Fort Va, was, for example, able to send a card to Cracow in mid-December. Instead of a stamp, he and other senders donated one crown per postcard and two crowns per letter to the Fortress Defenders' Widows and Orphans Fund. The Fortress Command's decision to regularize the transport of mail by aircraft was thus not motivated solely by a desire to raise morale. Certainly, the official airmail was fairer than the informal arrangements that were already common, for it opened up access to the pilots, giving men with no personal connection to them the chance to send letters to relatives. However, it also enabled the military authorities to control and censor all messages leaving the Fortress.[34]

The Fortress's air squadron, Flik 11, was equipped with primitive two-seater Albatros and Aviatik biplanes. Constructed of wood and canvas, with a top speed of 105 kilometers (65 miles) per hour and cargo space confined to whatever the airplane's observer could squeeze into his open cockpit, these craft were far from ideal for bulk mail delivery. Instead of regular letters, the new airmail service made use of special "flyer postcards," manufactured from thinner— and crucially, therefore lighter—paper than the standard military card stock. To ensure wide distribution across the garrison, the printed airmail postcards could be purchased only by military units, not by individuals, and to deter forgery each card was numbered. Control was clearly high up on the military's list of priorities, for the cards were to be twice censored, once within the soldier's unit, and then again in Przemyśl's main post office. Only messages about the sender's health and greetings were allowed. All other topics were strictly to be avoided. Officers were entitled to one card each. For other ranks, a single line on a postcard shared between five men was usually all that was permitted as a sign of life and love.[35]

After a run of poor weather, the first aerial postal mission took off on January 18. Three airplanes, together carrying a total of 140 kilograms (over 300 pounds) of mail, crossed over enemy-occupied territory and successfully flew the 206 kilometers (128 miles) to Cracow. At the city's main post office, one of the aircraft observers triumphantly handed the flyer postcards over for delivery to their recipients. This was the first of thirteen sporadic flights bringing mail from the Fortress. Although the Fortress Command wished for a regular service, neither it nor the Habsburg army could spare the aircraft or pilots. Instead, to help further satisfy the garrison's desperate desire for contact with home, a balloon delivery service was also introduced, on January 9. This method utilized improvised unmanned gas-filled balloons capable of carrying two kilograms (four and a half pounds) of post. The rules dictating content and censorship were the same as for the flyer postcards. However, for this service, fifteen soldiers had to share a single card. The first family to receive the message was expected to pass it on. That only applied, though, if the balloon, which was entirely at the mercy of favorable winds, reached friendly territory. The chance of that happening, as experience showed, was a mere fifty-fifty.[36]

Although pioneering, Przemyśl's airmail had serious limitations. For most of the garrison's Galician contingent—men like Stanisław Gayczak whose families lived under Russian occupation or were displaced—the airplanes could offer no help. For the others, whose homes were in places still safe from war, the chance to send a sign of life to loved ones was a comfort. Sadly, though, no provision was made for families' replies to be flown into the city. For fear of implying the Fortress's situation was hopeless, their letters and parcels were not returned by the imperial postal authorities but put into storage. A very few officers did receive word from home, but solely because aircrew sometimes agreed to bring messages in as a personal favor. Richard von Stenitzer, the doctor who so feared enemy airplanes, had great reason to thank the Austrian flyers, for he was one of the lucky ones. "The best day I have spent here," he jotted in his diary when a thick envelope from his wife arrived during the siege. "The charming photographs, composed with so much love and sympathy, the long letters that tell me that at home all is reasonably satisfactory," sent him into an ecstasy. "I really only now appreciate in what happiness I lived at home. God protect all and bring us together again!"[37]

TOWARD THE END of 1914, Stenitzer's wish suddenly looked like it might soon be granted. Through November, the Fortress's garrison had conducted the active defense Conrad had ordered. It had launched attacks to pin Russian strength around Przemyśl and to disrupt the movement of enemy troops westward. In the north, the defenses had been pushed forward. The new Na Górach–Batycze positions dug 3 kilometers (2 miles) in front of the main perimeter enabled the Fortress's artillery to fire on the highway running from the towns of Radymno to Rokietnica, forcing Russians marching westward to take a longer detour around the Fortress. From the command's perspective, this activity was useful, but to the people trapped in Przemyśl it had offered little confidence that the encirclement might soon be lifted. The only relief had come from wags who, seizing on the expanding perimeter and mimicking the language of the army bulletins, had cheerfully announced that Przemyśl was "gaining ground." If this continued, they joked, the garrison would be in Lwów by Christmas.[38]

At the start of December, however, the Habsburg field army opened an offensive that offered real grounds for hope. Radko Dimitriev's Russian Third Army stood at the gates of Cracow. With an assault force of four infantry and three cavalry divisions, Conrad launched a surprise attack into its underbelly at Limanowa, around 60 kilometers (40 miles) southeast of western Galicia's principal city. The Russians reeled back and retreated farther once the Habsburg Third Army, strung along the Carpathians, started to advance on December 8. Conrad's primary objective was to cut off the Russian withdrawal, and so he sent the Third Army marching north, rather than northeast toward Przemyśl. Nevertheless, if the ambitious plan succeeded, Dimitriev's force would be annihilated, forcing a further enemy retreat behind the San, which in turn would break Przemyśl's encirclement and free the garrison.[39]

The Fortress Command was not privy to Conrad's intentions. It hoped that the Third Army was coming directly to its relief. This hope was strengthened when, on the first day of the army's offensive, its commander, General Boroević, radioed a request for supporting operations to draw off enemy strength. In Przemyśl, people saw garrison troops departing on the 9th for a forty-eight-hour sortie to the southwest. Fierce gunfire echoed from the battlefield over the city. On the 11th, excitement reached fever pitch when a radio message arrived from the commander-in-chief of the Habsburg forces, Archduke Friedrich, announcing his "hope that I shall soon be able to free the Fortress from the enemy encirclement."[40]

The Fortress Command was further galvanized when, on December 14, a secret transmission arrived directly from the AOK. This message ordered the garrison to do "everything possible to disrupt enemy departures westward." All routes west of Sieniawa, Przemyśl, and Sambor were to be reconnoitered by its aircraft. Conrad's intention was to use the Fortress's strength to cover the Third Army's right wing as it passed by, heading north. However, his demand for reconnaissance reinforced the erroneous impression that these troops could well be heading northeast, straight for Przemyśl. Under its commander, Lieutenant-General Joseph Krautwald von Annau, the Third Army's right wing was, as Kusmanek knew from his flyers, already approaching Sanok and Lisko, 60 kilometers (40 miles) away. The fortress commander thus resolved to gather all available manpower for one great effort. A bare minimum of troops would be left to defend the perimeter. Everyone else was to be thrown southwest to open the way to Przemyśl.[41]

Led by Lieutenant-General Árpád Tamásy von Fogaras, the Fortress's strike force comprised seventeen and a quarter infantry battalions and two cavalry squadrons, supported by thirteen gun batteries. All the horsemen and three-quarters of the infantry were young, battle-hardened Honvéd troops. Their mission was to smash through the Russian encirclement and take control of the main road from Bircza, down which any relief force must pass. Three battle groups were organized. The strongest, on the right flank, had seven and a quarter battalions and six batteries. Its mission was to capture two sites overlooking the road, the fortified Hill 428 and the formidable 460-meter-high (1,509 feet) Paportenka summit. The center, with four battalions, and the left, with six, were to protect this key operation by occupying the Kopystańka and Szybenica, dominating hills with altitudes of 541 and 495 meters (1,775 and 1,624 feet), respectively. To the north, across the San River, a small separate sortie by two and a half battalions covered their backs. The troops had already fought in this terrain a week earlier and knew it was difficult. They would have to cross a frozen undulating landscape, keeping formation while passing through forest, before charging uphill into enemy guns. Even so, spirits were sky-high. If only they could grasp victory, the men thought, they could celebrate Christmas with the field army, or even, joy of joys, at home.[42]

The operation began on December 15 at 7:30 a.m. The all-important right wing, led by Major-General Rudolf Seide, one of the 23rd Honvéd Infantry Division's brigade commanders, advanced with four battalions to the fore. At first they met only light resistance, and by 10:30 a.m. they had already covered 8 kilometers (5 miles). Then, just north of Hill 428, they stumbled on entrenched Russian infantry. A fierce firefight ensued; it lasted two and a half hours until the surviving enemy upped and fled.[43]

The Russians' main hilltop position now loomed before the Honvéd troops. While their neighbors covered their flanks, two battalions of Honvéd Infantry Regiment 7 worked their way up the slope. Shells from their own artillery flew over their heads and hammered the position as they climbed. Their orders were unambiguous: "Do everything, even if it requires heavy sacrifice, to bring Hill 428 into our possession as quickly as possible. Forward!"[44]

By 4:30 p.m., the Honvéds had closed the distance to just 300 paces. Reinforcements were brought up and at 5:00 p.m. the assault restarted. The Russian positions could be seen clearly now. The strong entrenchments were equipped with shrapnel covers and surrounded by barbed wire. Two machine-guns traversed the approaches. Two more hours of blood and sweat brought the Honvéds to within 150 meters (about 500 feet). Some men lay only 50 meters (165 feet) away. Yet even this close, and hidden by darkness, they could not break in. When, at seven o'clock, a bugle call rose above the battle noise to signal the final storm, the assault troops went forward in fury, but were shot down at the wire.

At this critical point the commander on the spot, Lieutenant-Colonel Elek Molnár, resolved to retreat. His men were at the brink of exhaustion. Dead and wounded were strewn over the hillside. Yet, as he was issuing his order, something extraordinary happened. Cries of "Rajta! Rajta!"—"On! On!"—suddenly rose from the battlefield, followed by a heavy burst of fire. On its own initiative, the 4th Company, under Second Lieutenant József Magyary, had again stormed forward against the northeastern corner of the enemy positions.

Magyary's assault was beaten back by a hail of bullets, but the bravery of his men drew the defenders' attention. Two other Honvéd companies coming from the northwest seized the moment. They reached the wire, cut through it, and broke into the far end of the Russian position. Vicious hand-to-hand fighting followed, but the defenders now stood no chance. Sixty prisoners and their two machine-guns were captured. The triumphant Honvéds had surmounted the first major obstacle to taking control of the Bircza Road.[45]

Over the next two days, the breakout force made further gains. The operation's key objective, to puncture the Russian encirclement line, was achieved on the evening of the 16th, when, after a failed morning attack, reinforcements from Honvéd Infantry Regiment 5 conquered the Paportenka summit at the point of the bayonet. With Hill 428 and the Paportenka in their hands, the Hungarians had opened the road from Bircza. Strenuous efforts were made to bolster the operation's flanks and to keep the enemy off balance. To the north, a strong position was won 4.5 kilometers (just under 3 miles) from the road with the capture of the Namulowa hill. On the southeastern flank, Honvéd battalions were also winning heights, working their way toward the dominating Kopystańka. At dusk on December 17, the troops were frozen and fatigued but had every reason to feel proud. They had made great sacrifice, but stood ready to greet the Habsburg field army. Sentries on Hill 428 and the Paportenka strained their eyes looking down the Bircza Road, seeking a relief force that never came.

The Fortress's breakout party was living on borrowed time. The Russian blockade army's commander, General Andrei Selivanov, had been startled by the ferociousness of the garrison's assault but rapidly took countermeasures. Reinforcements were called and set marching toward the breakthrough point. A diversionary attack was also prepared in the north, against the Na Górach–Batycze positions. Worse, the Habsburg Third Army's right wing—which anyway had no order to relieve Przemyśl—had run into problems. Krautwald's group had ground to a halt in the face of strengthening opposition on the 16th, and on the 17th was forced into a 20-kilometer (12-mile) retreat. This then impacted the rest of the army farther west, which had to end its advance. Conrad's offensive had succeeded in pushing the Russians away from Cracow, but his greater plan to encircle and destroy Radko Dimitriev's army had clearly failed. During the night of December 17–18, the AOK radioed the Fortress Command with the grim news that Krautwald was withdrawing. Kusmanek now knew there would be no relief.

December 18 dawned, another bitterly cold and miserable day. In the north of the perimeter, far from the breakout battle, a diversionary assault on the Na Górach–Batycze position by two regiments of the Russian 82nd Reserve Division had already opened. The 82nd had fought in the abortive October storm on the Fortress. It would have its revenge that morning. Under cover of mist and darkness, the Russian infantry silently broke into the Habsburg forward trenches, which were more lightly garrisoned than usual because of the operation in the southwest, and massacred the defenders. Stunned survivors fled back to the main line. Fire from fort artillery saved the whole position from falling, but its advance defenses had been irredeemably lost. To be sure that no one was in any doubt about the menace they intended, a Russian aircraft had dropped a message over the city warning of what might come on the morrow: "Surrender yourselves, for on Nikolai's Day [December 19] Death is coming to you!"[46]

The retreat of the field army clearly made the continuation of the southwest breakout operation pointless. The Russian attack in the north showed that the Honvéd regiments were needed back in the Fortress. What added to the urgency to terminate the operation, though, was that on the 18th the breakout troops themselves started to come under severe pressure. The day had begun with the force still on the attack. The Kopystańka summit had been taken the day before, but then immediately lost, and so Molnár's men had been brought up to recapture and, this time, hold the summit. They went forward, yet by ten o'clock they were stuck in intense fire 400 paces from the Russian position. This was bad, but it was worse when, an hour later, twelve fresh enemy battalions suddenly launched a pincer attack from the south intended to crush and cut off the bulk of the breakout force.

The Honvéd battalions put up a bitter defense. However, on the right flank, II/Honvéd Infantry Regiment 5, firing from shallow trenches surrounded by a wood, suffered a disaster. Russian assault troops crept through the trees and then rushed the battalion, screaming "Rajta!" ("On!") and "Tüzet szüntess!" ("Cease fire" in Hungarian) to confuse the defenders. A melee began, and after much slashing and stabbing with swords and bayonets the Honvéds had lost a quarter of their strength and were forced out of their positions. Well-aimed artillery fire halted the Russian pursuit, and the battalion was able to form a new line of resistance 100 paces to the rear. Even so, panic spread. A ragtag force of sappers was hurriedly organized as a last line of defense. When the Russian attacks kept coming, and officers started to warn that they could hold no longer, the Honvéd units behind the Kopystańka were ordered to withdraw.[47]

The end was not far off. By midafternoon, most of the breakout force was strung out just south of the Bircza road. The Russians, now in overwhelming strength, had followed: instead of the welcome sight of friendly blue uniforms, it was hordes of soldiers in drab green whom sentries saw storming up the road. The breakout troops had in the past four days lost around 1,000 men killed and wounded. The Honvéds were saved from annihilation by the order, arriving at 7:30 p.m., to terminate the operation. The Russian attacks abated, and later that evening the force was able to withdraw, depressed but in good order, back to the Fortress. The 233 prisoners and five captured machine-guns they brought with them were scant compensation for the Habsburg soldiers' dashed dreams of relief and freedom.[48]

If one spends weeks in an encircled fortress
Peering down into the dang'rous precipice,
One has opportunity to think a lot
And becomes an Opti- or a Pessimist.

Trench newspaper doggerel[49]

As CHRISTMASTIDE APPROACHED, pessimists were ascendant within the Fortress. Less than a fortnight before, rescue had seemed so tantalizingly close. Expectations had rocketed. The fall when the breakout failed and the field army fell back was consequently hard. The Honvéds had given their all in the operation. They had achieved more than the AOK had thought possible, drawing significant enemy strength away from Conrad's advancing forces. They had even broken the Russian ring around Przemyśl. Failure in spite of all their sacrifice and exertion underlined that the Fortress's fate lay out of its hands. A debilitating feeling of impotence seized the soldiers.[50]

The heavy human losses sustained in the operations since the start of the second siege also permanently impacted on the Fortress. Well over 6,000 men had been killed or wounded, and the damage inflicted, particularly on the 23rd Honvéd Infantry Division, blunted the garrison's offensive capabilities. Some regiments were now just 40 percent of their original size. With the Fortress's best troops so depleted, the end of the year would see the cessation of sorties and spoiling operations outside the defensive perimeter. Citizens and garrison would passively await their fate.[51]

Christmas Eve—the day that Central Europeans traditionally gather to celebrate the Nativity—was thus a miserable affair. To be sure, the men made a heroic effort to foster a semblance of festive cheer. Christmas trees were decorated and quartermasters dug deep to scrape together a decent meal for the troops, but men's thoughts at this time were with their families, who seemed further away than ever. Stanisław Gayczak recorded in his diary that "the day was difficult . . . very difficult, so difficult that even just getting through it was hard." As soon as he woke up, he started wondering what his wife and children were doing, and whether he would ever again see them. When he spoke to his assembled company to mark the holy day, he and they all wept. At the officers' dinner afterward, emotions continued to run high. Rare was the colleague who did not need to step out to compose himself: "Mostowski, Stumpf, the captain, all quietly cried," Gayczak wrote in his diary. For all the candles and carols, this was nothing like the festivities of peace. It was a day of tears.[52]

Poignantly, the one ray of humanity at this desolate time came from the Russian troops encamped in the frozen wastes around the Fortress. They, too, were suffering from cold and homesickness. Around the holy celebrations, garrison patrols stumbled across messages with moving tidings of peace and goodwill left for them in no-man's-land. "Gallant knights!" opened one of these missives from the enemy:

> At so great a holiday as Christmas Eve we wish you and your families the best and that you return healthy to your nearest and dearest. We shall not disturb you on Christmas Day as you eat your supper and talk of your loved ones. As a mark of our fraternal greetings we break this holy wafer with you.
>
> *Your comrades outside the Siedliska forts.*[53]

Accompanying the notes were sometimes small packages—gifts for the garrison. These contained what the desperate people in the Fortress now needed most and most gravely lacked: sausage, sugar, bread—the stuff of life.[54]

CHAPTER SIX

STARVATION

Q. What is the difference between Troy and Przemyśl?
A. In Troy, the heroes were in the stomach of the horse,
and in Przemyśl the horses are in the stomach of the heroes!

A Przemyśl joke[1]

I t was the slaughter of the horses that most forcefully impressed on the Fortress's people, both soldiers and civilians, just how much trouble they were in. Of the 21,000 horses inside the Fortress, 10,000 were butchered around Christmas and the New Year, and a further 3,500 followed in mid-January 1915. Worrying news from the Quartermaster's Section prompted the cull. A bright spark in the section had scrutinized the inventory lists, checked the ration strength, and calculated that at the current rate of consumption, all the food in the Fortress would be eaten by January 15. Slaughtering horses freed up significant amounts of fodder that could be diverted to human consumption. It also provided an entirely new food source for the garrison. Horse suddenly became the staple of soldiers' diets. Their bread was baked from flour milled in part from horse bones and dried horse flesh, and horse liver pâté was issued to spread on it.

Their sausages were of horse intestine filled with horse offal. And as the only fat available for frying was horse fat, even the small share of fortress rations that were not equine still tasted of horse. The Russians soon got wind of their opponents' new diet. From across no-man's-land, Austrian soldiers in the front line heard chortling, along with the mocking sound of men whinnying and neighing.[2]

THE NEW YEAR opened in the Fortress with food on everyone's minds. For the command, the big question, asked rather late in the day, was how to stretch Przemyśl's scant supplies out as long as possible. The AOK was planning a new relief offensive over the Carpathian Mountains, but when that would begin and whether it would be successful, God only knew. After the alarm was raised in mid-December by the Quartermaster's Section, the Fortress's commander, Kusmanek, had formed a commission to check all the provisions thoroughly. The commission reported back with marginally more optimism: with the slaughter of 14,000 horses and other economies, it calculated, Przemyśl's garrison and destitute civilian population might be fed until February 18. The staff's most pressing task now was to find imaginative ways to push back that date, for when the storehouses were bare, the Fortress must fall.[3]

The garrison felt the change immediately. Quite apart from the sudden ubiquity of horse in their diet, from January 8 soldiers' rations were repeatedly reduced. Standard fortress rations had allowed each man 700 grams (25 ounces) of bread, 300 grams (10.5 ounces) of beef, and 200 grams (7 ounces) of vegetables daily. By the end of February, they were down to 300 grams of bread (10.5 ounces) supplemented by 50 grams (under 2 ounces) of hardtack, a tin of horse pâté, and 70 grams (2.5 ounces) of vegetables. To add to the soldiers' troubles, the physical demands of garrison duty increased. The killing and canning of most of Przemyśl's equine population left a severe shortage of draft animals. Those horses spared the cull were too few to meet all the Fortress's needs, and were usually in even worse condition than the humans imprisoned within the Fortress. These scrawny survivors subsisted off thatch salvaged from house roofs, straw from hospital bedding, and a mash of oats and wood shavings. The shavings, cooked in a weak salt solution, had no nutritional value but damped down hunger and aided digestion by encouraging thorough chewing. In the absence of any alternative, the men themselves thus became beasts of burden. It was common in these months to see starving soldiers harnessed to supply wagons, straining on snow-covered roads.[4]

The city had little food to offer. The few better-off among the populace retrenched and ceased entertaining, motivated not only by uncertainty about how long the siege would last, but also by the appearance of roving military commissions that went from house to house confiscating "excessive" stores. Everybody else was hungry. The three months' worth of provisions that most households had accumulated in the summer were long gone by January, and replenishment was near impossible. As a safety net, the Fortress Command opened its magazines to civilians at the end of the month, permitting every person to purchase 5 kilograms (11 pounds) of horsemeat at peacetime prices. All other foodstuffs were extremely scarce, and prices rocketed to terrifying heights. By March, milk rose to twelve times its prewar price; eggs rose to nineteen times their former price; and potatoes and bread to fifteen times and nearly forty times their prewar prices, respectively.[5]

Often people simply refused to sell. In mid-February, the resident Helena Jabłońska captured an evocative scene in her diary. A hungry soldier approached a Jew carrying a loaf of bread and asked how much it had cost. The Jew replied "10 crowns." The soldier thereupon produced a 20-crown note and tried to press it into his palm, but the Jew refused; he had eight children to feed, he explained. In despair, the soldier tore up the banknote and scattered the pieces to the wind.[6]

The deprivation brought manifestations of total war to Przemyśl early; the same scenes would become all too common across blockaded

Central Europe in 1917 and 1918. Deaths multiplied. The 928 deaths registered in the city in 1915 represented, given the reduced population, more than a doubling of peacetime civilian mortality. Food shortages pitted neighbor against neighbor and, as elsewhere later in the conflict, fueled an ominous explosion of anti-Semitism. Some of Przemyśl's Jews most likely were well positioned to source supplies; the Jewish community had dominated city commerce and industry before the war. Now, as prices spiraled, Poles complained bitterly of "terrible exploitation by the Jews." Worryingly, even hitherto reasonable people succumbed to prejudice. "Up to now," confessed Dr. Jan Stock, the thoughtful academic turned army supply clerk, "I have defended myself from anti-Semitism; in time of war, however, I have seen so much Jewish villainy, that in the future I shall not be ashamed of hatred toward the Jews. And in this, everyone agrees: Germans, Czechs, Poles."[7]

The garrison and citizens took refuge in food fantasies. The fairy tale circulated that, if only Przemyśl could be rescued, there were 200 wagons loaded high with every imaginable delicacy waiting to gallop into the starving city. The delusion, jealousies, and anger are explicable in the face of the immense hardship. "Only one who has lived through a struggle for bread can understand its true worth," reflected Stanisław Szopa, who was ten years old at the time of the siege. Near the end of a long life, he would vividly recall the winding queues, filled with old people and children, that formed anywhere food went on sale. One might stand for hours, and in the end get nothing. People dropped in the snow from hunger and exhaustion. Sixty years later, he recalled the childish elation of arriving home with a warm loaf under his arm. He could also still feel the "great sadness" of returning empty-handed. Boys and girls of Stanisław's age and younger were among the most heartrending victims of this vicious and undiscriminating war. Teachers reported that "their appearance spoke volumes: haggard little faces, threadbare clothing."[8]

Of course, not everybody went hungry. Army officers, especially in the Honvéd elite, still did themselves proud. A lavish dinner was

"Are you still asking how to get rich in wartime?" inquires the anti-Semitic mock advertisement at the top of this page from an unofficial fortress trench newspaper, circa end of 1914 or early 1915, p. 4. "Trust in Simi Slojmi's bank. Free consultation for only 100 crowns." Fake classified ads were used widely as a humorous device in the trench newspapers of the First World War. They were often dark and always topical. This example reflects the spiraling Jew hatred in Przemyśl during the siege fueled by food shortages and accusations of profiteering. The other advertisements are (middle) an offer of "prepared wood chips" as a substitute for horse feed—a supplement to equine diets actually used in the Fortress—and (bottom) an ironic invitation to soldiers to learn the piano.

held on January 6 to help officers of Honvéd Infantry Regiment
8 reconcile with their comrades in the artillery, who had acciden-
tally shot up the regiment in the December operations. After a liver
starter, the diners gorged themselves on roasted piglet with side
dishes, plum compote, a cheese selection, apples, and coffee and tea.
Officer privilege was the norm in early twentieth-century armies,
but under siege, when set against the deprivation in the ranks and
among civilians, such banqueting was obscene. The failure of the officers to behave paternalistically, to put their men first, undermined
respect for them in the ranks, especially with repeated revelations of
abuse. "Morale is starting to drop precipitately," one officer of the
23rd Honvéd Infantry Division observed glumly in February. "Not a
day goes by without one or two reports that officers are perpetrating
fraud and theft."⁹

Kusmanek appeared weirdly oblivious to the endemic corruption,
although it posed an existential threat to the Fortress. He did nothing to combat the blatant and colossal theft in the Quartermaster's
Section, where it was frankly admitted that "all supply officers would
end up in front of a court-martial." A few token arrests were made,
but in the face of its own failings the military administration was
mostly inert. With this example set by the leadership, corruption
quickly spread down the hierarchy. By the start of March, complaints about the troops not receiving their meager entitlement of
rations were increasing. NCOs and cooks were blamed for abusing
their positions and misappropriating food. Corporal Eduard Freunthaler, assigned to the stores of the Lower Austrian Landsturm
Infantry Regiment 21, could personally attest to the truth of these
grievances. At the end of the siege, this conscientious German was
passing lodgings belonging to the staff sergeant of a neighboring
Hungarian Landsturm regiment when there was a friendly tap on
the window and he was invited in:

I followed the call and inside found several NCOs sitting around a
table groaning with smoked ham, bread dumplings, and sauerkraut,

tucking in enthusiastically. While the rest of the Fortress starved, and ate only horse pâté without bread and flour, the Hungarians still had smoked ham, bread dumplings: things of which we could only dream. But that was how the Hungarians were. Their soldiers were half-starved, but their noncommissioned officers wallowed in abundance because they shamelessly stole from the men.

"Nonetheless," Freunthaler added—conceding that egoism, self-preservation, and dishonesty were not, after all, purely Magyar qualities—"at the sight of the feast I suppressed my moral outrage and quickly dug in, eating till I felt I would burst."[10]

Food shortages, inequality, and gross corruption shattered any solidarity within the Fortress. The command could not contemplate reducing officer rations and would not intervene effectively to halt abuses. Instead, it extended the Fortress's lifespan by requisitioning ever more ruthlessly from the villages around Przemyśl. Civilians were confronted by predatory parties of soldiers and gendarmes perpetrating acts that, had they not been sanctioned by high authority, could be described only as theft. The victims wept, pleaded, and employed all manner of trickery—from faking robberies to distracting the soldiers with a pretty, scantily clad young woman—to save their animals and property. As for the troops manning the defensive periphery, they saw little of these spoils. When resting in the rear, they were reduced to robbery or begging from house to house. In the line, they spent the long, black nights excavating frozen potatoes and turnips from the icy wastes of no-man's-land. Kusmanek forbade the dangerous practice, but by this point, as one man explained, "that was in the order, but no one cared about orders or about frost or about enemy bullets. The only thing that mattered was to eat."[11]

EVEN AS THE Fortress starved, its continued resistance behind Russian lines exerted a powerful and deeply malign influence on Habsburg military strategy. Back in November, when the field army had retreated from the San, General Conrad von Hötzendorf had made the comprehensible but cowardly decision to hold Przemyśl. So great was the prestige of Kusmanek's "heroes" after their October victory that abandonment of the city-fortress would inevitably have incited public and political scandal. Yet, of course, the problem posed by Przemyśl only became more acute once it lay beleaguered and surrounded. Capitulation was utterly unthinkable, for this would now mean the catastrophic loss of the 130,000-strong garrison. Consequently, Conrad had cornered himself into undertaking relief offensives under the most unfavorable of conditions. The operation he envisaged for late January was an attack from the south and southwest over the Carpathian Mountains.[12]

The Carpathian Mountains marked Galicia's boundary with Habsburg Hungary. At around 100 kilometers (60 miles) in breadth and with some peaks reaching heights of over 2,000 meters (6,500 feet), the range posed a very formidable obstacle. There had been fighting here already in late September, when the Russians briefly captured the important Uzsok Pass. The Habsburg army's retreat from the San at the beginning of November had brought the opponents back to the region. At the end of the month, Tsarist forces had seized the western Carpathians' other two major passes, at Łupków and Dukla, from General Boroević's Third Army, threatening an invasion of Hungary. Battle had seesawed through to the end of 1914. After Conrad's victory farther west at Limanowa at the start of December, Habsburg troops had surged out of the range, making the relief of Przemyśl appear possible. In spite of the Fortress's midmonth Honvéd breakout operations in its support, the field army had been halted by tough Russian opposition. A Tsarist offensive launched on December 21 pushed Boroević's troops deep into the range, and by the year's end the Uzsok Pass was again in the invaders' hands.[13]

Both sides believed much to be at stake in the Carpathians. The Habsburg Empire was at this time under intense diplomatic pressure. Italy, the distrusted erstwhile ally that had declared neutrality in

August, was now threatening to join the Habsburgs' enemies unless the empire ceded neighboring Trentino, South Tyrol, and extensive territories around the Adriatic coast. Conrad urgently needed a great success to make Austria-Hungary look strong and, above all, to rescue Przemyśl. The loss of so potent a symbol of Habsburg resistance would inevitably spur Italian interventionists, raising the likelihood of a new war on the southern border. The attack over the mountains was the most direct route to the Fortress. On the other side, General Nikolai Ivanov, the commander of the Russian southwestern front in charge of operations in Galicia, was adamant that the key to final victory lay hidden in the Carpathian snow. Defeating the Habsburg army here, Ivanov thought, would open the way for an invasion of Hungary. He fantasized about separate peace with the Magyars and hoped at least that Romania, which coveted Hungarian Transylvania, would then join the war against the Habsburgs.[14]

On January 23, 1915, Conrad's Carpathian relief offensive opened. A 175,000-strong Habsburg assault force attacked on a 160-kilometer (100-mile) front. Few armies in history have been ordered to fight in such a hostile environment. At altitudes of 800 meters (2,600 feet), in temperatures far below freezing, the troops scaled heights and waded through deep snow and blizzards to recapture the mountain passes. Conrad, who by this time was ensconced with the AOK in the comfort of the provincial Silesian town of Teschen 300 kilometers (around 190 miles) away, had reached a new low in sending men forward in such conditions. He wrote to his lover, Gina, complacently telling her that although service in the Carpathians was "certainly indescribably hard" on the troops, it was "a thousand times" preferable to his own "nerve-wracking mental work" at army headquarters.[15]

The general had no idea. It was sheer madness to attempt to throw troops over a mountain range in midwinter. Hasty and incomplete preparations only added to the operation's folly. The Carpathian front lacked the rail links necessary to serve a major offensive, and bringing supplies and artillery up from railheads along steep, icy mountain paths was always difficult and frequently impossible. Astoundingly, the Third Army, which was responsible for the primary attack, at first advanced and even briefly recaptured the Uzsok Pass. On the 26th, however, the Russians counterattacked. They sent Habsburg troops reeling, and in early February they smashed the offensive by capturing its main rail base at Mezőlaborcz. The Third Army lost two-thirds of its men in those two nightmarish weeks. At least half the casualties were through sickness or frostbite. Troops told of fighting for days without warm food or shelter. The only protection from the elements was to burrow into the snow. Weapons had to be thawed over a fire before they could be used. Men froze to death in their sleep. "Religious souls visualize hell as a blazing inferno with burning embers and intense heat," commented one veteran grimly. "The soldiers fighting in the Carpathian Mountains during that first winter of the war know otherwise."[16]

Undaunted and out of other ideas, Conrad renewed the offensive on February 27. Hoping that a change of leadership might help, he put the Second Army commander, General Eduard von Böhm-Ermolli, in charge and sent in more troops. The extreme climate continued to hamper operations. From February 8 there was a thaw, and flooding and mud made the mountain ways impassable. Then the temperature dropped again, and the troops found themselves freezing in -20°C (-4°F). Predictably, Böhm-Ermolli did no better than the Third Army's commander, Boroević. His army barely moved. The only success of the period was won in lower land 300 kilometers (around 190 miles) to the east, when on February 17 Czernowitz, capital of the Habsburg province of Bukovina, was liberated. This brought the operation no closer to achieving its primary objective, the relief of Przemyśl. A third, despairing offensive was vainly launched in March, just days before the Fortress's food supply was scheduled to expire. These reckless efforts to reach Przemyśl and save Conrad's dignity shattered the Habsburg field army. The sacrifice was extraordinary: total casualties amounted to 670,000 men.[17]

WHILE THE FIELD army flailed in the icy Carpathians, still 100 kilometers (60 miles) away, to the north Przemyśl's fortress commander waged the final attritional contest. Kusmanek ended all harassing operations beyond the defensive periphery. What strength remained to the Fortress must be preserved. Unclear to him, however, was the end objective: Should the garrison's aim be simply to survive as long as possible, or should it maintain an offensive capability in order to assist any renewed approach from the field army? The nub of the question revolved, as everything now in Przemyśl, around horses. The AOK was told that a further cull of 3,500 after the middle of January might help prolong resistance, but that with just 4,300 remaining afterward, the Fortress's operational capabilities would be seriously reduced. Conrad, however, never a man to permit reality to interfere with his plans, insisted on having his horse and eating it too. Kusmanek was commanded to build an offensive force and also told, in mid-February, to slaughter all but the last 4,300 horses.[18]

Treachery and tension defined the war around Przemyśl in these months. Through the dark arts of espionage, the Russians skillfully sought advantage. The commander of the southwestern front, General Ivanov, boasted after the siege to have been intimately aware of the Fortress's every move. His most valuable source of information was probably transmissions to and from the fortress radio station. The capabilities of Tsarist radio engineers and decoders was underestimated by Przemyśl's own technicians. Whether spies operated in the city and garrison remains a mystery. However, in mid-January, a known Tsarist agent, a woman named Bilińska, was captured in uniform with four Russian soldiers just north of the Fortress. Her mission may have been to infiltrate. Undeniably, the Russians did gain forewarning of some fortress operations. A sortie of December 27–28 was, testified peasants living in no-man's-land, already expected by Russian patrols passing through a day earlier.[19]

For both sides, the population trapped in no-man's-land between the Fortress's defensive perimeter and the blockading army's encircling trenches also offered copious intelligence. The biggest community was in Wapowce, a ruined village northwest of Przemyśl, where 1,660 people, mostly women and children, lived in starving purgatory. The Fortress Command carefully cultivated relations with these civilians, organizing charity and detailing Polish and Ruthenian noncommissioned officers to stay in contact. To survive, the desperate people in their turn exploited the belligerents' hunger for information. Peasants shuttled back and forth between the lines, offering nuggets of news from Przemyśl or stories of the siege army's activities in exchange for a crust of bread or some rice. Often, their tales were inventions that brought further suffering to the garrison: claims of imminent attack or the relief of an opposing unit invariably led to a night awake on high alert or a dangerous reconnaissance patrol.[20]

The exploitation of starving civilians for intelligence was only one of the lesser manifestations of the blurring of noncombatant-combatant boundaries in the war around the Fortress. Kusmanek escalated the struggle further by organizing illegal "bands": partisan-style groups of four or five volunteers, not always uniformed, with the mission to slip over enemy lines and wreak havoc. Railways were to be destroyed, depots blown up. In practice, the local Polish and Ruthenian soldiers who volunteered for the bands proved disappointing. Most never returned to the Fortress, and those who did told tall tales but inflicted negligible damage on the enemy. One officer suspected that they did nothing but slip into civvies and sell potatoes to the enemy. Even so, their presence unnerved the Russians. One band member was found hanged as a warning at the Niżankowice railway crossing south of the Fortress.[21]

Tension between besiegers and besieged climaxed at the end of January, when an emissary arrived at the Fortress's defenses bearing a letter from the commander of the Russian 81st Reserve Division. Addressed personally to Kusmanek, the letter accused fortress troops of firing internationally banned dumdum ammunition: bullets with a hollow or soft nose designed to expand or shatter on impact, inflicting horrendous wounds. Any Habsburg soldier captured with such ammunition would, on the orders of Grand Duke Nikolai Nikolaevich, supreme commander of the Russian army, immediately be executed. Kusmanek's reply was defiant. The AOK had authorized him to threaten that for every Habsburg soldier executed, two Russian prisoners would be shot (at this time, 8 Russian officers and 1,057 men languished within the Fortress). He also presented a catalog of counter-complaints: the Russians used dumdums, maltreated prisoners, and, he claimed, dressed in Habsburg uniforms to patrol no-man's-land. Even so, the Russian accusations were clearly justified, for a circular was hastily sent to all garrison units ordering the return to magazines of so-called expanding practice rounds, which, although illegal, were in limited use at the front.[22]

Possibly it was hunger-induced delusion, or perhaps it was the underhanded means of war practiced by both sides, but whatever the reason, around this time the paranoia already displayed by the Habsburg military at the war's opening surged to hysterical levels. The specter of treachery gripped the Fortress. At headquarters, Kusmanek was rumored to be decoding all the secret telegrams personally, for fear of a spy high up in the command. His staff wasted time investigating irrational ideas, such as the theory that enemy agents in Przemyśl were floating top-secret documents out in bottles. Similar outlandish stories circulated in the city and forts. Traitors and spies appeared to be ubiquitous: "The Russians," people asserted authoritatively, "know everything sooner than the subsector commanders." It was rumored that Przemyśl swarmed with Tsarist officers in disguise, with telephone connections to their own lines. Enemy troops were said to dress as women when on patrol. "Russophile" garrison soldiers were accused of betraying secret military passwords by tracing them in the snow.[23]

This lunacy had consequences. From the first days of January, the Fortress was seized by a bout of collective obsessive-compulsive disorder. The trigger was a fearful fantasy that Tsarist troops were donning Habsburg uniforms to patrol no-man's-land. To quell their surging anxiety, Kusmanek and his staff devised a new recognition system so intricate—and silly—that no enemy could hope to imitate it. It would have been funny, had it not put lives at risk.[24]

Under this new system, fortress troops stalking stealthily through no-man's-land were to halt on encountering an apparently friendly patrol and perform a three-part ritual to confirm its authenticity. First came the challenge: a top-secret acoustic signal. This was usually two or three blasts of varying length on a pipe. The attention of the patrol (and also presumably of any enemy lurking nearby) attracted, everybody would take cover.[25]

The ritual's second part, the answer, could then begin. One extremely unfortunate, and probably very scared, patrol member would stand up in no-man's-land and make a secret movement. The orders for one day instructed him to "swing [his] cap over his head in circles." On another, he would raise his rifle and wave it right and left. On yet another, the correct response was to balance a cap onto a rifle or saber and raise it high in the air. The order dictating this last move, for January 28, 1915, emphasized that the pose should be held for a full three march beats; perhaps to mitigate any risk that the anxious soldier might be over-hasty.

After the flawless performance of the answer came the final part of the ritual, confirmation. A soldier from the group that had initiated the challenge would stand up, revealing his patrol's position, too, and carry out a different but no less odd gyration. Holding a cap to the right and flapping it up and down three times, punching to either side three times with both arms, or raising a rifle once to the right and once to the left were just three of the moves troops were ordered to perform. The combinations were endless. Then, if nobody had been shot, both groups of soldiers could go on their way.

To be fair, the new recognition system was unquestionably an effective deterrent for anybody—Russian or otherwise—contemplating putting on a Habsburg uniform. However, as fortress troops trying to use the system quickly discovered, it suffered two fairly fundamental problems. First, it was really difficult to remember the complicated sequences of actions, let alone carry them out quickly under stress in no-man's-land. Unit commanders complained that no sooner had their men finally mastered one combination than the instructions changed and they were back to square one. This mattered terribly, for there were standing orders to open fire immediately on any patrol that erred in executing the movements.[26]

Though frontline officers were too polite to point it out, the other glaring problem with the new system was that standing in the middle of no-man's-land in broad daylight whistling and wildly gesticulating made troops sitting ducks. Quite what Russian sentries thought at the surreal sight of their enemy pirouetting in the open is sadly not recorded, but if they could overcome their astonishment there were easy kills to be had. Though the paranoid Fortress Command persisted in inventing ever more complicated moves, the troops eventually gave it up. They preferred, as one combat officer remembered, sensibly "to trust in . . . good luck."[27]

The New Year at least began quietly on the Fortress's defensive periphery. An exhausted stillness hung over the opposing lines. The garrison was spent after its breakout operations in December, and the Russians were, for now, content to wait for the defenders to starve. In some sectors, live-and-let-live truces prevailed. Occasionally in the festive period, troops from both sides could be seen together in no-man's-land peaceably digging up potatoes. Even so, the strength of the Fortress was fast fading. The weather was cold, in the second half of January hovering mostly below freezing. For troops still in ragged summer uniforms, service in the snow and water-logged interval trenches was hard, especially on reduced rations. Officers immediately noticed the effects. Weary companies returned from forward positions "like a procession of ghosts," as the adjutant of III/Landsturm Infantry Regiment 18 put it. "The soldiers creep forward, pale, like shadows, buckled like old men. . . . Words and speeches always meet with the same tired, hopeless silence."[28]

In February, the blockade army began to exert renewed pressure on the ailing Fortress. On the 9th, first the southern front, and then also the northwestern and northern fronts, came under heavy artillery bombardment. A week later, the Tsarist infantry moved forward, tightening the ring around Przemyśl. First to fall were the advance posts in the west and northwest. On February 18, Russian ambitions swelled, and a regiment was launched at the key southwestern Pod Mazurami position. The combat there was fierce. Assault troops swept forward and broke in, but the Honvéd stood firm and then beat them back. "In the strongpoints," wrote one Hungarian officer, "troops lay in piles, all had perished in bayonet fighting." In the end, 148 Russians held up their hands and surrendered.[29]

Lieutenant-General Tamásy, the Fortress's deputy commander, was willing to bet a thousand crowns on relief reaching Przemyśl by March 7, when the food was scheduled to run out, but few now shared his optimism. The small victory at Pod Mazurami at best only deferred the end. The Russians knew this too. Confidence was high in the blockade army. A letter smuggled into the Fortress from one of the garrison soldier's wives, who was living nearby under occupation, vividly captured the enemy's mood. "The Russians say they will lead our Emperor away from Vienna on a leash. They say, you must perish in Przemyśl . . . and that you in Przemyśl will give yourselves up."[30]

Wasyl Okolita[31] had had enough. In this regard, the company bugler was not alone. His unit, I/Landsturm Infantry Regiment 35, had suffered a trickle of desertions ever since the start of the second siege. The battalion had been raised from around the border town of Brody, on the northeastern edge of Galicia, and its officers tended reflexively to blame any indiscipline on Russophilia. This was a region where, one wrote gravely, "so far as patriotism and love of the Fatherland is concerned, there is much left to be desired." However, by January 1915, men had more pressing reasons than simple indifference to Emperor Franz Joseph in far off Vienna to feel disgruntled. There was the cold, the hunger, the homesickness, and the sheer hopelessness of the struggle. The 35th Regiment had fought in the breakout attempt of mid-December, the failure of which had depressed the morale of the entire garrison. One need not be a Russophile to decide, as Okolita now did, that it was time to get out.[32]

Leaving the Fortress would not be easy. Okolita and his comrades were manning trenches in the northeastern Defense Sector V. Belts of barbed wire in front of the position served to keep the garrison in, as well as the enemy out. Officers circulated the defenses during the day and checked on the men at least four times each night. A junior noncommissioned officer was responsible for each platoon's stretch of trench, and the soldiers were accommodated together in dugouts built into the line. Just leaving shelter could provoke a challenge, and any individual attempting to scramble over the trench parapet would be sure to attract the attention of tensed sentries, even before he came up against the wire. The only way forward out of the front line was through a channel that ran at ninety degrees, which was used by patrols to enter and exit no-man's-land. This channel cut right through the entanglements, but it was heavily guarded. A double gate with two sentries controlled access from the main line, and at the channel's mouth beyond the wire two soldiers manned a listening post. This was the dangerous route down which Okolita and five other want-to-be deserters would have to pass.

For the Greek Catholics in the regiment, January 6 was Christmas Eve, the day in the year on which men most missed their families. It was also a day on which the Orthodox Russians opposite the Fortress, who followed the same festive calendar, could be relied upon to be kind. The deserters planned their escape for the early morning. Okolita left his post (probably in the company HQ dugout) to join his co-conspirators in the frontline trench late on the prior evening. His excuse was flimsy—he claimed to be bringing up a pot of boiled potatoes for an NCO—but he was known as a steady man and popular with his platoon, and so his absence caused no concern. Okolita judged the deserters' best chance to be to pose as a legitimate patrol, so that they could use the channel into no-man's-land. He and his small band waited patiently through the dead of night in an adjacent shelter. At 3:45 a.m., at the noise of soldiers returning from operations in front of the wire, they sprang into action. There was not much time.

Mimicking the stentorian voice favored by NCOs, Okolita called his comrades out: "Zbyrajte sia i chodim na patrol" (Form up and march on patrol). The men quickly arrayed, kitted out to look the part with rifles, cartridge pouches, and rucksacks. Then, on a second crisp command from Okolita, "Nu ta chodim," they headed for the gate. The deserters had chosen their moment well. The sentries at the gate—two illiterate farmers—were expecting a new patrol to take the place of the one that had just returned. Moreover, they were coming to the end of a very long shift. The weather had been un-usually mild that day, and to avoid being repeatedly roused, the pla-toon had asked to do two-hour, rather than the normal one-hour, sentry stints. With five minutes to go, the sentries were tired and disinclined to question. Anyway, they had orders not to interfere with patrols leaving the line. Had they looked closer, however, they would have seen that this "patrol" had some suspicious characteris-tics. Why was the leader a lowly bugler? And where was the duty NCO, who usually accompanied patrols to the gate?[33]

For Okolita and his band, the sense of relief must have been im-mense when they were able to pass through the gate unchallenged. The wire entanglements were behind them; the only obstacle left was the listening post at the end of the channel. Here, again, the men had luck. The soldiers on duty were from another platoon, and so they did not recognize them. One did not even see them. Clouds had covered the moon, and the old dark-blue uniforms of the Landsturm merged into the inky blackness. The other sentry did halt the huddled line. Over a strong westerly wind, he demanded the day's password. Okolita gave it correctly and the men were al-lowed to go on. The small band headed toward the Russian lines, into the gloom.

THE ESCAPE OF Wasyl Okolita and his comrades marked the beginning of a flood of desertions from the Fortress. How many men left, or tried to leave, is no longer known, but from early January reports of absconding multiplied. East Galician units were badly affected. A week after Okolita's departure, his 35th Landsturm lost another ten soldiers from a forward post. Landsturm Infantry Regiment 33 and Landwehr Infantry Regiment 19, two other units with many Ruthenes, also reported a spate of desertions. Yet disturbingly for Kusmanek, such gross disobedience could no longer be dismissed as just Ruthenian Russophilia, for troops of other nationalities began going over to the enemy too. In the elite Honvéd Infantry Regiment 8, a unit with many Romanians, thirty soldiers deserted en masse to the Russians at the end of January. That same month in the 16/II Honvéd March Battalion, five ethnic Hungarians fled for enemy lines. Soldiers from every part of the empire were conspiring to defy their superiors and make their getaway. Any forward position without an officer now appeared vulnerable to desertion.[34]

The Russians did their best to hasten the disintegration. Propaganda leaflets were dropped in no-man's-land for Habsburg patrols to find. Although psychological warfare was in its infancy, these were skillfully framed. One siren call to the whole multiethnic garrison centered on material conditions. A "well-intentioned appeal" purporting to be from a Habsburg prisoner extolled the comforts of captivity. Incarceration in Russia, the leaflet emphasized, could not really be called "imprisonment." "As soon as we arrive," asserted the "prisoner," "we walk free and whosoever wishes can get employment and receives full board and a ruble a day." Guaranteed to capture the starving garrison's attention were mouth-watering descriptions of prisoners' meals: tea with sugar for breakfast; a meaty soup, vegetables, and a half-liter of wine for lunch; and then more meat and 500 grams (a little over a pound) of delicious bread every day for dinner. It all sounded very tempting.[35]

The Russian propagandists' second theme was hope. This worked better for some Habsburg nationalities than others. Grand Duke

Nikolai Nikolaevich's September 1914 message to the "Peoples of Austria-Hungary," which had cast Russia as a land that "bled heavily for the freedom of other peoples," set the tone. "Slavs of the Austro-Hungarian army" were called upon to throw away their weapons and be received as "brothers." Serbs and Romanians in the garrison, who shared a faith with their opponents, were promised that "the war is being prosecuted for the liberation of the Orthodox peoples from Austrian and Hungarian rule." To Poles, the propagandists framed their message as an appeal from co-nationals in the Tsarist Empire, tried unconvincingly to drum up some Pan-Slavic solidarity, and repeated the supreme army commander's empty promises for a unified Poland.[36]

What the Russians really excelled at, though, was the propaganda of despair. Fake news was a part of their armory already in 1915. Cracow was, like Przemyśl, said to be encircled. Russian troops were flooding over the Carpathians and marching on Budapest. The German and Habsburg armies had been defeated. For garrison troops who had only the barely more trustworthy fortress newssheets for information, these lies were deeply unsettling. The Russians manufactured a sense of urgency to act and played on soldiers' anxieties about survival. "Brothers, all is lost," warned one leaflet. "The Russian heavy guns are already roaring and I hear that in a few days a storm will be launched against the Fortress. You have no other salvation than at an opportune moment to go over to the Russian side." "Now is the time," admonished another. "Later it will be hard, for soon the forts will be bombarded and nobody will escape alive."[37]

The cleverest propaganda of despair was directed toward the men of Galicia. The approach in this case was to delegitimize the Habsburg regime without resorting to lies, as they were unnecessary. Leaflets for these soldiers cast Franz Joseph's state and army as incompetent and brutal. Through this Habsburg-initiated war, Galicia had been devastated, they claimed, and there was truth to the charge. "Remember," demanded one leaflet emotively, "you are no longer defending the land but just bare walls. You are the enemies of your own land and your families!" To Ruthenes, the propagandists adopted a tone of sympathy and righteous anger in order to foster resentment and undermine discipline. "Your villages have been burned by Austrian troops, your families abandoned to frost and starvation," asserted one propaganda flyer, entirely truthfully. "They would have starved if we had not given them a warm roof and bread. . . . The sooner the forts fall, the better we can rescue your unhappy compatriots from freezing—from death! It depends on you!"

The Fortress Command fought back in this information war. The *Kriegsnachrichten* and *Tábori Újság* newssheets were its prime weapons. Officers were ordered to keep men's hopes of relief alive. Through their unit translators, they passed on the newssheets' bulletins about the progress of the field army. Inspirational articles with titles like "The Impregnability of Przemyśl" were read aloud. The Fortress's daily orders countered Russian propaganda about the joys of captivity by publishing accounts of soldiers who had escaped from enemy hands, emphasizing that prisoners of war were badly underfed and maltreated. Cynically, the fiction was spread that the blockade army was no less hungry than the men in the Fortress, and just as cold and miserable. Officers disingenuously claimed that it was actually the fortress garrison that was pinning the Russians. "Make sure the Russians don't escape, because they have nothing left to eat," commanders dishonestly admonished their troops. For good measure, the smear was circulated that the enemy used prisoners, especially deserters, as human shields in the front line.[38]

The Fortress Command also searched for ideological reinforcement to steady its troops, especially to hold the Ruthenes, whom it greatly distrusted. In reaction to Okolita's desertion, Kusmanek appealed to the Greek Catholic bishop of Przemyśl, Father Konstantyn Czechowicz. The bishop was a staunch Habsburg loyalist and eager to help. Since taking charge of the Przemyśl diocese in 1897, he had stood in the front line of the Eastern European culture wars, fending off aggressive proselytizing by the rival Russian Orthodox Church. The stakes had risen exponentially in 1914. Czechowicz was painfully conscious of Tsarist persecution of his church, and of the arrest of its Metropolitan, Archbishop Andrei Sheptits'kyi, in Lwów in September. As he assured Kusmanek, "the safety of the Fortress, the defeat of the enemy is for me a vital issue. . . . I know . . . that the Russians would respect neither my Catholic faith nor my nationality, nor, what concerns me personally, my position."[39]

Unfortunately, the command's request for support was distinctly tardy. The rampant repression Kusmanek had ordered at the outset of the war had alienated ordinary Ruthenes and gravely weakened the same church which he now hoped would provide them with a reason to fight. Before the war, Przemyśl and its environs had been tended by fifty-five Greek Catholic priests. By the start of 1915, arrests, evacuation, and internment had left only seven to assist Bishop Czechowicz. With food running short too, spiritual nourishment was unlikely to be sufficient; the bishop really needed to repeat the miracle of the Feeding of the Five Thousand. Even so, the sixty-seven-year-old Czechowicz went about his morale-raising work with vigor. After insisting to Kusmanek that most of the garrison's 35,000 Greek Catholic Ruthenian soldiers discharged "their duty . . . with the fullest devotion," he prepared a program of sermons for eastern Galician regiments to strengthen their resolve. In his preaching, Czechowicz emphasized the sacredness of the oath the troops had sworn to their monarch and stressed the oppressive nature of Russia. The empire to the east, he warned, was "the prison of unfree nations." The Tsars "never kept promises to subordinated peoples."[40]

As will waned and convincing reasons to continue to resist became harder to find, the Fortress fell back on coercion to keep men in line. The Habsburg army had reformed its justice system shortly before the war, but it was still one of the forces most likely to carry out the death penalty. No fewer than 754 Habsburg soldiers would be executed for military crimes between 1914 and 1918. Within the Fortress, the power to levy the ultimate penalty was intimidating, and it was exploited to the fullest as a deterrent against desertion.

Every sentence of execution was read out to the garrison on three consecutive days to ensure that all the soldiers heard it. It was even more blood-curdling to be present at the solemn ritual of a firing squad. Lieutenant Stanisław Gayczak, shaken and upset by the experience, left an account:

Today I was witness to an execution. Captain Gibiš was the commander; our battalion provided the soldiers. The feeling was horrid—but there was nothing to be done about it. At 3 o'clock a young boy of 23 years—name Józef Medecki—was led out from the cell to the detention room, after which he walked slowly from the garrison court over the wooden bridge to Winna Góra. The condemned man had [his] hands cuffed behind him, he was pale, but he walked the whole time alone, quietly, only from time to time throwing a vacant glance around. . . . The journey, which lasted almost half an hour, was awful for us. What was this poor individual thinking to himself? And why did he walk calmly to death? Why did he not weep, not cry out, not thrash about? It is a puzzle to me! . . .

We came to the first curve in the river, and here the judge indicated the place, a small depression in the hillside. The captain commanded "Battalion, form the execution square," [and] a square was formed in the middle of which stood the felon, surrounded by eighteen soldiers. The judge read out the sentence (convicted of desertion), after which the priest offered the felon a cross to kiss. The poor little soldier planted his lips on Jesus the Lord and then kissed the priest on the hand. One of the soldiers tied a dirty cloth over his eyes. At the same time, the rear of the square parted, the captain stood at the side and lifted his saber into the air, [and] from the front and side stepped out four soldiers in absolute silence. Two aimed [their] rifles at the [condemned man's] head, while two [aimed at his] chest. Somebody ordered the [condemned] soldier to kneel, he crouched on one knee, and at this rang out the command "fire." The executed man did not even twitch. He was knocked over on his face, very disfigured, because [his] head was nearly shattered. . . . The doctor noted the death, after which the priest spoke briefly to the assembled men. The captain commanded, "To prayer," a prayer was said, and then, "Company, form up!"

There was a coda to Gayczak's experience that made the episode even more awful. It could be harder to kill a man than one might think:

Suddenly Lieutenant Tyro approached and said that "the dead man" was [still] alive. That had a terrible effect on us. The idiot doctor had not checked properly and had issued his confirmation of death too soon. Then one of the soldiers was summoned from the ranks and the captain ordered him to fire a shot into the head again, from right up close. When that had happened, the corpse was put into a coffin and taken away to the cemetery.[41]

In his appeal to Bishop Czechowicz, Kusmanek had talked of introducing further "strict military measures" if desertion continued to threaten the security of the Fortress. In February, he acted. To amplify the deterrent effect of the death penalty, soldiers were warned that deserters' home communities would be telegrammed so that their "cowardice" could be made publicly known. Not only they, but also their relatives, would be made to suffer. All state support would be withdrawn from their parents and wives. To prevent further disobedience, officers were urged to keep a close eye on their men's mood, to be alert for conspiracies to desert, and to report any special agitation among their soldiers to the Fortress Command.[42]

By this stage, however, officers, too, were disheartened. To desert was unthinkable. Instead, as a confidential order from the Fortress Command complained, those unable to face the grim reality of life shut into the Fortress sought refuge in the rear. Hospitals became hotbeds of officer shirking. A favorite method to gain admittance was to catch a venereal disease, which was no great challenge in the blockaded city. One doctor recorded with fury at the siege's end that among his fifty-eight officer patients, only one was wounded. Half were being treated for gonorrhea.[43]

On the Fortress's front lines, even the officers still struggling on with their duty did all they could to keep their heads, quite literally, below the parapet. Lieutenant Jan Vit told a revealing tale of the trouble his battalion, the III/Landsturm Infantry Regiment 18, had in finding an officer to lead an elite patrol group filled with the unit's best soldiers. Nobody wanted to be the hero. By Vit's account, the officers embraced their national stereotypes as they attempted to wriggle out of the responsibility. A fellow Czech given the task insisted to anyone who would listen that he was far too incompetent. When his protests were ignored, he fell into a depression. His colleague, a Jewish second lieutenant, was more cunning. When he realized there was no possibility of talking his way out, he patrolled so badly, taking such care to avoid the Russians, that he was fired. His replacement, a sullen Pole, had seen the misery and destruction inflicted by the Habsburg army in Galicia and, as Vit explained with heavy sarcasm, also "did not burn with hatred for the enemy." Eventually, despairing of his useless officers, the battalion commander admitted defeat. Leadership of the patrol group was placed in the hands of two staff sergeants.[44]

As MARCH BROKE, the Fortress still loomed dark and defiant over a desolate white landscape. Somehow, the command had contrived to prolong its resistance. Through drastic cuts in rations, the slaughter of more horses, and the dilution of flour with turnip, bran, or 20 percent birch wood, the food had been stretched well beyond the initial estimated end date of February 18. Systematic searches of the fortress area, ruthless confiscations from the city, and the discovery of thousands of kilograms of sugar beets buried in frozen land just south of the defensive perimeter had helped, step by step, to extend stocks. March 7, and then March 23, seemed to be the last possible day to feed everyone, but then one more day was won through the collection of animal bones and the grinding of those bones into the garrison's flour. Finally, the definitive date on which rations would end was March 24, 1915.[45]

Though its hard carapace remained intact, over the Fortress hung the unmistakable stench of decay. By March 1, 15,469 men—one in every eight soldiers in the garrison—were hospitalized. The deluge had begun in early February, when a temporary thaw set in and the perimeter trenches filled with mud and water. The undernourished men collapsed in droves. Horrified doctors saw severe exhaustion. As one doctor later opined, such conditions could "scarcely have been observed in the same qualitative or quantitative magnitude anywhere else in this war." Some patients' whole bodies were swollen with hunger. Kidney disease was common. So, too, were rheumatism and lung inflammations. What shocked medics most was the utter apathy of the sick men. To Dr. Josef Tomann, they appeared to be turning to corpses before his very eyes: "They silently and without complaint accept a cold place in the hospital, drink the slop which passes here for tea; the next day, they are moved to the morgue."[46]

Through March the sickness swelled. By the middle of the month, 24,000 soldiers lay incapacitated. Just 2,500 were wounded. The vast majority of the hospitalized men were suffering from starvation and exposure. The immense psychological strain of the siege also claimed its victims. The Fortress's psychiatric unit registered a surge of exhaustion-related mental disease in March. The case notes of "Infantryman P.V.," who was admitted to the hospital dangerously undernourished and delusional, reveal movingly how physical weakness could combine with deep longing for families to break men:

Infantryman P.V., thirty-one years old, has, according to the statements of the men who accompanied him in, since midday on March 14 not been himself, constantly calling for his wife and children, whom he says he saw here today. On admission (morning of March 15), the patient gave [his] name, age, place of birth, [and] regiment correctly. He can focus well, [and] makes outwardly a calm and reasonable impression. He believes he is in his home town's school, [and] cannot understand why he has been brought here. [He told the doctors:] "I was lying in the dugout, had rifle and cartridges, I was lucky. My daughter entered the dugout. She's two years old, little Stephanie. She brought me flowers and said that her mother would soon come, bring me something to eat, bread and bacon, and take me home. Then the Russians started shooting terribly and little Stephanie disappeared."[47]

The Fortress Command attempted to reduce the strain on the troops in the defensive perimeter. Artillerymen and labor battalions were retrained as infantry in order to spread the burden of frontline service and permit more regular relief. Yet the exodus of the exhausted men meant that company strengths were very low. Frontline units fielded, at best, two-thirds of their complement, and those soldiers still in service were extremely weak. The fortress garrison had become a zombie army. Major Ferdinand Reder von Schellmann, the artillery commander of the southern sector of Przemyśl's inner defensive core, the *Noyau*, described ranks of walking dead. "The men are looking very bad," he wrote in consternation. "They have deeply sunken cheeks, bulging eyes, ears transparent like paper. They drag themselves laboriously forward. One sees their feebleness."[48]

Determined to seize advantage from the garrison's distress, on the night of March 12–13 the Russians again went forward. This time, their attack was against the north of the Fortress, on the Na Górach–Batycze positions 3 kilometers (2 miles) in front of the main perimeter defenses. Here, after a December operation had taken the position's forward line, besieger and besieged had been living in uneasy proximity. Now, just after midnight, an assault brigade's infantry advanced through a whirling snowstorm. The men carried unloaded rifles with fixed bayonets; their leaders wanted no accidental or anxious firing to alert the enemy. As quickly and noiselessly as they could, the soldiers of the first wave waded through the snow. Their plan was to massacre the trenches' garrison in its sleep.

At Batycze, the Russians faced alert Honvéd troops and were thrown back. However, against the Na Górach side of the position, garrisoned by the East Galician I/Landwehr Infantry Regiment 35, they achieved a complete success. This battalion was weak and demoralized. Over half its strength, 533 soldiers, were already out of action owing to exhaustion. Blinded by the snow flying into their faces, freezing and apathetic, the unit's sentries did not see the attackers until it was too late. When Tsarist storm troops leaped into the trenches brandishing naked steel, the shock was total. There was a brief brawl, and then capitulation. Not many survivors made it back to the main perimeter defenses.

There was no hope of retaking the position. Kusmanek had wanted to, and Landwehr Infantry Regiment 19, resting as the Fortress Command's reserve, was alerted, but the regiment's malnourished soldiers took three hours to march the 7 kilometers (a little over 4 miles) from the city to the perimeter. By the time they arrived, utterly exhausted, the opportunity had passed. In any case, even if by some miracle the trenches had been won back, the Fortress's low combat strength doomed the defense. They could never have been held.[49]

HOPES OF RELIEF had by this point long dissipated. It was clear to all who were trapped in the Fortress that General Conrad's field army was not going to come. As if preparing for extinction, Kusmanek ordered the establishment of a fortress museum to showcase the struggle of the garrison and the citizens. What would go in it was a mystery. There was little left in Przemyśl but obsolete weaponry and rags of old uniforms. Empty shelves would have best represented what the garrison had left to subsist on and warm itself with anyway. In the city, a middling-sized dog now cost 20 crowns, a mouse 10 hellers. All the cats had already been sold and eaten. In the front lines, freezing soldiers were dismantling their defenses—tearing down wooden trench wall cladding, wire entanglement posts, even dugout roof props—just to have something to burn.[50]

The nights were long that last month in the Fortress. A few officers worked by the hazy light of acrid horse-fat candles, writing the daily report of men who had collapsed or died that day. Everybody else was plunged into darkness. In those eerie hours, Przemyśl seemed to shrink in on itself, becoming even more claustrophobic and oppressive. Thoughts of family weighed heavily on men's minds. So, too, did fear of the future. They all knew the Fortress was lost. "Who will survive, only God knows," wrote one of the 23rd Honvéd Infantry Division's officers, capturing the garrison's despair. "Already for a few days I've been walking like a drunk, or, to speak precisely, like a man condemned to death. I walk here and there, I can never find a place for myself, I find no delight in anything, I am apathetic, just like the general staff. . . . There is nowhere to hide, the end is coming."[51]

CHAPTER SEVEN

ARMAGEDDON

The column of soldiers marched through the night. In front of them stretched the main road to the east, the same road along which the Habsburg field army had ingloriously retreated six months previously. The spring thaw had now begun and the cobbles were slippery with mud and half-melted ice. The men were heavily laden. Besides the regulation knapsack, rifle, bayonet, and spade, each man carried extra ammunition and, if through dire hunger he had not already devoured them, rations for five days. They were exhausted. At every halt, soldiers sank into the snow-filled ditches by the road, incapable of further exertion. Their leaders did not bother to raise them. Yet this was an assault force. The order that had set them marching told them there was no more food, and that there would be no return. "Forward—at all costs forward!" it had urged. Yet they were marching east, away from Austro-Hungarian forces. Beyond them lay occupied Lwów, then Kiev and Moscow. And they were tired and weak. It all made no sense.[1]

IDEAS FOR A final breakout had been bouncing between the AOK and the Fortress Command since early January, when the Habsburg general staff chief, Conrad, had demanded the Fortress build a powerful offensive group of five divisions, each of 12,000–15,000 men and backed by artillery. The fortress commander, Kusmanek, had immediately set to work reorganizing the garrison. Przemyśl's troops and equipment proved insufficient to create the large force imagined at the AOK, but two assault divisions and three brigades were formed, ready to concentrate at short notice for a decisive operation outside the defenses. What mission they would receive depended on whether the Habsburg field army could strike out of the Carpathians. If the army approached Przemyśl as in December, the group would sally out in support. However, if the army stuck in the snow, the Fortress's offensive group would be sent on an altogether more desperate enterprise. Then, its task would be to act as a spearhead, penetrating enemy lines. Troops left behind in Przemyśl would blow their own defenses and follow in its wake, and the entire garrison would try to cut a way through to the field army.[2]

Conrad had originally promised to make a decision by mid-February concerning which operation the fortress offensive group would undertake, but as Kusmanek and his staff managed to stretch the garrison's rations, and as the Carpathian battles dragged on, the decision was postponed for as long as possible. Only on March 13, when barely ten days of food remained in Przemyśl, did Conrad at last settle on a course. Blaming the bad weather in the mountains, in a telegram to Kusmanek he conceded that the field army was unlikely to reach Przemyśl in time. The fortress commander was ordered to wait until the 17th. Then, if it was clear no relief was coming, "honor of arms" dictated that the garrison must launch its own offensive to break through to friendly territory.[3]

The general staff chief's appeal to honor was an intimation of the real objective of the operation. Even Conrad, a perennial optimist, had sufficient grasp of reality to know the breakout force had no chance of reaching Habsburg lines. Rather, what he intended was to manufacture a myth. A final glorious death ride should mute all criticism of the Fortress's inevitable surrender. It might even cement for all time the legend of the heroes of Przemyśl. At the Fortress Command, some of the officers balked. The staff intelligence officer, Lieutenant Felix Hölzer, reacted to the order to break through with disbelief: "What has proven impossible for the field army with young well-equipped forces, we should do with Landsturm men 50 percent of whom are laid low through exhaustion?" Unit reports made grim reading. Although regiments had been broken up and their soldiers redistributed to bring all the assault battalions up to a nominal strength of 800 men, actual field strengths were far lower. On the eve of the operation, Landsturm Infantry Regiment 33 reported that only half of its soldiers were fit for service. In Hungarian Landsturm Infantry Regiments 9 and 16, just a third of the troops were capable of offensive action.[4]

The fortress commander understood Conrad's thinking. General Kusmanek had been delegated the authority to decide where the attack should be launched. His initial instinct was to thrust southeast, toward Sambor, the headquarters of the Russian Eighth Army, and into the Carpathian Mountains. However, the more he considered the operation, the less attractive this plan appeared. Early on the afternoon of March 16, he telegraphed the AOK with a new plan. To Conrad's surprise, Kusmanek now wanted to attack to the east.[5]

If, like Conrad and Kusmanek, one cold-bloodedly ignores the central question of whether sending Przemyśl's starved garrison into battle was anything but criminal folly, there was logic to this bizarre proposal. The fortress commander knew the 40,000 infantry of his attack group could never beat through 90 kilometers (around 56 miles) of enemy-held territory to the field army. Instead, his drive eastward would satisfy honor and, as he promised Conrad, "do one more service for the army." If his force penetrated the encirclement line, it could destroy crucial enemy infrastructure—above all, the railways radiating from Lwów. It would also help itself to the large Russian food depots situated in this direction. Lastly, and poignantly, the weakness of the soldiers meant there really was no other option. Southeast of Przemyśl lay bog, and to the west and southwest hills. In the east, however, the land was flat and mostly firm. At this late hour, that was all the exhausted troops could drag themselves over.[6]

Needless to say, for the soldiers there would be no return. Death or captivity were inevitable. To avoid opposition, Kusmanek avoided acknowledging this when he spoke with his generals. Nor did he speak about "honor." When he summoned them to his headquarters for an emotional meeting on the morning of March 18, he presented the operation as a *bona fide* breakout attempt aimed in a direction where the Russians were weakest and would least expect it. Objections from two generals that the troops were too exhausted were overruled.[7]

The offensive was set for the small hours of March 19, the last date possible, on account of the imminent expiry of the Fortress's food stocks. Surprise and secrecy were supposed to guarantee success. Elaborate efforts were made to deceive the enemy. In the days before the operation was to begin, agents were dispatched to convince the Russians that an assault was imminent in the southwest, the place where in December the Honvéds had briefly broken the encirclement line. During the night of March 18–19, the artillery of Defense Sector VIII in the southwest ferociously bombarded the encirclement line with the same diversionary intent. For the real operation in the east, security was tight; indeed, the precautions passed over into characteristic paranoia. Especially telling of Kusmanek's fear of betrayal was that he unveiled his plan to his closest confidants a mere fourteen hours before the offensive was scheduled to begin. As Kusmanek's chief of staff, Lieutenant-Colonel Ottokar Hubert, handed out orders of attack and operational maps to the generals, each was made to swear a solemn oath of silence.[8]

Those top-secret orders and maps set out how the operation was to unfold. At 1:00 a.m., the offensive was scheduled to open under Kusmanek's command. The Combined Division led by Lieutenant-

General Karl Waitzendorfer—a formation of central and eastern Galician units—was to advance from the eastern perimeter along the Lwów Road; it would be accompanied by an armored train, built by the Fortress's Engineering Directorate, on the railway that ran parallel to the road. To the south, the Hungarian 97th Landsturm Brigade would also move forward. Farther south still, the 23rd Hungarian Honvéd Infantry Division would wait inside Defense Sector VI's forward defensive crescent—the scene of the bitterest fighting back in October—and, once the rest of the assault group drew level, would join the attack eastward. Eighteen artillery batteries were allocated as fire support. The 108th (Austrian German) and Major-General Friedrich Kloiber's Combined Brigades comprised the reserve in the south and north of the attack front.[9]

There would be no preparatory bombardment. Instead, as an order issued by the Fortress Command on March 18 emphasized, for the eyes of company commanders and their superiors only, everything hinged on speed, stealth, and surprise. The troops were to creep forward silently under cover of darkness. Special detachments of sappers and the units' most skilled soldiers would rush ahead to cut gaps in the enemy's wire. No one was to shoot. Instead, aping the tactic employed by the Russians a week earlier in their capture of the Fortress's Na Górach positions, assault troops were to head straight for enemy lines and attack with the bayonet. "Then," the order claimed hopefully, "we shall find the Russians sleeping and shall overpower them easily."[10]

Kusmanek's public confidence about the ease with which Russian positions could be broken contrasted sharply with his obvious fear that Przemyśl's regiments would refuse to participate in this suicide mission. "The breakthrough will succeed only if officers and men are instilled with the conviction of the absolute necessity of breaking through," his order to commanders asserted. Officers were told to explain that there was nothing left to eat in the Fortress. To stay meant to surrender or to perish from hunger. Nowhere in the order was it mentioned that the troops would be marching east, away from Austria-Hungary, only that there could be no return. Just behind enemy lines, it was emphasized, were depots brimming with food. All that stood between the starving assault force and this abundance were ancient Russian militiamen and untrained reservists who "every time run at the first shot." Should this encouragement fail to animate the men, officers were to enforce iron discipline. Any soldier who turned to retreat was to be shot on the spot. Any soldier who ate more than a day's rations in twenty-four hours was to be summarily executed.[11]

The AOK had telegraphed its assent to the operation on the 16th, and on the following day the assault group's units were withdrawn from the perimeter and began to concentrate. The Fortress's defense was left with two infantry regiments, one of them the distrusted Landsturm Regiment 35, a few other low-grade Landsturm battalions, and labor units given crash courses in infantry combat. On the 18th, while their officers rushed to make eleventh-hour preparations, the troops rested. Extra rations were distributed. Everyone waited nervously for what was to come.[12]

The fortress commander spent the final hours before the attack working up his own legend. Kusmanek, like Conrad, understood that defeat is a sensitive matter. Handled wrongly, reputations can suffer. Done right, with pathos and heroism, they can soar. Throughout the long siege, Kusmanek had been a remote figure. He rarely inspected the garrison. Some company officers complained that not once during the ordeal had the men set eyes on their commander. Now, however, Kusmanek penned an order with all the familiarity and warmth of Napoleon's address a hundred years earlier to his Old Guard. "My Soldiers!" the message began ringingly. What followed was a breathtakingly cynical piece of self-promotion from a man ruthlessly dispatching the fathers of thousands of families on a futile death march. The promise that they were marching to the Habsburg field army, the implication that Kusmanek was leading them personally into the mouths of the enemy guns: both were cheap deceits.

So late was the order issued that it failed to reach most of the units, as they had already departed for their jump-off positions. Yet this mattered little, for it was aimed primarily at posterity:

My Soldiers!

A full half year is gone, in which we—children of nearly all the nations of our beloved Fatherland shoulder to shoulder—stand without pause before the enemy.

With God's help and thanks to your courageous devotion, I have been able to hold our Fortress despite heavy enemy storms, despite cold and deprivation, against every attack by the raging, ruthless foe.

Trustingly, you have followed my leadership. You have stood defiant against all dangers and unending hardships.

You have already won in ample measure the recognition of our All Highest Warlord [the Emperor], the thanks of the Fatherland—and the respect of the enemy.

Thousands of loyal hearts beat and fret for you—away in the dear Fatherland.

Millions wait with bated breath for any news which comes from you to home.

Once again—my Bravehearts—I am forced to demand the utmost from you!

The honor of our Fatherland commands it! . . .

I am leading you out to smash with steel fist the enemy's iron ring around our Fortress, and then with irresistible strength to push ever farther and farther until we reach our army, which in hard battles has already forced its way close to us.

A bitter fight stands before us, for the enemy will want to hold fast to what he believed was his certain prize.

He will only now truly come to know the garrison of Przemyśl.

Each of you must be animated by just one single thought—

Forward! At all costs forward![13]

THE 3RD BATTALION, Landsturm Infantry Regiment 18, had passed through hell during its seven months in the Fortress. That scorching August, when the battalion had first arrived in Przemyśl, when the war was new and innocence still intact, now seemed to belong to a different age. The unit's baptism of fire in September had quickly been followed by the fury of the Russians' October storm. There had been further hard fighting and casualties in February, when the Russians conquered an advance position on the wooded hill of Nadgrodzenie to the northwest, and the III/Landsturm 18 was sent in to retake it.[14]

No one in the battalion, neither officers nor men, was overweight anymore. All were gaunt and pasty, worn down by service in the interval lines, the cold, a horse diet, and unceasing worry for their families around the unit's home base of Czerteż, now under Russian occupation. By March, the middle-aged soldiers were collapsing on duty and dying of exhaustion. Officers repeatedly warned their superiors that the battalion was barely capable of combat. Yet disconcerting rumors circulated, fueled by baffling orders to construct light sledges for carrying munitions, by new allocations of horses, and by the arrival of unrequested wire cutters. Men whispered that the High Command was plotting a desperate breakout from the Fortress.

On the night of March 17–18, 3rd Battalion companies garrisoning the perimeter were suddenly pulled out and replaced with armed labor soldiers. The whole regiment was gathered and, at 3:00 a.m., left its barracks in the Fortress's northwest and marched down to the city of Przemyśl. There, on the 18th, it rested and prepared to attack. Special rations and extra ammunition were issued, adding another couple of kilograms to the weak Landsturm men's heavy loads. As evening fell, the last of the battalion's liquor was handed out. The officers retired to their mess, a desolate, unheated room half-illuminated by flickering candlelight. From the wall, a portrait of Emperor Franz Joseph stared down disapprovingly at these shadows of soldiers. Sad Slavic songs wafted from the men's barracks.

No one wanted to die. So much hardship had already been endured, so many dangers survived; now, at what was obviously the end, it seemed perverse to have to perish.

The officers were roused from their brooding by the arrival of the regiment's commander, Colonel František Kralíček, and his adjutant, Lieutenant Balka. With a face like stone, the colonel read aloud the orders for the imminent operation. The breakthrough, he announced, would take place in the direction of Medyka. A murmur rippled round the room. Medyka? But that was to the east. It was entirely the wrong direction. Moreover, the Russians had built strong positions in that direction back in October, when the Habsburg field army had tried to hammer through to Lwów. No easy way forward was to be found there.

Some subalterns pondered whether the regiment's mission was a feint to distract the enemy from a real attack southward. Others were less sure. There appeared to be no limit to the madness of the senior commanders. Any idea of a breakthrough, in whatever direction, was ridiculous. "Everyone," fumed Lieutenant Jan Vit of the 10th Company, "from the highest commander to the ordinary soldier, knew very well that our starved and physically exhausted men and emaciated horses were incapable of undergoing a single day's march, not to speak of several days of battle."[15]

There was not much time to ponder these questions or to organize the troops. The regiment was to depart at 9:20 p.m., barely an hour away. The entire assault force had to be past the perimeter defenses and arrayed in no-man's-land no later than 12:30 a.m., and ready thirty minutes later to go into the attack. At the appointed hour, the regiment paraded, ready to march. The 3rd Battalion formed the tail of the column. Its commander was now Major Kazimierz Ładosz, a popular Pole who had been in charge since the October storm, when his predecessor, the autocratic Vinzenz Zipser, had been wounded by shrapnel. Ładosz tried to inspire the men with a few hurried words. Then the dark ranks moved forward slowly and painfully onto the road to the east.

The stupidity of the escapade was laid bare soon enough. During the long, debilitating siege, the troops had lost the strength to hike any distance. By the time the 3rd Battalion was halfway to Defense Sector VI, a third of its heavily laden soldiers had dropped out through exhaustion. Progress was slow, and not only because neither men nor horses had much energy. The roads were choked. Artillery, supply wagons, and columns of troops jostled for space and blocked each other's paths. Halts were frequent. Only at 1:00 a.m. did the 1st Battalion, at the head of Landsturm Infantry Regiment 18's column, arrive at the perimeter. Now, just half the soldiers were left in the ranks.[16]

There were further delays as the regiment struggled through the Fortress's forward defenses. Guides were provided to help the men through the maze of trenches and then past minefields and barbed wire. In single file, with no lanterns or torches, they were led down the narrow channels running out of the main line for patrols and raiding parties to access no-man's-land. One by one, the soldiers climbed out into the open.

Waitzendorfer's Combined Division, to which Landsturm Regiment 18 belonged, was only in place on the left of the attack front at 2:35 a.m. At 3:15 a.m., more than two hours behind schedule, its assault began. The 3rd Battalion, the last unit on the division's right wing, strung out into skirmisher lines and went forward.

Imagine yourself, for a moment, in the patched boots of a Landsturm man slowly pacing forward in the skirmisher line that night. It is a solitary experience. The sky is dead. There are no stars, no moon. Each soldier walks apart. The line is spaced like this so as to limit casualties. Everyone carries a heavy rucksack. Everyone advances with fixed bayonet. By strict command, the rifles are unloaded; officers reckon the chances of reaching the Russians' position are slim enough without an accidental shot betraying them. The terrain is unfamiliar. Nobody knows exactly where the enemy lies, or whether he is already watching.

Suddenly, from out of the inky darkness, loom soldiers. A brief shock: the Russians already? They turn out to be a company of the neighboring battalion, who have missed their way and are traveling perpendicular to the rest of the attack. It was fortunate the men of the Third had no bullets loaded, or somebody would have been shot. The advance goes on, slowly. The only sound is the wheezing of overburdened men as they struggle through the undergrowth.

Eventually, after what feels like an interminable trek, the battalion comes to a large stream crossing its path. Nobody has warned Landsturm Regiment 18's commander that this stream is there and, as a result of the intense secrecy surrounding the attack, he has had no opportunity to reconnoiter. The battalion stops. It has nothing with which to bridge the stream. A few brave soldiers jump in, but the water is too broad, too deep, and too cold to cross. They sink in up to their chests. Only with great difficulty can they be rescued. The officers send out patrols to try to find a way around. Failing that, if the patrols can locate a ruined house, they can rip out materials so that the stream can be spanned. Everybody waits.

While this farce is underway, the battle begins. It is 4:30 a.m. Over on the right, where the Hungarian 97th Landsturm Brigade and the 23rd Honvéd Division have not been seen since the start of the operation, a cry of "Rajta!"—On!—rises. Moments later, far to the left, another thunderous shout echoes, signaling the storm of Waitzendorfer's troops on the other side of the Lwów Road. Shells start falling. The Russians entrenched outside Medyka switch on a powerful searchlight. As its beam swings toward the Landsturm soldiers trapped at the stream, everyone dives to the ground. The men lie motionless in the dirty snow, hoping not to be noticed, hoping to avoid the hail of shrapnel and bullets that must follow.

III/Landsturm Regiment 18 was now in extreme danger. Dawn was approaching, and as the sun's pale rays slid languidly over the battlefield, they revealed a landscape devoid of cover or refuge. There was no way forward; the stream made sure of that. The ground was still too frozen to dig; to stay motionless meant being picked off by snipers or blown to pieces. Already, the Russian guns were shooting. At first, they aimed well to the rear, blocking off retreat. Then, step by step, the gunners reduced their range. With awful deliberation, the curtain of fire and brimstone rumbled closer and closer to the helpless men of the 3rd Battalion.

With a deafening roar, the shells came crashing down around the stream, throwing up columns of earth and water. There were screams from wounded. Men started to flee. Lieutenant Vit looked on with disgust as one of his brother officers, a "crafty swine," turned tail, followed helter-skelter by his platoon. Any sense of superiority the Czech lieutenant felt was short-lived, however, for when he called out to his own company, he discovered that it, too, had mostly "legged it." Just six soldiers remained. Scanning the area through binoculars, he saw Ładosz and a few other officers, each with a tiny group of soldiers, still grimly hanging on to the stream's bank.

Quite what possessed those few survivors to hold is difficult to know. Duty? Courage? Manly pride? Sheer bloody-mindedness? Vit, a good officer but an arch cynic when it came to the Habsburg military, never explained. Perhaps he himself did not know. As the day grew lighter, nothing but a miracle could save them. Though the embattled Habsburg soldiers still could not see their enemy's positions, he certainly had them in his sights. Machine-gun and rifle fire was whistling over their heads.

Then, a miracle did happen. It began to snow. At first just a few flakes drifted down onto the unhappy men. Then from heaven fell a thick snowfall. It was as if an impenetrable white veil had been dropped between the doomed Landsturm soldiers and their enemy. Ładosz took his chance and pulled the remnants of the battalion back.

The final rout began after the snow stopped, shortly after 6:00 a.m. The Russians counterattacked in the Na Błonie Wood over on the right, contested by the 3rd Battalion's Hungarian neighbors. There was fierce fighting and hellish noise. The ground shook. Then the Hungarians fled. Shellfire exploded among them as in panic they ran. Landsturm Regiment 18's Colonel Kraliček knew all was lost. To stay was to die. He organized a disciplined withdrawal. Regiments on the left, when they saw the 18th Landsturm go back, also gave up the hopeless struggle and followed, so that soon an entire brigade was in retreat. The soldiers did not run. They were too broken for that. Haltingly, harassed by shells, they limped back to the safety of the Fortress.

ON THE RIGHT of the attack front, the Fortress's elite, the 23rd Honvéd Infantry Division under Lieutenant-General Árpád Tamásy, suffered a similarly crushing defeat. Its debacle was in part a result of poor coordination. The 23rd Honvéd Division was supposed to wait inside Defense Sector VI's forward crescent until the formations to the north drew level. Tamásy, who had based himself in Fort I, "Salis-Soglio," heard that the Combined Division was running late, and so he held his men behind the front. Unfortunately, he waited too long. At 3:15 a.m., when Waitzendorfer's Galician units began their advance, Tamásy's soldiers were mostly still filing through the fortress defenses. Not until 4:40 a.m. was the bulk of the Honvéd Division ready to begin its attack. Exacerbating the confusion, one unit, Honvéd Infantry Regiment 2, went forward far earlier. This unit, entirely by itself, launched its assault at 3:30 a.m.[17]

Colonel Géza von Szathmáry, the commander of Honvéd Infantry Regiment 2, was, by all accounts, something of a lunatic. At 3:15 a.m. he already had his regiment deployed in no-man's-land and was impatiently champing at the bit, wondering why the rest of the division was still not ready. Unlike most officers, who regarded the operation with reactions ranging from intense skepticism to dull dread, Szathmáry felt inspired and was determined to triumph or go under. At 3:30 a.m., he could stand it no longer: the division's attack should have begun a full hour and a half earlier. The colonel ordered an advance on his own authority. No other regiment went forward. His own assault battalions were not positioned quite correctly and within minutes of setting off they split into two groups, losing contact with each other in the darkness. None of this mattered to Szathmáry. Heady with thoughts of death and glory, he stormed to the fore.

Szathmáry led the bulk of his soldiers straight at a Russian field watch, capturing its men before they had time to alert their comrades to the rear. Further on, the Honvéd put to flight another Russian post, which retreated to the main encirclement line. However, at 300 paces from this line, Szathmáry's assault stuck fast. The defenders were alarmed. Bullets were flying. He had no contact with Tamásy back in Fort I, or with his own 2nd Battalion, which had disappeared into the night. For hours, first in snow and then broad daylight, the troops lay pinned in front of the enemy positions. They annihilated one Russian counterattack against them. At 8:00 a.m., however, the Russians again charged, advancing on the flanks and encircling the isolated Honvéd. Szathmáry was lightly wounded and the commander of his 1st Battalion, Major Johann Sztodola, was beaten to death by an angry Russian infantryman as he tried to surrender. Most of the remainder of the regiment, those who had not yet been killed or incapacitated, were taken prisoner.

The rest of the 23rd Honvéd Infantry Division did no better. Indeed, Szathmáry's impulsive advance an hour before the other regiments moved made progress much more difficult, for they now faced alert opponents aware that an offensive operation was underway. Although at 5:00 a.m. Tamásy ordered the Fortress's artillery to obliterate the Russian guns, these were too far back for its mostly worn and obsolete pieces to hit. Honvéd Infantry Regiment 5 was stopped by fire from the side, and Regiment 7 also ground to a halt. Only Infantry Regiment 8 managed to advance, and after 6:00 a.m., its flanking fire permitted the right of the 97th Hungarian Landsturm Infantry Brigade to move forward too over the Medyka–Byków road. The left of the brigade did not follow. It had disappeared into Na Błonie, the nightmarish wood where Vit and the men of Landsturm Regiment 18 witnessed the vicious fighting.

At 8:00 a.m., as Szathmáry was going under, the Russian 58th Reserve Infantry Division crashed into the right flank of Tamásy's division. Honvéd Infantry Regiments 5 and 7 and the wandering 2nd Battalion of Szathmáry's Regiment 2 were encircled. Groups of dazed and frightened soldiers scurried back to the Fortress. As in the north, there was no opportunity to commit the brigade that had been kept back in reserve. At 9:45 a.m., Kusmanek conceded that the breakthrough had failed and ordered a general retreat. All that could be hoped for was that the exhausted and abused troops could hold the Fortress's eastern perimeter against the Russian counterattack swelling all along the line.

WHILE THE FAILURE of the final offensive of March 19 came as no surprise to anybody, from senior commanders to subalterns, the speed and totality of the collapse did startle higher ranks. Nowhere had the Fortress's assault group even penetrated the Russian line. From its launch until the senior commanders issued orders to retreat, the operation had lasted less than seven hours. Once they were back inside the defensive perimeter, what was left of the assault units had to be urgently ordered to man the interval trenches for fear the Russians would seize on the garrison's disarray and attempt to breach them. Whatever Habsburg military leaders might claim, talk of "honor" had little place in this operation; it was an abject, humiliating defeat.

The Fortress Command's fundamental mistake had been its willful disregard for the utter exhaustion, both mental and physical, of its troops. The failure was worsened, however, by Kusmanek's obsessive fears of betrayal. By not revealing his attack scheme to the commanders until the morning of March 18, Kusmanek left no time for reconnaissance. Only the 97th Hungarian Landsturm Brigade was familiar with the terrain it would cross and the Russian positions on the other side. The other units of the assault group had little or no experience of service in the eastern defenses. This resulted in a series of disasters; indeed, Landsturm Infantry Regiment 18's surprise at encountering an unfordable stream was just one of many signs of the lack of planning. Most spectacularly, the secrecy also rendered the improvised armored train useless. Its task had been to support Waitzendorfer's Combined Division by sallying forth down the track to Lwów, guns blazing.

The Fortress Engineering Directorate had expended considerable energy on building the armored train, based around a small tender engine onto which thick steel plate had been painstakingly riveted. However, the Fortress Command had not thought to check the state of the track. No traffic had run on it since the beginning of September. The armored train was scheduled to arrive at Fort XIV, "Hurko," at 1:00 a.m. In the event, it did not leave Przemyśl station until 1:50 a.m. because sudden concerns were raised about whether a bridge over the Wiar River, which had been wired for demolition, was safe to cross. Once this had been checked and the train was permitted to steam forward, the Combined Division discovered a second problem. Where the track crossed the defensive lines, the garrison had thrown up a sandbank, which prevented any traffic rolling through. Troops were sent out to do some midnight shoveling, but further precious time was wasted. Not until 3:00 a.m. did the armored train steam up to Hurko, where it waited in vain for the obstruction to be cleared. Ultimately, the opportunity was missed and the Fortress's wonder weapon was never committed to the battle.[18]

Had Kusmanek's intense secrecy safeguarded the surprise of the breakout operation, then perhaps it would still have been worthwhile. Yet it did not even achieve this. In fact, the command's hysterical fears of human treason distracted attention from the greatest of all security vulnerabilities: the Fortress's radio station.

As Kusmanek ruefully warned Conrad after the defeat, the Russians' countermeasures clearly indicated that they had the Habsburg military's codes and had been reading his correspondence with the AOK. To counter the attack, the Russians had transferred the entire

58th Reserve Division from the Carpathians. This formation knew the terrain, for it had already fought against Przemyśl's eastern defenses during the October storm. Prior to the arrival of the 58th Reserve, the 48th Militia Brigade had stood alone in this sector. This brigade was composed of old, unenthusiastic militiamen: Kusmanek had promised his assault troops that these would be the only force standing against them. The 58th Reserve Division's better-equipped, battle-hardened soldiers, some doubtless keen to avenge their defeat of the previous autumn, were a far more formidable opponent. Their counterattack against the Hungarians in the south definitively smashed the Fortress's final offensive.[19]

The operation had been a calamity. Not only had it failed utterly, but casualties had been extraordinarily heavy. Among the 40,000 infantry in the assault group, over 10,000 were killed, wounded, or captured. On the north side of the battlefield, Waitzendorfer's Combined Division lost around 3,000 men. In the center, the 97th Hungarian Landsturm Infantry Brigade lost 1,500–2,000 soldiers. The 23rd Honvéd Infantry Division in the south of the battlefield had suffered most of all. From its 8,500 soldiers who marched out of the Fortress in the early hours of March 19, some 5,838 never returned: a casualty rate of nearly 70 percent in just five hours. Two of its regiments had a little over 900 men, one-third of their complement, left. Through Szathmáry's reckless attempt to take on the Tsarist Empire alone, Regiment 2 was nearly obliterated, with just 380 traumatized survivors managing to reach safety. All in all, the futile operation was, observed one subaltern bitterly, "a poor thanks to the soldiers for their loyalty and copious sacrifices during eight months of service in the Fortress."[20]

THE FAILURE OF the breakthrough operation sent a collective shudder through Przemyśl. The sight of ragged bands of defeated soldiers—"wounded, weary, worn-out"—returning through the city dismayed the inhabitants. Rumors of utter catastrophe passed from mouth to mouth. Tamásy was said to be captured, Waitzendorfer killed. Casualties were inflated to some 20,000 men. The word on the street was that Kusmanek lay dangerously ill. Everything appeared to be on the verge of complete collapse.[21]

The reality was scarcely less apocalyptic. Worse, the Russians were stirring. The blockade army had, over the past months, accumulated 148 heavy artillery pieces. Most were obsolete armaments from the Russians' own fortifications of Kronstadt, Brest-Litovsk, and Kovno (Kaunas), but they nevertheless gave the force more than double the heavy firepower it had deployed during the storm of early October 1914. Through March 19 and 20, these guns hammered not only Przemyśl's defenses, but also the city. A hundred shells fell on the first day alone. Several exploded on the pavilions of the garrison hospital. Others damaged houses. Frightened residents packed valuables and clothes, ready to flee for their lives.[22]

Early on the evening of March 20, the enemy's infantry advanced against the Fortress's northwest. In the small hours of the 21st, more action followed against the northern front. Senior officers insisted there had been major assaults here and even also in the east. Somehow the depleted garrison had held them at bay. A different story was told at the front. Officers of Landsturm Regiment 18, which was deployed to reinforce the most threatened sector, believed that unheroic soldiers of the armed labor battalions had been spooked by shadows and triggered a panic. Mistaking Russian patrols for attacking regiments, they had begun shooting so wildly that the enemy had become alarmed that another breakthrough attempt was underway and had laid down a barrage. The Landsturm men were again the victims. They took casualties and were forced to spend a last night pointlessly freezing in the interval trenches.[23]

Kusmanek prepared for the end. On the 20th, he had summoned unit commanders to fortress headquarters to present final reports on the state of their troops. "Physically and morally broken," was how Major-General Artur Kaltnecker described his 93rd Landsturm Brigade. Most of the other thirty officers present spoke in similar, devastating terms. The report of Colonel Kraliček of Landsturm Infantry Regiment 18, back from the breakthrough operation, can stand for them all:

> The men are physically and psychologically broken and deaf to any attempt to influence or encourage them. At most, 500 men of the regiment still possess the moral strength to be used under shrapnel covers in defense against an enemy attack. All others are, at the moment, just likely to spread panic.
>
> The officer corps is also utterly physically exhausted and, in particular, the constant strains which are conditioned by fortress warfare and which have lasted for eight months have engendered insomnia and advanced nervous fatigue among all officers.[24]

On the following day, March 21, a far smaller but no less somber meeting of the Fortress's six-man Defense Council convened. Kusmanek, his chief of staff, Lieutenant-Colonel Ottokar Hubert; his artillery and engineering staff chiefs, Colonels Camil and Schwalb; and the garrison's two most senior officers, Generals Tamásy and Waitzendorfer, made a final decision to surrender the Fortress. Tamásy was reluctant. He and a few other Magyar officers favored a suicidal last stand. They vowed to carry the fight from the forts and the interval lines into the heart of the city itself, if this helped to prevent a Russian invasion of Hungary. Yet Kusmanek, sobered by the debacle on the 19th, rejected his deputy's romantic fantasy of self-immolation.[25]

The minutes of this last meeting spelled out the Fortress's hopeless plight. Capitulation was inevitable and imminent on two grounds. First, after months of unbroken struggle with the enemy, worn-out clothing, poor accommodation, and severe undernourishment, the troops were finished. Their enfeeblement had undergone a marked acceleration since the 19th, when first the breakout operation and then the enemy assault on the perimeter had broken the best remaining troops and consumed what little energy survivors had left.

In the judgment of the Fortress's senior commanders, the garrison was now in such poor physical condition and so demoralized that it could not withstand Russian assault for more than one final night.[26]

The second factor that made immediate capitulation necessary was, of course, food. In Przemyśl's magazines were, per head, only seven portions of tinned horsemeat and four of hardtack. While these scanty stocks would just about keep the men alive until March 24, Kusmanek and his council calculated that two days' worth of rations needed to be set aside so that, once they were prisoners, the garrison would still have something to eat. Without this reserve, there was a genuine risk that the men would starve before they could be brought to the nearest Russian food depots in Jarosław, Mościska, and Dobromil.

For both these reasons, Kusmanek and the Defense Council determined that the Fortress's last day would be March 22, 1915. They meant this in the most literal sense. On this date, Przemyśl would be surrendered to the Russian army. Yet it would fall with a bang, not a whimper. In a final act of *Götterdämmerung*, everything of military value would be destroyed. Forts, magazines, even the city's bridges would be blown. The bulwark of Habsburg defense would be wiped from the face of the earth. The Russians would march into ruins.

PREPARATION FOR THE destruction of the Fortress had begun at the end of December 1914, when Colonel Hans Schwalb's Engineering Directorate had worked up demolition plans. By the last days of February, the necessary explosives, and sealed orders for how to use them, had been placed inside the forts. As the end approached, the Fortress Command began to clear anything of military value from Przemyśl. First to go was easily combustible paper. On March 17, all units were ordered to hand in their diaries and documentation. The secret life of the Fortress during the siege was not to be revealed to the Russians. Two days later, on the 19th, the Fortress burned its money. The troops were paid a double wage to cover March and

April, and then the remaining funds were brought to Przemyśl's meat-smoking facility and incinerated: 6.7 million crowns went up in flames.[27]

The pace of destruction quickened after the failure of the break-out operation. On March 20 and 21, the Fortress's telephone and telegraph equipment was smashed. So, too, was the city's rail infrastructure. Gasoline and ammunition were dumped in the San. With no further hope of escape from the doomed bulwark, most of the surviving horses were shot. At 3:00 p.m. on the 21st, the Defense Sectors' engineering officers were called to Schwalb's office and presented with the final demolition schedule. That evening, the artillery would fire off all its remaining ammunition and, on the following morning at five o'clock, destroy its guns. At 6:00 a.m., the forts, the munitions depots, and the bridges over the San and Wiar Rivers would be blown up. In the interval lines, infantry would keep sharp watch to stop the Russians from trying to intervene. Then they would douse their own trenches and shelters with paraffin and burn them out. All weapons and equipment were to be destroyed. Rifle butts would be broken, cartridges trodden into the ground. Nothing should be left to the enemy.[28]

That last night was filled with earth-shattering impressions. Helena Jabłońska, the fifty-one-year-old widow and avid diarist, was not alone in thinking that "these dozen or so hours were surely unique in the history of the entire world." Everybody who lived through them agreed that they were unforgettable, although so extraordinary, staggering, and shocking were the events that no one quite remembered exactly how they had unfolded.[29]

The night of destruction was heralded by the menacing rumble of fortress artillery. By ten o'clock that evening, this had risen to an almighty, unprecedented crescendo. It was "a lunatic bombardment," the president of Przemyśl's district court, Władysław Grzędzielski, recalled. "Not even during the 72-hour storm [of] October 1914 was there such a fire as then." To Jabłońska, it seemed that every gun in the Fortress "roared simultaneously without a second's pause."

Together with her neighbors from above, she cowered in her block's ground-floor apartment, full of dread that the building would collapse. Nobody undressed. Nobody slept. The cacophony drowned out any attempt at conversation. The bass tones of the heaviest guns sounded amid the salvos of smaller, quick-firing pieces. From time to time, there rose a piercing whine, a hum which, to Jabłońska, sounded like "powerful falling water" or "a whole swarm of airplanes." This was the machine-guns shooting off their ammunition. For hours and hours, the noise reverberated from all sides and never stopped.[30]

Around 3:30 a.m. there were shouts from the street. "Get up! Get up! Everyone outside! Open all windows! They're going to blow the forts! They're going to blow the bridges!" The police were hammering on doors, warning all residents. Grzędzielski was outraged. The shock waves shattered many thousands of panes of glass that night, he thought, because the authorities had given neither time nor adequate instructions to permit citizens to prepare. Instead, the sudden alarm in the early hours, rousing people from bed and hastily evacuating those on the roads closest to the danger—among them the thoroughfare 3rd May Street, which ran to the San road bridge—inflamed panic. Jabłońska joined the chaos. "Crowds of terrified people with trunks, bundles, and children" were fleeing down the main Słowacki Street, "eyes bulging with fear."[31]

The crowds stood and froze. Some people prayed. Daylight began to filter through the darkness. Then, at last, after the night of deafening noise, the fire began to slacken. The artillerymen had moved on to the next phase of their program, the destruction of their guns. This was quickly completed. For around fifteen minutes, there was total quiet. In the streets, in barracks, in the interval lines, the citizens and soldiers of Przemyśl nervously watched and waited. It was, thought one soldier in the forward trenches, "the silence of the grave."[32]

Armageddon began on the dot of six o'clock, when to the north a shaft of flame suddenly shot from the earth. A mighty roar followed.

This was Fort XI, "Duńkowiczki," exploding. Before the shocked onlookers had time to realize what they had witnessed, another ear-splitting boom followed, then another and another. To Józefa Prochazka, Jabłońska's neighbor, it was as if Przemyśl were ringed by erupting volcanoes. Crimson fire and thick clouds of black smoke rose in the sky, and enormous boulders were hurled up with incredible force. Others had similar thoughts. Two airmen, the last people to leave the Fortress, had just taken off and were at an altitude of only 100 meters (about 325 feet) when the explosions began. It was "a spectacle," wrote the pilot Rudolf Stanger, "horrible and yet of incomparable beauty, eternally sad and yet of such sublime greatness that the destruction of Pompeii or Herculaneum could not have offered a sight more awesome."[33]

On the ground, citizens were rocked by a terrific detonation from Powder Magazine No. 1 at Zniesienie just south of the city center. When this went up, the earth shifted below their feet. In the streets, windows shattered. Glass shards went flying. Clouds of dust and plaster came down in the houses. Unfortunates who had been ordered out of their homes by the police and had sought refuge farther south down Słowacki Street, near the old Jewish cemetery, were smothered in thick smoke. Countess Ilka Künigl-Ehrenburg, who was there, described with terror how rubble and branches had rained down on them. How many people expired that night simply from nervous shock will never be known. Helena Jabłońska knew of one such mortal victim of fright. His corpse lay in her block until the following afternoon, when someone spirited it away, either to the depths of a cellar or to be abandoned on a rubbish tip.[34]

The greatest and most horrific spectacle was the blowing of Przemyśl's three San bridges. These were the arteries of the city, uniting the historic center south of the river to its most important suburb, Zasanie, north of (or, literally, "behind") the San. Przemyśl could not live without them. The airmen, in their frail canvas, wood, and wire contraption, had the bad luck to fly over one bridge at 300 meters (about 985 feet) just as it went up, and the debris climbed right up to their height. Still, the shock was even worse on the ground. Grzędzielski, who lived only a few hundred meters from the bridges, resolved to leave his home for fear that the explosions would cave in its walls.

I was still in the vestibule when the mines placed under the wooden [road] bridge exploded. I tumbled into the street and amid the cloud rising above the epicenter of the explosion I saw the broken beams of the bridge falling to earth. Five minutes later, the most terrible of the series of explosions rent the air. By this point, I was standing in the middle of Krasiński Street. The ground swayed beneath my feet and the impact of the blast wave was so powerful that I staggered. The aural effect almost took second place behind the strong effect of the concussion, which spread throughout my entire body. That mine burst apart the masonry pillars of the railway bridge and broke the central iron spar. . . . Pieces weighing tens of kilograms fell. . . . One piece weighing over 100 kilograms [220 pounds] fell onto Krasiński Street, at the place where the railway bridge runs over this street.[35]

When the smoke cleared, Przemyśl's iron girder railway bridge lay mangled and twisted in the river. The 3rd May Bridge, the city's main crossing point for road traffic, was blown immediately after that. The explosion sliced through it and this central thoroughfare came to rest at a surreal 45-degree angle in the water. The wooden bridge farther downstream had vanished completely. The city had been rent asunder.[36]

By seven o'clock on the morning of March 22, 1915, it was all over. The demolition program was complete, although throughout the day dense smoke billowed from the ruins of the Fortress's perimeter and munitions magazines continued to pop, bang, fizz, and whistle as ordnance ignited. In the city, disorder immediately broke out. Honvéd soldiers looted houses and civilians mobbed military food magazines. In the external Defense Sectors, by contrast, all was eerily still. On the hills and over the forts' ruins around the perimeter, white flags fluttered. The front troops had filed back, smashed their personal weapons and equipment, and shot their last horses; now they sat quietly, exhausted in their barracks. A few NCOs wept; many of the men were simply grateful that the ordeal was over. Everyone wondered what would happen next. At long last, the Russians were coming.[37]

General Kusmanek had selected his right-hand man, Staff Chief Lieutenant-Colonel Ottokar Hubert, and the ruthless commander of the 108th Landsturm Brigade, Colonel August Martinek, to negotiate Przemyśl's surrender. They departed at 7:00 a.m. for the blockade army's headquarters in the Strachocki Palace outside Mościska, to the east. When the two officers arrived, after passing through the Russian encirclement lines, they received a hostile reception. General Andrei Selivanov, the commander of the blockade army since the end of the October storm, was livid. The demolition of the fortress defenses, he shouted, was an act of wanton vandalism. He was not interested in negotiating: he demanded an unconditional surrender.[38]

Hubert and Martinek did their best to coax a few concessions. The Habsburg army's fortress regulations set out the conditions that a defeated garrison should request. The Russians would never concede to some of these, however. Freedom for the troops to depart or occupation of only some of the ruined outer defensive works was clearly never going to be on the table. Remarkably, the emissaries did win agreement that, as a mark of honor for their prolonged resistance, garrison officers should be permitted to retain their swords; it was a chivalric gesture from another era, and a gift to Conrad's and Kusmanek's efforts to present Przemyśl's siege publicly as a tragic and heroic saga.

The dialogue was terminated by a loud detonation, a secondary blast from the demolitions, which sent Selivanov back into a rage.

Though Hubert and Martinek explained that the Fortress's destruction program had already been completed, the Russian general warned them that if they were wrong, he would have them shot. The two Habsburg officers were disarmed and held captive for twenty-four hours. When they protested that such treatment contravened international law, Selivanov ominously retorted that he was indifferent to legal niceties. "Vaë victis," he told them, quoting with unintended irony the barbarians who had sacked Rome in the fourth century: "Woe unto the vanquished."

While this exchange was taking place, Russian units were already feeling their way forward into the Fortress. Almost everywhere, the victors were calm and even friendly, joking with the garrison's Ruthenes and Poles and sharing tobacco. Only in Defense Sector VII, in the south, was the mood tenser. There, a Tsarist patrol had crept up to Fort IV, "Optyń," just before its demolition. When the fort was ripped apart by four explosions—in the left and right armored artillery batteries, in its well, and in its munitions magazine—the forty Russians were killed by the blast. A Habsburg party that had tried to approach under a white flag immediately after the explosions was fired upon. Russian officers suspected foul play and threatened that if they discovered booby traps in the sector, all the garrison officers would be shot.[39]

At nine o'clock, the Russians arrived in Przemyśl's center. The first unit came from the southwest, down the Sanok Road and along the river. Another group marched from the southeast, up Słowacki Street. The men of one Cossack squadron made a particularly memorable entrance. They were led by an exotic young nobleman mounted on a magnificent Arab steed who was clothed in a long, loose-fitting robe and brandished a jewel-encrusted sword. The Cossacks rode six abreast through the city center, their voices imposingly lifting in song. Some citizens shouted, "Hurrah!" Others simply did not know what to think. Should one feel fear for the coming occupation? Sadness at a defeat that many assumed spelled the imminent end of the

Habsburg Empire? Or relief at the promise of a return to law and order and the end of the suffering of the siege?[40]

The Russians themselves were in no doubt about the significance of the moment. A brigadier of the Tsarist 81st Reserve Division who arrived at the Fortress Command surrounded by Cossacks euphorically captured the day's joy and gravitas. "Przemyśl belongs to us now for ever," he crowed. Yet as the following months, years, and decades would bloodily show, such triumphalism was distinctly premature.[41]

INTO THE DARK

Send them along for just one bloody night—
Your zealous heroes spoiling for a fight.
For just one bloody night:
[. . .] When hell's hot jaws in paroxysm expand
And vomit blood and horror on the land.
[. . .] And reeking mists are made of Magyar gore,
They may scream out in tears: "My God, no more!"

Géza Gyóni, "For Just One Night,"
composed in Przemyśl, November 1914[1]

rzemyśl buries its dead to the south. Today, if one walks from
the city's clock tower down what used to be called Dobromil Street, whose end destination now lies cut off across the
Ukrainian border, the municipal cemetery soon comes into view.
Turn right up a twisting, undulating road which in 1914 led past
some of the Fortress's main powder magazines, and very soon you
reach the military burial ground. For all its tranquility, this is a sad
place. A pretty, lightly wooded field lies at the top of the sloping
grounds. Only a monument, flanked by two imposing Byzantine

crosses, warns visitors that below their feet is the mass grave of some 9,000 Russian soldiers. The Austro-Hungarian cemetery across the road appears more organized, with row on row of dark stone crosses. Yet no plaque records how many men lie here—as if that were still a military secret—and the crosses have no inscriptions; these peasant soldiers are in death, as in life, anonymous. The empires for which they fell would within just a few years both lie in ruins. Yet the violence unleashed by their war would live on. Silent witnesses to future, even greater horrors lie nearby: in a Polish military cemetery for soldiers killed fighting German invaders in 1939 and Ukrainians in the 1940s, and, just to the east, in the city's eerily beautiful Jewish burial grounds.

THE NEWS OF Przemyśl's capitulation quickly spread. Grand Duke Nikolai Nikolaevich, the Russian army's supreme commander, was euphoric when, that same morning of March 22, 1915, a report from the besieging force arrived at Stavka. He ran to the Tsar's railway carriage to share the great tidings. All over occupied Galicia, along the front and in Russian newspapers, triumphal notices were immediately posted. These emphasized the significance of the victory by detailing the huge number of prisoners: 9 Habsburg generals, 2,500 officers, and 117,000 other ranks had all fallen into Russian hands. St. Petersburg's leading conservative daily, *Novoe Vremya* (The New Times), excitedly speculated that Przemyśl's surrender could hasten the end of the war. The Fortress's fall, it wrote, was decisive for "the fate of the whole Habsburg Empire."[2]

In Austria-Hungary, the first announcements of the disaster were published early that evening. By the following morning, March 23, Przemyśl was on every front page. The official narrative circulated by the Habsburg army was that the Fortress had fallen with honor: "The defense of Przemyśl will forever remain an illustrious and glorious chapter in the history of our army." The garrison had been heroic to the end, even daring to launch a final attack in order to break the enemy's encirclement. Its prolonged resistance "to the outer limit of human endurance" had inflicted immense losses on the Russians. Starvation, not storm, had finally forced the end. The heroes remained undefeated. Everything of military value—"forts, bridges, weapons, ammunition, and war materiel of all kinds"—had been destroyed. The enemy had captured only ruins. The loss of the Fortress, the official pronouncements were at particular pains to emphasize, would have no impact on the wider prosecution of the war.[3]

Newspaper editorials loyally followed the official line. Vienna's upper classes, sitting down to breakfast over their copies of the *Neue Freie Presse* (New Free Press)—the daily morning read for the metropolitan elite—had nearly six full pages on the Fortress to digest. Readers were reminded of glorious October, when Przemyśl's garrison had bravely withstood the Russian storm. "Przemyśl annihilated a Russian army," asserted the paper's war correspondent inaccurately but grandly.

Serendipitously, however, the *Neue Freie Presse* could report that Przemyśl had been neither as strong nor as essential as people had believed. Doubtless, many of its readers were among those harboring such mistaken ideas, for embarrassingly, just two days earlier the *Neue Freie Presse* itself had carried an article irrefutably proving Przemyśl's "unbroken strength" and crucial role in pinning down Russian troops. The paper now revealed that the Fortress had been armed with antique ordnance, the destruction of which was unimportant. Its military value had sunk further during the long siege. Of course, the loss of the heroic garrison was greatly regretted. Strangely, though, nowhere in the lengthy reportage devoted to the Fortress did the editor note how many Habsburg soldiers had been consigned to captivity. Instead, ranks of retired generals were wheeled out to reassure the public that Przemyśl's capitulation was of no consequence. The fall of the Fortress was entirely predictable. Doubtless the High Command had made careful preparations. The army, not the Fortress, was the empire's principal defender, and inspired by the garrison's courageous example it would steadfastly bar the Russians' way and hold them in the Carpathian Mountains.[4]

Of course, no one believed any of it. In eastern Galicia, Jews wept openly. Deep despair gripped the provincial capital, Lwów, which occupiers were busily transforming into a Russian city. Defiant Przemyśl had been a rare beacon of hope for those who longed for liberation. Its fall triggered nervous breakdowns, even suicides. Farther west, in Cracow—Galicia's other great fortress-city, which was still in Habsburg hands and blocked the way into inner Austria—there was panic. A Russian siege threatened. An evacuation, the third which its citizens had endured, was prepared. Frustration and anger toward Habsburg military commanders boiled. "The arrogance and conceit, contempt for societal forms, disregard for the civilian population etc. which characterizes higher commanders—all this was, in a way, punished at Przemyśl," reflected one shrewd diarist in Cracow, the historian Klemens Bąkowski. He feared that "Ruthenian or Polish treason" would, as usual, be scapegoated for the defeat. The army's claim that it would have no effect on the wider war was absurd. Quite apart from the obviously huge loss of men and guns through capitulation, Bąkowski rightly worried that the 100,000 men of the Russian blockade army, released from the siege, were already now preparing to march against Hungary, or to Cracow.[5]

The mood was scarcely better in the heart of the empire. A deep depression hung over Vienna. Confidence in the Army Command was again severely shaken. People wondered aloud how the Fortress could have been left so inadequately provisioned. Rumors of Kusmanek's sloth and incompetence would persist throughout the war. The army's propaganda portraying the capitulation as honorable and heroic also badly backfired. In particular, the story of the garrison's breakout operation on March 19 did not, as Conrad and Kusmanek had hoped and expected, inspire. Instead, the public reacted with horror that starving men had been put through the vain ordeal. When casualty figures for the operation were misunderstood and word circulated that 10,000 had been killed, an outcry threatened.

Within a week, the army had to release the Russians' prisoner totals. That 117,000 soldiers had been captured, its press bureau explained, proved that most of the losses of the breakout attempt were not dead. Soothing relatives, but with damning implications for the judgment of the commanders who had ordered the assault, the bureau argued that most casualties were men who had dropped from exhaustion and been left behind when the assault force withdrew, falling alive into enemy hands.[6]

The failure of the Habsburg authorities to construct a more compelling narrative around the Fortress's fall was in part a reflection of their—and especially the army's—distance from public opinion. State propaganda would prove ineffectual throughout the war. However, a more fundamental reason was that the capitulation was a genuine disaster. To be sure, the Russian blockade army's third-line troops released from the siege were themselves unlikely to make any decisive impact on the front. Much of Przemyśl's equipment had indeed been obsolete, and its garrison old. Yet the Habsburg army could ill-afford such a large net shift in strength on the eastern front, especially after the severe losses sustained in the Carpathians trying to relieve the Fortress. In April 1915 the army's strength, at just 892,693 soldiers, was little more than half what it had been upon mobilization in August 1914. To sustain the war effort, even older men now had to be drafted. New legislation, passed on May 1, raised the upper limit of military eligibility from forty-two to fifty years of age.[7]

Even worse than the military consequences was the blow the Fortress's fall inflicted on Habsburg prestige. This was immense. The surrender was a painfully public demonstration to the world of Austria-Hungary's weakness. Predators circled. Italy had vast ambition to take any Habsburg territory in which there lived, no matter as how tiny a minority, Italian-speakers. A month after Przemyśl's surrender, its government signed a secret pact with the Entente, the Treaty of London, promising to join the war within a month in return for lands stretching through southern Austria deep into modern-day Croatia and Slovenia. On May 23 Italy declared hostilities against its erstwhile ally, opening a new southern front by deploying its 750,000-strong army against the already hard-pressed Habsburg Empire. At home, too, the humiliation was felt deeply. Przemyśl had become a symbol of the empire's heroism and strength. Throughout the 181-day siege, newspapers had constantly reminded readers of the fortress garrison's courage and resilience. Emperor Franz Joseph himself, a man who in his sixty-six-year reign had faced many disasters, understood this defeat as different and ruinous. For two full days after the Fortress's fall he wept inconsolably.[8]

IN PRZEMYŚL, THE defeated garrison was not permitted to linger long. The fortress commander, General Kusmanek, who had the dubious distinction of being the highest-ranking Habsburg officer captured by the Russian army during the First World War, was whisked away immediately. He arrived in Kiev on March 26. To forestall any rebelliousness, the Russian conquerors also quickly separated regimental officers from their men. On the day of the capitulation, several hundred officers were sent to railheads for transfer to camps. Feeding so many prisoners posed huge difficulties, and so the Russians hurried with the evacuation. Nearly all the remaining officers and over half the garrison, 68,438 soldiers in total, departed in the second week of the occupation. The rest of the prisoners followed throughout April. Last to leave were the seriously ill and wounded lying in Przemyśl's hospitals. In May, however, accompanied by a few Habsburg medical personnel, they, too, were transported away, to be swallowed up by the vast empire to the east.[9]

Captivity was less difficult for fortress officers than it was for soldiers, because the Russians granted them special privileges. Generals were permitted to bring 114 kilograms of baggage with them, staff officers were allowed 82 kilograms, and all the other officers 49 kilograms (250, 180, and 108 pounds, respectively). Carts were provided to carry the officers to the railheads at Jarosław, Lwów, or, just south of Przemyśl, Niżankowice, whereas the men of the other ranks had to march. Certainly, the officers felt the humiliation, confusion, and anxiety of being taken prisoner as much as the other men. Nonetheless, it was a relief to have survived the siege. Grief at separation from their soldiers was not especially noticeable. In some units, the inequality of suffering during the siege, along with the harsh discipline and the ethnic persecutions, had fueled a fierce and festering loathing in the ranks for their superiors. "The mood of our soldiers, especially among the Ruthenes, is openly revolutionary," observed one Polish lance corporal three days after the surrender. "You can feel in their every action hatred toward the officers."[10]

The Fortress Command staff and nearly all the generals from Przemyśl were incarcerated in European Russia. Kusmanek spent nearly three years in Nizhny Novgorod, 400 kilometers (250 miles) east of Moscow and 1,700 kilometers (over 1,000 miles) from Przemyśl. Most regimental officers were held many thousands of kilometers farther away in Siberia and the Far East. They were subjected to some petty abuses. The Russians soon regretted their chivalry in permitting Przemyśl's officers to keep their swords, and on April 14 withdrew the privilege. This was presented as a reprisal for Habsburg troops on the Carpathian front supposedly cutting out the tongue of a captured Russian telephonist after he refused to speak under interrogation. Of greater significance was the confiscation of officers' money. In besieged Przemyśl, many had gathered substantial savings. Lieutenant Stanisław Gayczak, for example, brought nearly 6,000 crowns with him into captivity. Coveting the cash, and fearing that it could be used to escape, during the summer of 1915 Tsarist military authorities ordered its surrender.[11]

Even so, an officer's existence in captivity, although psychologically straining, was generally not physically arduous. The Hague Convention of 1907, the international treaty governing the laws and customs of war on land, to which both Russia and Austria-Hungary were signatories, dictated that officers could not be forced to work and guaranteed them a regular salary. Generals received 125 rubles per month. Regimental officers were paid an entirely adequate 50 rubles. Especially in 1915 and 1916, living conditions were fairly comfortable. Some officers were permitted to live in houses. In the prisoner-of-war camps, they could afford extra furnishings and had soldier-servants. Sports and educational activities were organized. The Berezovka camp in Siberia became famous for its "extraordinarily rich" library, which was well stocked thanks to "officers from Przemyśl who brought with them a major part of the Fortress's library." Not only post but also telegraphic services were accessible. For Gayczak, this easily compensated for all the other hardship. At long last, after eight months of aching worry, he was able to contact his family in Russian-occupied Lwów. On April 19, 1915, he received a five-word telegram from his wife that left him euphoric with relief: "Everyone alive and healthy, Lucy."[12]

The fate of Przemyśl's other ranks was far grimmer. For them the war was by no means over. The Russian army took 2.1 million Habsburg prisoners during the First World War. Horrifyingly, one in every five—around 470,000 men—died during their captivity. At the start of their imprisonment, the Fortress's starved soldiers were already in far worse physical condition than its officers. Standing by Przemyśl's Grand Café Stieber, a special correspondent for the *London Times*, Stanley Washburn, witnessed the sorry departure of these "warn and ragged ranks." "Their faces were pinched and drawn," he observed, "and many of them tottered under their loads as they marched out of the town." One man, whom Washburn thought looked about sixty, but knew could not be more than forty-five, stumbled. "He tried to get up, but collapsed, and, placing his head on his arms, he lay prone in the mud and filth of the street and from sheer misery and weakness cried like a baby. Two of his companions lifted him up, but his knees hung limp beneath him and he could not stand. They put him in a cart and took him away."[13]

The Russian army was merciless in its treatment of these exhausted men. Jan Lenar, a peasant from the village of Handzlówka about 50 kilometers (30 miles) northwest of Przemyśl, who served in

Landsturm Infantry Regiment 17, recorded the abuses. He noticed that Hungarians, whom the Russians feared, were handled especially badly by their captors: "whipped and thrown to the ground for the least offense." Russian guards led Lenar's regiment to Radymno, north of where the Fortress's outer perimeter had run. The men were left in the open overnight, but the next morning were at least fed. The conquerors were clearly struggling with supply, for food was scant over the following days, and Lenar and his comrades became extremely hungry. In an odd way, this may have been of some benefit to them. South of Przemyśl, prisoners were immediately fed better, but the rich food upset their stomachs, which had been inured by months of siege to starvation rations. The new diet brought an outbreak of mass vomiting. To keep them meek, the Russians told the Galician soldiers that they would soon be allowed to return home. "That was how they seduced us," reflected Lenar grimly.[14]

After a few days, the men of Landsturm Regiment 17 were split into groups of 100 and set marching in snow and rain north to Jarosław. Lenar saw how Habsburg double-headed eagles had been ripped down from official buildings and replaced by Russian inscriptions. He was shocked at the devastation of the land: "The destroyed villages and hamlets seemed to scream to heaven for revenge." The prisoners were forced to walk without food; at night they were packed "like herring" into barracks. The coughing of sick comrades kept everyone awake. When the prisoners reached the town of Przeworsk, locals urged them to escape. Lenar knew he was just 25 kilometers (15 miles) from his home village, and when the guards went to their own night quarters he fled. He had acquaintances in the area, and so was able to borrow civilian clothes. On the road, he met many men he knew who had also absconded from prisoner columns and dumped their uniforms to sneak home. Lenar made it back to Handzlówka and lay low for the rest of the occupation. When, a couple of months later, the region was liberated by the German army, he was deeply impressed. Unlike the enemy and the Habsburg army, these troops were polite and paid for everything.

"They behaved extremely progressively, displaying their civilization in every regard in a model fashion."[15]

For less fortunate men, a hell awaited. The prisoners were driven by knout-wielding Cossacks "like cattle" on long marches to rail stations. Most entrained at Lwów or, another 90 kilometers (around 56 miles) to the northeast, at the Galician frontier town of Brody. Nearly all passed through the Tsarist army's large transit camp at Kiev, 600 kilometers (370 miles) from Przemyśl. Here, prisoners' names, ranks, and regiments were recorded. Above all, the Russian army was avidly interested in prisoners' ethnicity. Its officers' racialized thinking had already been evident in Przemyśl. There, first the Hungarian regiments were sent away—for the Russians regarded them as the most dangerous—then the Austrian Germans. Slavic units, whom the conqueror hoped were less hostile, were dispatched last. In Kiev, a more thorough sorting took place. Magyars, Germans, and Jews were separated to be cast into the harshest camps. Serbs and Romanians in Honvéd uniforms were sought out and earmarked for privileged treatment as "friendly" peoples. Hundreds of Przemyśl prisoners were transported to Russia's capital, St. Petersburg, where they were paraded humiliatingly before the public along the main thoroughfare, the Nevsky Prospekt. Then they, too, were made invisible.[16]

Most of the Przemyśl prisoners were incarcerated deep in Asian Russia, in the region of Turkestan (in today's Kazakhstan and Uzbekistan). The rail journey lasted two to four weeks. Cattle wagons, those functional items of the nineteenth-century industrial revolution that, in the dehumanizing twentieth, became icons of ethnic cleansing and genocide, were provided for transport. Cold, dark, overcrowded, and stinking, they were breeding grounds for disease-carrying parasites. The wagons rolled slowly. Food was distributed only irregularly and could be barely edible. When the weak men eventually disembarked, they found themselves in a strange climate. Turkestan was a place of extremes. In the winter, it could feel like the arctic. In summer, temperatures soared up to 45°C (113°F).

Its unsanitary camps were overseen by brutal guards, and epidemics raged through them in 1915. Everybody contracted malaria. Dysentery, cholera, and typhus killed thousands.[17]

The Russian hell had many circles. There were prisoners who spent years in Turkestan. Others were moved around the Tsar's empire. Sometimes Slavic prisoners—although not Poles, who were distrusted by the Russians—were set above their fellows and given privileged conditions; they themselves then became instruments of suffering. Many prisoners volunteered to work as a means of escaping the camps and earning money so they could supplement their meager rations. They might end up felling trees or plowing the fields on big landed estates. Those most fortunate were handed over to small peasant farmers who would treat them as one of the family. In contrast, labor in the mines of southern Russia could be lethal. Whether benevolent or brutal, however, employers had total power over their prisoners. For sure, they had duties of care, but often there were no checks to ensure these were observed. Instead, official regulations emphasized that "it is the duty of all prisoners to carry out all work to which they are commanded, no matter how heavy. If one refuses, he is to be . . . treated as a convict, and this punishment shall . . . last the entire period of his captivity."[18]

The deepest circle was the Tsar's own Death Railway to Murmansk. This place of suffering was reserved largely for Hungarians and Germans. The line was urgently needed to transport war materials left by British ships at the northern port to the Russian armies at the front. Over 50,000 prisoners worked here until 1917 in conditions that in their hardship equaled, and even exceeded, those of the later Soviet Gulags. One Przemyśl prisoner who labored there described his comrades' dread as they surveyed "the eerie white plains" of Archangel. For accommodation, primitive huts with bare boards to sleep on had been sloppily erected. There were not enough of them, so many prisoners slept in burrows dug into the earth. Each day of forced labor lasted eighteen hours. The digging in the frozen soil was "inhumanely hard." Clad in worn-out uniforms and shod in broken boots wrapped in rags, in a pathetic attempt to keep out the cold, the frail men could not withstand it. Frostbite cases were evacuated in a constant flow. Men died in droves. Anyone perceived not to be working hard enough was whipped or beaten bloody. Anyone judged to be simulating sickness was denied food. Despair ruled in the icy wilderness.[19]

The Bolshevik Revolution in the autumn of 1917 at last brought release. In March 1918, Austria-Hungary, Germany, and the Bolsheviks signed the Treaty of Brest-Litovsk, ending the war in the east and paving the way for the prisoners' homecoming. Many men did not wait for officially organized transportation. Instead, they struck out by themselves. Around 700,000 prisoners, among them some soldiers who had fought at Przemyśl, returned before November 1918, in time to see the Habsburg Empire also collapse. Many other hundreds of thousands were delayed in Russia by the revolutionary chaos and the outbreak of civil war. Only in 1921 did the last prisoners reach home. The empire was gone. The world had changed. The survivors were altered as well. The fighting, the long separation, and the incarceration, first in a besieged city and then in a prison state, had all left their mark. One son, twelve years old at the time, remembered the return of a father he barely knew, a gunner in the Fortress's artillery: "He came in the door buckled like a centenarian." In not every case was trauma so visible. Yet the mental scars always ran deep.[20]

THE CITY OF Przemyśl's occupation proved far shorter than anyone—especially the Russians—expected, but it was also radical and extraordinarily brutal. Like Lwów, Przemyśl was, in the conquerors' eyes, a "Russian city liberated again after long centuries of slavery." Without any formal declaration of annexation, they immediately busied themselves incorporating it into their empire. Przemyśl was designated the capital of a new Russian governorate and an acting governor was appointed, the experienced administrator

Sergei Dmitriyevich Yevreinov. Within the city and its environs, the Russian army retained real power. Although the defenses had been destroyed, a "fortress" commander was the absolute authority. Three generals held this post in quick succession. Below them, the city council continued in operation. At first, this was led by a Pole, but on April 19 he was summarily dismissed. Signaling ominously their determination to shift power permanently between Przemyśl's ethnicities, the Russians chose an extremist Galician Russophile, Dr. Maryan Glushkievich, to serve as mayor of the city.[21]

The Russians quickly asserted an iron grip over Przemyśl. The new fortress commander, General Leonid Artamonov, warned the population on March 24 that he expected absolute obedience. Should his orders not be followed—or, worse, if there was active resistance—the consequences would be severe: "the siege artillery will open up on Przemyśl at a prearranged signal from me and will shoot the city into ruins." This was no idle threat. The Russian army had used exactly this punishment against the town of Neidenburg during its invasion of the German province of East Prussia seven months earlier, a campaign in which Artamonov had served. To show he was serious, the fortress commander executed sixteen soldiers, Habsburg and Russian, who had been caught plundering on the first day of the occupation. An 8:00 p.m. curfew was enforced. Intimidating Cossacks on horses joined local police on patrols. The prompt delivery of food also helped to quell unrest among the starving populace quickly. With order restored, the occupiers could get on with transforming Przemyśl into a "Russian" city. The ruble was introduced. Clocks were put forward an hour. Citizens now lived on St. Petersburg time.[22]

The Russian occupiers at first acted with caution. The Tsarist governor general of Galicia, Count Bobrinskii, had promised religious toleration, and Artamonov echoed it. Schools were permitted to reopen, and the population was promised protection. Nevertheless, Przemyśl's citizens quickly felt the military authorities' arbitrary hand. The Russian army suspected, with good reason, that some of

Kusmanek's troops had evaded capture and were living as civilians. The first surprise house searches were launched on April 7, and 600 men were arrested. Thereafter, the sound of military police furiously hammering at doors in the small hours was an ever-present dread. Ultimately over 4,000 men, many of whom had never held a gun, were deported into Russia. The other ubiquitous peril for male residents was impressment into work parties. When labor for road repair or other menial jobs was needed, Tsarist soldiers simply pulled men and boys off the streets. Children as young as eight years old were handed shovels and forced to work under overseers brandishing whips.[23]

Jews suffered especially badly. Despite assurances of religious toleration, the Russians' rabid anti-Semitism was manifest everywhere. Their discrimination was, and was intended to be, deeply divisive within the city. At the outset of the occupation, only Christian traders, not Jews, were granted permission to travel to Lwów to fetch stock. In early April the Russians were "joking"—as the diarist Helena Jabłońska overheard—that "they'll let [the Jews] eat up their matzahs in peace, and after Easter they'll take them and send them to Siberia." In fact, Jews never were left in peace. Przemyśl's chief of police, Eugen Wierzbowski, collaborated with the occupiers to make life hellish for the Jews of the city, above all for those who were members of the upper classes. He recommended their homes as billets for officers and singled them out for compulsory street-sweeping, bridge-building, or fortification work. The Sabbath became a special day of humiliation. Every Saturday, a day of rest and worship for Jews, Cossacks lay in wait for synagogue-goers wearing their best clothes and forced them to do the filthy job of carting the town's waste away. No horses were provided, and so the Christian populace was treated to the sight of finely dressed Jews straining to move heavy rubbish carts.[24]

On Friday, April 23, Tsar Nikolai II visited Przemyśl. The occupation authorities made frenetic efforts to present him with a "Russian" city. The Greek Catholic bishop, Father Konstantyn Czechowicz, was pressured to hold a celebratory joint service with a Russian Orthodox cleric in the city marketplace. The theater of two clergymen of rival eastern rite churches uniting before the Tsar and an assembled public in the heart of the city would have possessed a powerful symbolism. Residents living along the procession route were ordered to collect Russian red, blue, and white flags from the town hall and hang them outside their homes. No fewer than three triumphal arches were set up. However, the authorities distrusted the populace. Strict orders were issued that all windows facing onto the route must remain shut, with blinds down. The lines of soldiers arrayed on both sides of the road served as a security force as well as a guard of honor. Nevertheless, the organizers needed some local participation. To gather a submissive crowd, instructions were circulated to Przemyśl's schools. Teachers and schoolchildren were commanded to welcome their new ruler.[25]

The reception was a big disappointment. Bishop Czechowicz denied the Tsar his propaganda coup and rejected the Russians' demands. Rather than the public joint celebration he desired, or even an Orthodox Mass in Przemyśl's Greek Catholic cathedral, Nikolai II had to make do with a service in a temporary chapel set up in a warehouse. Few members of the public turned out, and the enthusiasm of those who did was doubtless dampened by being corralled all afternoon. Only at 7:30 p.m. did the Tsar arrive, with Grand Duke Nikolai at his side. His car swept past his soldiers and intended subjects, smothering them in a cloud of dust. To be sure, the welcome at the Fortress Command pleased the visitors. The new Russophile mayor, Glushkievich, gave a speech expressing fervent loyalty to the Tsar and to Russia. A bunch of overawed peasants from the surrounding villages were then pushed forward to present him with bread and salt, the traditional Slavic greeting to guests. Even so, Nikolai II must have been glad to get away the following morning to tour the city's ruined fortifications. His uncle was simply relieved that no one had tried to assassinate him. Neither would ever again return to Przemyśl.[26]

Following the Tsar's visit, the authorities pursued a radical form of Russification in Przemyśl. Nikolai II devotedly believed, as he announced in a speech in Lwów that same month, that "there is no Galicia, rather a Great Russia to the Carpathians." Possibly he impressed this on Russian officers at Przemyśl during his brief stay; or perhaps embarrassment at the way his reception had betrayed the assertion's patent falsity moved them to action. Either way, it was at this time, in the second half of April, that they stepped up the Russification program. Schooling had already been targeted. Ukrainian was to be replaced by Russian-language education. Polish schools were permitted to reopen only if they gave five hours of Russian-language instruction weekly and taught heavily politicized history and geography from Polish-language textbooks produced in Russia. The schools had resisted these demands. The city's prestigious Polish secondary school, for example, refused the conditions and stayed shut. In the women's teacher training college, the arrival of a Russian-language teacher provoked a mass walkout by the students. The Russians' conduct then became more vicious. They began to eliminate their enemies.[27]

The Greek Catholic bishop, Czechowicz, was a particular thorn in the occupiers' side. He had refused to surrender any of his churches to Orthodoxy. Humiliatingly for conquerors determined to spread the Tsar's true faith, Orthodox services had been banished to the ticket hall of the disused main rail station. There are clear signs that in the aftermath of the imperial visit, Czechowicz was marked for deportation. Most menacingly, a military guard was posted in his palace and stood permanently outside the door of his bedroom. Days before the Tsar's arrival, the military had already arrested all Przemyśl's Polish political elite, including Włodzimierz Błażowski, the dismissed Polish mayor, and the president of the district court, Władysław Grzędzielski. Błażowski had been immediately deported to Russia. Czechowicz only avoided the same fate because he died. On April 24, the day after the Tsar's visit, under intense stress, he suffered a stroke, and he passed away four days later. Of course, for

Poster, written in Russian, Polish, and Yiddish, issued by the Tsarist Military Occupation Authorities, expelling all Jews from the city and district of Przemyśl at the end of April 1915.

the residents this appeared far too convenient for the Russians to be a coincidence. Popular rumor circulated that the Russians had driven the bishop to suicide.[28]

A solution was also found for Przemyśl's Jews. On April 28, a large poster appeared around the city. Written in three languages, Russian, Polish, and Yiddish, and signed by the local district commander, Guard Colonel Kiriakov, it ordered them to get out. The Russian occupiers, like the Nazis with their ghetto "Jewish Councils" a quarter-century later, calculated that forcibly co-opting local Jewish leadership was the most effective means of achieving their designs. Therefore, to lead the exodus, a so-called Jewish Executive Committee had been named by Kiriakov, headed by the respected rabbi Gedalyah Schmelkes. The Russian army would provide empty wagons, but Schmelkes and his committee were handed responsibility for ensuring that every Jew left Przemyśl. The penalty for not leaving "voluntarily," as Kiriakov disingenuously put it, would be bloody. "If Jews . . . do not fulfill the orders of the committee," he threatened, "I shall be forced to resort to the most energetic measures: a regiment of Cossacks will carry out the evacuation in the course of a few hours. The disobedient will have only themselves to blame."[29]

Wider Tsarist ethnic cleansing formed the backdrop to this action. The Russian army deported hundreds of thousands of people from the empire's own western borderlands during the autumn and winter of 1914, and in January 1915 it began uprooting Jewish communities in Galicia. Nonetheless, the expulsion of Jews from Przemyśl was distinctive. It was the largest single forced removal of a community perpetrated by the Russian military on occupied soil. Austrian authorities later estimated that over just ten days nearly 17,000 Jews were made to leave the city and surrounding district. By May 8, there was not a Jew to be seen in Przemyśl. Most of the refugees, desperate and impoverished, ended up in Lwów, where their arrival triggered a mini-humanitarian crisis.[30]

The Russian army's precise motives for ordering the expulsion of Jews from Przemyśl were, and remain, opaque. However, the timing is telling. Coming so soon after the Tsar's visit, and concurrent with the planned deportation of the city's Greek Catholic bishop and the arrest of its Polish political elite, the expulsion should be seen as the most extreme act of a radicalized and violent Russification. The army was turning Przemyśl politically and ethnically into a "Russian" city: a step toward the realization of the Tsar's imagined "Great Russia to the Carpathians." Greed was an additional reason. Through the expulsion, Russian officers were able to plunder the apartments of wealthy Jews unimpeded. They stole huge quantities of furniture and some 300 pianos. Happily, there was no conflict between ideology and the base desire to loot. Quite to the contrary, the Russians won support for their regime by permitting Poles and Ruthenes a share of the spoils. Despairing Jews unable to take all their possessions with them were fleeced by their Christian neighbors, who offered derisory prices before their departure. Afterward, those same people stole anything left behind. The Russian occupation authority was only too willing to transfer ownership of Jews' homes to their Christian cooks and caretakers.[31]

Of course, as elsewhere in Galicia, the occupiers tried to justify the expulsion on security grounds. The Jews themselves were told, as one expellee remembered, "the reason was that Przemyśl was a fortified city, and Jews were forbidden to enter any fortified city." Yet this excuse was hardly credible. Przemyśl was denuded of its fortifications. It was also now far from any fighting. At the end of April 1915, the city was 80 kilometers (50 miles) behind the stable Carpathian front and around 120 kilometers (75 miles) from the opposing lines in western Galicia. For the first time in months, no gunfire could be heard. Nevertheless, cynically or gullibly, the Russians spread fantastical rumors about Jews' perfidy. This people were spies and traitors. They had a secret underground telephone line between Lwów and Przemyśl. The intelligence they gathered, so Tsarist officers claimed, was delivered to Cracow by pigeons.[32]

Ironically, even as the Russians tightened their grip on Przemyśl, their hold on Galicia was slipping. On the morning of May 2, the

German Eleventh Army, supported by the Habsburg Fourth and Third Armies, attacked on a 50-kilometer (30-mile) front between the western Galician towns of Gorlice and Tarnów. Russian intelligence had noticed the German deployment, but Stavka was complacent and the army commander in charge of the sector, General Radko Dimitriev, was told not to worry. When the assault came, however, it was like nothing yet seen on the eastern front. Overall, the forces were evenly matched, but on the decisive sector the Germans concentrated 107,000 soldiers, more than twice the number of defenders, and more than 500 guns, against the defenders' 145. Most important was the sophistication of the operation. A whirlwind bombardment by modern artillery, which had been carefully targeted and organized for mobility, blew Dimitriev's troops from their shallow front line, and the German infantry pushed them out into open country. In just a week, the Russian Third Army lost 200 guns and 210,000 men, 140,000 of whom were prisoners. The survivors were forced into a headlong rout east toward the San.[33]

Signs of the Russians' disaster were soon apparent in Przemyśl. As early as May 5, the rumble of artillery could again be heard. A week later, everyone knew the Tsarist army was in general retreat. The German advance cut behind the Russian armies in the Carpathians, making their position untenable, and so they too withdrew. Helena Jabłońska, watching the mass of imperial soldiers retreating through the city on May 14, commented that "yesterday we thought that there must be a million filing past, and today one can say there must be half of Russia and half of Asia." At this time, too, German aircraft appeared over Przemyśl. They dropped cards promising no ill will against inhabitants; but they also dropped bombs, which exploded in populated areas. One landed in the marketplace, killing five. Others fell on the garrison hospital, the rail station, and the barracks, inflicting many military and civilian casualties. The Germans had more aircraft than the Russians did, and their bombs were far more powerful than anything the Russians had dropped on the city earlier in the year. The bombing ignited fires and panic.

Przemyśl's occupiers had great trouble extinguishing either one, as by now they had arrested and deported the municipal police and the fire brigade.[34]

As the German army neared, terror spread. Tsarist commanders were divided about whether Przemyśl could be held. Confusion reigned. Glushkievich, the Russophile mayor, became hysterical and fled to Kiev on May 12, taking with him what was left of the municipal funds. Preparations were made to evacuate the garrison. On the 18th, to prevent them from being conscripted into the Habsburg army if Przemyśl were lost, local boys and men from the age of twelve upward were seized and set marching east. Tsarist officers told bloodcurdling stories of German savagery. "The Hungarians are supposed to be lambs compared with the Prussians," they fretted. Driven by fear, the Russians lashed out. The Jews had left the city, so they could not be scapegoated for the debacle. Instead, suspicion embraced the remaining residents. The order was issued "to clean the city of harmful elements." Houses and even the cemetery were obsessively searched for secret telephone lines. Arrests and deportations multiplied. There were also at this time many executions for spying and sabotage. On one day alone, May 17, Tsarist troops summarily shot thirty-two citizens for disobeying published orders.[35]

After much vacillation, Grand Duke Nikolai ordered Przemyśl to be held at all costs. At Habsburg High Command, Conrad was no less determined that the city should be taken, and desperate that the conquest and glory should go to his army. The Habsburg Third Army was advancing south of the Germans. It had made haste and on May 15 already stood on the Pod Mazurami heights southwest of the old fortress perimeter. The following day, the X Corps, which had been based in Przemyśl before the First World War, launched an assault against Russian defenses around Fort VII, "Prałkowce." This was repulsed. The Austrians then waited for their heavy artillery. Once this arrived on the 28th, Conrad, wanting to beat the Germans as much as the Russians, pushed urgently for another attack. The X Corps went forward again against Prałkowce on the evening of the 30th, earlier than its commander liked. The price of attacking without adequate preparation was, as Conrad never learned, failure. The soldiers of the Galician infantry captured the Russians' positions, but were forced out the following morning by a furious bombardment and counterattacks.[36]

In the end, it was the Germans who conquered Przemyśl. An unnatural thunder announced their coming. To the north of the city on May 29, they positioned 42 cm "Big Bertha" howitzers, a superweapon larger than anything possessed by either ally or enemy. Residents compared the shells fired by these monstrosities to "goods trains": they seemed to hang in the air before hurtling downward and detonating with devastating force. All the qualities that made the German army so formidable were on display in this final assault. The Eleventh Army had carefully planned its operation. Unlike the Austrians, when the Germans deemed their bombardment unsatisfactory, they extended it for twenty-four hours. Then, on June 1, their well-trained infantry stormed the fortress perimeter between Forts X, "Orzechowce," and XI, "Duńkowiczki." The Russians did not stand a chance. By the evening of the 2nd, they were retreating, burning the temporary bridges they had built over the San. German troops reached the city center in the early hours of the 3rd. General August von Mackensen, the army commander, mockingly laid Przemyśl "at the feet" of the Habsburg Emperor. To mark their victory, disciplined ranks of German soldiers, looking for all the world like Nietzschean supermen, goose-stepped past city hall to public acclaim. A new power was rising in the east. Przemyśl would, for the remainder of the war, lie under Habsburg rule before passing, on the empire's collapse in 1918, to a new, independent Polish Republic.[37]

THE GERMANS WOULD return to Przemyśl. On September 7, 1939, German bombers attacked the city. They missed the rail station and bridges, but they hit a school and a gymnastics club, killing eight people. A follow-up raid destroyed the Hotel Royal and, on its ground floor, that relic of Habsburg civility, Grand Café Stieber. Worse was to follow. Within days, the German army was motoring toward the city. Despite resistance from the Poles, by the afternoon of September 14 the whole northern suburb of Zasanie was in German hands. The Polish army blew the 3rd May Bridge over the San that night, creating a scene almost identical to that of 1915, and then retreated east. The victorious Wehrmacht took possession of the old town on the morning of the 15th. Behind it came a so-called operational group (*Einsatzgruppe*)—a unit of security police and the feared Nazi secret state police, the Gestapo. The Nazi and Soviet governments had sealed a nonaggression pact a month earlier and had agreed to partition Poland. This special unit's mission was to drive as many Jews as possible from German-occupied territory through terror. From September 16 to 19—less than three weeks into the Second World War—targeting the elite especially, it murdered between 500 and 600 Jewish men in and around Przemyśl.[38]

The hatred and violence unleashed in East-Central Europe by the First World War simmered and spat for decades before exploding in a crescendo of unimaginably vicious bloodshed. Przemyśl, like everywhere in the region, was cast under the shadow. The siege of 1914–1915, with its danger, starvation, and divisive imperial repressions, inflamed antagonisms that only sharpened further with time. Though the city never again stood in the front line during World War I, hunger and death stalked the later war years too. Polish nationalism flared. Ominously, for they also claimed Przemyśl, the desire for nationhood grew as well among the Ukrainians (as Ruthenes now universally became known). When, in the autumn of 1918, the Habsburg Empire disintegrated and the war's Western victors—and above all, US President Woodrow Wilson—promised "self-determination" for the peoples of East-Central Europe, Przemyśl's community turned on itself. A Ukrainian coup to seize the city was launched on the night of November 3–4, 1918. Poles resisted. There were scores of casualties. Five civilians died. When the Ukrainian insurrectionaries were chased out of town on the 11th and

12th, the victors celebrated with a pogrom, one of many in Poland at this time. Jewish shops were plundered. Their owners were beaten. One Jew, an old man named Abraham Rotter, was killed.[39]

Przemyśl never regained the civility that had been shattered by war in 1914. To be sure, ethnic tensions had predated the conflict, but life had now been cheapened, and the stakes were higher in a world of nation-states. Jews and Ukrainians were no longer subjects of a multinational empire, but instead the distrusted and disadvantaged minorities of a state built for Catholic Poles. To win eastern Galicia, Poland immediately fought a nasty war with the fledgling West Ukrainian Republic. Final victory in July 1919 and recognition of its claim in 1923 at the League of Nations cemented its grip on the region, which it pointedly renamed "Eastern Little Poland" (*Małopolska Wschodnia*). Ukrainian radicals never accepted this result. The Polish government's broken promises of autonomy, and its assimilationist policies, which were far harsher than any that had existed before 1914, pushed others into their arms. Terrorism began to take root. Around Przemyśl in the early 1920s, there were attempts to blow up trains and attacks on Polish soldiers stationed in the remnants of the old Habsburg forts. The extremists sought not only to contest Polish rule but also to make Polish-Ukrainian coexistence impossible. Prominent Ukrainians cooperating with Poles in any way were assassinated. In Przemyśl, the most tragic victim was the revered educator Sofron Matwijas, director of the Ukrainian Women's Teacher Training College, who was murdered on September 1, 1924.[40]

On the face of it, after the two-day pogrom of November 1918 Przemyśl's Jews did rather better. Jews continued to be represented on the city council, and in the municipal elections of 1928 a pro-government "Block of Three Nationalities" (*Blok Trzech Narodowości*) preaching interethnic harmony won every seat. However, this apparent victory for toleration only veiled underlying anti-Semitism. Anger against the minority had first surged during the siege of 1914–1915, fueled by accusations of food speculation. War in

1920 with the Soviet Union—which Polish nationalists caricatured as a "Judeo-Bolshevik" state—escalated hostility. The difficult economic conditions throughout the interwar period also exacerbated jealousy against Jews who—though many were poor—continued to dominate Przemyśl's commerce and professions. Through the democratic early 1920s and in the second half of the oppressive 1930s, public boycotts of Jewish businesses were repeatedly and widely promoted in the city. A week-long campaign at Christmas 1937 was run under the menacing slogan "Przemyśl without the Jews."[41]

To any middle-aged citizen of Przemyśl, the outbreak of the Second World War on September 1, 1939, and the subsequent invasion and occupation must have seemed wearily familiar. The panic as the enemy approached, the hordes of frightened refugees, and, once the Germans arrived, the immediate appearance of posters in several languages taking away freedoms, setting out arduous regulations, and warning citizens to obey the occupiers on pain of death were little different from those they had seen a quarter-century earlier. The two totalitarian regimes that partitioned Poland in September 1939 did not, for all their revolutionary credentials, stand outside history. The frontier they drew ran roughly down the old blurred fault line between Western and Eastern Christendom, or between the Poles on one side and, on the other, Ukrainians and Belorussians. In the south, it followed the San River, cutting Przemyśl in two. The Germans retained Zasanie, giving it the discordant name "Deutsch-Przemysl" (German Przemyśl). The old city, its Jewish quarter, and the modern eastern suburb of Lwowskie all fell under Soviet rule until 1941.[42]

That frontier was a potent symbol of the agony of the city and of all East-Central Europe. Even at Przemyśl, one of only two major transit points between the two evil empires (the other was at the city of Brest—before the war in Poland and today in Belarus), it was a scar of ugly concrete bunkers, artillery emplacements, and tangled barbed wire. It screamed the end of centuries of cultural exchange, ethnic intermixing, and fluidity. In their place it promised permanent terror and oppression. Behind this frontier began two new, bloody projects to reshape the occupied populations. The Soviet and Nazi designs were—as should by now be clear—not the first brutal ideological transformations implemented in Przemyśl and the wider region. To residents who had faced the Tsarist army's Russification efforts twenty-five years earlier, there was much to recognize. Assaults on schooling and religion, divisive ethnopolitics, arbitrary violence, corruption, and looting were all shared features of these occupation regimes. However, while the Tsarist army had been limited in what it could achieve by a lack of central state guidance, the Soviet and Nazi regimes pursued unchecked, expansive, vicious ideological aims with single-minded, systematic lethality. In East-Central Europe, their policies of mass murder would together kill some 14 million people.[43]

The Soviets took control of Przemyśl south of the San on September 28, 1939. Their occupation, which lasted until June 1941, was built on an ideology far removed from the monarchism, Russian nationalism, and anti-Semitism of the Tsar's army in 1915. On November 1, 1939, the USSR did what Nikolai II had never dared, formally annexing "Eastern Little Poland," along with other former Polish state territory farther north. For the Soviet regime, unlike its imperial precursor, a façade of popular support was always important. To give the annexation a veneer of legitimacy, on October 22 "elections" had been held for a National Assembly of what was now to be "Western Ukraine." Voter turnout was claimed at a totalitarian 92.83 percent. In Przemyśl and across the annexed lands, the administration and economy were reorganized along Soviet socialist lines. In the countryside, landowners were chased out and collective farms were set up. In the towns, banks, industry, and the property of political parties and charitable organizations were expropriated by the state. Even small artisans were ordered to join collectives "voluntarily." Apartments were confiscated.[44]

The defining characteristic of the Soviet occupation was extraordinary violence, not merely to pacify but as the essential instrument to effect radical transformation of the population. Indeed, in occupied Poland up until the summer of 1941, Soviet mass murder victims, numbering nearly 500,000 dead, exceeded three- or fourfold those of the Nazis. As with the Tsarist regime before it—though applied by the Soviets far more systematically for ideological ends and, especially in the lands that had been eastern Galicia, also more extensively—deportations were a favorite tool. Three-quarters of a million people were forced from the occupied territories into the USSR. Deportations began almost immediately, at the turn of October–November 1939, after which there were four major waves, in February, April, and June 1940 and in June 1941. Some deportees were taken only as far as Soviet eastern Ukraine or Belarus. Most were transported in crowded cattle wagons much farther. Many ended up in Kazakhstan, just like much of the Fortress's garrison twenty-five years before. Intelligentsia, state officials, army and police officers, clergy, business owners, small merchants, farmers, settlers, and refugees, and all their families, were taken: anyone whose mentality was at odds with Soviet reality. From Przemyśl and its environs 10,000 people were deported and a further 2,000 arrested, of whom between 500 and 1,000 were murdered by Stalin's security police, the NKVD.[45]

The northern part of Przemyśl was incorporated into Hitler's racial empire along with the rest of western Poland. The whole city would fall under Nazi control once Hitler launched his attack on the Soviet Union, "Operation Barbarossa," on June 22, 1941. Then, Przemyśl again found itself in a battle front. After a week of heavy bombardments and savage to-and-fro fighting that destroyed two-fifths of the houses and razed the old Jewish quarter to the ground, the Germans captured the districts south of the San. The Nazi occupation's guiding principle was, as one Wehrmacht general ruthlessly put it, "Germans are the masters, and Poles are the slaves." Deutsch-Przemysl's principal importance in the first two years of occupation had been as a conduit for grain and oil exports from the Soviet Union and as the main reception point for *Volksdeutsche*—ethnic Germans who had been Soviet subjects who were "returning" to Hitler's Greater Germany. The indigenous Christian population of Poland was of interest solely as a source of slave labor. The Nazis, like the Soviets, immediately slated for death Poland's elite and killed more than 50,000 educated people. For the rest of society, brutal repression, exploitation, and starvation rations defined everyday life. From Przemyśl and the surrounding district, 26,431 Poles and Ukrainians were taken for forced labor into Germany. Some 5,000 people— Jews excluded—were murdered or went missing during the city's Nazi occupation.[46]

At the core of Nazi ideology was anti-Semitism. It was a more rigidly biological racial form of anti-Semitism, even more prone to radicalized violence, than that of the Tsarist army. Nevertheless, in this key regard, in the lands that had been eastern Galicia it was the Germans rather than the Soviets who were the most obvious successors to the Tsarist occupation of 1915. Indeed, at the outset, the Nazis, like the Russians twenty-five years before, though with much greater force, expelled rather than exterminated the Jews. In Zasanie, they did this extremely successfully. Before the war, over 2,500 Jews lived in the suburb; by 1941, only 66 remained. There was no overlap in occupation personnel between 1915 and 1939; nor is there evidence that earlier Russian military actions inspired Nazi policy. Instead, the similarity is best explained by a shared imperialist perception of multiethnic eastern Galicia as a land of experimentation and transformation, a common logic of extreme anti-Semitism, and nationalism and military ruthlessness. All of these components were present early in the First World War.[47]

Only in the second half of 1941 did Nazi Jewish policy turn genocidal. In July 1941, Przemyśl's Jews were forced from their homes and concentrated in the Garbarze district behind the rail station. Some 22,000 unfortunates were crammed into its few streets. A "Jewish Council" was ordered to run the district at the occupiers' bidding. The life here was one of brutality, hard labor, impoverishment, disease, and starvation. There were many executions from the spring of 1942, carried out by Gestapo men in the city's historic Jewish cemetery to the south. After a year, on July 16, 1942, the district was turned into a sealed ghetto; less than two weeks later, the "resettlement of Jews for forced labor"—a euphemism for extermination—was announced. In two clearance actions, at the turn of July–August and in November 1942, most of Przemyśl's Jews were taken 100 kilometers (60 miles) to the northeast to the Bełżec Extermination Facility, which in its year-long existence gassed 434,508 Polish Jews. In September 1943, the last Jews in Przemyśl, numbering barely 5,000, were nearly all, to a man, woman, and child, sent to Auschwitz-Birkenau—the last 1,580, who dodged the transport, were shot in the ghetto. As for the 66 Jews who had stayed in Zasanie under Nazi occupation since 1939, in June 1942 they were driven to Fort VIII, "Łętownia," where the Nazis had set up an execution site. Here, at the first of the forts to be built for the outer perimeter of the Habsburg fortress, they were killed: just one small way in which the history of the Fortress intertwines with the mid-twentieth-century destruction of East-Central Europe.[48]

If today one walks through Przemyśl, the old world of 1914, the safer world before the bloodletting began, can still seem graspable. The city's eighteenth-century clock tower still stands, with views over the city and to the east. One can stroll down Mickiewicz Street, past fine Habsburg military buildings, or wander around the old town and sightsee its historic churches. Yet the Jewish quarter and Old Synagogue are gone. The Greek Catholic cathedral, where Tsar Nikolai II never was permitted to enjoy an Orthodox Mass, is bereft of its eastern dome and serves as a Roman Catholic church. The population, too, is much changed. At the end of the Second World War, there were just 28,144 people—around half what there had been in 1939—left in the city. Only 415 Jews had survived. The Ukrainians vanished soon after. Poland's communist government, operating within new borders imposed by the USSR, mindful of horrific violence that Ukrainian paramilitaries had just perpetrated against Poles in contested lands around, and determined to make Poland ethnically pure, threw them out. Its ethnic cleansing was completed in 1947. Some 15,000 Poles displaced from territories seized by the USSR were brought to Przemyśl to replace its murdered and deported citizenry and to create a purely Polish city.[49]

The remains of the old fortress perimeter outside the city offer a reminder of the conflict that set East-Central Europe on this cycle of horror. Here, in 1914, raged the first of the twentieth century's ferocious struggles for the region, fought by men from all across the continent. Taboos were broken; a new barbarity was unleashed. These military ruins are powerful testimony to the fragility of a civilization that no one could ever have imagined would end so suddenly or so terribly. The rubble might serve as a fitting memorial to all that followed.

THE ORGANIZATION OF THE HABSBURG ARMY IN 1914

The Habsburg army, or, to give it its proper grand title, the "Imperial and Royal" (*kaiserlich und königlich*) Army, reflected the complexities of the multiethnic dynastic empire that it served. The Habsburg Empire was reformed into a "dual monarchy" in 1867, dividing into two parts, Austria and Hungary, each with its own parliament and government but sharing a monarch (who was known as Emperor in Austria, but King in Hungary), a foreign minister, and a war minister. They also had a common trade policy. One year later, the Habsburg army, which remained under the Emperor's exclusive control, underwent a thorough restructuring to reflect the new political constellation. It was divided into three main forces. The largest and most important of these was the Imperial and Royal Common Army, which contained within it the General Staff—the elite body of specially trained officers responsible for operational planning, mobilization, and direction—and received three-quarters of the conscripts from all over the empire. In 1914, it numbered

110 infantry regiments, 30 battalions of light infantry, 42 cavalry regiments, and most of the forces' artillery. The two much smaller forces, initially intended as reserves, were the Imperial-Royal Austrian Landwehr (37 infantry and 6 cavalry regiments in 1914) and the Royal Hungarian Honvéd (32 infantry and 10 cavalry regiments), which recruited only from their own halves of the empire.[1]

The army was also reformed in 1868 to raise its performance. In 1866, the force had been smashed by the Prussians at the Battle of Königgrätz. To improve, it copied the Prussians' model of short-service universal conscription, a system all the armies of continental Europe would adopt in the following decade. A core of professional officers and noncommissioned officers provided leadership and training. The rank and file were drafted from among the population. Every male Habsburg subject was formally liable for military duty, at first from the ages of seventeen to thirty, and then, after further reform in 1886, from nineteen to forty-two. In peacetime, men were conscripted in the year they turned twenty-one. They served for three years in the Common Army or two in the Landwehr and Honvéd, a short period by past standards. Trainee reserve officers, drawn exclusively from the middle classes and above, who alone were able to meet the criterion of a secondary school education, enlisted for just a year. Once service was completed, the men were released and placed in the reserve for a decade. Thereafter, they were transferred to a third-line Reserve status, the Landsturm.[2]

The period between 1868 and 1914 saw further developments to Habsburg military organization. Most notable was the rise of the Honvéd and Landwehr. At the outset, these had been envisioned as reserve formations. However, Hungarian parliamentarians aspired to establish their own national army and gradually built up the Honvéd. The Austrian parliament followed their example. Already by 1892, both forces were regarded as first-line formations, and in 1912 both for the first time were permitted their own artillery. A second major change was the introduction of territorialization in 1882. Past practice had been to transfer units away from their home areas. Under the new system, the empire was divided into sixteen military districts. The corps commands in charge of each district managed training and supply, and the regiments raised there were stationed in these districts. The reform was intended to accelerate mobilization, but it also gave regiments, which each had their own recruitment areas within the wider district, close links with particular towns and localities.[3]

On the eve of war in 1914, the Habsburg army numbered 18,000 career officers and around 430,000 noncommissioned officers and men. A frequent refrain in histories of the force is that its ethnic diversity was a major weakness. Certainly, as in the wider empire, nationalist sensitivities and linguistic heterogeneity posed challenges. Officers, who were disproportionately of Austrian German descent, were divided by education and ethnicity from their men. Moreover, fewer than half (142) of the Common Army's regiments were monolingual; 162 regiments had two languages (both of which, it is often forgotten, a proportion of the men would have spoken, for after territorialization they came from mixed communities in which both tongues were in everyday use); and 24 had three languages. However, the Habsburg army's primary problem was not its diversity but simply that it had neither enough guns nor enough soldiers. Conscription may formally have been universal for adult males, but in practice the force was denied the funding to draft more than around a quarter of those young men eligible for service each year. This was a far lower proportion than in France (83 percent), Germany (just over 50 percent) or—ominously, with its far greater population—Russia (around 30 percent).[4]

The Habsburg army in 1914 was thus distinguished by the desperate contortions it undertook in order to maximize its strength in the opening and, it was expected, decisive period of war. To boost its pool of trained manpower, since 1883 the force had annually given an extra 10,000 men—designated *Ersatzreservisten* (replacement reservists)—basic military instruction lasting eight weeks. To achieve a mobilized strength of 1,687,000 officers and men in

August 1914, the army called up every trained reservist immediately. Units were heavily diluted by men whose peacetime service was years behind them. In the German army, standing regiments were kept at three-quarters strength and, on mobilization, completed using the two most recently trained reservist year groups. The Habsburg force, by contrast, spread its "active" manpower—the men currently undertaking their peacetime conscription—thinly, which inevitably impacted negatively on its units' combat readiness. "Active" soldiers comprised a mere 25 percent of personnel in any Common Army or Landwehr regiment, and just eighteen percent in Honvéd regiments after mobilization.[5]

Third-line units were also added to the Habsburg army's order of battle to boost numbers. Central to this book are the Landsturm regiments. The Landsturm Law of 1886 had extended military obligation to men over thirty for use as troop replacements and, in the initial concept, for lines-of-communication work and home defense. In 1914, seventy Landsturm regiments were raised across the empire from the oldest contingent liable for military service: men aged between thirty-seven and forty-two years old. Each Landsturm regiment was composed of three or four battalions. An Austrian Landsturm battalion had 986 soldiers. The Hungarian Landsturm—known in Magyar as Népfelkelő—battalions were larger, each fielding 1,107 men. From the outset of war, the Habsburg army treated the Landsturm as combat troops. Despite this, their equipment levels, as well as their fitness and training, were far inferior to those of Common Army, Landwehr, and Honvéd regiments. They were formed into brigades of eight to twelve battalions each, which had just ten field guns in support, less than half the norm for first-line brigades. They had no transport, not much medical provision, no mobile field kitchens, no signals equipment, and no machine-guns.[6]

The March Battalions were another unit type established by the army to increase its strength. These were immortalized for later generations thanks to the writer Jaroslav Hašek's bumbling *Good Soldier Švejk*. They were units of replacement troops and often contained a high proportion of the barely trained *Ersatzreservisten*. However, rather than being used as drafts for depleted established formations, they were formed into March Regiments and March Brigades and thrown into combat. This was no stopgap, but rather a measure that had been planned long before the war. At most, the March Brigades had just six light field guns to support them and, like the Landsturm, they had no machine-guns. Hurriedly formed, hastily trained, lacking fire support, and without veteran leaders, they were generally wiped out quickly upon entering active service. In the Fortress of Przemyśl, Honvéd March Regiments 3, 4, and 6 (all belonging to the 23rd Honvéd Infantry Division), Honvéd March Regiment 16, and Landwehr March Battalion 35 made up a minor part of the garrison.[7]

The Habsburg army was distinctive in both its organization and many of its formations. Nonetheless, in basic structure and terminology it also had much in common with other continental short-service conscript forces. For the Common Army, Landwehr, and Honvéd, as for allies and enemies, the basic tactical unit in 1914 was the division, with an establishment strength of around 18,000 men. Landsturm Brigades, the highest formation for Landsturm troops, possessed approximately 8,000 soldiers. Each corps had two or three divisions. Divisions had below them two brigades. A standard brigade (excluding Landsturm and March Brigades) was two regiments. A regiment was three or four battalions. While minor variations existed between the Common Army, Landwehr, and Honvéd, a full-strength battalion numbered approximately 1,100 soldiers. The full strength of the Habsburg army after mobilization in 1914 consisted of 48 infantry divisions, 11 cavalry divisions, and 36 Landsturm or March Brigades supported by 2,600 artillery pieces of all calibers.[8]

THE ORGANIZATION OF THE RUSSIAN ARMY IN 1914

The Russian army had long been the Tsar's personal possession. The Fundamental Laws of 1906—the constitution hastily introduced to quell the revolution that broke out a year earlier—named the Tsar as "supreme commander of all the armies and fleets," in whose hands alone lay the direction of "all military matters." This sounds archaic today, but the imperial German and Habsburg armies too lay under their emperors' exclusive authority in 1914. Nonetheless, the Tsar's force was a more extreme mix of ancient and modern. Nine of every ten generals came from the nobility, the traditional warrior caste. In the 45,582-strong professional officer corps as a whole, the proportion was lower at 51 percent, but this still made it by far the most aristocratic of any European army's leadership. Yet these men were simultaneously the modernizing vanguard of a rapidly changing empire. The general staff, though not so powerful as its more famous German namesake, was an elite institution, among the most meritocratic and professional of any in the Russian

Empire. The Tsar's officers still held traditional feudal loyalty, but they were increasingly preoccupied with the new ideals of Russian nationalism.[1]

The army had made a great leap forward in the 1870s, when Minister of War General Dmitry Miliutin had forced through reform. For the officer corps, there had been vast improvements in education. A broad curriculum, incorporating not only strategy, tactics, and fortification but also languages, the natural sciences, and the liberal arts, was introduced. Ominously, military statistics and geography, which disaggregated populations by ethnicity and ascribed characteristics to each people, were particularly prominent, first for general staff officers and, from 1903, as a mandatory subject for cadets as well. Miliutin's interest in demographics and ethnicity was not merely academic, for the centerpiece of his reforms was the 1874 Conscription Law, which followed other European states in introducing a Prussian-style model of universal short-service conscription into the Russian Empire. Previously, the term of service had been a life-robbing twenty years. The new Conscription Law initially set a six-year period of active service, followed by nine years in the reserves. By the First World War, this had been adjusted to three years of active service, which men started at the age of twenty-one, followed by fifteen years in the reserves and a final five years (up to age forty-three) in a militia, or *opolchenie*.[2]

The 1874 Conscription Law ringingly proclaimed that "the defense of the throne and the country is the sacred duty of every Russian subject," but imposing a military system designed for a modern nation-state onto the Tsarist Empire was an immense challenge. The population, at 167 million souls, was huge and highly diverse. Ethnic Russians constituted only 44 percent of the overall population, even if the imperial regime's insistence on also counting Ukrainian- and Belorussian-speakers as "Russians" raised the official total to a more reassuring-sounding 66 percent. The Tsar's subjects were uneducated. Over 70 percent of the recruits drafted in the mid-1890s were illiterate, in contrast to 22 percent in the Habsburg Empire and 0.2 percent in Germany. The revolution of 1905 made manifest the seething discontent in the towns and among the impoverished peasant masses. The empire was divided into 12 military regional commands along with a separate (Don Cossack) military province and subdivided into 208 recruiting districts, but territorialization was never introduced; Russian regiments, unlike their Habsburg and German counterparts, were rarely stationed in their home areas during peacetime. Partly this was due to Russia's thin rail network, which made it necessary to position units near the borders, but it was also to ensure that, if faced with internal disorder, soldiers would not side with rebellious populations.[3]

The Tsar's military embodied, in the eyes of its commanders, the Russian nation in arms. Though its soldiers, and even its officers, were hardly less diverse than those of its Habsburg enemy, there was no concession to multilingualism; this army's single official language was Russian. The army was well aware that even the "Russian" peasants in its ranks often had scant conception of a Russian Motherland, and particularly after the 1905 revolution it strove to inculcate a Russian national identity. Partly in consequence, Tsarist regiments tended to be far less locally rooted than those of the Habsburg army; even units raised in the ethnic Russian heartlands frequently mixed men from more than one recruitment district. Toward non-Russian minorities the army generally evinced distrust. A few groups, notably the Central Asian Muslim nomadic peoples, were judged to be too dangerous to be conscripted. For those many non-Russians who were drafted, the firm rule was that they should not make up more than one-quarter of any regiment. Polish recruits, who were regarded with particular suspicion, were banned from constituting more than one-fifth of any military unit.[4]

Cossacks were the outstanding exception. This "warrior people" was regarded as the most loyal of all the Tsar's subjects. Their origins lay in the small communities established around 1500 on the steppes north of the Black Sea by serfs who had fled from the Muscovy and Polish-Lithuanian states. Their name came from a Turkish word for "brigand." The Tsars had extended their rule over the Cossacks in the late seventeenth and eighteenth centuries, and recognizing their martial utility, had cultivated a special relationship. The Cossack *voiskos*—as the various scattered communities were known—entered imperial service in return for land and privileges, most famously as light cavalry. From the 1870s, when their military obligations were updated, Cossacks passed through three four-year "turns." The first turn was active service, for which the men had to bring their own horses and equipment. The second and third turns were spent off duty at lower levels of readiness. On reaching thirty-two, the men were transferred to the reserve and later the militia. By 1914, the training, uniforms, and armament of the Cossack squadrons were similar to those of the regular Russian cavalry, but they retained their own élan. Cossacks had a reputation for superb horsemanship as well as for indiscipline, brutality, and violent anti-Semitism.[5]

The Russian army was the world's largest in 1914. Thanks to the empire's huge population and Miliutin's conscription system, it had a standing strength of 1.4 million soldiers, exceeding Germany's and Austria-Hungary's peacetime armies combined. Once mobilized, the Russian field army reached 3.4 million men led by 70,000 professional and reserve officers. In the summer of 1914, it was able to commit some 98 infantry divisions and 37½ cavalry divisions on the eastern front. The force was the pride of the Tsarist state. A third of the empire's entire budget had been spent preparing it between 1909 and 1913. It was technologically sophisticated. Although the Russian army lagged behind its opponents in the development of heavy howitzers—an oversight that would cost it dearly at Przemyśl—it had a huge artillery park of 7,088 mostly modern, highly mobile, quick-firing pieces. Owing to the war against Japan in 1904–1905, the army also had recent experience of combat that its enemies a decade later lacked. However, the force also suffered grave weaknesses in 1914, both in its command and, most fundamentally, in terms of institutional and doctrinal cohesion. Throughout the First World War, the army consequently found great difficulty at all levels in executing coordinated action, a problem that severely retarded its operational performance.[6]

Like other countries, Russia fielded both standing and wartime-raised formations. The peacetime Tsarist army had 37 corps, most of which were formed of 2 infantry divisions (each of 2 brigades), a cavalry division (4,500 men at war strength), 2 heavy howitzer batteries (each with 6 howitzers), and engineers. Alongside 3 elite Guards and 4 Grenadier and 11 Siberian infantry divisions, there were 52 active (peacetime standing) infantry divisions and 18 independent rifle brigades. The active infantry divisions—2 of which, the 12th and the 19th, along with the active 3rd Rifle Brigade, would attack Przemyśl in October 1914—were marginally stronger in manpower than their Habsburg equivalents, each fielding 16 battalions and totaling 20,000 men. However, their major advantages lay in firepower, training, and fitness. Each Russian active infantry division had 60 artillery pieces to the Habsburg divisions' 48, and 32 against 28 machine-guns. Their 4 regiments each had a war strength of 79 officers and 4,036 men; they were kept at half strength in peace, so that in the field they had a higher proportion of young active service soldiers than their Habsburg opponents, although fewer professional noncommissioned officers.[7]

In contrast to the Habsburg army, which struggled to fill all its first-line units, the Russian military also raised 35 reserve divisions on mobilization, including those which formed the bulk of the blockade army around Przemyśl in the early autumn of 1914. These were of equal strength to active divisions but less well equipped. They had 48 field guns, which still made them vastly superior to the Habsburg Landsturm. Around two-thirds of their complement were reservists, with the remainder serving soldiers. The Russians' lowest-grade units were militia (*opolchenie*) brigades. These were equivalent to the

Landsturm. They were filled with the oldest men or with previously undrafted reservists with six weeks' wartime training. These militia-men shared the Landsturm's unheroic reputation. During the second siege, from November 1914 until March 1915, such units were deployed to blockade the Fortress.[8]

NOTES

INTRODUCTION

1. I. S. Bloch, *Is War Now Impossible? Being an Abridgment of "The War of the Future in Its Technical, Economic and Political Relations,"* ed. W. T. Stead (London, 1899), esp. lxiii. More generally, see H. Afflerbach and D. Stevenson, eds., *An Improbable War: The Outbreak of World War I and European Political Culture Before 1914* (New York, 2007).

2. For population, see W. Kramarz, *Ludność Przemyśla w latach 1521–1921* (Przemyśl, 1930), 109.

3. For the quotation about Przemyśl as "symbolic point," see F. Molnár, *Galicja, 1914–1915: Zapiski korespondenta wojennego,* trans. A. Engelmayer (Warsaw, 2012), 148. The other quotations are from the German army's plenipotentiary, Lieutenant-Colonel Karl von Kageneck, reports of April 6 and May 31, 1915, quoted in H. H. Herwig, *The First World War: Germany and Austria-Hungary, 1914–1918* (London, 1997), 140.

4. See O. Bartov and E. D. Weitz, *Shatterzone of Empires: Coexistence and Violence in the German, Habsburg, Russian and Ottoman Borderlands* (Bloomington, IN, 2013); also M. Levene, *The Crisis of Genocide,* vol. 1, *Devastation: The European Rimlands, 1912–1938,* and vol. 2, *Annihilation: The European Rimlands, 1939–1953* (Oxford, 2013).

5. See the brilliant study by T. Snyder, *Bloodlands: Europe Between Hitler and Stalin* (New York, 2010). For excellent studies tracing the violence to 1917–1923, J. Böhler, W. Borodziej, and J. von Puttkamer, eds., *Legacies of Violence: Eastern Europe's First World War* (Munich, 2014); and R. Gerwarth, *The Vanquished: Why the First World War Failed to End, 1917–1923* (London, 2016).

6. See L. Hauser's pioneering *Monografia miasta Przemyśla* (Przemyśl, 1991 [1883]), 93–105, 124–141. The quotation from Nestor is given in A. Kunysz, "Pradzieje Przemyśla," in F. Persowski, A. Kunysz, and J. Olszak, eds., *Tysiąc lat Przemyśla: Zarys historyczny,* vol. 1 (Rzeszów, Poland, 1976), 51–58. The Lyakhs,

rendered as "Lachy" in Polish, are sometimes translated as "Poles," though this implies a misleading affinity between these people and the modern Polish nation. They are better described as a West Slavic tribe.

7. For Christian churches and the Early Modern town, see F. Persowski, "Przemyśl od X wieku do roku 1340," and K. Arłamowski, "Stosunki społeczno-gospodarcze w Przemyślu staropolskim od końca wieku XIV do roku 1772," both in Persowski et al., eds., *Tysiąc lat Przemyśla*, 1:130–136, 176, 192, 207. Also Hauser, *Monografia*, 182–184, 225–227; M. Orłowicz, *Illustrierter Führer durch Przemyśl und Umgebung: Mit besonderer Berücksichtigung der Schlachtfelder und Kriegsgräber, 1914–15* (Lemberg, 1917), 18. For the early Jewish community, see C. Dunagan, "The Lost World of Przemyśl: Interethnic Dynamics in a Galician Center, 1868 to 1921," PhD thesis, Brandeis University, 2009, 22–37.

8. These and the following passages on the early plans for Przemyśl's fortification rest on F. Forstner, *Przemyśl: Österreich-Ungarns bedeutendste Festung*, 2nd ed. (Vienna, 1997 [1987]), 41–51, 95–103. The best discussion of the first modern fortifications built in 1854–1855, during the Crimean War, is T. Idzikowski, *Twierdza Przemyśl: Powstanie—Rozwój—Technologie* (Krosno, Poland, 2014), chap. 2. For Galicia's size and geography, see A. von Guttry, *Galizien: Land und Leute* (Munich, 1916), 28.

9. J. E. Fahey, "Bulwark of Empire: Imperial and Local Government in Przemyśl, Galicia (1867–1939)," PhD thesis, Purdue University, 2017, 33–34, 38–39, 44–57.

10. For the building of the Fortress, see Forstner, *Przemyśl*, 105–107. For Habsburg-Russian relations in the 1870s, see C. A. Macartney, *The Habsburg Empire, 1790–1918* (London, 1968), 588–594.

11. Idzikowski, *Twierdza Przemyśl*, chaps. 4–9, offers the most detailed and up-to-date account of the development of the Fortress and of individual forts. See also Fahey, "Bulwark of Empire," 78–80; and Forstner, *Przemyśl*, 105, 153.

12. Forstner, *Przemyśl*, 117–118; B. Gudmundsson, "Introduction," in S. Marble, ed., *King of Battle: Artillery in World War I* (Leiden, 2015), 1–34; M. Baczkowski, *Pod czarno-żółtymi sztandarami: Galicja i jej mieszkańcy wobec austro-węgierskich struktur militarnych 1868–1914* (Cracow, 2003), 272–273, 449–450. The conversion to today's money has been made by using the exchange table in the cover of K. Baedeker, *Austria-Hungary: Handbook for Travellers* (Leipzig, 1911) (which gives £1 as equivalent to 23 crowns), to convert to a contemporary sterling figure and then the Bank of England's Inflation Calculator (www.bankofengland.co.uk /monetary-policy/inflation/inflation-calculator) to translate this total to a modern pound sterling equivalent. The dollar figure is based on the Bank of England's sterling–dollar exchange rate for January 21, 2019.

13. For Conrad's fortification priorities, see G. Kronenbitter, *"Krieg im Frieden": Die Führung der k.u.k. Armee und die Großmachtpolitik Österreich-Ungarns, 1906–1914* (Munich, 2003), 186–189. For Przemyśl specifically, see Forstner, *Przemyśl*, 120–122.

14. Kramarz, *Ludność Przemyśla*, 54–55, 108. Confessional statistics are more reliable than language data as a marker of ethnicity at this time, primarily because

Yiddish, the language of most of the city's Jews, was not an option on the Austrian census forms. Most Jews therefore entered Polish, the tongue of Przemyśl's (and Galicia's) politically dominant nationality, as their language, swelling the "Polish" share of the city. Language data for 1910 gives misleading totals of 39,155 (85.2 percent) "Poles," 5,229 "Ruthenes" (Ukrainians), and 1,490 "Germans" in the city. See ibid., 110.

15. I. von Michaelsburg, *Im belagerten Przemysl: Tagebuchblätter aus großer Zeit* (Leipzig, 1915), 18–19, 67 (September 19 and November 14, 1914). Künigl-Ehrenburg's description reflects some contemporary anti-Semitic tropes, but for a Gentile at this time she was unusually open, curious, and sympathetic toward Jews.

16. For the city's key buildings, see the directories in Orłowicz, *Illustrierter Führer*, 5–6; and *Kalendarz pamiątkowy z czasów oblężenia Przemyśla w r. 1914 na rok pański 1915* (Przemyśl, 1914). The figure for military buildings comes from Fahey, "Bulwark of Empire," 78.

17. For the Austrian reforms, especially the Imperial Municipalities Law of March 5, 1862, see J. Deak, *Forging a Multinational State: State Making in Imperial Austria from the Enlightenment to the First World War* (Stanford, CA, 2015), 151–160. The politics of the Polish Democrats (Polskie Stronnictwo Demokratyczne) are discussed in H. Binder, *Galizien in Wien: Parteien, Wahlen, Fraktionen und Abgeordnete im Übergang zur Massenpolitik* (Vienna, 2005), 63–73. For Przemyśl's late nineteenth-century development, see F. Persowski, "Przemyśl pod rządami austriackimi, 1772–1918," in F. Persowski et al., eds., *Tysiąc lat Przemyśla*, vol. 2, *Zarys historyczny* (Warsaw, 1976), 102–104; Orłowicz, *Illustrierter Führer*, 23.

18. Ruthenian identities are discussed in K. Bachmann, *Ein Herd der Feindschaft gegen Rußland: Galizien als Krisenherd in den Beziehungen der Donaumonarchie mit Rußland (1907–1914)* (Vienna, 2001), 18–28, 138–159, 196–212; and I. L. Rudnytsky, "The Ukrainians in Galicia Under Austrian Rule," in A. S. Markovits and F. E. Sysyn, eds., *Nationbuilding and the Politics of Nationalism: Essays on Austrian Galicia* (Cambridge, MA, 1982), 23–67. For Ruthenes in Przemyśl, see Z. Felczyński, "Rozwój kulturalny Przemyśla, 1772–1918," in Persowski et al., eds., *Tysiąc lat Przemyśla*, 2:189–198. National indifference may be reflected in Przemyśl's 1910 census, where 3,000–4,000 Greek Catholic residents declared their everyday language to be Polish. This rejection of Ukrainian identity may have been motivated by indifference or by the financial and career advantages that could be won by identifying as a Pole. See Kramarz, *Ludność Przemyśla*, 108, 110.

19. Michaelsburg, *Im belagerten Przemysl*, 77 (November 16, 1914).

20. Details on Jewish Przemyśl from Dunagan, "Lost World," 62–64, 117–137, 164–177, 221–235. For Jews' place in Przemyśl's economy, Persowski, "Przemyśl pod rządami austriackimi," 110–112, offers data. Among twenty manufacturing concerns registered from 1910 to 1918, ten were in Jewish ownership, two jointly owned by Jews and Christians, and eight owned by Christians. Only four of twenty-one trading and services firms were owned by Christians.

21. Baedeker, *Austria-Hungary*, 378; Orłowicz, *Illustrierter Führer*, 5, 62–63. Przemyśl's infrastructure was, by Galician standards, not unduly behind the times.

Its electrification, which took place 1896–1907, was relatively early, albeit partial. Cracow, a much larger and more important city, had put a modern waterworks into operation only in 1901 and an electricity-generating power plant only in 1905. See (for Przemyśl) M. Dalecki, "Rozbudowa urządzeń komunalnych Przemyśla w latach 1867–1914," *Rocznik Historyczno-Archiwalny* 6 (1989): 50–55, and (for Cracow) J. M. Małecki, "W dobie autonomii Galicyjskiej (1866–1918)," in J. Bieniarzówna and J. M. Małecki, eds., *Dzieje Krakowa*, vol. 3, *Kraków w latach 1796–1918* (Kraków, 1979), 349, 351.

22. Orłowicz, *Illustrierter Führer*, 51; Michaelsburg, *Im belagerten Przemysl*, 65 (November 14, 1914).

23. A. Kunysz, "Pradzieje Przemyśla," in Persowski et al., eds., *Tysiąc lat Przemyśla*, 1:16.

24. Fahey, "Bulwark of Empire," 94; Orłowicz, *Illustrierter Führer*, 5–6, 48; Michaelsburg, *Im belagerten Przemysl*, 67–68 (November 14, 1914). For the late nineteenth-century Habsburg Empire's architecture, see A. Nierhaus, "Austria as a 'Baroque Nation': Institutional and Media Constructions," *Journal of Art Historiography* 15 (2016): 1–22, https://arthistoriography.files.wordpress.com/2016/11/nierhaus.pdf on January 9, 2019.

25. Macartney, *Habsburg Empire*, 562–563. For a recent analysis of how the system functioned to win legitimacy for the state among its peoples, see P. M. Judson, *The Habsburg Empire: A New History* (Cambridge, MA, 2016), esp. chap. 7.

26. Fahey, "Bulwark of Empire," 161–167. For details of Potocki's assassination, see L. Wolff, *The Idea of Galicia: History and Fantasy in Habsburg Political Culture* (Stanford, CA, 2010), 331–336.

27. Felczyński, "Rozwój kulturalny Przemyśla," 218–219, 232, 234; J. E. Fahey, "Undermining a Bulwark of the Monarchy: Civil-Military Relations in Fortress Przemyśl (1871–1914)," *Austrian History Yearbook* 48 (2017): 155–156. Bilingualism and intermarriage between Greek and Roman Catholics were fairly common in Galicia on the eve of war. In 1910, there were 22,114 Roman Catholic, 26,744 Greek Catholic, and 5,090 mixed Catholic weddings in the province. See K.k. Statistisches Zentralkommission, *Österreichische Statistik: Bewegung der Bevölkerung der im Reichsrate vertretenen Königreiche und Länder im Jahre 1910* (Vienna, 1912), 9.

28. For spying and antagonism toward Russia, see Bachmann, *Herd der Feindschaft*, 227–233; Forstner, *Przemyśl*, 123–127. For the mobilization of Przemyśl's X Corps during the Balkan Crisis, see G. E. Rothenberg, *The Army of Francis Joseph* (West Lafeyette, IN, 1998 [1976]), 166–167.

29. E. M. Remarque, *All Quiet on the Western Front*, trans. B. Murdoch (London, 1996), 14. For analysis of rival "lost generation" narratives, see G. L. Mosse, *Fallen Soldiers: Reshaping the Memory of the World Wars* (New York, 1990), esp. chap. 4; and R. Wohl, *The Generation of 1914* (Cambridge, MA, 1979).

30. W. Winkler, *Die Totenverluste der öst.-ung. Monarchie nach Nationalitäten. Die Altersgliederung der Toten. Ausblicke in die Zukunft* (Vienna, 1919), 48–54. For comparison, men under twenty-five constituted 52 percent of Habsburg military

fatalities. The single year group to suffer most (7.15 percent of all fatalities) was born in 1895, and so was aged just nineteen at the outbreak of hostilities.

31. J. Vit, *Wspomnienia z mojego pobytu w Przemyślu podczas rosyjskiego oblężenia, 1914–1915*, trans. L. Hofbauer and J. Husar (Przemyśl, 1995), 31.

32. See S. Stępień's introduction in ibid., 21–25.

33. J. J. Stock, *Notatnik z Twierdzy Przemyśl, 1914–1915*, ed. J. Bator (Przemyśl, 2014), 13–17.

34. S. Gayczak, *Pamiętnik Oberleutnanta Stanisława Marcelego Gayczaka*, ed. J. Gayczak (Przemyśl, n.d.), 5–6.

35. See the editor's preface in I. Künigl-Ehrenburg, *W oblężonym Przemyślu: Kartki dziennika z czasów Wielkiej Wojny (1914–1915)*, ed. S. Stępień and trans. E. Pietraszek and A. Siciak (Przemyśl, 2010), 26–33.

36. F. Dzugan, "Chamäleons im Blätterwald: Die Wurzeln der ÖVP-ParteijouralistInnen in Austrofaschismus, Nationalsozialismus, Demokratie und Widerstand. Eine kollektivbiographische Analyse an den Beispielen 'Wiener Tageszeitung' und 'Linzer Volksblatt' 1945 bzw. 1947 bis 1955," PhD thesis, University of Vienna, 2011, 130.

CHAPTER ONE: A BROKEN ARMY

1. This description is based on a mix of eyewitness accounts, esp. V. Nerad, *Przemysl: Erinnerungen des Genieoffiziers Viktor Nerad* (Salzburg, 2015), 18–19; Kusmanek, "Die beiden Belagerungen von Przemyśl durch die Russen," 10, KA Vienna: NL Kusmanek B/1137/14; and Michaelsburg, *Im belagerten Przemysl*, 10 (diary entry for September 15, 1914). The first elements of the retreating army reached Przemyśl on September 12, and the bulk arrived on September 13 and 14, 1914. See F. Stuckheil, "Die Festung Przemyśl in der Ausrüstungszeit," *Militärwissenschaftliche und technische Mitteilungen* 55 (1924): 216–217.

2. T. Pudłocki, "Działalność inteligencji Przemyśla na tle życia mieszkańców miasta między sierpniem a listopadem 1914 r.," in J. Polaczek, ed., *Twierdza Przemyśl w Galicji: Materiały z konferencji naukowej. Przemyśl, 25–27 kwietnia 2002* (Przemyśl, 2003), 109–110. For the press report of Archduke Franz Ferdinand's assassination, see "Ohydna zbrodnia," *Echo Przemyskie* 19, no. 53 (July 1, 1914): 1.

3. Pudłocki, "Działalność inteligencji," 110, 112. Some of the August proclamations on hygiene, post, and telegraph measures survive in AP Przemyśl: Akta Miasta Przemyśla (129): 1594: fos. 26–33, 38. The quotations are from: W. Zakrzewska, *Oblężenie Przemyśla rok 1914–1915: Z przeżytych dni* (Lwów, 1916), 50; and Stock, *Notatnik*, 26 (diary entry for August 27, 1914).

4. The first quotation is from Zakrzewska, *Oblężenie*, 50. The rest of the paragraph draws on A. Krasicki, *Dziennik z kampanii rosyjskiej, 1914–1916* (Warsaw, 1988), 29 (diary entry for August 10, 1914).

5. Michaelsburg, *Im belagerten Przemysl*, 6 (diary entry for September 11, 1914).

6. "Z kraju," *Nowa Reforma: Wydanie Popołudniowe* 33, no. 378 (September 1, 1914): 2; Krasicki, *Dziennik*, 39 (diary entry for August 27, 1914).

7. H. z Seifertów Jabłońska, *Dziennik z oblężonego Przemyśla, 1914–1915*, ed. H. Imbs (Przemyśl, 1994), 38–41 (diary entries for August 24 and 28, September 4 and 6, 1914).

8. Krasicki, *Dziennik*, 43–44 (diary entry for August 30, 1914), and 46 (diary entry for September 1, 1914); Stock, *Notatnik*, 27–28 (diary entry for September 5, 1914). More generally for Lwów on the eve of Russian occupation, see C. Mick, *Kriegserfahrungen in einer multiethnischen Stadt: Lemberg, 1914–1947* (Wiesbaden, 2010), 77–80.

9. For "the times of panic," see Sweryna z Kozłowskich Kapecka (a teacher), memoir, reproduced in M. Dalecki, "Wspomnienia przemyskich nauczycielek z okresu I wojny światowej," *Przemyskie Zapiski Historyczne* 18 (2010–2011): 156. For the admonitions to evacuate and to stockpile food (the first of which was given as early as August 2), see C.i.k. Komendant twierdzy, poster entitled "Obwieszenie," n.d., AP Przemyśl: 397 (Afisze, plakaty i druki ulotni): 483, and (for a version of this Polish poster in German), 484, the "Nakaz" of August 14, 1914, in the same file (397): 482. Also, C.k. Starostwo, poster entitled "Obwieszenie," September 11, 1914, AP Przemyśl: (Afisze, plakaty i druki ulotni): 19. More generally, see W. Mentzel, "Kriegsflüchtlinge in Cisleithanien im Ersten Weltkrieg," PhD thesis, University of Vienna, 1997, 75–78.

10. For civilians remaining in Przemyśl, see Forstner, *Przemyśl*, 160. The figure of 18,000 is improbable because, in the second siege, after further evacuation in November, there remained 30,000 people in Przemyśl. Michaelsburg, *Im belagerten Przemysl*, 10 (diary entry for September 15, 1914), and Jabłońska, *Dziennik*, 43 (diary entry for September 14, 1914), described the sight of the field army in Przemyśl. The last quotation, from the Russian-Polish prisoner, comes from Jabłońska, *Dziennik*, 42 (diary entry for September 12, 1914).

11. See L. Sondhaus, *Franz Conrad von Hötzendorf: Architect of the Apocalypse* (Boston, 2000). For an insightful discussion of Conrad's relationship with Gina and the formidable legal challenges of divorce and remarriage in Austria, see U. Harmat, "Divorce and Remarriage in Austria-Hungary: The Second Marriage of Franz Conrad von Hötzendorf," *Austrian History Yearbook* 32 (January 2001): 69–103.

12. Conrad started rehearsing exculpatory arguments already during the disaster in the autumn of 1914. See J. Redlich, *Schicksalsjahre Österreichs, 1908–1919: Das politische Tagebuch Josef Redlichs*, ed. F. Fellner, vol. 2 (Graz, 1953), 271 (diary entry for September 9, 1914). For prewar military underfunding and underrecruitment, see G. Kronenbitter, *"Krieg im Frieden": Die Führung der k.u.k. Armee und die Großmachtpolitik Österreich-Ungarns, 1906–1914* (Munich, 2003), 145–178. For mobilization figures in 1914, see A. Watson, *Ring of Steel: Germany and Austria-Hungary in World War I* (New York, 2014), 117, 141.

13. Kronenbitter, *"Krieg im Frieden,"* 317–324, 361–367.

14. Ibid., 330–331, 334–356, 389–428; H. Strachan, *The First World War*, vol. 1, *To Arms* (Oxford, 2001), 69. The final quotation from Conrad appears in C. Clark, *The Sleepwalkers: How Europe Went to War in 1914* (New York, 2013), 392.

15. N. Stone, "Die Mobilmachung der österreichisch-ungarischen Armee 1914," *Militärgeschichtliche Mitteilungen* 16, no. 2 (1974): 67–95.

16. P. Tscherkassow, *Der Sturm auf Przemysl, 7.X.1914. Stab der Roten Armee. Abteilung für die Erforschung u. Auswertung de Kriegserfahrungen* (Moscow, 1927), 10, 30, KA Vienna: Übersetzung Nordost Nr 14.

17. L. von Fabini, "Die Feuertaufe des Eisernen Korps: Der erste Tag der Schlacht von Złoczów am 26. August 1914," *Militärwissenschaftliche Mitteilungen* 61 (1930): 787–789.

18. Stone, "Mobilmachung," 94–95. Conrad's quotation about being shot comes from G. Wawro, *A Mad Catastrophe: The Outbreak of World War I and the Collapse of the Habsburg Empire* (New York, 2014), 231.

19. M. Rauchensteiner, *The First World War and the End of the Habsburg Monarchy* (Vienna, 2014), 153. For the big map, see F. Conrad von Hötzendorf, *Aus meiner Dienstzeit 1906–1918, vol. 4, 24. Juni 1914 bis 30. September 1914. Die politischen und militärischen Vorgänge vom Fürstenmord in Sarajevo bis zum Abschluß der ersten und bis zum Beginn der zweiten Offensive gegen Serbien und Rußland* (Vienna, 1923), 415.

20. N. Stone, *The Eastern Front, 1914–1917* (London, 1998 [1975]), 80, and Rauchensteiner, *First World War*, 180–183.

21. Rauchensteiner, *First World War*, 180; Wawro, *Mad Catastrophe*, 169–215 (with Auffenberg's quotation on p. 180; emphasis in Wawro).

22. For the purported intelligence and advice, see K.u.k. 3. Armeeoberkommando, Op. Nr 76, "Eindrücke über die russ. Truppen (mitgeteilt vom Kmdtn der deutschen Ostarmee)," c. August 17, 1914; and K.u.k. 3. Armeeoberkommando, Op. Nr 71, "Direktiven für Kommandanten," August 15, 1914, both in KA Vienna: NFA 30 ITD (August 1914): Karton 1721. Regarding Russian commanders' combat experience, see B. W. Menning, *Bayonets Before Bullets: The Imperial Russian Army, 1861–1914* (Bloomington, IN, 1992), 249. For example, the commander of the southwestern front, General Nikolai Ivanov, and the commander of the Russian Third Army, General Nikolai Ruzski, opposite Brudermann, had both fought in the Manchurian War ten years earlier.

23. Bundesministerium für Heereswesen und Kriegsarchiv, *Österreich-Ungarns letzter Krieg*, vol. 1, *Vom Kriegsausbruch bis zum Ausgang der Schlacht bei Limanowa–Łapanów* (Vienna, 1931), 172, 207–208; and J. R. Schindler, *Fall of the Double Eagle: The Battle for Galicia and the Demise of Austria-Hungary* (Lincoln, NE, 2015), 191.

24. J. E. Romer, *Pamiętniki* (Warsaw, 2011), 37–39.

25. The 11th Division staff officer's quotation is from P. Broucek, ed., *Ein General im Zwielicht: Die Erinnerungen Edmund Glaises von Horstenau, vol. 1, K.u.k. Generalstabsoffizier und Historiker* (Vienna, 1980), 298. For the weakness of the Habsburg artillery's cooperation with the infantry, see Romer, *Pamiętniki*, 40–41. For Russian training and tactics, see Menning, *Bayonets*, 256–262, 264–265. See also D. R. Stone, *The Russian Army in the Great War: The Eastern Front, 1914–1917* (Lawrence, KS, 2015), 37–39.

26. For Conrad's tactical vision and infantry training, see Sondhaus, *Conrad von Hötzendorf*, chap. 3; Watson, *Ring of Steel*, 117–120; W. Wagner, "Die k.(u.) k. Armee—Gliederung und Aufgabenstellung 1866 bis 1914," in A. Wandruszka and P. Urbanitsch, eds., *Die Habsburgermonarchie 1848–1918*, vol. 5, *Die Bewaffnete Macht*, (Vienna, 1987), 627–628. For "outstanding feats of arms," see "Gefechtsbericht über das Gefecht bei Busk und Kozłów an 26. und 27. August 1914. K.u.k. 30 I.T.D. Kmdo. Op. Nr 23," KA Vienna: NFA 30 ITD (1914): 31. Cf. III Corps' experience outside Złoczów in Schindler, *Fall*, 192–194.

27. See the shortcomings listed in the AOK's Op. Nr 2610, "Erfahrungen aus den bisherigen Kämpfen," September 28, 1914, esp. Points 2, 10, and 12, KA Vienna: NFA 43, Sch.D. (1914): 2180. For an example and criticism of officer heroics, see Broucek, ed., *General im Zwielicht*, 298. Casualty figures are from Schindler, *Fall*, 192–193.

28. Entries for August 30–September 2, 1914, KA Vienna: NFA Tagebuch Ausrüstung Festung Lemberg 1914. See also order of 3. Armeekommando, August 31, 1914, at 5:00 p.m., reproduced in Conrad, *Dienstzeit*, 4:598.

29. Bundesministerium, *Österreich-Ungarns letzter Krieg*, 1:249–253, and Conrad, *Dienstzeit*, 4:608–609. The quotation that begins the paragraph is from E. Ludendorff, *My War Memories, 1914–1918*, vol. 1 (London, 1919), 75.

30. Conrad, *Dienstzeit*, 4:666–668. Further details supplied by Broucek, ed., *General im Zwielicht*, 302.

31. [C. Komadina], *Dziennik oficera Landsturmu*, trans. M. Wichrowski (Przemyśl, 2004), 48–49.

32. This account of Landsturm Infantry Regiment 10 is taken from Emerich von Laky, "Aus dem Tagebuch eines Offiziers: Aus dem Weltkriege," trans. into German by C. Komadina, HL Budapest: II.169 M.kir. 23 HG: 4 Doboz.

33. Schindler, *Fall*, 219–220, 224–225.

34. For the Fourth Army's establishment, see Conrad, *Dienstzeit*, 4:903. For the casualties, see M. von Auffenberg-Komarów, *Aus Österreichs Höhe und Niedergang: Eine Lebensschilderung* (Munich, 1921), 332. Wawro, *Mad Catastrophe*, 232–236, provides a good analysis of the flaws in Conrad's planning. The quotation is from P. Broucek, ed., *Theodor Ritter von Zeynek: Ein Offizier im Generalstabskorps erinnert sich* (Vienna, 2009), 187.

35. Schindler, *Fall*, 225–231. For the Third Army's mission, see Conrad's Op. Nr 1605 of September 5, 1914, reproduced in Conrad, *Dienstzeit*, 4:643.

36. Wawro, *Mad Catastrophe*, 239; Bundesministerium, *Österreich-Ungarns letzter Krieg*, 1:311, 313–314, 319. For justified criticism of the march battalions, see A. Krauß, *Die Ursachen unserer Niederlage: Erinnerungen und Urteile aus dem Weltkrieg*, 3rd ed. (Munich, 1923), 92–94.

37. The following is from B. Zombory-Moldován, *The Burning of the World: A Memoir of 1914*, trans. P. Zombory-Moldovan (New York, 2014), chap. 6 and 147–148.

38. Kassa is today known as Košice, and is the second-largest city in modern Slovakia.

39. Bundesministerium, *Österreich-Ungarns letzter Krieg*, 1:314. Conrad's quotation is given in Redlich, *Schicksalsjahre Österreich*, 2:271 (diary entry for September 9, 1914).

40. Ibid., 294–298.

41. Redlich, *Schicksalsjahre Österreich*, 2:271 (diary entry for September 9, 1914). On the operational situation, see Bundesministerium, *Österreich-Ungarns letzter Krieg*, 1:279, 299–300.

42. Bundesministerium, *Österreich-Ungarns letzter Krieg*, 1:284–289, 303, 305–306. For Conrad's front visit, see Wawro, *Mad Catastrophe*, 244.

43. Schindler, *Fall*, 251–252; Stone, *Eastern Front*, 90; Bundesministerium, *Österreich-Ungarns letzter Krieg*, 1:305–310.

44. For the casualties of the initial campaign, see Bundesministerium, *Österreich-Ungarns letzter Krieg*, 1:319, and Stone, *Eastern Front*, 91. The Russians lost around a quarter of a million men, 40,000 of whom were prisoners. Their losses were easier to replace with already trained reinforcements and they surrendered only 100 guns, against the Habsburg army's 300 captured artillery pieces. Fleischer's account of the retreat is in R. Fleischer, "Rückzug nach Przemysl im Herbst 1914. (Erinnerungen eines Truppenoffiziers)," *Militärwissenschaftliche und technische Mitteilungen* 55 (1924): 19–20.

45. Ibid., 24.

46. For Ruthene conversion and spy scandals, see Bachmann, *Herd der Feindschaft*, 219–233. Conrad's quotation is from Redlich, *Politische Tagebuch*, 1:265 (diary entry for September 2, 1914). For further details, see Watson, *Ring of Steel*, 145–146, 151–155.

47. See, respectively, A. V. Wendland, *Die Russophilen in Galizien: Ukrainische Konservative zwischen Österreich und Rußland 1848–1915* (Vienna, 2001), 546; and A. Holzer, *Das Lächeln der Henker: Der unbekannte Krieg gegen die Zivilbevölkerung, 1914–1918* (Darmstadt, 2008), 74–75. The examples come from Laky, "Tagebuch," HL Budapest: II.169 M.kir. 23 HG: 4 Doboz; and R. Völker, *Przemysl: Sieg und Untergang der Festung am San* (Vienna, 1927), 54.

48. See K.u.k. 3. Armeekommando to k.u.k. Festungskommando Przemysl, September 13, 1914, KA Vienna: NFA Przemysl 1321: fo. 624. Also, in the same file and illustrating the confusion when the fortress became overwhelmed with stragglers, III. Vert. Bezirk, Res. Nr 129 to k.u.k. Festungskommando in Przemyśl, September 16, 1914. The final quotation is from Nerad, *Przemysl*, 18.

49. Conrad, *Dienstzeit*, 4:752, 754, 777–779.

50. See Bundesministerium für Heereswesen und Kriegsarchiv, *Österreich-Ungarns letzter Krieg*, vol. 2, *Vom Ausklang der Schlacht bei Limanowa–Łapanów bis zur Einnahme von Brest–Litowsk* (Vienna, 1931), 10–11; Bundesministerium, *Österreich-Ungarns letzter Krieg*, 1:337–338; Wawro, *Mad Catastrophe*, 239. For the long-term impact of the death on Conrad, Sondhaus, *Conrad von Hötzendorf*, 156.

51. Conrad, *Dienstzeit*, 4:780.

CHAPTER TWO: "THE HEROES"

1. The quotation is from Vit, *Wspomnienia*, 33.

2. For the arrival of the wartime garrison, see K.k. 17 Landsturm Rgt, diary, KA Vienna: NFA Przemysl 1322: fo. 207 (reverse); Vit, *Wspomnienia*, 35; [Komadina], *Dziennik oficera Landsturmu*, 39. For Habsburg military equipment, see J. S. Lucas, *Austro-Hungarian Infantry, 1914–1918* (London, 1973), 19. For the problems of uniforming the Landsturm units, see K.u.k. 3. Verteidigungsbezirkskommando, "Auszug aus dem Berichte über die Aktion im III. Verteidigungsbezirke während der Einschließung," KA Vienna: NFA Przemysl 1322: fo. 36. The difficulties were not universal, however. The adjutant of II/Landsturm Regiment 18 thought his battalion, kitted out entirely in pike gray, looked smart enough to be "Guards," and was well pleased with their brand-new boots and underwear. Krasicki, *Dziennik*, 28 (diary entry for August 9, 1914).

3. The following description of III/Landsturm Infantry Regiment 18 comes from the wonderful details in Vit, *Wspomnienia*, 32–35.

4. Ibid., 32.

5. M. Schmitz, *"Als ob die Welt aus den Fugen ginge": Kriegserfahrungen österreichisch-ungarischer Offiziere, 1914–18* (Paderborn, Germany, 2016), esp. 51–55. While obviously self-serving, these arguments were not without merit. For explanations of how socially elite officer corps functioned extremely effectively through a paternalism-deference exchange in other contexts, see G. Sheffield, *Leadership in the Trenches: Officer-Man Relations, Morale and Discipline in the British Army in the Era of the First World War* (Basingstoke, 2000); and A. Watson, "Junior Officership in the German Army During the Great War, 1914–1918," *War in History* 14, no. 4 (November 2007): 429–453. The French officer corps, which pursued a far more egalitarian and open recruitment policy than either its British ally or its German enemy, performed notably less well than either throughout the conflict.

6. Information on the composition of III/Landsturm Infantry Regiment 18 is given in Vit, who mentions that Poles constituted half the battalion, and Ukrainians the other half (*Wspomnienia*, 79–80). The adjutant of the regiment's 2nd Battalion noted that most of his men were local peasants, and "Jews [were] relatively few." Krasicki, *Dziennik*, 26 (August 4, 1914). On language issues in the Habsburg army, see T. Scheer, "K.u.k. Regimentssprachen: Institutionalisierung der Sprachenvielfalt in der Habsburgermonarchie in den Jahren 1867/8–1914' in K.-H. Ehlers, M. Nekula, M. Niedhammer, and H. Scheuringer, eds., *Sprache, Gesellschaft und Nation in Ostmitteleuropa: Institutionalisierung und Alltagspraxis* (Göttingen, Germany, 2014), 75–92. An exception was Yiddish, which was not an officially recognized language within the Habsburg Empire.

7. B. Wolfgang, *Przemysl: 1914–1915* (Vienna, 1935), 98. Złoczów, today Ukrainian Zolochiv, lies 60 kilometers (40 miles) east of Lviv. For biographical information on Prochaska, see Dzugan, "Chamäleons," 130. For Jews as translators, see B. Wolfgang, *Batjuschka: Ein Kriegsgefangenenschicksal* (Vienna, 1941), 15. For "Army Slavic," see E. Suchorzebska, "Zur Geschichte der polnischen

Militärsprache in der Habsburgermonarchie," Diplomarbeit, University of Vienna, 2009, 24–26, 90–91, 96.

8. *Eine Helden Sage: Przemysl*, 1915, 4–5, MNZP Przemyśl: Archiwum Molnara. The saga, written with humor reminiscent of Hašek's famous *The Good Soldier Švejk* (1921–1923), has been digitalized at Podkarpacka Biblioteka Cyfrowa (Podkarpacka Digital Library), www.pbc.rzeszow.pl/dlibra/docmetadata ?id=11060&from=&dirids=1&ver_id=&lp=1&QI=.

9. "Hermann Kusmanek von Burgneustädten," *Österreichisches Biographisches Lexikon* (1968): 372, Austrian Academy of Sciences, www.biographien.ac.at/oebl ?frames=yes.

10. F. Stuckheil, "Ausrüstungszeit," 202–204, 211–212. Also Kusmanek, "Die beiden Belagerungen," 4, KA Vienna: NL Kusmanek B/1137/14. Little is known about the military laborers in Przemyśl, but a surviving muster roll for the IV Detachment of I/1 Landsturm Fortress Labor Group offers some insight. Most of the 221 men on this list came from Budapest. A surprisingly high number—seventy-six (34 percent)—had served in peacetime, and their average age was thirty-one. See "Névjegyzék" for I/1 népf. erőd. munk. csoport IV. osztag parancsnokság in HL Budapest: II.169 M.kir. 23 HG: 3 Doboz.

11. H. Schwalb, "Die Verteidigung von Przemyśl, 1914/15," Sonderabdruck aus den *Mitteilungen über Gegenstände des Artillerie- und Geniewesens* 59, Jahrgang, Heft 9 (1918): 2–3; Forstner, *Przemyśl*, 146–550; Bundesministerium, *Österreich-Ungarns letzter Krieg*, 1:379; K.u.k. Geniedirektion in Przemysl, "Folgerungen," KA Vienna: NFA Przemysl 1322: fo. 38.

12. Military buildings in the city are detailed at "Wykaz ulic i placów miasta Przemyśla," in *Kalendarz Pamiątkowy*, and 1907 city plan of Przemyśl at Center for Urban History of East Central Europe, Urban Maps Digital, www.lvivcenter .org/en/umd/map/?ci_mapid=121. For the administration of the Fortress's defense, see "Instruktion für den Kommandanten des Verteidigungsbezirkes," KA Vienna: NFA Przemysl 1321: fos. 580–586.

13. M. de Paula, *Der österreichisch-ungarische Befestigungsbau, 1820–1914* (Vienna, 1997), 57–73, 82–112; Idzikowski, *Twierdza Przemyśl*.

14. The following tour of Fort I is based on Idzikowski's excellent *Twierdza Przemyśl*, 93–102, 217, 278–279; T. Idzikowski, *Fort I "Salis-Soglio"* (Przemyśl, 2004); and also a trip to the fort made by the author on August 6, 2015.

15. Fort I's nickname is given in E. von Laky, "Die Erste Belagerung von Przemysl: Aus dem Tagebuch eines Offiziers. Aus dem Weltkriege," trans. into German by C. Komadina, HL Budapest: II.169 M.kir. 23 HG: 4 Doboz. The scathing judgment at the end of the paragraph is in Wolfgang, *Przemysl*, 57. Fort I was unusual in having been named after a soldier. Most other forts were known by the names of the villages adjacent to them.

16. C. Hämmerle, "'. . . Dort wurden wir dressiert und sekiert und geschlagen . . .': Vom Drill, dem Disziplinarstrafrecht und Soldatenmisshandlungen im Heer (1868 bis 1914)," in L. Cole, C. Hämmerle, and M. Scheutz, eds., *Glanz—Gewalt—Gehorsam: Militär und Gesellschaft in der Habsburgermonarchie (1800 bis 1918)* (Essen, 2011), 37–39, 51.

17. Tscherkassow, *Sturm*, 44.

18. Kusmanek, "Die beiden Belagerungen von Przemyśl durch die Russen," 5–7, KA Vienna: NL Kusmanek B/1137/14; H. Heiden, *Bollwerk am San: Schicksal der Festung Przemysl* (Oldenburg i.O, 1940), 40–41.

19. Tscherkassow, *Sturm*, 9.

20. Schwalb, "Verteidigung," 2; Tscherkassow, *Sturm*, 14; K.u.k. 3. Verteidigungsbezirkskommando, "Auszug aus dem Berichte über die Aktion im III. Verteidigungsbezirke während der Einschließung," KA Vienna: NFA Przemysl 1322: fo. 31.

21. K.u.k. Geniedirektion in Przemyśl, "Arbeitsrapport," September 9, 1914, and K.u.k. Festungskommando in Przemyśl, September 21, 1914, KA Vienna: NFA Przemysl 1321: fos. 515, 850. The village Hermanowice appears on both lists.

22. See J. Lenar, *Pamiętnik z walk o Twierdzę Przemyśl* (Przemyśl, 2005), 12–13; Wolfgang, *Przemysl*, 26–31.

23. For the Habsburg Empire's treatment of its refugees, see Mentzel, "Kriegsflüchtlinge," 5, 258, 291–296; Watson, *Ring of Steel*, 201–202. For the population trapped outside the Fortress's walls during the siege, K.u.k. 3. Verteidigungsbezirkskommando, "Auszug aus dem Berichte über die Aktion im III. Verteidigungsbezirke während der Einschließung," KA Vienna: NFA Przemysl 1322: fo. 36 (reverse).

24. C. Führ, *Das k.u.k. Armeeoberkommando und die Innenpolitik in Österreich, 1914–1917* (Graz, 1968), 17–23. See also "Nachtrag zum Festungskommandobefehl Nr 190," August 16, 1914, KA Vienna: NFA Przemysl 1321: fos. 387–388.

25. J. Z. Pająk, *Od autonomii do niepodległości: Kształtowanie się postaw politycznych i narodowych społeczeństwa Galicji w warunkach Wielkiej Wojny, 1914–1918* (Kielce, Poland, 2012), 84; A. Szczupak, *Greckokatolicka diecezja Przemyska w latach I wojny światowej* (Cracow, 2015), 44–45, 50–55.

26. M. Zubrycki, "Dziennik," in A. A. Zięba and A. Świątek, eds., *Monarchia, wojna, człowiek: Codzienne i niecodzienne życie mieszkańców Galicji w czasie pierwszej wojny światowej* (Cracow, 2014), 67–68.

27. Szczupak, *Greckokatolicka diecezja Przemyska*, 49; "Belagsziffer der Internierungs- und Unterbringungsorte am 18. September 1914," KA Vienna: MKSM (1914): 69–11/1.

28. The final quotation is from Jabłońska, *Dziennik*, 38 (diary entry for August 18, 1914). For the examples of trials, see "Referatsbogen in der Strafsache des Julian Połoszynowicz wegen Verbrechen des Störung des offent. Ruhe," mid-August 1914, and the same for Katarzyna Ilków; for Agnes Szczęsna. "Wegen des Verbrechens der Majestätsbeleidigung," end of August 1914, AGAD Warsaw: 417–281: fos. 10–12, 28–30, and 417–297: fos. 17–19. Kusmanek routinely signed the court case paperwork.

29. Kusmanek's alleged quotation is given in Szczupak, *Greckokatolicka diecezja Przemyska*, 70. The order to expel Ruthenes is K.u.k. Festungskommando, "Op. Nr 35/3: Entfernung der ruthenischen Bevölkerung," September 4, 1914, HL Budapest: II.169, M.kir. 23 HG: 3 Doboz, fo. 31 (underlining in the original). Cf. Mentzel, "Kriegsflüchtlinge," 75–76, who presents further evidence on the totality

of the Fortress Command's evacuation plans for Ukrainians. For the Ruthenian laborers and the shift in language, see K.u.k. Festungskommando, "Inhalt: Abschub ruthenischer Lstpflichtiger Arbeiter," September 13, 1914, and the following telegrams to and from Feldtransportleitung Krakau on September 13 and 14, which refer to "russophile Landsturmpflichtige Arbeiter," KA Vienna: NFA Przemysl 1321: fo. 573 and reverse, and 641.

30. The *Kriegsnotwehrrecht* is discussed in J. E. Gumz, *The Resurrection and Collapse of Empire in Habsburg Serbia, 1914–1918* (Cambridge, 2009), 31–33, 53. Kusmanek's orders are Festungskommandobefehl Res. Nr 2231, September 9, 1914, KA Vienna: NFA Przemysl 1321: fo. 845 (reverse) (underlining in original) and Festungskommandobefehl Nr 227, September 22, 1914, KA Vienna: NFA Przemysl 1322: fo. 399. The term "useless eaters" appears in Befehle u. Abfertigungen des V.B. VII, September 26, 1914, KA Vienna: NFA Przemysl 1322: fo. 298. For the wider shift in policy, see B. Geőcze, *A przemysli tragédia* (Budapest, 1922), 70–71.

31. See Laky, "Tagebuch," HL Budapest: II.169 M.kir. 23 HG: 4 Doboz; and Oberst Martinek, Defense District Command VII, Order No. 166, October 2, 1914, KA Vienna: NFA Przemysl 1322: fo. 311.

32. The documentation on which the following account rests is: (1) a copy of the Przemyśl police report: C.k. Komisaryat Policyi w Przemyślu do c.k. Prokuratoryi Państwa w Przemyślu, September 16, 1914, in AVA Vienna: Min.d.Innern, Präs., 22/Galiz. (1918): 2119; (2) Interpellation des Abgeordneten Dr. Zahajkiewicz und Genossen in 5. Sitzung, June 13, 1917, *Stenographische Protokolle über die Sitzungen des Hauses der Abgeordneten des österreichischen Reichsrates im Jahre 1917. XXII. Session. 1. (Eröffnungs-) bis 21. Sitzung. (S. 1 bis 1155)*, 4 vols. (Vienna, 1917), 1:520–521, accessed at Österreichische Nationalbibliothek, http://alex.onb.ac.at /cgi-content/alex?aid=spa&datum=0022&page=6167&size=45; (3) the Thalerhof Almanac, *Талергофскій альманахъ: Пропамятная книга австрійскихъ жестокостей, изуверствъ и насилий надъ карпато-русскимъ народомъ во время Всемірной войны 1914–1917 гг.* (Lviv, 1924), 102–110, which contains useful press reports presenting Ruthenian and Polish eyewitness accounts, the most notable of which was by a councillor of the Higher Regional Court, Roman Dmohowski.

33. Interpellation des Abgeordneten Dr. Zahajkiewicz und Genossen, June 13, 1917, in *Stenographische Protokolle*, 1:520.

34. Ukrainian sources blamed Hungarian troops for the massacre. The Reichsrat complaint in 1917 referred specifically to a "Honvéd unit," and there was general agreement that Hungarian was the nationality of the first soldier to approach the prisoners. However, the two most immediately contemporary sources, the police report of September 16 and Helena z Seifertów Jabłońska's diary, do not mention Hungarians. Both identify the main perpetrators as dragoons, although the police report states that men of other units were also present. There were no Hungarian dragoon units. It is possible, but not probable, that police confused Hungarian Hussar uniforms for those of dragoons. A more likely explanation is that some Honvéd were present, one of whom first approached the prisoners,

but that most of the perpetrators were Austrian dragoons. The prior brutality of Honvéd troops across Galicia may have encouraged commentators to assume that they also bore primary blame for this massacre.

35. The first quotation is from *Prikarpatskaya Rus* 1539 (1915), reproduced in the Thalerhof Almanac (Талергофскій альманахъ), 103; the second is from Jabłońska, *Dziennik*, 43 (diary entry for September 14 [*sic*], 1914).

36. Conrad, *Aus meiner Dienstzeit*, 4:729, 780. For a full discussion of garrison strength, see Forstner, *Przemyśl*, 152–153.

37. Available casualty statistics are as follows. The 93rd Landsturm Infantry Brigade, from an establishment strength of just under 12,000, had lost 122 officers and 4,400 men. Landsturm Infantry Regiment 21 (in the 108th Landsturm Infantry Brigade) had dropped from 2,934 to 1,930 soldiers. Hungarian Landsturm Infantry Regiment 10 (in the 97th Landsturm Infantry Brigade) had dropped from 3,357 to around 2,200 soldiers. Its losses included twenty-six officers. See Stuckheil, "Ausrüstungszeit," 220; [Komadina], *Dziennik oficera Landsturmu*, 49, 53 (entries for September 1 and 10, 1914). See also Kusmanek, "Die beiden Belagerungen," 12, KA Vienna: NL Kusmanek B/1137/14. Landsturm establishment strengths are provided in R. Hecht, "Fragen zur Heeresergänzung der gesamten bewaffneten Macht Österreich-Ungarns während des Ersten Weltkrieges," PhD thesis, University of Vienna, 1969, 43; and Völker, *Przemysl*, 25. The examples of a commander's attempts to spin defeat positively are from K.k. 108 Landsturm-Infanterie-Brigade, Brigadekommandobefehl Nr 4, September 19, 1914, NFA Przemysl 1322: fos. 287–288 (reverse).

38. Versecz is now Vršac in Serbia. Lugos is today Lugoj, in western Romania. For the language distribution of the populations of the surrounding districts, Krassó-Szörény and Temes, see Magyar Kir, Központi Statisztikai Hivatal, *A magyar szent korona országainak 1910. évi népszámlálása. Első rész: A népesség főbb adatai községek és népesebb puszták, telepek szerint* (Budapest, 1912), 23*, accessed at Klimo Theca, University of Pécs, Hungary, http://kt.lib.pte.hu/cgi-bin /kt.cgi?konyvtar/kt06042201/0_0_3_pg_23.html. For the panic outside Lwów, see Conrad, *Dienstzeit*, 4:620, 648. See also Bundesministerium, *Österreich-Ungarns letzter Krieg*, 1:253.

39. Kusmanek, "Die beiden Belagerungen," 12–13, KA Vienna: NL Kusmanek B/1137/14; Secret order to Commanders of IV–VIII Defensive Districts, September 16, 1914; Armee Oberkommando—Telegram discussing Landsturm Regiment 19, mid-September 1914, KA Vienna: NFA Przemysl 1321: fos. 727, 772.

40. Festungskommando in Przemyśl to 3. Armeekmdo and 44 ITD (September 18, 1914), and accompanying documentation, KA Vienna: NFA Przemysl 1321: fos. 771–773. See also, for the composition, R. Nowak, "Die Klammer des Reiches: Das Verhalten der elf Nationalitäten Österreich-Ungarns in der k.u.k. Wehrmacht 1914 bis 1918," 331, KA Vienna: NL Nowak B/726/1.

41. For the order, see K.k. 108 Landsturm-Infanterie-Brigade, Brigadekommandobefehl No. 4, September 19, 1914, NFA Przemysl 1322: fo. 287 (reverse) (underlining in original). For Tyrol (especially the Italian-speaking parts) and the military in peacetime, see L. Cole's excellent *Military Culture and Popular*

Patriotism in Late Imperial Austria (Oxford, 2014), esp. 68–75, 92–94, 130, 169–216, 314–322.

42. The Tyroleans' disciplinary problems and dissatisfaction is addressed in O. Stolz, *Das Tiroler Landsturmregiment Nr. II im Kriege, 1914–15, in Galizien* (Innsbrück, 1938), 144–149, 156–165. For the end quotation, see Stock, *Notatnik*, 51 (diary entry for October 6, 1914).

43. Such nationalist rhetoric is near universal in Hungarian officers' memoirs of Przemyśl. For contemporary reportage with the same characteristics, see Molnár, *Galicja*, 138. For rival views of Hungarians as thugs and medal-hoggers, see Stock, *Notatnik*, 58 (diary entry of October 13, 1914), and, more gently, *Eine Helden Sage: Przemysl*, 1915, 22, MNZP Przemyśl: Archiwum Molnara. More generally, P. Szlanta "'Najgorsze bestie to są Honwedy': Ewolucja stosunku polskich mieszańców Galicji do monarchii habsburskiej podczas I wojny światowej," in U. Jakubowska, ed., *Galicyjskie spotkania 2011* (n.p., 2011), 161–179.

44. The officer's quotation is from M. von Kozma, *Mackensens ungarische Husaren: Tagebuch eines Frontoffiziers, 1914–1918*, trans. M. von Schüching (Berlin, 1933), 18–19. For the Hungarian government's appeal, see "Proklamation der ungarischen Regierung," *Pester Lloyd* 61, Jahrgang, Nr 177, Morgenblatt (July 28, 1914): 1. More generally, see J. Galántai, *Hungary in the First World War* (Budapest, 1989), 56–71.

45. Geőcze, *A przemysli tragédia*, 41–42.

46. Stuckheil, "Ausrüstungszeit," 224–225; Tscherkassow, *Sturm*, 27, KA Vienna: Übersetzung Nordost Nr 14.

47. For the fortress garrison's hygienic deficiencies, see Festungskommandobefehle Nr 230, 233, 235 (September 25, 28, and 30, 1914), KA Vienna: NFA Przemysl 1321: fos. 39, 413, 420 (underlining in original). See also A. Pethö, ed., *Belagerung und Gefangenschaft: Von Przemyśl bis Russische-Turkestan. Das Kriegstagebuch des Dr. Richard Ritter von Stenitzer, 1914–1917* (Graz, 2010), 34, 40–45. Stenitzer, who worked in Przemyśl's Fortress Hospital No. 4, recorded seventy cases of cholera in the whole Fortress up to October 11. Typhus was a bigger problem, with twenty new cases every day (diary entry for October 11, 1914). The cholera mortality rate provided in the text is that for the Austro-Hungarian army in the first year of the war, given in S. Kirchenberger, "Beiträge zur Sanitätsstatistik der österreichisch-ungarischen Armee im Kriege, 1914–1918," in C. Pirquet, ed., *Volksgesundheit im Kriege*, 2 vols. (Vienna, 1926), 1:68. Information on the disease's symptoms is taken from H. Elias, "Cholera Asiatica," in ibid., 2:48, and J. B. Harris, Regina C. LaRocque, Firdausi Qadri, Edward T. Ryan, and Stephen B. Calderwood, "Cholera," *The Lancet* 379 (2012): 2466–2476, accessed at www.thelancet.com/pdfs/journals/lancet/PIIS0140–6736(12)60436-X.pdf.

48. Stuckheil, "Ausrüstungszeit," 214–215, 226, and idem, "Die zweite Einschließung der Festung Przemyśl," *Militärwissenschaftliche und technische Mitteilungen* 57 (1926), 167–168. Extrapolating from ration norms supplied by Stuckheil ("Zweite Einschließung" [1926]: 171, fn 6), the 17,000 quintals of flour given to the field army by the Fortress in the first months of war would have fed the 131,000-strong garrison for forty-three days. The information on wagons

and on the disastrous Jarosław evacuation mission is from Major Artur Poeffel, "Chronologische Zusammenstellung meiner Kriegsdiensttätigkeit in Przemysl vom 4–8.1914 bis 22–3.1915," KA Vienna: NL Kusmanek B/1137/12: fos. 42–44. For the losses, see Forstner, *Przemyśl*, 153–154.

49. Kusmanek, "Die beiden Belagerungen," 5–6, KA Vienna: NL Kusmanek B/1137/14; Forstner, *Przemyśl*, 155–157; "Beilage zum Festungskommandobefehl Nr 226" (September 21, 1914), KA Vienna: NFA Przemysl 1321: fo. 397.

50. Kusmanek, "Die beiden Belagerungen," 14–15, KA Vienna: NL Kusmanek B/1137/14; K.u.k. Geniedirektion in Przemysl, "Verlauf der Kämpfe," NFA Przemysl 1322: fo. 40. See also T. Idzikowski, "Fortyfikacje polowe Twierdzy Przemyśl—Problematyka ochrony reliktów pola bitwy 1914–1915," in W. Brzosk-winia. ed., *Fortyfikacja austriacka—Twierdza Przemyśl. Materiały z konferencji naukowej Towarzystwa Przyjaciół Fortyfikacji Przemyśl 30 IX–2 X 1999 roku* (Warsaw, 1999), 101–109.

51. Stuckheil, "Ausrüstungszeit," 226–227; Kusmanek, "Die beiden Belagerungen," 17–18, 20, KA Vienna: NL Kusmanek B/1137/14.

52. These orders are Kusmanek, "Kurze Orientierung über die Führung des Verteidigungskampfes" circa end of September 1914, KA Vienna: NFA Przemysl 1322: fos. 497–498; and K.u.k. Festungskommando in Przemyśl, "Verhalten der Werkkommandanten," October 1, 1914, HL Budapest: TGY 18, István Bielek.

53. The incapacitated Magyar battalion commander is mentioned in Laky, "Erste Belagerung," HL Budapest: II.169 M.kir. 23 HG: 4 Doboz. The experience of III/Landsturm Infantry Regiment 18 is recounted in Vit, *Wspomnienia*, 42, and Wolfgang, *Przemysl*, 46–47.

54. K.k. 17 Landsturm Rgt, diary, September 25, 1914, KA Vienna: NFA Przemysl 1322: fos. 210 (reverse)–214. Today Medyka is a main crossing point on the Polish-Ukrainian border.

55. See Vit, *Wspomnienia*, 43; Wolfgang, *Przemysl*, 48–49. A similar Hungarian account is in Laky, "Erste Belagerung," HL Budapest: II.169 M.kir. 23 HG: 4 Doboz.

56. The following is based on Heiden, *Bollwerk*, 105–109, and an account by the Fortress's staff chief, Lieutenant-Colonel Ottokar Hubert, on February 23, 1926, in KA Vienna: NL Kusmanek B/1137/11. Sources differ on the date of the Russian emissary's arrival. *OÜLK*, vol. 1, 381, gives October 4, while Schwalb, "Verteidigung," 3, states he arrived a day earlier. However, Kusmanek ("Die beiden Belagerungen," 18, KA Vienna: NL B/1137/14) remembered the emissary arriving on October 2, and his recollection is confirmed by both Hubert and the fortress staff section's intelligence officer, Felix Hölzer, in a diary entry for October 2, in KA Vienna: NL B/486.

57. For Dimitriev, see R. C. Hall, "Dimitriev, Radko (1859–1918)," in R. C. Hall, ed., *War in the Balkans: An Encyclopedic History from the Fall of the Ottoman Empire to the Breakup of Yugoslavia* (Santa Barbara, CA, 2014), 92. The quotation is from B. Pares, *Day by Day with the Russian Army, 1914–15* (London, 1915), 86.

CHAPTER THREE: STORM

1. Heiden, *Bollwerk*, 104–105. For the position of the Habsburg field army, see Bundesministerium, *Österreich-Ungarns letzter Krieg*, vol. 1, Beilage 14: "Lage am 30. September abds."

2. Kusmanek, "Die beiden Belagerungen," 21, KA Vienna: NL Kusmanek B/1137/14. Kusmanek claims the Russian preparatory bombardment began on October 3, but his memory failed him. Neither the Russian heavy artillery nor the infantry were in position at that time. The fortress intelligence officer, Lieutenant Felix Hölzer, laconically noted that there was "no event worth mentioning" in his diary on October 3; other contemporary diaries also report mostly calm on this and the next day. See KA Vienna: NL Hölzer B/486.

3. T. C. Dowling, ed., *Russia at War: From the Mongol Conquest to Afghanistan, Chechnya, and Beyond*, vol. 1, *A–M* (Santa Barbara, CA, 2015), 152. See also C. Johnston, "Brusiloff, Hero of the Hour in Russia, Described Intimately by One Who Knows Him Well," *New York Times* (June 18, 1916), https://timesmachine.nytimes.com/timesmachine/1916/06/18/99440704.pdf on April 13, 2018.

4. Tscherkassow, *Sturm*, 29. Also A. A. Brussilov, *A Soldier's Note-Book, 1914–1918* (London, 1930), 76, 79. Alfred Knox, the British military attaché in Russia, highlights the importance of the main Galician railway to the Fourth and Ninth Armies to the north. See idem, *With the Russian Army, 1914–1917: Being Chiefly Extracts from the Diary of a Military Attaché* (London, 1921), 168. The Stavka quotation comes from an order of September 15 (28), 1914, issued by Ianushkevich, quoted in P. Robinson, *Grand Duke Nikolai Nikolaevich: Supreme Commander of the Russian Army* (DeKalb, IL, 2014), 172.

5. Tscherkassow, *Sturm*, 28, 34, 75. For Stavka, see Robinson, *Grand Duke*, 171.

6. Kusmanek, "Die beiden Belagerungen," 4, KA Vienna: NL Kusmanek B/1137/14. See also A. Pavlov, "Russian Artillery," in S. Marble, ed., *King of Battle: Artillery in World War I* (Leiden, 2015), 255–280. For the use of German and Habsburg siege artillery in Belgium, see H. H. Herwig, *The Marne, 1914: The Opening of World War I and the Battle That Changed the World* (New York, 2009), 116–117, 129–130.

7. Tscherkassow, *Sturm*, 36–37, 41–43, 76; cf. Brusilov, *Soldier's Note-Book*, 76, 79–80.

8. Tscherkassow, *Sturm*, 8, 11–13, 43–54.

9. T. Idzikowski, "Grupa Siedliska," in Polaczek, ed., *Twierdza Przemyśl w Galicji*, 83–106; Tscherkassow, *Sturm*, 34–36, 47, 75, 164–165.

10. Ibid., 30–32, 34, 54–57, 152–155. Captured and translated examples of prisoner statements given to the Russians just before their October assault are in KA Vienna: NL Kusmanek B/1137/15.

11. The following description is based on the accounts of two officers of III/Landsturm Infantry Regiment 18, Wolfgang, *Przemysl*, 54–58, and Vit, *Wspomnienia*, 46.

12. Wolfgang, *Przemysl*, 55.

13. By the end of the battle on October 8, Fort I had taken 122 hits. See Idzikowski, *Fort I*, 46.

14. The standing orders are "Kurze Orientierung über die Führung des Verteidigungskampfes," KA Vienna: NFA Przemysl 1322: fo. 497. For the other details, see Tscherkassow, *Sturm*, 57–70, 79.

15. J. Lévai, *Éhség, árulás, Przemyśl* (Budapest, 1933), chap. 8, translated and reproduced in T. Pomykacz, "Jenő Lévai: Bój o fort I/1 'Łysiczka,'" *Nasz Przemyśl* 3 (March 2014): 10.

16. K.u.k. Geniedirektion in Przemysl, "Charakteristik des Russischen [*sic*] Angriffes," and VI Vert. Bez. Art. Kmdo to k.u.k. VI Vert. Bez. Kmdo, "Bericht über stattegefundene Kämpfe," November 2, 1914, both in KA Vienna: NFA Przemysl 1322: fos. 42–43, 50. For Russian training precepts as laid down in the 1912 Field Regulations, see Menning, *Bayonets*, 257–258. For the 19th Division's casualties, see Tscherkassow, *Sturm*, 62, 140–141.

17. Kusmanek, "Die beiden Belagerungen," 22, KA Vienna: NL Kusmanek B/1137/14; Tscherkassow, *Sturm*, 59. See also Bundesministerium, *Österreich-Ungarns letzter Krieg*, vol. 2, 1, Beilage, Skizze 21.

18. K.u.k. Geniedirektion in Przemysl, "Wirkung des feindlichen Artilleriefeuers," KA Vienna: NFA Przemysl 1321: reverse of fo. 25; Tscherkassow, *Sturm*, 94, 122–124, 149–150. For the southern front's casualties, see K.u.k. Verteidigungsbezirkskommando VII, Order No. 206, October 6, 1914, KA Vienna: NFA Przemysl 1322: fo. 322.

19. Nerad, *Przemysl*, 27; Laky, "Erste Belagerung," HL Budapest: II.169 M.kir. 23 HG: 4, Doboz; F. Hölzer, diary, October 6, 1914, KA Vienna: NL Hölzer B/486; Stock, *Notatnik*, 49 (diary entry for October 5, 1914).

20. Vit, *Wspomnienia*, 46. Atmospheric descriptions of the night are in Wolfgang, *Przemysl*, 58–59; and Laky, "Erste Belagerung," HL Budapest: II.169 M.kir. 23 HG: 4 Doboz.

21. Tscherkassow, *Sturm*, 69.

22. Ibid., 67–68, 84.

23. For Fort XV's construction and armament, see T. Idzikowski, *Fort XV "Borek"* (Przemyśl, 2004), 33–46.

24. Tscherkassow, *Sturm*, 9, 45–47, 63, 79–81, 149. For defenders' instructions, "Kurze Orientierung," KA Vienna: NFA Przemysl 1322: fo. 498. For the battle's topography, see Tomasz Idzikowski's short film showing a bird's-eye view of Fort XIV and its immediate environs in 1914 at Cross-border Cooperation Programme, Poland–Belarus–Ukraine, 2007–2013, www.pogranicze.turystyka.pl/fort-xiv-hurko-.html.

25. See Tscherkassow, *Sturm*, 79–80, 83, 122, 147. The assumption is that total munitions expenditure mirrored that of the 69th Artillery Brigade, for which detailed statistics are available. Tscherkassow's numbers for expenditure are at slight variance with estimates from the Fortress's defenders, who thought 45,000 shells were fired into the (southeastern) Defense District VI alone. See Art. Kmdo., VI Vert. Bez. to k.u.k. VI Vert. Bez. Kmdo, November 2, 1914, KA Vienna: NFA Przemysl 1322: fo. 52.

26. Lenar, *Pamiętnik*, 14. For the Russian gunners' rhythm, see K.u.k. Genie-direktion in Przemysl, "Wirkung des feindlichen Artilleriefeuers," KA Vienna: NFA Przemysl 1321: fo. 26, which states that the Russian guns fired from dawn until 11:00 a.m., and then from midday until dusk. Fire ceased at dusk in order to avoid muzzle flashes, which would be clearly visible in the darkness, revealing the guns' positions. For comparison, the German army delivered over 1 million shells into British lines in just five hours at the opening of its Spring Offensive in March 1918. See Watson, *Ring of Steel*, 293–300, 310–326, 519.

27. Wolfgang, *Przemysl*, 59–60, 62. For the "fight-or-flight" instinct in trench warfare, see A. Watson, *Enduring the Great War: Combat, Morale and Collapse in the German and British Armies, 1914–1918* (Cambridge, 2008), 22–34.

28. [Komadina], *Dziennik oficera Landsturmu*, 65 (diary entry for October 7, 1914). There is some chronological confusion in this diary, but internal evidence and cross-referencing with von Laky's memoir reveals that the entries dated October 7 and 8 refer, respectively, to October 6 and 7. The following account is derived from this diary and Laky, "Erste Belagerung," HL Budapest: II.169 M.kir. 23 HG: 4 Doboz.

29. Locations from sketch map in MNZP Przemyśl: Archiwum Molnara: DVD 9: T. Nr 1 MP. HIST 388: fo. 2a.

30. [Komadina], *Dziennik oficera Landsturmu*, 65 (diary entry for October 7 [6], 1914).

31. Laky, "Erste Belagerung," HL Budapest: II.169 M.kir. 23 HG: 4 Doboz.

32. G. Stiefler, "Über Psychosen und Neurosen im Kriege (I.)," *Jahrbücher für Psychiatrie und Neurologie* 37 (1917): 405–407. For prewar and wartime debates on the causes of psychiatric disorders, see H.-G. Hofer, *Nervenschwäche und Krieg: Modernitätskritik und Krisenbewältigung in der österreichischen Psychiatrie (1880–1920)* (Vienna, 2004), esp. 231–236, 242–252, 383.

33. For the opposing artillery forces and the Russians' concern about the in-effectiveness of their guns, see Kusmanek, "Die beiden Belagerungen," 22, KA Vienna: NL Kusmanek B/1137/14; Tscherkassow, *Sturm*, 76, 86. Only twelve of Przemyśl's forts were capable of withstanding shells of greater than 15 cm caliber. For the panic among fortress commanders and in the city, see K.u.k. Geniedirek-tion in Przemysl, "Wirkung des feindlichen Artilleriefeuers," KA Vienna: NFA Przemysl 1321: fo. 25, and Festungskommandobefehl Nr 242, Pkt. 6, October 7, 1914, KA Vienna: NFA Przemysl 1322: fo. 445 (reverse). The quotation is re-ported in Jabłońska, *Dziennik*, 60–61. For Shcherbachev's order, see Tscherkas-sow, *Sturm*, 90, 157–158. All times in this chapter have been converted to the clock used by Habsburg troops, which was an hour behind the St. Petersburg time used by the Russian blockade army.

34. B. G. Offz., k.u.k. IV Verteidigungsbezirkskommando, November 2, 1914, and K.u.k. Geniedirektion in Przemysl, "Verlauf der Kämpfe," KA Vienna: NFA Przemysl 1322: fo. 48 (reverse)–49 (reverse) and fo. 40 (reverse), respectively; Tscherkassow, *Sturm*, 108–110, 125, 158.

35. T. Idzikowski, "Uniwersalny fort pancerny Twierdzy Przemyśl—Fort IV 'Optyń' w świetle ostatnich badań terenowych i archiwalnych," in Brzoskwinia, *Fortyfikacja austriacka*, 79–90; Nerad, *Przemysl*, 58–59.

36. Tscherkassow, *Sturm*, 87–88, 103–108; Schwalb, "Verteidigung," 8.

37. For the bombardment, see Tscherkassow, *Sturm*, 55; Gayczak, *Pamiętnik*, 12 (diary entry for October 7); Jabłońska, *Dziennik*, 59–60; Stiefler, "Über Psychosen und Neurosen (I.)," 375. For the southern and eastern assaults, see Tscherkassow, *Sturm*, 92–95, 101–103, 138–139. Defenders' views of these two attacks are provided in Völker, *Przemysl*, 87–101.

38. T. Idzikowski, "Grupa Siedliska," in J. Polaczek, ed., *Twierdza Przemyśl w Galicji*, 83–107; Tscherkassow, *Sturm*, 91. The final quotation is from POW Nibefer Padalka, interrogation, October 6, 1914, HL Budapest: II.169, M.kir. 23 HG: 3 Doboz, fo. 188.

39. A good example is Laky, "Erste Belagerung," HL Budapest: II.169, M.kir. 23 HG: 4 Doboz.

40. See the interrogations of men from I.R. 73, 76, and 274 in HL Budapest: II.169. M.kir. 23 HG: 3 Doboz: fos. 154–169, 177–188.

41. J. A. Sanborn, *Drafting the Russian Nation: Military Conscription, Total War, and Mass Politics, 1905–1925* (DeKalb, IL, 2002), 25–29, 96–119, 142–145. For an example of leadership from the front in the 19th Division, see the inspirational action of one of IR 76's battalion commanders in leading his men onto the glacis on Fort I/3. Tscherkassow, *Sturm*, 98. See also the account of the storming of Fort I/1 below.

42. For prerevolutionary military training in Russia, see J. Bushnell, "Peasants in Uniform: The Tsarist Army as a Peasant Society," *Journal of Social History* 13, no. 4 (Summer 1980): 565–576. The tales of Habsburg brutality and coercion experienced by Russian reservists are detailed in E. Freunthaler, diary, October 1, 1914, KA Vienna: NL Freunthaler, B/497; Vit, *Wspomnienia*, 50–51. Cf. F. Hölzer, diary, October 7, 1914, KA Vienna: NL Hölzer, B/486.

43. The narrative of Fort I/1 with Švrljuga as hero developed very early, in Roda Roda, "Der Sturm auf Przemysl: Geschildert nach den Erzählungen der Mitkämpfer," *Neue Freie Presse* 18016, Morgenblatt (October 20, 1914), 1–2. Influential works took up the narrative and cemented it in historiography, notably Bundesministerium, *Österreich-Ungarns letzter Krieg*, 1:382; and Heiden, *Bollwerk*, 120–130. A photograph of Švrljuga is in G. Graf Vetter von der Lilie, "Die erste Belagerung von Przemyśl," in A. Veltzé, ed., *Die Geschichte des großen Weltkrieges unter besonderer Berücksichtigung Österreich-Ungarns*, 3 vols. (Vienna, 1917), 1:446, available at Landesbibliothek, Digital State Library of Upper Austria, http://digi .landesbibliothek.at/viewer/image/AC04533540/493/LOG_0454. For Švrljuga's prewar military career, see K.u.k. Kriegsministerium, *Schematismus für das k.u.k. Heer und für did k.u.k. Kriegsmarine für 1914: Amtliche Ausgabe* (Vienna, 1914), 888, 914. He is listed here in February 1914 as a second lieutenant (*Leutnant*) serving in Fortress Artillery Regiment 5, in the Temesvár district.

44. A photograph of Bielek is in Lévai, *Éhség, árulás, Przemyśl*, 46. Austrian accounts, and later German-language historiography, mostly name artillery officer Otto Altmann as the fort commander, while Hungarian accounts name Bielek. My account makes use, for the first time, of Bielek's memoir, dated March 25, 1922, and held in HL Budapest: TGY 18, István Bielek. Bielek states that he

was the commander and his claim is proven by an order entitled "Verhalten der Werkkommandanten," dated October 1, 1914, and addressed to him, which he enclosed with his memoir. Tomasz Pomykacz first highlighted the divergence in Austrian and Hungarian accounts. For further details, see his "Kontrowersje wokół dowódcy obrony Fortu I/1 'Łysiczka,'" *Rocznik Przemyski* 51, no. 3 (2015): 135–148.

45. Between one-quarter and one-fifth of Fortress Artillery Regiment 1 would have been very young conscripts undergoing peacetime service. Many of the others were reservists in their twenties. See Bundesministerium, *Österreich-Ungarns letzter Krieg*, 1:25, and Hecht, "Heeresergänzung," 32–38. For Munkács (now Mukachevo, in Ukraine), see B. Varga, *The Monumental Nation: Magyar Nationalism and Symbolic Politics in Fin-de-siècle Hungary* (Oxford, 2016), chap. 5, 242.

46. Idzikowski, "Grupa Siedliska," 84–92. See also the account by R. Rieser, "Przemyśl: Der Kampf um das Werk I/1 der Gruppe Siedliska am 7. Oktober 1914," *Oesterreichische Wehrzeitung* 29 (July 17, 1925): 3–4. Rieser was a reserve corporal in the artillery garrison. It is a strong indication of the lack of contact between artillery and infantry in Fort I/1 that not only did this NCO erroneously name Altmann as the fort commander, but he was also unable to name the infantry unit he was fighting alongside. (He claimed Landsturm Regiment 10 supplied the infantry.)

47. Bielek, memoir, 7–10, HL Budapest: TGY 18, István Bielek. Pomykacz, "Kontrowersje," 140, provides the unit. See also, Rieser, "Przemyśl," 3; Laky, "Erste Belagerung," HL Budapest: II.169 M.kir. 23 HG: 4 Doboz.

48. These details come from Rieser, "Przemyśl," 3.

49. Bielek, memoir, 8, and statements of Zugsführer Péter Gorzó and Imre Bernáth, HL Budapest: TGY 18, István Bielek. See also Laky, "Erste Belagerung," HL Budapest: II.169 M.kir. 23 HG: 4 Doboz. Sources diverge about the time of the assault's start. Bielek, and the NCOs whose statements (taken down in Bielek's presence in August 1915) accompany his memoir, insist that they were aware of the Russians' approach from 2:00 a.m., but these claims were likely motivated by a desire not to appear to have been negligent and cannot be squared with Russian sources, which state that IR 73 arrived at Fort I/1's glacis undetected at 4:35 a.m. (St. Petersburg time—around 3:30 a.m. for the Habsburg troops). See Tscherkassow, *Sturm*, 96. More credible in this light is the Habsburg official history's statement (Bundesministerium, *Österreich-Ungarns letzter Krieg*, 1:382) that it began shortly after 3:00 a.m. A Fortress Engineering Directorate report blamed the fort's sentries for sleeping on watch. See K.u.k. Geniedirektion in Przemyśl, "Verlauf der Kämpfe," KA Vienna: NFA Przemyśl 1322: fo. 40 (reverse).

50. Lévai, *Éhség, árulás, Przemyśl*, chap. 8, in T. Pomykacz, "Jenő Lévai: Bój o fort I/1 'Łysiczka,'" *Nasz Przemyśl* 3 (March 2014): 10–11. See also, Zugführer Imre Bernáth's statement in HL Budapest: TGY 18, István Bielek. Lévai's account is sensationalist and heavily biased toward Hungarian troops, but it was also well researched. He very likely used Bielek's memoir and his NCOs' statements, and possibly Laky's memoir, as part of the source material informing his own account.

51. Tscherkassow, using Russian sources, is categorical on the silence of Fort I/1's artillery. See his *Sturm*, 96. While Hungarian sources blame a crisis among Fort I/1's artillery officers for the silence of the fort's guns, there is an alternative explanation. Fort I/1's turrets were fully traversable, but they were situated on the fort's left, and the Russian attackers advanced against its right shoulder, protected by a small valley. The gunners may thus have been unable to see or fire at targets. My thanks to Tomasz Idzikowski for this point, personal email, August 18, 2018. For the discussion of Švrljuga, see Bielek, memoir, 12, HL Budapest: TGY 18, István Bielek; and Lévai, *Éhség, árulás, Przemyśl*, chap. 8, in Pomykacz, "Jenő Lévai," *Nasz Przemyśl* 3 (March 2014): 11.

52. Statements of Zugsführer Péter Gorzó and Imre Bernáth, HL Budapest: TGY 18, István Bielek.

53. Schwalb, "Verteidigung," 7; Bielek, memoir, 13–14, 16; and statement of Gefreiter Aladár Végh (1922), HL Budapest: TGY 18, István Bielek. Cf. Pomykacz, "Jenő Lévai," *Nasz Przemyśl* 4 (April 2014): 15. Figures for dead and wounded in the ditch from Roda Roda, "Sturm," 2.

54. Bielek, memoir, 13–14, HL Budapest: TGY 18, István Bielek. Casualty figures from Lévai, *Éhség, árulás, Przemyśl*, chap. 9, in Pomykacz, "Jenő Lévai," *Nasz Przemyśl* 4 (April 2014): 14. Estimates of the Russian troops who reached the top of the fort vary. Lévai suggests 450–500 (ibid., 15) whereas Tscherkassow (*Sturm*, 96) states 150. My estimate of 250 is based on prisoners captured and corpses and wounded around the fort.

55. Tscherkassow, *Sturm*, 130–131.

56. The first quotation is from Bielek, memoir, 15, HL Budapest: TGY 18, István Bielek. Both Bielek and Rieser agree that the telephone connection had long been broken, making a nonsense of the story, which appears in some secondhand accounts, that Švrljuga telephoned for reinforcements or to bring Austrian fire down on the roof of the fort. See Roda Roda, "Sturm," 2, and "Die Belagerung vor Przemysl," *Fremden-Blatt* 68, Jahrgang, Nr 290, Morgenblatt (October 20, 1914): 1. An atmospheric description of conditions inside Fort I/1 during the battle is in Pomykacz, "Jenő Lévai," *Nasz Przemyśl* 4 (April 2014): 14–15. For Suchy, see "Franz Suchy, der Held bei den Kämpfen bei Przemysl," *Die Neue Zeitung* 7, Jahrgang, Nr 290 (October 21, 1914): 5.

57. This and the following paragraphs draw on Pomykacz, "Jenő Lévai," *Nasz Przemyśl* 4 (April 2014): 15, and 5 (May 2014): 9. Also Statement of Gefreiter György Buskó, HL Budapest: TGY 18, István Bielek. For Russian commanders at Fort I/1, see Tscherkassow, *Sturm*, 96.

58. The officers' suicide is well attested by both Hungarian and Austrian sources. See Lévai in ibid.; Laky, "Erste Belagerung," HL Budapest: II.169 M.kir. 23 HG: 4 Doboz; and also Roda Roda, "Sturm," 2.

59. General agreement on the number of Russian prisoners taken at Fort I/1 exists, though less on the Russians' dead. See K.u.k. Geniedirektion in Przemysl, "Verlauf der Kämpfe," KA Vienna: NFA Przemysl 1321: fo. 40 (reverse).

60. The defining account of the battle for Fort I/1 was Roda Roda's report, "Sturm," 1–2. Notable also is Švrljuga's account of the battle in "Die Belagerung

vor Przemysl," *Fremden-Blatt* 68, Jahrgang, Nr 290, Morgenblatt (October 20, 1914): 1–2. For Švrljuga's award, see "Der erste Orden der Eisernen Krone für einen Subalternoffizier," *Reichspost* 21, Jahrgang, Nr 259, Morgenblatt (November 6, 1914): 6; Pomykacz, "Kontrowersje," 143. See also Pomykacz, "Jenő Lévai," *Nasz Przemyśl* 5 (May 2014): 10. Lévai claimed an inquiry into Švrljuga's conduct was held at the behest of the Fortress's deputy commander, General Árpád Tamásy, but that its results were suppressed for the sake of the army's reputation. Bielek and Altmann both received the lesser *Signum laudis*. Altmann's faith was not mentioned in any of the mainstream reportage. However, he appears on a list of decorated Jewish soldiers and officers published in *Jüdisches Archiv: Mitteilungen des Komitees "Jüdisches Kriegsarchiv,"* Lieferung 2–3 (August 1915): 40. Bielek's role was remembered in Hungary, although nowhere else. Hungary's interwar dictator, Admiral Horthy, later compensated him for his wartime neglect by ennobling him and conferring on him the *Tiszti arany vitézségi érem* (Golden Officer's Medal for Courage). Pomykacz, "Jenő Lévai," *Nasz Przemyśl* 5 (May 2014): 11.

61. Tscherkassow, *Sturm*, 147.

62. [Komadina], *Dziennik oficera Landsturmu*, 66 (diary entry for October 8 [7], 1914); K.u.k. Geniedirektion in Przemysl, "Verlauf der Kämpfe," KA Vienna: NFA Przemysl 1322: fo. 40 (reverse); Forstner, *Przemyśl*, 176, suggests that Fort I/2, "Byków," was abandoned, but this is clearly a misreading of the contemporary documentation.

63. Vit, *Wspomnienia*, 47–49.

64. Variants of this episode appear in Wolfgang, *Przemysl*, 68–69; Pomykacz, "Jenő Lévai," *Nasz Przemyśl* 5 (May 2014): 11; and Vit, *Wspomnienia*, 54.

65. Tscherkassow, *Sturm*, 111–116; [Komadina], *Dziennik oficera Landsturmu*, 66 (diary entry for October 9, 1914).

66. Heiden, *Bollwerk*, 134–135.

67. Bundesministerium, *Österreich-Ungarns letzter Krieg*, 1:357–358, 449; Gayczak, *Pamiętnik*, 14 (diary entry for October 14, 1914).

68. Tscherkassow, *Sturm*, 75, 114, 117–118, 144. For the inflated Russian casualties reported to the public, see, for example, Roda Roda, "Die Belagerung von Przemyśl," *Neue Freie Presse* 18015 (Nachmittagblatt), October 19, 1914, 3; "Die Verluste der Russen vor Przemysl," *Die Neue Zeitung* 7, Jahrgang, Nr 290 (October 21, 1914): 1. The quotation eulogizing the garrison's "courage" and "resolve" is in "Die Helden von Przemysl," *Neue Freie Presse* 18016 (Abendblatt), October 20, 1914, 1.

69. Quotation from [Komadina], *Dziennik oficera Landsturmu*, 67 (diary entry for October 9, 1914). Also cf. Vit, *Wspomnienia*, 52–53; and F. Hölzer, diary, October 9, 1914, KA Vienna: NL Hölzer B/486. For casualties, see the official figures provided by Hauptmann i. R. Ferencz Stuckheil, which cover the entire first siege, on p. 46 of a draft manuscript, "Die zweite Einschliessung der Festung Przemysl. II. Zeiten des Niedergangs," December 19, 1925, in HL Budapest: II.169 M.kir. 23 HG: 4 Doboz. The Hungarians—the 23rd Honvéd Infantry Division and 97th Landsturm Infantry Brigade—who defended key points on VI Sector, the focus of the attack, suffered the heaviest losses. Landsturm Infantry Regiment 10,

which belonged to the latter formation, alone had 60 killed and 140 wounded. By contrast, the artillery in the sector had very low casualties (36 dead and 54 wounded). So, too, did units defending secondary fronts. Thus, VII (southern) Defense District recorded only 20 killed, 75 wounded, and 8 missing during the entire first siege. See, for these other statistics, Laky, "Erste Belagerung," HL Budapest: II.169 M.kir. 23 HG: 4 Doboz; K.u.k. Verteidigungsbezirkskommando VII to k.u.k. Festungskommando, November 1, 1914, and Art. Kmdo., VI Vert. Bez. to k.u.k. VI Vert. Bez. Kmdo, November 2, 1914, KA Vienna: NFA Przemysl 1322: fos. 45, 52. See also [Komadina], *Dziennik oficera Landsturmu*, 67, 70 (entries for October 9 and 12, 1914).

CHAPTER FOUR: BARRIER

1. "Tartarenwirtschaft in Galizien," in AN Cracow: Naczelny Komitet Narodowy: 279 (Mikrofilm: 100,477), 34.

2. Pethö, ed., *Belagerung und Gefangenschaft*, 49 (diary entry for October 21, 1914).

3. For contemporary views on Grand Duke Nikolai Nikolaevich, see Robinson, *Grand Duke*, 3–5, 15. For his proclamations, see posters entitled "Polacy!" (August 14, 1914) and "Do ludów Austro-Węgier" (dated August 1914, but in fact issued on September 16, 1914), in *Odezwy i rozporządzenia z czasów okupacyi rosyjskiej Lwowa, 1914–1915* (Lwów, 1916), 18–19. For the wide dissemination, see Brussilov, *Soldier's Note-Book*, p. 107.

4. Imperial Russia's treatment of its minorities is covered in A. Kappeler, *The Russian Empire: A Multiethnic History* (Harlow, UK, 2001), 247–282. For discussion of Russia's wartime objectives, see W. A. Renzi, "Who Composed 'Sazonov's Thirteen Points'? A Re-examination of Russia's War Aims of 1914," *American Historical Review* 88, no. 2 (April 1983): 348–350.

5. Bobrinskii's speech is reported in "Generał gubernator rosyjski dla Galicyi," *Ziemia Przemyska* 40 (October 22, 1914), 2. Article 43 of the 1907 Hague Convention on the Laws and Customs of War on Land conferred on occupants the obligation of "respecting, unless absolutely prevented, the laws in force in the country." Available at Yale Law School, Lillian Goldman Law Library, Avalon Project, http://avalon.law.yale.edu/20th_century/hague04.asp. For Galicia's population, see Bachmann, *Herd der Feindschaft*, 30. The Russian army distributed a brochure to its officers at the start of the war containing this caricature of ethnic relations in Galicia. See Kriegszensuramte des Generalquartiermeisters beim Stabe des Oberkommandanten des Südwestarmeen, *Das Galizien der Gegenwart* (July 1914), translated by Nachrichtenabteilung des Operierenden Oberkommandos, KA Vienna: MKSM 69–8/9 1914: fos. 28–37.

6. "Ciekawe wieści ze Lwowa," *Ziemia Przemyska* 41 (October 25, 1914): 2. See also the further installments of this article (originally published in *Głos Narodu*) in the editions of October 27, 29, and 30 and November 3, 5, and 7, 1914. Ruthenian voting in the 1907 parliamentary elections is discussed in Bachmann, *Herd der Feindschaft*, 129.

7. M. von Hagen, *War in a European Borderland: Occupations and Occupation Plans in Galicia and Ukraine, 1914–1918* (Seattle, 2007), 37–40, 52. Illuminating comparison can be made with the later Nazi and Soviet elimination of Polish intelligentsia in 1939. See Snyder, *Bloodlands*, 126, 128, 133–141, 146–147, 153–154.

8. K.k. Statthalter für Galizien, "Planmäßige Bedrückung und Verfolgung der Ukrainer und ihrer Anstalten; Verfolgung der griechisch-katholischen Kirche und ihrer Seelsorger," October 5, 1915, in K.u.k. Ministerium des Äussern, *Sammlung von Nachweisen für die Verletzungen des Völkerrechts durch die mit Österreich-Ungarn Krieg führenden Staaten. III. Nachtrag. Abgeschlossen mit 30. Juni 1916* (Vienna, 1916), 34–41.

9. "Bericht des Legationsrates Baron Andrian über seine Informationsreise nach Ostgalizien" (July 26, 1915), 24–25, AVA Vienna: Min.d.Innern, Präs., 22/Galiz. (1914–1915): 2116: Doc. 19644; Von Hagen, *War*, 26–27; Mick, *Kriegserfahrungen*, 95–96; "Das Schulwesen in Galizien," *Prikarpatskaja Rus* 1402, translated in KA Vienna: NFA Przemysl 1323: fo. 30 and reverse.

10. T. R. Weeks, "Between Rome and Tsargrad: The Uniate Church in Imperial Russia," in R. P. Geraci and M. Khodarkovsky, eds., *Of Religion and Empire: Missions, Conversion, and Tolerance in Tsarist Russia* (Ithaca, NY, 2001), 70–91.

11. Rudnytsky, "Ukrainians," 25–30, 39, 46–47.

12. Wendland, *Russophilen*, 558; Mick, *Kriegserfahrungen*, 116–118.

13. Evlogii, quoted in von Hagen, *War*, 37–38. See also Mick, *Kriegserfahrungen*, 121–122.

14. See von Hagen, *War*, 7–8, 34–35; Mick, *Kriegserfahrungen*, 122–127. See also K.k. Statthalter für Galizien, "Planmäßige Bedrückung und Verfolgung der Ukrainer," in K.u.k. Ministerium des Äussern, *Sammlung von Nachweisen ... III. Nachtrag*, 40, and "Bericht des Legationsrates Baron Andrian" (July 26, 1915), 22, in AVA Vienna: Min.d.Innern, Präs., 22/Galiz. (1914–1915): 2116: Doc. 19644. The number of Greek Catholic parishes in Galicia is taken from T. Olejniczak, "Die kirchliche Verhältnisse in Galizien," in S. Bergmann, ed., *Galizien: Seine kulturelle und wirtschaftliche Entwicklung* (Vienna, 1912), 149.

15. Mick, *Kriegserfahrungen*, 87–89, 98. For Bobrinskii's complaints about Evlogii, see Robinson, *Grand Duke*, 209–210.

16. Letter to Kazimierz Baran from Nienadowa, January 1915, KA Vienna: NFA Przemysl 1323: fos. 316 (reverse) and 317.

17. S. Ansky, *The Enemy at His Pleasure: A Journey Through the Jewish Pale of Settlement During World War I*, ed. and trans. J. Neugroschel (New York, 2002), 68–70; "Bericht über Brody," by Dr. B. Hausner, in CAHJP Jerusalem: HM2–9177: fo. 23.

18. Numerous examples of the Russian army's violence against civilians, and especially against Jews, are reproduced in K.u.k. Ministerium des Äussern, *Sammlung von Nachweisen für die Verletzungen des Völkerrechts durch die mit Österreich-Ungarn Krieg führenden Staaten. Abgeschlossen mit 31. Jänner 1915* (Vienna, 1915), and the three supplementary (*Nachtrag*) volumes. These documents need to be treated with caution, as the material was selected to influence international opinion, and there is usually no way to verify specific incidents. However, the similarity

between these reports, Ansky's *Enemy*, and Hausner's reports in CAHJP Jerusalem leave no doubt that they are valuable and illuminating sources. For the cultural and historical roots of Cossacks' anti-Semitism, see W. W. Hagen, *Anti-Jewish Violence in Poland, 1914–1920* (Cambridge, 2018), 78; R. H. McNeal, *Tsar and Cossack, 1855–1914* (Basingstoke, 1987), 74–83. The description of Jews in the war zone is from O. C. Tăslăuanu, *With the Austrian Army in Galicia* (London, n.d.), 65, 85. Cf. Ansky, *Enemy*, 8. For refugee numbers, see B. Hoffmann-Holter, *"Abreisendmachung": Jüdische Kriegsflüchtlinge in Wien 1914 bis 1923* (Cologne, 1995), 29.

19. Mick, *Kriegserfahrungen*, 105–106. For the Przemyśl spy's account of Lwów, see report by Julian Walczak on his observations in occupied territory in December 1914 (January 8, 1915), 23, KA Vienna: NFA Przemysl 1323: fo. 245. News of the pogrom also reached the garrison. See Gayczak, *Pamiętnik*, 73 (March 8, 1915).

20. A. S. Lindemann, *Esau's Tears: Modern Anti-Semitism and the Rise of the Jews* (Cambridge, 1997), 279–305. For the rise of "racial" ideas in imperial Russia, see E. M. Avrutin, "Racial Categories and the Politics of (Jewish) Difference in Late Imperial Russia," *Kritika: Explorations in Russian and Eurasian History* 8, no. 1 (Winter 2007): 13–40; and R. Weinberg, "Look! Up There in the Sky: It's a Vulture, It's a Bat. . . . It's a Jew: Reflections on Antisemitism in Late Imperial Russia, 1906–1914," in E. M. Avrutin and H. Murav, eds., *Jews in the East European Borderlands: Essays in Honor of John D. Klier* (Boston, 2012), 167–186. For state anti-Semitism during the 1905 revolution and Trepov, see S. Lambroza, "The Pogroms of 1903–1906," in J. D. Klier and S. Lambroza, eds., *Pogroms: Anti-Jewish Violence in Modern Russian History* (Cambridge, 1992), esp. 219–239.

21. Generally, Avrutin, "Racial Categories," 24, 28–29, 31; P. Holquist, "To Count, to Extract, and to Exterminate: Population Statistics and Population Politics in Late Imperial and Soviet Russia," in R. G. Suny and T. Martin, eds., *A State of Nations: Empire and Nation-Making in the Age of Lenin and Stalin* (Oxford, 2001), esp. 124–125. For the conversations at Stavka and Russian military anti-Semitic actions in Galicia, see P. Holquist, "The Role of Personality in the First (1914–1915) Russian Occupation of Galicia and Bukovina," in J. Dekel-Chen, D. Gaunt, N. M. Meir, and I. Bartal, eds., *Anti-Jewish Violence: Rethinking the Pogrom in East European History* (Bloomington, IN, 2010), 59.

22. A. V. Prusin, *Nationalizing a Borderland: War, Ethnicity, and Anti-Jewish Violence in East Galicia, 1914–1920* (Tuscaloosa, AL, 2005), 38–39.

23. Ibid., 39–45. One Habsburg soldier who hid behind Russian lines was told by a Jewish sergeant in the Tsar's artillery that orders for requisitioning reflected the ethnic hierarchy of the occupied zone: "The men must pay the Ruthenes, they could pay the Poles, [but] they should take from the Jews." See Fähnrich i.d. Res. Dr. Hermann Löw, testimony to k.u.k. Kriegsministerium, June 20, 1915, reproduced in K.u.k. Ministerium des Äussern, *Sammlung von Nachweisen für die Verletzungen des Völkerrechts durch die mit Österreich-Ungarn Krieg führenden Staaten. II. Nachtrag. Abgeschlossen mit 30. November 1915* (Vienna, 1916), 122.

24. Von Hagen, *War*, 27–28. Ansky mentions a case of a son being forced by Cossacks to hang his own father. See *Enemy*, 91. The other examples are from Hausner's report for Horodenka in CAHJP Jerusalem: HM2–9177: fos. 3–4.

25. Ansky, *Enemy*, 91. See also "Bericht des Legationsrates Baron Andrian" (July 26, 1915), 17, in AVA Vienna: Min.d.Innern, Präs., 22/Galiz. (1914–1915): 2116: Doc. 19644.

26. Mick, *Kriegserfahrungen*, 109. See also the report to 2. Armee-Etappen-kommando (Doc. 102, Beilage 2) and Dr. Ludwig B.'s testimony of January 9, 1915 (Doc. 109) in K.u.k. Ministerium des Äussern, *Sammlung von Nach-weisen . . . Abgeschlossen mit 31. Jänner 1915*, 146–147, 153–154. The Russian occupation in Jarosław was reported on in Przemyśl. See "Moskale w Jarosławiu," *Ziemia Przemyska* 46 (November 3, 1914): 1.

27. For the Tsarist military's deportations in Russia's western borderlands, see E. Lohr, *Nationalizing the Russian Empire: The Campaign Against Enemy Aliens During World War I* (Cambridge, MA, 2003), 122–137. For its deportations in Galicia, see Holquist, "Role of Personality," 65. For the Russians' estimates of interned and executed Ruthenes, see Wendland, *Russophilen*, 546.

28. Grand Duke Nikolai's order is quoted in Holquist, "Role of Personality," 65. The other details in this paragraph are from "Bericht aus Mościska," by Dr. B. Hausner and k.k. Landesgendarmeriekommando Nr 5 to c.k. Starostwa w Mościska[ch], May 10, 2016, CAHJP Jerusalem: HM2–9177: fos. 9, 51–52. There may at this time have been a deliberate effort to remove Jews from all around Przemyśl. Prusin (*Nationalizing*, 51) notes that 4,000 Jews were expelled from neighboring Dobromil at the end of February 1915.

29. Holquist, "Role of Personality," 66–67. Dimitriev's Order No. 289 to the 278 Kromski Infantry Regiment, April 8 (21), 1915) (Doc. 39) is translated and reproduced in K.u.k. Ministerium des Äussern, *Sammlung von Nachweisen . . . II. Nachtrag*, 82–83.

30. Holquist, "Role of Personality," 67; Prusin, *Nationalizing*, 62. For a failed attempt to drive Jews into Habsburg lines, see "Bericht über Tyśmienica," by Dr. B. Hausner, in CAHJP Jerusalem: HM2–9177: fos. 56–57.

31. F. Conrad von Hötzendorf, *Aus meiner Dienstzeit 1906–1918*, vol. 5, *Oktober–November–Dezember 1914. Die Kriegsereignisse und die politischen Vorgänge in dieser Zeit* (Vienna, 1925), 87–88, 92.

32. Reichsarchiv, *Der Weltkrieg, 1914–1918*, vol. 5, *Der Herbst-Feldzug 1914: Im Westen bis zum Stellungskrieg; Im Osten bis zum Rückzug* (Berlin, 1929), 411–416, 420. For the East Prussia campaign, see Reichsarchiv, *Der Weltkrieg, 1914–1918*, vol. 2, *Die Befreiung Ostpreußens* (Berlin, 1925). For Conrad's jealousy, see Rauchensteiner, *First World War*, 246–247.

33. Bundesministerium, *Österreich-Ungarns letzter Krieg*, 1:370–377; Robinson, *Grand Duke*, 176–182; Reichsarchiv, *Weltkrieg*, 5:550.

34. Bundesministerium, *Österreich-Ungarns letzter Krieg*, 1:413, 425–430, 440–450, 471–483. See also Skizze 24 in the accompanying "Beilagen." Thirty-six and a half Habsburg divisions faced 25½ Russian divisions between the mouth of the

San and the town of Stary Sambor. The map (Skizze 24) shows another four Habsburg divisions and one Russian brigade southeast of Stary Sambor.

35. Forstner, *Przemyśl*, 184–185, 197–198; Stuckheil, "Zweite Einschließung" (1926), 168–169. Stuckheil notes that twenty-six fortress ration days of oats were taken, of which two-thirds could have been diverted to bread production for the garrison's soldiers.

36. Forstner, *Przemyśl*, 200–201; Stuckheil, "Zweite Einschließung" (1926), 170–171; G. A. Tunstall, *Written in Blood: The Battles for Fortress Przemyśl in WWI* (Bloomington, IN, 2016), 105.

37. Forstner, *Przemyśl*, 189, 197; Bundesministerium, *Österreich-Ungarns letzter Krieg*, 1:448.

38. Bundesministerium, *Österreich-Ungarns letzter Krieg*, 1:435, 448–449. See also Gayczak, *Pamiętnik*, 17 (October 27, 1914). For the 23rd Honvéd Infantry Division's overall losses, see Kusmanek, "Die beiden Belagerungen," 27, KA Vienna: NL Kusmanek B/1137/14. Detailed casualty returns for III/Honvéd Infantry Regiment 2 and III/Honvéd Infantry Regiment 8 survive in MNZP Przemyśl: Archiwum Molnara: DVD 4: T. Nr 4 MP. HIST 391: fo. 55 (reverse) and 60. In both battalions, cholera accounted for nearly one-fifth of losses.

39. Wawro, *Mad Catastrophe*, 280–281; Stone, *Eastern Front*, 99; Bundesministerium, *Österreich-Ungarns letzter Krieg*, 1:430–435.

40. Bundesministerium, *Österreich-Ungarns letzter Krieg*, 1:450–470.

41. Ibid., 1:489–501; Op. Nr 3834, reproduced in Conrad, *Dienstzeit*, 5:362–363.

42. For the machinations to remove Conrad, see Rauchensteiner, *First World War*, 253–255. For the railway bridges, see Heiden, *Bollwerk*, 153. The final quotation is from Kusmanek, "Die beiden Belagerungen," 30, KA Vienna: NL Kusmanek B/1137/14.

43. See Stuckheil's draft manuscript, "Zweite Einschliessung II," December 19, 1925, in HL Budapest: II.169 M.kir. 23 HG: 4 Doboz, fo. 108.

44. F. Stuckheil, "Die strategische Rolle Przemyśls auf dem östlichen Kriegsschauplatze," *Militärwissenschaftliche und technische Mitteilungen* 54 (1923): 76–78.

45. Thus, for example, the influential *Neue Freie Presse* published reports on Przemyśl's victorious resistance under siege and the fighting around it every day, with one exception (October 25), from October 8 to 30, 1914.

46. For the order to write farewell letters, see Forstner, *Przemyśl*, 205. Quotation from Op. Nr 3854, reproduced in Conrad, *Dienstzeit*, 5:363–364.

CHAPTER FIVE: ISOLATION

1. The first quotation is from Gayczak, *Pamiętnik*, 21 (diary entry of November 4, 1914). The second comes from "W obecnej chwili," *Ziemia Przemyska* 47 (November 5, 1914): 1. An example of the evacuation posters, issued by the c.k. Starostwo, is in AP Przemyśl: 397 (Afisze, plakaty i druki ulotni): 20.

2. F. Stuckheil, "Die zweite Einschließung der Festung Przemyśl," *Militärwissenschaftliche und technische Mitteilungen* 55 (1924): 302–303.

3. Stuckheil's draft manuscript, "Zweite Einschliessung II," December 19, 1925, 27, in HL Budapest: II.169 M.kir. 23 HG: 4 Doboz; Kusmanek, "Die beiden Belagerungen," 48, KA Vienna: NL Kusmanek B/1137/14. For frostbite cases, see diary of unknown Hungarian officer (diary entry for November 25, 1914), in I. Lagzi, ed., *Węgrzy w Twierdzy Przemyskiej w latach 1914–1915* (Warsaw, 1985), 124. For warm underwear production in the Fortress, see Festungskommandobefehl Nr 236 (October 1, 1914), Pkt. 5 in KA Vienna: NFA Przemysl 1322: fo. 422; "Fabryka bielizny w . . . Sali sądowej," *Ziemia Przemyska* 38 (October 18, 1914): 3–4. For the end of the work, see M. Dalecki and A. K. Mielnik, eds., "Dziennik Józefy Prochazka z okresu oblężenia i okupacji rosyjskiej Przemyśla w 1915 roku jako źródło historyczne," *Archiwum Państwowe w Przemyślu. Rocznik Historyczno-Archiwalny* 17 (2003): 274–276 (entries for January 27 and 31 and February 18, 1915).

4. Stuckheil's draft manuscript, "Zweite Einschliessung II," December 19, 1925, 28–30, in HL Budapest: II.169 M.kir. 23 HG: 4 Doboz; Schwalb, "Verteidigung," 13–14. For the matches, see Roda Roda, "Die zweite Einschließung von Przemysl," *Neue Freie Presse* 18158 (Morgenblatt), March 12, 1915, 4.

5. Maximum food prices laid out in "Obwieszczenie!" issued by Komisarz rządowy Lanikiewicz, November 2, 1914, AP Przemyśl: 397 (Afisze, plakaty i druki ulotni): 47. For foodstuffs' peacetime prices, see Michaelsburg, *Im belagerten Przemysl*, 81. Discussion of the difficulties of purchasing food is in "Z miasta," *Ziemia Przemyska* 53 (November 15, 1914): 3–4.

6. Information on these initiatives is in "Dla najbiedniejszych," *Ziemia Przemyska* 53 (November 15, 1914): 1; "Kuchnia dla ubogich," *Ziemia Przemyska* 73 (December 29, 1914): 3–4; "Tania kuchnia," *Ziemia Przemyska* 8 (January 17, 1915): 3–4; "Erhebungen über Verpflegsvorräte bei der Übergabe von Przemyśl" (September 14, 1915); Testimony of Dr. Sigismund Szłapacki, KA Vienna: NL Kusmanek B/1137/13.

7. The quotation about prehistoric times is in "W obecnych stosunkach," *Ziemia Przemyska* 9 (January 19, 1915): 1.

8. This account is from "Nad miastem rosyjskie latawce" and "Migawki: Straszna przygoda z . . . bombą," *Ziemia Przemyska* 63 (December 3, 1914): 2–4; and Jabłońska, *Dziennik*, 95–97 (diary entry for December 1, 1914).

9. "Nad miastem rosyjskie latawce," *Ziemia Przemyska* 63 (December 3, 1914): 3. For other accounts of this first bombing, see Jabłońska, *Dziennik*, 95–96 (diary entry for December 1, 1914); Michaelsburg, *Im belagerten Przemysl*, 90 (diary entry for December 4, 1914). Lieutenant Stanisław Tyro, who visited the scenes of the bombing in the hours after the raid, was told that a boy had been very badly injured by bomb fragments, in KA Vienna: NFA Przemysl 1321: fos. 205–206. The number of bombs dropped during the siege comes from Schwalb, "Verteidigung," 11. For early aerial bombing, see C. Geinitz, "The First Air War Against Noncombatants: Strategic Bombing of German Cities in World War I," in R. Chickering and S. Förster, eds., *Great War, Total War: Combat and Mobilization on the Western Front, 1914–1918* (Cambridge, 2000), 207–226.

10. For the posters, see "Ogłoszenie!," signed by Komisarz rządowy Dr. Bła-żowski, December 6, 1914, AP Przemyśl: 397 (Afisze, plakaty i druki ulotni): 49. Countermeasures are laid out in Stuckheil's draft manuscript, "Zweite Ein-schliessung II," December 19, 1925, in HL Budapest: II.169 M.kir. 23 HG: 4 Doboz; H. Schwalb, "Improvisationen zur Bekämpfung von Luftfahrzeugen in der Festung Przemyśl 1914/15," *Mitteilungen über Gegenstände des Artillerie-und Geniewesens* 49, no. 10 (1918): 1539, 1544–1545. For apocalyptic rumors, see Jabłońska, *Dziennik*, 95–96 (diary entry for December 1, 1914); Stock, *Notatnik*, 92 (diary entry for December 2, 1914).

11. See the detailed reports of raids on January 18 and 20, 1915, by K.u.k. Militär-Polizeiwachabteilung in Lemberg derzeit in Przemyśl, KA Vienna: NFA Przemysl 1323: fos. 481–486, 514–517. For an example of a rumor claiming the deaths of a mother and her six children, see S. Tyro's notes of December 19, 1914, in KA Vienna: NFA Przemysl 1321: fo. 232 (reverse). Total casualties in the raids are given in Orłowicz, *Illustrierter Führer*, 94. Stenitzer's reaction is recounted in Pethö, ed., *Belagerung und Gefangenschaft*, 56 (diary entries for December 2 and 3, 1914).

12. Künigl-Ehrenburg's quotation comes from Michaelsburg, *Im belager-ten Przemyśl*, 121 (diary entry for February 15, 1915); the other quotations, from Stanisława Baranowicz and Maria Golińska, are in Dalecki, "Wspomnienia Prze-myskich nauczycielek," 153–155.

13. R. Biedermann, "Kriegstagebuch," vol. 2, c. 1946, p. 234, KA Vienna: NL Biedermann, B/608.

14. Gayczak, *Pamiętnik*, 29, 32 (entries for November 24 and December 4, 1914). For the rumor of peace negotiations, see ibid., 46 (diary entry for January 4, 1915); Stock, *Notatnik*, 110 (January 4, 1915); Jabłońska, *Dziennik*, 115 (diary entry for January 12, 1915).

15. Gayczak, *Pamiętnik*, 35–36 (December 14, 1914). See also esp. 29–31 (No-vember 25 and 28 and December 1 and 2). For the other ranks' distress, see also Lenar, *Pamiętnik*, 17. For the negative rumors referred to at the start of the para-graph, see Stuckheil, "Zweite Einschließung" (1924), 303; Jabłonska, *Dziennik*, 99 (entries for December 3 and 4, 1914).

16. "A kino gra...," *Ziemia Przemyska* 50 (November 10, 1914): 4. For the the-ater, see "Z teatru," *Ziemia Przemyska* 5 (January 10, 1915): 3.

17. Michaelsburg, *Im belagerten Przemysl*, 82 (diary entry for November 24, 1914). See also *Ziemia Przemyska* 50 (November 10, 1914): 4, and 54 (Novem-ber 17, 1914): 4. For music more generally in the besieged Fortress, see "Kronika," *Ziemia Przemyska* 10 (January 21, 1915): 4. See also Michaelsburg, *Im belagerten Przemysl*, 114–115 (diary entry for January 29, 1914). One notable musician who played at these events was Béla Varkonyi, a renowned Hungarian composer, who after the war emigrated to the United States.

18. For balls, see T. Pudłocki, "'Lolu, gdzie mój frak?' Prowincjonalne bale Galicji wschodniej w latach 1867–1914 jako przkład synkretyzmu estetyki życia codziennego," in A. Seweryn and M. Kulesza-Gierat, eds., *Powinowactwa sztuk*

w kulturze oświecenia i romantyzmu (Lublin, Poland, 2012), esp. 94, 96–97. More generally, see Fahey, "Bulwark," 84, 96–97, 138–140.

19. See "Die Poterne: Unabhängiges Heldenblatt," and the mainly Hungarian-language mock advertisements and story in MNZP Przemyśl: Archiwum Molnara. The humor uses many wordplays and in-jokes, some of them in two languages. For example, the Hungarian "Uncle Göre" might also be a reference to the German word "Göre" meaning a cheeky little girl. An alternative interpretation is that it refers to a Captain Adalbert Göre who served in Honvéd Infantry Regiment 8. The mock advertisements are digitalized at Podkarpacka Biblioteka Cyfrowa (Podkarpacka Digital Library), www.pbc.rzeszow.pl /dlibra/docmetadata?id=11063&from=&dirids=1&ver_id=&lp=4&QI=08DE F6A08A5A690265DD27653520EC30-3.

20. The hotelier's letter appears in the papers of S. Tyro, no date, KA Vienna: NFA Przemysl 1321: fo. 200. The description of the city is in "To i owo . . . ," *Ziemia Przemyska* 54 (November 17, 1914): 3. For the price of sex, see R. Biedermann, "Kriegstagebuch," vol. 2, c. 1946, p. 236, KA Vienna: NL Biedermann B/608. Cf. Laky, "Erste Belagerung," HL Budapest: II.169 M.kir. 23 HG: 4 Doboz. For food prices, see chap. 6.

21. For Amy, see R. Biedermann, "Kriegstagebuch," vol. 2, c. 1946, 237–238, KA Vienna: NL Biedermann B/608. The other information comes from Stock, *Notatnik*, 112 (diary entry for January 11, 1915); Laky, "Erste Belagerung," HL Budapest: II.169 M.kir. 23 HG: 4 Doboz; Gayczak, *Pamiętnik*, 51 (diary entry for January 13, 1915). Underlining in original.

22. See S. Tyro, notes, December 2, 1914, KA Vienna: NFA Przemysl 1321: fo. 206. For Wilk and Haas, see "Erhebungen über Verpflegsvorräte bei der Übergabe von Przemyśl," September 14, 1915, KA Vienna: NL Kusmanek B/1137/13: fos. 124–138. Wilk's lover, Captain Georg Fenyö, was arrested at the start of February because Wilk was caught selling some of the food and fattening hogs with army rusks that she had received from him. See the diary entry of February 2, 1915, in Lagzi, ed., *Węgrzy*, 144. E. Schwarz makes the point about expressing love with sardines and cigarettes in his story "Helden," in *Frauen in Przemysl: Sittenbilder aus der belagerten Festung, 1914/15* (Darmstadt, 1936), esp. 137.

23. For nurses, see J. Tomann, diary, January 13, 1915, KA Vienna: NFA Przemysl 1322: Fasz. 1345. Tomann records in his diary entry of February 17, 1915, that military doctors were at last banned from forming relationships with nurses in order to halt the reputational damage to the army medical organization. For "Mici," see the diary entries of November 12, 16, and 21, 1914, and February 6 and 7, 1915, in Lagzi, ed., *Węgrzy*, 117, 120, 122, 146.

24. Helena's notoriety across the garrison was such that she even appears in the trench newspapers as author of one of the imaginary erotic books for fortresses, *Recollections from Married Lives: Fascinating Disclosures from Prof. Hella*, MNZP Przemyśl: Archiwum Molnara. She is the subject of Schwarz's story "Der Fesselballon" (see p. 120 for the quotation here). She also appears in the anonymous Hungarian officer's diary reproduced in Lagzi, ed., *Węgrzy*, 146 (diary entry for

February 7, 1915): "In the evening I partied hard again, as Kálmán [the officer's billet mate], Ella and Hella arrived." This may not have been Ella's and Hella's first visit. Kálmán had brought two young women back to the billet with him in the early hours a few months previously (November 21—an experience clearly both intense and exhausting, for the officer mentions sleeping into the afternoon of the following day).

25. Sadly, this investigation is now lost, but it, and some details about the women, are mentioned in K.u.k. Feldgericht in Przemyśl to Haupt K.Stelle des k.u.k. Brückenkopfkommandos in Przemyśl, August 26, 1915 (K.Nr 36/15) and the reply of September 12, 1915 (K.Nr 594), KA Vienna: NL Kusmanek B/1137/13: fos. 136, 130.

26. This account draws on Schwarz's story "Der Fesselballon" in his *Frauen in Przemysl*, 117–130.

27. This and the following paragraphs are based on Oberleutnant Walfried Hahn von Hahnenbeck's "Bericht über die stabile Radiostation Przemyśl," in KA Vienna: NL Kusmanek B/1137/15.

28. Forstner, *Przemyśl*, 210–211.

29. Michaelsburg, *Im belagerten Przemysl*, 111 (diary entry for January 26, 1915). For examples of overzealous poetry, see "Ein Landsturmlied 'Kusmanek Hurrah!' and 'Przemyśl,'" in *Kriegsnachrichten* 112 and 116 (February 9 and 13, 1915). A full run of the paper is preserved in KA Vienna: NL Kusmanek B/1137/8.

30. The *Tábori Újság* is discussed at length in Geőcze, *A przemysli tragédia*, 41, 86–88. For Künigl-Ehrenburg's quotation, see Michaelsburg, *Im belagerten Przemysl*, 111 (diary entry for January 26, 1915). The skill of reading between the lines of official bulletins is most explicitly addressed in Wolfgang, *Przemyśl*, 101–102, but the same thought processes can also be seen in, for example, Stock's *Notatnik* and Jabłońska's *Dziennik*.

31. See *Ziemia Przemyska* 33, 34, 36 (October 6, 8, and 11, 1914) and 12 and 14 (January 26 and 31, 1915). The paper appeared with four pages on Tuesdays, Thursdays, and Sundays. It cost 10 hellers, like the military newssheets. In the interwar period it was known for being rabidly anti-Semitic (so much so that for half a year in 1936 it had to be published in Poznań, because no printer in Przemyśl, Lwów, or Cracow would have it), but there is no sign of Jew-hatred in its siege issues of 1914–1915.

32. "Kiedy skończy się wojna?," *Ziemia Przemyska* 53 (November 15, 1914): 3. On December 11, a day before the war's end was supposed to happen, the newspaper addressed the issue again, running an article exploring the length of previous conflicts. See "Jak długo może trwać obecna wojna?," *Ziemia Przemyska* 68 (December 11, 1914): 1–2. A further article on the theme was stopped by the censor. See *Ziemia Przemyska* 8 (January 17, 1915): 4. The paper's mystical calculation of the war's end clearly had huge appeal, for it spread beyond the Polish-speaking population to others in the garrison. An (unattributed) version appears in German in Völker, *Przemyśl*, 142–143, and the date is also referenced in the trench newspaper poem "Der Opti und die Pessimisten," by Bruno Prochaska: "On 12/XII is the war at an end / as can be proven mathematically." MNZP Przemyśl: Archiwum Mol-

nara. Digitized at Podkarpacka Biblioteka Cyfrowa (Podkarpacka Digital Library), www.pbc.rzeszow.pl/dlibra/show-content/publication/edition/11062?id=11062.

33. F. Czernin von Chudenitz, *Das Postwesen in der Festung Przemysl während der beiden Belagerungen 1914/1915* (Vienna, 1985), 17–18.

34. See "Beilage zum Festungskommando-Befehl Nr 9," January 4, 1915, KA Vienna: NFA Przemysl 1323: fo. 109; Stock, *Notatnik*, 101–102 (diary entry for December 19, 1914). See also Nikolaus Wagner von Florheim, "Als Flieger in Przemysl," 14, KA Vienna: Luftfahrtarchiv: Ms. 72.

35. P. Gray and O. Thetford, *German Aircraft of the First World War* (London, 1962), 17–19, 253, 278–279; "Beilage zum Festungskommando-Befehl Nr 9," January 4, 1915, KA Vienna: NFA Przemysl 1323: fo. 109.

36. Czernin von Chudenitz, *Postwesen*, 23–26, 28; K. Wielgus, "Lotniska Twierdzy Przemyśl," in Brzoskwinia, *Fortyfikacja austriacka*, 124; "Beilage zum Festungskommando-Befehl Nr 14," January 9, 1915, KA Vienna: NFA Przemysl 1323: fo. 261; Forstner, *Przemyśl*, 223.

37. Czernin von Chudenitz, *Postwesen*, 39–42. The quotation is from Pethö, ed., *Belagerung und Gefangenschaft*, 65 (diary entry for January 12, 1915).

38. Stuckheil, "Zweite Einschließung" (1924), 292–302. For the joke, see Stock, *Notatnik*, 97 (diary entry of December 8, 1914).

39. The Battle of Limanowa and its aftermath is dealt with in detail in Bundesministerium, *Österreich-Ungarns letzter Krieg*, 1:774–812, 2:33–43. For the Fortress's perspective and the December 9–10 operation, see Stuckheil, "Zweite Einschließung" (1924), 413–415.

40. Stuckheil, "Zweite Einschließung" (1924), 395–410; Jabłońska, *Dziennik*, 103 (diary entry for December 10, 1914). Archduke Friedrich's announcement was reported in the *Kriegsnachrichten* issue of December 11, 1914, in KA Vienna: NL Kusmanek B/1137/8. For the reaction, see Stock, *Notatnik*, 98–99 (diary entry of December 14).

41. Stuckheil, "Zweite Einschließung" (1924), 416–417; Kusmanek, "Die beiden Belagerungen," 36–37, KA Vienna: NL Kusmanek B/1137/14.

42. F. Stuckheil, "Die zweite Einschließung der Festung Przemyśl," *Militärwissenschaftliche und technische Mitteilungen* 56 (1925), 1–3; Geőcze, *A przemysli tragédia*, 100.

43. The following account of the storming of Hill 428 is drawn from Stuckheil, "Zweite Einschließung" (1925), 4–8, and Heiden, *Bollwerk*, 172–176. See also Molnár's battle report of December 21, 1914, in MNZP Przemyśl: Archiwum Molnara: DVD 11: T. Nr 13 MP, HIST 400: fos. 13–14.

44. Heiden, *Bollwerk*, 174.

45. For the number of prisoners, see the telegram from the Fortress Command to AOK, December 16, 1914, KA Vienna: NL Kusmanek B/1137/14. Stuckheil states that between forty-two and eighty prisoners were taken.

46. This attack and its aftermath are recounted in Stuckheil, "Zweite Einschließung" (1925), 120–133. For the message dropped by the Russian airplane, see K.u.k. Festungskommando in Przemyśl, Op. Nr 129/8 to Noyaukommando in Przemyśl, December 12, 1914, KA Vienna: NFA Przemysl 1321: fo. 86.

47. See the battalion commander Major Berdenich's report in D. Nónay, *A volt m. kir. szegedi 5. honvéd gyalogezred a világháborúban* (Budapest, 1931), University of Szeged, Klebelsberg Library, www.bibl.u-szeged.hu/bibl/mil/ww1/nonay /fejezet18.html.

48. For losses and captures, see Stuckheil, "Zweite Einschließung" (1925), 116. The losses of Honvéd Infantry Regiment 7 in the operation amounted to 1 officer and 23 soldiers killed and 3 officers and 141 soldiers wounded.

49. Bruno Prochaska, "Der Opti und die Pessimisten," MNZP Przemyśl: Archiwum Molnara. Digitized at Podkarpacka Biblioteka Cyfrowa (Podkarpacka Digital Library), www.pbc.rzeszow.pl/dlibra/show-content/publication/edition/11062 ?id=11062.

50. Stuckheil, "Zweite Einschließung" (1925), 18–19, 226–227.

51. Little information on losses in November is available, but they seem not to have been great. The December losses, by contrast, were heavy and included 700–800 men in the sortie of December 9–10; over 1,000 men in the breakout attempt of December 15–18; another 2,000 on other fronts (mainly the north) from December 15 to 20; and around 2,000 injured or killed (there may be some overlap with the previous figure here) in the counterattacks on the northern Na Górach positions, as well as 724 men in the operations of December 27–28. See Stuckheil, "Zweite Einschließung" (1924), 410, and (1925), 116, 222, 224, 355. The anonymous Hungarian diarist notes that before Christmas, Honvéd Infantry Regiment 8 had suffered 60 percent losses. See Lagzi, ed., *Węgrzy*, 137 (diary entry for December 21, 1914).

52. Gayczak, *Pamiętnik*, 40–41 (diary entry for December 24, 1914).

53. Original note in KA Vienna: NFA Przemysl 1323: fos. 46–47. The message is written in Polish and the word used is *opłatek* (pl. *opłatki*). The *opłatek* is a thin wafer similar to the Eucharistic wafers used in the Catholic Holy Mass. The Polish tradition is that before the Christmas Eve family meal, family members break the *opłatki* together, giving each other wishes as they share the wafer. It is an intimate moment. The Tsarist troops' use of it was an extremely powerful and emotional way to signal peace and fraternity to the garrison. (Among the Tsarist troops, of course, there were many Poles.)

54. See Wolfgang, *Przemyśl*, 117; Stolz, *Tiroler Landsturmregiment Nr. II*, 200.

CHAPTER SIX: STARVATION

1. Pethö, ed., *Belagerung und Gefangenschaft*, 66 (Stenitzer's diary entry for January 16, 1915).

2. Stuckheil, "Zweite Einschließung" (1926), 287–290; Forstner, *Przemyśl*, 216, 219. For the mocking neighing, see "Przemysls Kapitulation," 4, KA Vienna: NL Páger, B/737.

3. Stuckheil, "Zweite Einschließung" (1926), 288.

4. For human rations, see "Beilage zum Fskmdobefehl Nr 282," November 7, 1914, KA Vienna: NFA Przemysl 1321: fo. 100; Völker, *Przemyśl*, 183–186. Stuck-

heil, "Zweite Einschließung" (1926), 286, states that rations were modified already on December 1, 1914, but evidence from Vit, *Wspomnienia*, 88–90, shows that reductions were marginal before January. For the horses, see Kusmanek, "Die beiden Belagerungen," 42; Poeffel, "Chronologische Zusammenstellung," 10–12, KA Vienna: NL Kusmanek B/1137/14 and B/1137/12: fos. 51–53. See also "Beilage zum Festungskommando-Befehl Nr 28," January 22, 1915, in KA Vienna: NFA Przemysl 1323: fo. 572. Lenar, *Pamiętnik*, 16, describes soldiers being harnessed to wagons. See also Vit, *Wspomnienia*, 76–77, stating that each battalion retained just ten horses.

5. Inflation figures based on diary comparisons, especially the detailed information in Gayczak, *Pamiętnik*, 73 (March 10) and Geőcze, *A przemysli tragédia*, 111–112. Prewar prices are given in Michaelsburg, *Im belagerten Przemysl*, 81. The roving commissions are mentioned in Schwarz, *Frauen*, 142, and Jabłońska, *Dziennik*, 118 (diary entry for January 28, 1915). For the military's sale of food to civilians, see Völker, *Przemysl*, 181; Jabłońska, *Dziennik*, 117 (diary entry for January 23, 1915).

6. Jabłońska, *Dziennik*, 122 (diary entry for February 13, 1915).

7. Civilian mortality is recorded in Kramarz, *Ludność Przemyśla*, 115. For anti-Semitism and accusations of Jewish profiteering, see Dalecki and Mielnik, eds., "Dziennik Józefy Prochazka," 275 (diary entry for January 31, 1915). For Jews' economic position in Przemyśl before the war, see the Introduction. The final quotation is from Stock, *Notatnik*, 57 (October 10, 1914).

8. Good examples of food fantasies are in Jabłońska, *Dziennik*, 112, 127 (entries for January 3 and March 9, 1915). See also, for a child's experience of the siege, S. Szopa, "Wspomnienia z dziecinnych lat" (1976), 16. Extra details from Jabłońska, *Dziennik*, 126 (diary entry for March 6, 1915). The final quotation is from Stefania Zaborniak, in Dalecki, "Wspomnienia Przemyskich nauczycielek," 160.

9. The Honvéd officers' menu of January 6, 1915, is in HL Budapest: II.169 M.kir. 23 HG: 2 Doboz. For the rest, see the diary of an unknown Hungarian officer, February 14, 1915, in Lagzi, ed., *Węgrzy*, 147.

10. For corruption in the Fortress Quartermaster's Section, see testimony of Stefanie Haas (quoting her fiancé), August 27, 1915, in KA Vienna: NL Kusmanek B/1137/13: fo. 126 (reverse). Cf. Hungarian officer's diary entry of January 1, 1915, in Lagzi, ed., *Węgrzy*, 139. For theft in units, see Verteidigungsbezirk No. VIII, Order, Res. No. 591, March 5, 1915, MNZP Przemyśl: Archiwum Molnara: DVD 8: T. Nr 11 MP. HIST 398: fo. 62. The quotation is from E. Freunthaler, diary, March 19, 1915, KA Vienna: NL Freunthaler, B/497. For similar corruption in a Galician regiment, see Lenar, *Pamiętnik*, 16.

11. For the confiscation of civilians' food and their ploys to save it, see Szopa, "Wspomnienia," 16, and Freunthaler, diary, March 20, 1915, KA Vienna: NL Freunthaler, B/497. More generally, see Stuckheil, "Zweite Einschließung" (1926), 294. For theft, see Stationskmdobefehl No 1, Żurawica, January 27, 1915, and K.u.k. IV Vert.Bez.Kmdo., February 5, 1915, in MNZP Przemyśl: Archiwum

Molnara: DVD 12: T.nr. 7 MP. HIST 394, fos. 17a–b and 39a–b. For begging, see Jabłońska, *Dziennik*, 117 (diary entry for January 23, 1915); Stock, *Notatnik*, 142 (diary entry for March 4, 1915). The final quotation comes from Lenar, *Pamiętnik*, 17. Cf. Wolfgang, *Przemysl*, 122.

12. Stuckheil, "Strategische Rolle," 138, 140–141.

13. G. A. Tunstall, *Blood on the Snow: The Carpathian Winter War of 1915* (Lawrence, KS, 2010), 6–8, 23; Bundesministerium, *Österreich-Ungarns letzter Krieg*, 1:348, 373–377, 574–588, 2:58–72, 103–144. The Uszok Pass is today in Ukraine, just behind the border beyond Poland's southeastern corner.

14. Rauchensteiner, *First World War*, 357–370; Bundesministerium, *Österreich-Ungarns letzter Krieg*, 2:123; Stone, *Eastern Front*, 111.

15. Quoted in Sondhaus, *Conrad von Hötzendorf*, 165.

16. Tunstall, *Blood on the Snow*, chap. 2, esp. 66, 82. The quotation comes from the artillery colonel Georg Veith of the 43rd Landwehr Division.

17. Of these casualties, 238,000 were killed, missing, or captured. A full breakdown is given in Bundesministerium, *Österreich-Ungarns letzter Krieg*, 2:270. More generally on the battles, see Rauchensteiner, *First World War*, 303–306; Tunstall, *Blood on the Snow*, chaps. 2 and 3.

18. Stuckheil, "Zweite Einschließung" (1926), 291–293.

19. For Russian espionage, see ibid., 358; Forstner, *Przemyśl*, 210–211. Cf. A. Marshall, "Russian Military Intelligence, 1905–1917: The Untold Story Behind Tsarist Russia in the First World War," *War in History* 11, no. 4 (November 2004): 393–408. Bilińska is mentioned in K.u.k. Festungskommando, Telephondepesche, January 19, 1915, KA Vienna: NFA Przemysl 1323: fo. 492. The betrayal of the sortie of December 27–28 is recounted in k.u. 23 Honvéd Inf. Brigade, "Verrat des Ausfalls am 27–28/12/1914," January 1, 1915, KA Vienna: NFA Przemysl 1323: fo. 76.

20. Information on Wapowce is in K.u.k. Festungskommando, Nr 284, "Referatbogen," January 29, 1915, KA Vienna: NFA Przemysl 1323: fo. 271. For civilians' trading of information and the consequences for the troops, see Vit, *Wspomnienia*, 59; Stuckheil, "Zweite Einschließung" (1926), 295–296; exchange between k.u.k. Festungskommando and k.u.k. Verteidigungsbezirkskommando VII, January 19 and 22, 1915, KA Vienna: NFA Przemysl 1323: fos. 502, 504. Also, fo. 602.

21. Geőcze, *A przemysli tragédia*, 101, 146, and Hungarian officer's diary entries of November 17 and 27, 1914, in Lagzi, ed., *Węgrzy*, 120, 126.

22. See the 81st Division commander's note, dated January 25, 1915 (January 12 by the old Russian calendar), in KA Vienna: NFA Przemysl 1323: fo. 615; K.u.k Festungskommando, Op. Nr 179/6 "Völkerrechtswidrige Handlungen—Parlamentär," January 26, 1915, KA Vienna: NFA Przemysl 1323: fo. 637–639, and other relevant documentation in fo. 581, 625, 641 (this last a list of illegal munitions in units' inventories). Most likely, the "Ü-Munition" referred to in the documents was the M8 target practice cartridge. See K.k. Landwehrinfanterieregiment Nr 35 to Festungskommando, January 23, 1915, KA Vienna: NFA Przemysl 1323: fo. 561. Prisoner totals for January 28, 1915, are given in K.u.k. Etappenstationskommando in Przemyśl, KA Vienna: NFA Przemysl 1323: fo. 735.

23. Wolfgang, *Przemysl*, 108; J. Tomann, diary, February 11, 1915, KA Vienna: NFA Przemysl 1322: Fasz. 1345; K.u.k. Festungskommando, Telephondepesche, January 7, 1915, KA Vienna: NFA Przemysl 1323: fo. 173 (reverse); "Bericht," by Kusmanek, November 14, 1914, KA Vienna: NFA Przemysl 1321; Gayczak, *Pamiętnik*, 47 (diary entry for January 4, 1915); Jabłońska, *Dziennik*, 113 (diary entry for January 7, 1915).

24. K.u.k. Festungskommando, Op. Nr 157/3, "Akustische und optische Abfertigungszeichen," January 4, 1915; Op. Nr 166/4, "Akustische und optische Abfertigungszeichen, Abänderung," January 13, 1915, KA Vienna: NFA Przemysl 1323: fos. 83–84, 347 (and reverse).

25. The examples here are from orders of 13 (Op. Nr 166/4), 15 (Op. Nr 167/4), and January 27 (Op. Nr 180/8) and February 7 (Op. Nr 186), in KA Vienna: NFA Przemysl 1323: fos. 347 (and reverse) and 379 and MNZP Przemyśl: Archiwum Molnara: DVD 12: T. Nr 7 MP HIST 394: fos. 14a and 47.

26. K.u.k. III. Verteidigungsbezirkskommando, "Akustische und optische Abfertigungszeichen, Erfahrungen," January 18, 1915, KA Vienna: NFA Przemysl 1323. For the order to shoot if incorrect replies were given, see K.u.k. Festungskommando, Op. Nr 157/3, "Akustische und optische Abfertigungszeichen," January 4, 1915, in the same box, fos. 83–84.

27. Wolfgang, *Przemysl*, 109.

28. For potato digging, see F. Reder von Schellmann, diary, January 5, 1915, KA Vienna: NL Reder von Schellmann, 763(B,C). Cf. Gayczak, *Pamiętnik*, 56 (January 18 and 19, 1915). For the troops' condition and the quotation, see Wolfgang, *Przemysl*, 124. Temperatures for 7:00 a.m., 2:00 p.m., and 9:00 p.m. each day were recorded in the Festungskommandobefehle, preserved in KA Vienna: NFA Przemysl 1323.

29. Kusmanek, "Die beiden Belagerungen," 49, KA Vienna: NL Kusmanek B/1137/14; Hungarian officer's diary, February 19, 1915, in Lagzi, ed., *Węgrzy*, 150–151.

30. Letter to Kazimierz Baran from Nienadowa, January 1915, KA Vienna: NFA 1323, fo. 316 (reverse) and 317. For Tamásy's bet, see Hungarian officer's diary, February 26, 1915, in Lagzi, ed., *Węgrzy*, 152.

31. This may be a landmark moment in historiography: the first time in over a hundred years that the name of an ordinary Ukrainian-speaking soldier has appeared in a book on the First World War. This is remarkable, as perhaps 2.5 million Ukrainian-speakers served in the Russian Army and around 500,000 in the Habsburg army in 1914–1918 (together, more than the entire male population of contemporary Ireland). I make this point to emphasize how buried Eastern Europeans' wartime history still is, especially in comparison to the voluminous literature on the rank and file of the British and other Western nations' armies. The following account of Wasyl Okolita's desertion is based on reports from 2 Feldkompanie, K.k. Landsturminfanterieregiment Nr 35, January 6, 1915, including a letter and sketch of the position from the second lieutenant commanding the company and interviews with the sentries on duty on the night of the desertion, KA Vienna: NFA Przemysl 1323: fos. 202–208.

32. Kommandant der 5. Feldkompanie, Landsturminfanterieregiment Nr 35 to V Vert.-Bezirks-Kommando, January 15, 1915. For desertion, see Festungskommando, Op. Nr 159/5, January 6, 1915. Seven men had deserted from the battalion between November 10 and December 3, 1914. Respectively, KA Vienna: NFA Przemysl 1323: fos. 415, 135–136.

33. Throughout January temperatures dropped to freezing or below in the evenings. However, on January 5 the temperature ranged between 0.5 and 2°C (32.9–35.6°F), and in the evening rose to 4°C (39.2°F). See Festungskommandobefehl Nr 11, January 6, 1915, KA Vienna: NFA Przemysl 1323: fo. 172.

34. 5. Feldkompanie, Landsturminfanterieregiment Nr 35, "Protokoll," January 15, 1915, KA Vienna: NFA Przemysl 1323, fos. 410–411; Vit, *Wspomnienia*, 79; IV. V.B. Kmdo, "Bezirkskommandobefehl," February 15, 1915, MNZP Przemyśl: Archiwum Molnara: DVD 12: T. Nr 7 MP HIST 394: fo. 61a. Cf. Stolz, *Tiroler Landsturmregiment Nr. II*, 200–201; Hungarian officer's diary, January 31, 1915, in Lagzi, ed., *Węgrzy*, 143; 1. Kompagnie, k.u. 16/II Honvéd Marschbaon to V Verteidigungsbezirkskommando, January 14, 1915, KA Vienna: NFA Przemysl 1323, fo. 417.

35. The following is based on the German translations of these leaflets in MNZP Przemyśl: Archiwum Molnara: DVD 6: T. Nr 23 MP HIST 410.

36. For more on Nikolai's appeal to the Poles, see Chapter 4. Regarding Serbs and Romanians, the importance of shared Orthodox faith with the Russians should not be underestimated. There were Habsburg Serb soldiers in the Fortress who for this reason refused to shoot at the enemy. See A. Szczupak, "W pamiętnych dniach Przemyśla. Wojenne zapiski Bp. Konstantyna Czechowicza, Ks. Mirona Podolińskiego i Ks. Aleksandra Zubryckiego z lat 1914–1915," *Rocznik Przemyski* 51, no. 3 (2015): 183.

37. Some believed these stories. See Gayczak, *Pamiętnik*, 72 (diary entry for March 8, 1915).

38. Vert.Bez. VIII, orders of February 3 and 16, 1915, MNZP Przemyśl: Archiwum Molnara: DVD 7: T. Nr 11 MP HIST 398: fos. 13, 29; Wolfgang, *Przemysl*, 149; Festungskommandobefehle Nr 7 and 11 (January 2 and 6, 1915), KA Vienna: NFA Przemysl 1323: fos. 66, 117; Hungarian officer's diary, February 2, 1915, in Lagzi, ed., *Węgrzy*, 144. For prisoners as human shields, see ibid., 152 (February 27, 1915); and Vert.Bez. VIII, order of February 16, 1915, MNZP Przemyśl: Archiwum Molnara: DVD 7: T. Nr 11 MP HIST 398: fo. 29.

39. The correspondence between Kusmanek and the bishop, dated January 7 and 8, 1915, is in KA Vienna: NFA Przemysl 1323: fos. 133, 137. For a full discussion of Czechowicz and his prewar struggle against Russian Orthodoxy, see Szczupak, *Greckokatolicka diecezja Przemyska*, 16–40.

40. Szczupak, *Greckokatolicka diecezja Przemyska*, 55; "Programm für die Predigten Sein Exzellenz des griechisch-kath. Bischofs," KA Vienna: NFA Przemysl 1323: fos. 413–414. Additions to the bishop's notes by Reverend Aleksander Zubrycki quoted in Szczupak, *Greckokatolicka diecezja przemyska*, 97.

41. Gayczak, *Pamiętnik*, 26–27 (diary entry for November 18, 1914). A second account of this execution exists, left by Lieutenant Tyro, in KA Vienna: NFA

Przemysl 1321: fos. 203–204. Tyro states that Medecki was a Ruthene who belonged to Infantry Regiment 15. He had deserted on November 5–6 when his unit had left for Hungary. For the reading out of execution sentences, see Stock, *Notatnik*, 132 (diary entry for February 16, 1915). For comparison of Habsburg discipline with that of other armies, see A. Watson, "Morale," in J. Winter, ed., *The Cambridge History of the First World War*, vol., 2, *The State*, vol. 2 (Cambridge, 2014), 179. The British army executed 346 of its own soldiers, the French around 600, and the Germans just 48 between 1914 and 1918. No figures are available for the Russian army.

42. Festungskommando, "Massnahmen gegen Desertion" Op. Nr 188/10, February 6, 1915, MNZP Przemyśl: Archiwum Molnara: DVD 7: T. Nr 11 MP. HIST 398: fo. 18.

43. Res.-Festungskommando-Befehl Nr 11, March 5, 1915, MNZP Przemyśl: Archiwum Molnara: DVD 7: T. Nr 11 MP. HIST 398: fo. 17; J. Tomann, diary, March 10 and 19, 1915, KA Vienna: NFA Przemysl 1322: Fasz. 1345.

44. Vit, *Wspomnienia*, 62–63.

45. Stuckheil, "Zweite Einschließung" (1926), 290, 294–295; Major Artur Poeffel, "Chronologische Zusammenstellung," KA Vienna: NL Kusmanek B/1137/12: fos. 13–14.

46. Hospitalization figures from Stuckheil's draft manuscript, "Zweite Einschliessung II," December 19, 1925, in HL Budapest: II.169 M.kir. 23 HG: 4 Doboz; Geőcze, *A przemysli tragédia*, 176. (March 15: 2,447 wounded, 10,614 sick, 8,919 "weak," and a further 3,000 suffering "exhaustion," based on records for the surrounding days.) Cf. the slightly different figures in Forstner, *Przemyśl*, 220–221. For the start of the influx of sick, see Pethö, ed., *Belagerung und Gefangenschaft*, 71 (entries for February 8, 12, 13, and 15, 1915). The quotation in the middle of the paragraph is from Stiefler, "Über Psychosen und Neurosen (I.)," 376, and the final one is from J. Tomann, diary, March 8, 1915, KA Vienna: NFA Przemysl 1322: Fasz. 1345.

47. G. Stiefler, "Über Psychosen und Neurosen im Kriege (III.)," *Jahrbücher für Psychiatrie und Neurologie* 38 (1917): 399, 409–410.

48. Honvéd Infantry Regiment 8, for example, had a regulation strength of 3,334 men, but in mid-March the reported daily shortfall amounted to 1,000 soldiers. See "Betegjelentés [sick reports]," March 6–16, 1915, MNZP Przemyśl: Archiwum Molnara: DVD 1: T. Nr 14 MP HIST 401: fos. 1–3, 5–6, 8–9, 13–15. The final quotation is from F. Reder von Schellmann, "Memoiren eines Kriegsgefangenen nach der Übergabe von Przemyśl," 12 (diary entry for March 5, 1915), KA Vienna: NL Reder von Schellmann, 763(B,C).

49. Stuckheil's draft manuscript, "Zweite Einschliessung II," December 19, 1925, 94–100, in HL Budapest: II.169 M.kir. 23 HG: 4 Doboz.

50. For the museum, see *Wiadomości wojenne. Nr 143* of March 11, 1915, reproduced in Archiwum Państwowe w Przemyślu, *Wojenna skrzynka pocztowa* (Przemyśl, 2014), 52. For the consumption of dogs, cats, and mice, see Vit, *Wspomnienia*, 79, and (with lower prices) J. Tomann, diary, March 12, 1915, KA Vienna: NFA Przemysl 1322: Fasz. 1345. The complaint about troops burning wooden trench materials is in Verteidigungsbezirkskommando VIII, Res. Nr 466,

471, February 3 and 4, 1915, MNZP Przemyśl: Archiwum Molnara: DVD 7: T. Nr 11 MP HIST 398: fos. 14, 16.

51. Hungarian officer's diary, March 6, 1915, in Lagzi, ed., *Węgrzy*, 157. See also Wolfgang, *Przemysl*, 150.

CHAPTER SEVEN: ARMAGEDDON

1. K.u.k. Festungskommando, Op. Nr 227/1, "Meine Soldaten!," March 18, 1915, KA Vienna: NL Kusmanek B/1137/13: fo. 118. See also Wolfgang, *Przemysl*, 156, 161–164.

2. Forstner, *Przemyśl*, 224.

3. Kusmanek, "Die beiden Belagerungen," 50, KA Vienna: NL Kusmanek B/1137/14; Stuckheil's draft manuscript, "Zweite Einschliessung II," December 19, 1925, 64, in HL Budapest: II.169 M.kir. 23 HG: 4 Doboz.

4. See k.u.k. Festungskommando to AOK, Op. Nr 230/15, sent 11:30 p.m. on March 18, 1915, KA Vienna: NL Kusmanek B/1137/13: fo. 117; Stuckheil's draft manuscript, "Zweite Einschliessung II," December 19, 1925, 56–57, in HL Budapest: II.169 M.kir. 23 HG: 4 Doboz. The quotation is from F. Hölzer, diary, March 14, 1915, KA Vienna: NL Hölzer, B/486.

5. See k.u.k. Festungskommando to AOK, Op. Nr 228/3, sent 1:40 p.m. on March 16, 1915, KA Vienna: NL Kusmanek B/1137/13: fos. 113–114.

6. For Kusmanek's full justification, see his "Die beiden Belagerungen," 50–51, KA Vienna: NL Kusmanek B/1137/14.

7. The meeting is recounted in Stuckheil's draft manuscript, "Die zweite Einschliessung der Festung Przemysl. III. Das Ende," February 11, 1926, 11–14, in HL Budapest: II.169 M.kir. 23 HG: 4 Doboz.

8. Ibid., 10–11, 13–14.

9. The order setting out the attack group's dispositions is reproduced in ibid., 89–94. See also k.u.k. Festungskommando to AOK, Op. Nr 231/29, March 19, 1915, KA Vienna: NL Kusmanek B/1137/13: fo. 106.

10. K.u.k. Festungskommando, Op. Nr 230/11: "Direktiven für die Durchführung des Durchbruches. Höhere Kmdos, Rgts-, Baons-, Komp.-Kmdten.," March 18, 1915, KA Vienna: NL Kusmanek B/1137/4.

11. Ibid.

12. Stock gives an atmospheric description of the garrison's nervous mood on the eve of the attack in *Notatnik*, 150–151 (diary entries for March 16 and 17, 1915). Cf. also Wolfgang, *Przemysl*, 156.

13. K.u.k. Festungskommando, Op. Nr 227/1 "Meine Soldaten!," March 18, 1915, KA Vienna: NL Kusmanek B/1137/13: fo. 118 (underlining in original). For Kusmanek's invisibility to the garrison, see Stolz, *Tiroler Landsturmregiment Nr. II*, 207, and for the order's failure to reach most troops, Geőcze, *A przemysli tragédia*, 189.

14. This section draws on Vit, *Wspomnienia*, 78–85; Wolfgang, *Przemysl*, 154–179; and Stuckheil's draft manuscript, "Zweite Einschliessung III," February 11, 1926, 19–32, in HL Budapest: II.169 M.kir. 23 HG: 4 Doboz.

15. Vit, *Wspomnienia*, 81.

16. The high drop-out rate was common throughout the assault force. See Nerad, *Przemysl*, 45. The chaos on the roads was mostly the fault of Honvéd Field Artillery Regiment 2, which lost its way in the night. It had been ordered that after 8:00 p.m. on March 18, only traffic heading in the direction of the eastern front was permitted on the Lwów Road. This Field Artillery Regiment, recognizing its mistake, had tried to struggle back on the road against the flow of the 93rd Landsturm Brigade (the formation to which Landsturm Infantry Regiment 18 was assigned). See Stuckheil's draft manuscript, "Zweite Einschliessung III," February 11, 1926, 20–21, in HL Budapest: II.169 M.kir. 23 HG: 4 Doboz.

17. The following is taken from ibid., 32–46, which includes a translated account by the commander of II/Honvéd Infantry Regiment 2, Captain Eugen von Marschalkó.

18. Ibid., 22, 92.

19. Festungskommando to AOK, telegram Op. Nr 231/32, March 19, 1915, KA Vienna: NL Kusmanek B/1137/13: fo. 108. British sources close to the Tsarist army offer a different explanation for the Russians' foreknowledge of the breakthrough operation. Both Captain J. F. Neilson, the military attaché, and Bernard Pares, the professor of Russian history appointed as an official British observer with the Russian armies in the field, reported that the Russians learned of it through a message carried by a shot-down fortress airman. Pares claimed that a staff officer's letter to his wife mentioning the attack and a copy of Kusmanek's March 18 order to the men were found among captured airmail. However, as planning for the operation east began so late (from March 16) and was so secretive, and as there were no airmail flights dispatched after this date, this cannot be correct. Most likely, the Russians wished to hide their prowess in code-breaking from their British allies and used this as a cover story. Stuckheil offered an analysis and further evidence confirming Kusmanek's suspicion that Russian interception of his radio communications with the AOK was the source of the leak. See Neilson's despatch on Przemyśl, TNA London: WO106/1122; Pares, *Day by Day*, 157–160; and Stuckheil's draft manuscript, "Zweite Einschliessung III," February 11, 1926, 14–16, 44–45, in HL Budapest: II.169 M.kir. 23 HG: 4 Doboz.

20. Vit, *Wspomnienia*, 81. For casualty figures, see Stuckheil's draft manuscript, "Zweite Einschliessung III," February 11, 1926, 48; Geőcze, *A przemysli tragédia*, 195. The Russians, according to Stuckheil, claimed to have captured 107 officers, 3,954 soldiers, and 16 machine-guns in the operation. Neilson's despatch (TNA London: WO106/1122) confirms this, stating that 4,000 prisoners were taken and "exceedingly heavy losses" inflicted.

21. The quotation is from Dalecki and Mielnik, eds., "Dziennik Józefy Prochazka," 278 (diary entry for March 19, 1915). For the rumors, see Jabłońska, *Dziennik*, 133–137 (entries for March 19–21, 1915); Pethö, ed., *Belagerung und Gefangenschaft*, 76 (Stenitzer's diary entry for March 19, 1915); Gayczak, *Pamiętnik*, 80 (diary entry for March 20, 1915).

22. Pavlov, "Russian Artillery," 265. Jabłońska, *Dziennik*, 133–134 (March 19, 1915); Stiefler, "Über Psychosen und Neurosen (I.)," 376. The number of shells comes from F. Hölzer, diary, March 19, 1915, KA Vienna: NL Hölzer, B/486.

23. For the official view, see K.u.k. Festungskommando to AOK, Op. Nr 233/5, March 21, 1915, KA Vienna: NL Kusmanek B/1137/13: fo. 109. Front accounts are in Wolfgang, *Przemysl*, 177–179; Vit, *Wspomnienia*, 85.

24. Stuckheil's draft manuscript, "Zweite Einschliessung III," February 11, 1926, 61, in HL Budapest: II.169 M.kir. 23 HG: 4 Doboz.

25. Geőcze, *A przemysli tragédia*, 204.

26. The minutes of this meeting are published in Stuckheil, "Die zweite Einschließung der Festung Przemyśl. III. Das Ende," *Militärwissenschaftliche und technische Mitteilungen* 57 (1926): 406–407.

27. For the demolition plans, see Schwalb, "Verteidigung," 16. For documents, see "Res-Festungskommando-Befehl Nr 15," March 17, 1915, MNZP Przemyśl: Archiwum Molnara: DVD 8: T. Nr 11 MP HIST 398: fo. 83. For money, see Stuckheil, "Ende," 408–409.

28. Stuckheil "Ende," 530–532. For details of the meeting with Schwalb, see Nerad, *Przemysl*, 46; Stock, *Notatnik*, 155–156 (diary entry for March 21, 1915).

29. While there exists general agreement among sources about the rough order in which the events in the early hours of March 22 took place, there are wide disparities in the times given. The quotation is from Jabłońska, *Dziennik*, 140 (diary entry for March 22, 1915).

30. W. Grzędzielski, "22. Marca 1915. Przeżycia i wrażenia," originally published in nine parts in *Echo Przemyskie* 21, Nr 24–31, 33 (March 23, 26, and 30 and April 2, 6, 9, 13, and 16 1916) and republished in abridged form in *Nasz Przemyśl* 4 (April 2014): 16–20, here at p. 18; Jabłońska, *Dziennik*, 139 (diary entry for March 22, 1915).

31. The first quotation is from Michaelsburg, *Im belagerten Przemyśl*, 143 (diary entry for March 22, 1915). Other sources (including Jabłońska and Józefa Prochazka, who were sheltering together but differ by an hour) record the time as 3:00 or 4:00 a.m. Also, Grzędzielski, "22. Marca 1915," 18; Jabłońska, *Dziennik*, 139 (diary entry for March 22, 1915).

32. Gayczak, *Pamiętnik*, 82 (diary entry for March 22, 1915).

33. Dalecki and Mielnik, eds., "Dziennik Józefy Prochazka," 280 (diary entry for March 22, 1915); R. Stanger, "Der letzte Flug aus Przemysl," reproduced in A. Hemberger, *Der europäische Krieg und der Weltkrieg: Historische Darstellung der Kriegsereignisse von 1914/15*, vol. 2 (Vienna, 1915), 201–203.

34. Jabłońska, *Dziennik*, 139–140, 144 (March 22 and 23, 1915); and Michaelsburg, *Im belagerten Przemyśl*, 145–146 (diary entry for March 22, 1915).

35. Grzędzielski, "22. Marca 1915. Przeżycia i wrażenia V.," *Echo Przemyskie*, Rok 21, Nr 28 (April 6, 1916): 1.

36. A detailed description of the bridges appears in Michaelsburg, *Im belagerten Przemyśl*, 146–147 (diary entry for March 22, 1915).

37. For events in the city the fullest account is Jabłońska, *Dziennik*, 141–142 (diary entry for March 22, 1915). The atmosphere at the front at the time of surrender is vividly portrayed in Wolfgang, *Batjuschka*, 7–15. See also Vit, *Wspomnienia*, 86; and Lenar, *Pamiętnik*, 20–21.

38. The following is based on Stuckheil, "Ende," 682–688.

39. Ibid., 680 (which reproduces the account of Fort IV's commander, Lieutenant Gottfried Hohn), and F. Reder von Schellmann, "Memoiren eines Kriegsgefangenen nach der Übergabe von Przemyśl," 13–14 (March 22, 1915), KA Vienna: NL Reder von Schellmann, 763(B,C). For the peaceful atmosphere elsewhere, see Wolfgang, *Batjuschka*, 16–18; Vit, *Wspomnienia*, 87; and Gayczak, *Pamiętnik*, 82 (diary entry for March 22, 1915).

40. For the Cossacks' entry into the city, see Nerad, *Przemysl*, 48–49. Cf. also Stock, *Notatnik*, 159 (March 23, 1915). Grzędzielski states from which directions the first Russian units arrived in his "22. Marca 1915," *Nasz Przemyśl* (April 2014): 19. For civilians cheering, see Stuckheil, "Ende," 680. Grzędzielski denied this, claiming that "the whole population of Przemyśl, without any distinction of nationality and faith, behaved entirely irreproachably" (Grzędzielski, "22. Marca 1915," 20). In fact, civilian reactions probably did divide along ethnic lines. Jews had most to fear from Russian occupation (see, for example, Jabłońska, *Dziennik*, 133, diary entry for March 18, 1915, where Jews are described taking down shop signboards to make their owners' ethnicity less obvious). After vicious persecution by Habsburg authorities, some Ruthenes had good reason to welcome the Russians. Polish reactions were complex. Jabłońska, a Pole, certainly remained proud of the fortress garrison's resilience, though she feared and despised Honvéd looters (see *Dziennik*, 145, diary entry for March 25, 1915).

41. Stuckheil, "Ende," 681.

EPILOGUE

1. Extracts from stanzas 1, 4, and 5 of Géza Gyóni's "For Just One Night," reproduced and translated in T. Cross, ed., *The Lost Voices of World War I: An International Anthology of Writers, Poets and Playwrights* (London, 1998 [1988]), 349–350. Gyóni served in Przemyśl and died of a nervous breakdown in June 1917 in Russian captivity. He is Hungary's most famous war poet, and his "For Just One Night," which is about the fighting at Przemyśl, occupies a place in the Hungarian literary canon equivalent to Wilfred Owen's "Dulce et decorum est" in England.

2. *Novoe Vremya*, quoted in A. J. May, *The Passing of the Hapsburg Monarchy, 1914–1918*, vol. 1 (Philadelphia, PA, 1966), 99. For Grand Duke Nikolai Nikolaevich's reaction, see Robinson, *Grand Duke*, 224–225, and for the notices at the front and in occupied Galicia, see Brussilov, *Soldier's Note-Book*, 123, and, as examples, the posters issued by the military commander of the occupied Galician town of Tarnów. AN Cracow: Naczelny Komitet Narodowy: 282 (Mikrofilm: 100,480).

3. Order of the commander of the army, Archduke Friedrich, and statement by the deputy chief of the general staff, General von Höfer, published in *Pester Lloyd* 62, Jahrgang, Nr 82, Morgenblatt (March 23, 1915): 1. The latter message was already published in an evening extra edition of the *Neues Wiener Tagblatt* (49, Jahrgang, Nr 81 [March 22, 1915]).

4. *Neue Freie Presse* 18169 Morgenblatt (March 23, 1915): 1–6. See also "Die Kämpfe bei Przemysl und in Galizien," in 18167 Morgenblatt (March 21, 1915): 8–9.

5. Ansky, *Enemy*, 64; Mick, *Kriegserfahrungen*, 128; K. Bąkowski, diary, March 22 and 23, 1915, Biblioteka Jagiellońska w Krakowie: rps 7283. More generally, see Małecki, "W dobie autonomii Galicyjskiej," 388–390.

6. For the mood at home, see Redlich, *Schicksalsjahre Österreichs*, 2:26–28 (diary entries of March 24, 26, and 28, 1915); *Pester Lloyd* 62, Jahrgang, Nr 88, Morgenblatt (March 29, 1915): 1. An Austrian commission investigating derelictions of duty that examined Kusmanek in the immediate aftermath of the First World War cleared him. However, doubts persisted, with good reason, as early chapters of this book show. Even former garrison officers argued that he had wasted early opportunities to gather food into the fortress. See Stolz, *Tiroler Landsturmregiment Nr. II*, 178–179, 189–191. For the postwar investigation, see Forstner, *Przemyśl*, 290–291.

7. For Habsburg propaganda, see Watson *Ring of Steel*, 241–255, and, for the Habsburg army's War Press Bureau, C. Tepperberg, "War Press Office (Austria-Hungary)," in U. Daniel, P. Gatrell, O. Janz, H. Jones, J. Keene, A. Kramer, and B. Nasson, eds., *1914–1918 Online: International Encyclopedia of the First World War*, https://encyclopedia.1914–1918-online.net/article/war_press_office _austria-hungary. For the raising of the upper age for military service, see Hecht, "Heeresergänzung," 199–210.

8. Rauchensteiner, *First World War*, 370–381; M. Thompson, *The White War: Life and Death on the Italian Front, 1915–1919* (London, 2008), 22–33, 62, 64. For Franz Joseph weeping, see Redlich, *Schicksalsjahre Österreichs*, 2:27 (diary entry of March 26, 1915).

9. R. Nachtigal, *Rußland und seine österreichisch-ungarischen Kriegsgefangenen (1914–1918)* (Remshalden, Germany, 2003), 34. The officers of the VII (southern) Defense District left on March 22, among them all the officers of the 108th (Austrian German) Landsturm Brigade. They marched south to Niżankowice and from there were taken by rail first to Dobromil and then through Lwów into the Russian Empire. See Stolz, *Tiroler Landsturmregiment Nr. II*, 209.

10. Nachtigal, *Rußland*, 33–34. For examples of officer emotions, see Wolfgang, *Batjuschka*, 7–25; Gayczak, *Pamiętnik*, 83–84 (esp. diary entry for March 24, 1915). For the final quotation, see Stock, *Notatnik*, 161 (diary entry for March 25, 1915).

11. Nachtigal, *Rußland*, 36–37, 143; Stuckheil, "Ende," 688; Gayczak, *Pamiętnik*, 91–93 (entries for April 19 and May 8, 1915). Gayczak was left with 1,000 crowns after the confiscation.

12. For the books, see prison camp newspaper *S'Vogerl*, quoted in A. Rachamimov, *POWs and the Great War: Captivity on the Eastern Front* (Oxford, 2002), 99. See also G. Wurzer, *Die Kriegsgefangenen der Mittelmächte in Russland im Ersten Weltkrieg* (Göttingen, Germany, 2005), 151–160. The final quotation is from Gayczak, *Pamiętnik*, 89–91 (entries for April 15 and 19, 1915).

13. R. Nachtigal, "Zur Anzahl der Kriegsgefangenen im Ersten Weltkrieg," *Militärgeschichtliche Zeitschrift* 67 no. 2 (2008): 368. For comparison, death rates of prisoners held during the First World War in German captivity were 5–6 percent, in Austria-Hungary 7.5–10 percent. In France, 5.8 percent of prisoners died

and in Britain around 4 percent. During the Second World War, 57.5 percent of Soviet Army prisoners would die in German camps through a deliberate policy of starvation. See ibid., 356–357, 361, 372, 374; Snyder, *Bloodlands*, 175–182. The quotation is from S. Washburn, *On the Russian Front in World War I: Memoirs of an American War Correspondent* (New York, 1982), 91–93.

14. The following is based on Lenar, *Pamiętnik*, 22–35 (quotation at p. 23). For the vomiting, see Forstner, *Przemyśl*, 259. The lie about permitting Galicians to return home is echoed in J. Tomann, diary, March 25, 1915, KA Vienna: NFA Przemysl 1322: Fasz. 1345; Stock, *Notatnik*, 160 (diary entry for March 23, 1915); and Wolfgang, *Batjuschka*, 18.

15. Lenar, *Pamiętnik*, 26, 27, 35.

16. The first quotation is from Franz Hentschel, quoted in Wurzer, *Kriegsgefangenen*, 62. For the rest, see E. Brändström, *Unter Kriegsgefangenen in Rußland und Sibirien, 1914–1920* (Berlin, 1922), 17–18; Stock, *Notatnik*, 161 (diary entry for March 25, 1915); R. Nachtigal, "Privilegiensystem und Zwangsrekrutierung: Russische Nationalitätenpolitik gegenüber Kriegsgefangenen aus Österreich-Ungarn," in J. Oltmer., ed., *Kriegsgefangene im Europa des Ersten Weltkriegs* (Paderborn, Germany, 2006), 172–176; Nachtigal, *Rußland*, 332. Stenitzer noted, too, that in his hospital, Galicians (including, interestingly, Jews) were separated from other personnel and not immediately evacuated. See Pethö, ed., *Belagerung und Gefangenschaft*, 109 (diary entry for March 29, 1915).

17. Wurzer, *Kriegsgefangenen*, 63–74; Brändström, *Unter Kriegsgefangenen*, 48–50. Brändström, the Swedish aid worker who became known as the "Angel of Siberia" for her tireless efforts to improve the conditions of German and Habsburg prisoners of war in Russia, recorded that of the 200,000 prisoners incarcerated in Turkestan, 45,000 died.

18. Nachtigal, "Privilegiensystem," 176–179; Directive of Irkutsk Military District, quoted in Brändström, *Unter Kriegsgefangenen*, 55. More generally, see Wurzer, *Kriegsgefangenen*, 345–368, 381–385.

19. Quotations from L. Ehrenstein, *Der Fall der Festung Przemysl*, ed. E. Portisch (Bratislava, 1937), 65–71. Extra details from Brändström, *Unter Kriegsgefangenen*, 62; Wurzer, *Kriegsgefangenen*, 368–381. In October 1916, 53 percent of the prisoners working on the railway were Hungarians, 35 percent Germans, 7.4 percent Slavs, and 3.6 percent Romanians.

20. Wurzer, *Kriegsgefangenen*, 507–519; Brändström, *Unter Kriegsgefangenen*, 62. The quotation is from E. A. Welles, *Der verblasste Krieg: Vom Feld der Ehre in die Dunkelheit. Geschichte einer Familie in der Zeit des Ersten Weltkriegs* (Mödling, Austria, 2014), 71.

21. The quotation is from Orłowicz, *Illustrierter Führer*, 98. See also ibid., 100; von Hagen, *War*, 25; departure speech of the outgoing Polish mayor of Przemyśl, Dr. Włodzimierz Błażowski, to city council officials. AP Przemyśl: 129 (Akta Miasta Przemyśla): 1382.

22. For a copy of Artamonov's order, March 11 (24), 1914, see Pethö, ed., *Belagerung und Gefangenschaft*, 108. For Artamonov's actions in Przemyśl, see Gayczak, *Pamiętnik*, 83 (March 24, 1915); Pethö, ed., *Belagerung und Gefangenschaft*,

107 (diary entry for March 26, 1915); Michaelsburg, *Im belagerten Przemysl*, 152–153 (entries for March 24 and 25, 1915). Lieutenant-General Martos, one of the corps commanders in the Second Army—in which Artamonov also served as a corps commander—fired 300 shells into Neidenburg on August 22, 1914, as punishment for what he erroneously believed to be shooting by residents at his troops. See A. Watson, "'Unheard of Brutality': Russian Atrocities Against Civilians in East Prussia, 1914–15," *Journal of Modern History* 86, no. 4 (December 2014): 806–807.

23. A.R. "Jak wyglądała Wielkanoc 1915 w Przemyślu?," *Echo Przemyskie*, 21, Nr 33 (April 23, 1916): 2; Orłowicz, *Illustrierter Führer*, 98; Jabłońska, *Dziennik*, 162–163 (diary entry for April 18, 1915); Dalecki and Mielnik, eds., "Dziennik Józefy Prochazka," 281 (diary entries for April 9 and 12, 1915).

24. For the quotation, see Jabłońska, *Dziennik*, 151 (diary entry for April 1, 1915). For the persecution of Jews, see Szopa, "Wspomnienia" (1976), 20. Cf. Jabłońska, *Dziennik*, 162–163 (diary entry for April 18, 1915); also the anonymous denunciation headed "Polnische Politik!" sent to the Viennese Police and forwarded to the Austrian Interior Ministry in the summer of 1917, and the reply of K.k. Bezirkshauptmannschaft in Przemyśl, Polizeiabteilung, "Verhalten der Polen in Galizien gegenüber der jüdischen Bevölkerung," September 27, 1915, AVA Vienna: Min.d.Innern, Präs., 22/Galiz. (1914–1915): 22/Galiz.: 2116 (doc. 15635) and (1916–1917): 22/Galiz.: 2117 (doc. 26250). Local authorities denied Wierzbowski had displayed bias against Jews, but he was found guilty of collaboration and sentenced to twenty-two months in prison.

25. Szczupak, *Greckokatolicka diecezja Przemyska*, 130–132; Dalecki and Mielnik, eds., "Dziennik Józefy Prochazka," 282–283 (diary entry for April 23, 1915). Documentation concerning the preparations for the Tsar's visit are held in TsDIAL Lviv: 645/1/16.

26. Details from Jabłońska, *Dziennik*, 165–166 (diary entry for April 23, 1915); Michaelsburg, *Im belagerten Przemysl*, 168 (April 30, 1915); and the school chronicle written by Headmaster Grzegorz Piotrowski, a fragment of which is reproduced in M. Dalecki and A. K. Mielnik, eds., "Oblężenia i okupacja Przemyśla przez Rosjan w latach 1914–1915 według kroniki Szkoły Ludowej Czeroklasowej Męskiej Imienia Św. Jana Kantego," *Archiwum Państwowe w Przemyślu: Rocznik Historyczno-Archiwalny* 23 (2011–2012): 186. Glushkievich's speech is mentioned in the draft memorandum by the governor of the Przemyśl Governorate to the military governor-general of Galicia, June 24 (July 7), 1915. TsDIAL Lviv: 645/1/148, fo. 29. Grand Duke Nikolai's fears of an assassination attempt are in Robinson, *Grand Duke*, 229. Lastly, newsreel of the Tsar's visit is available at YouTube, www.youtube.com/watch?v=QzLZQNdJxY0.

27. The Tsar is quoted in P. Szlanta, "Der Erste Weltkrieg von 1914 bis 1915 als identitätsstiftender Faktor für die moderne polnische Nation," in G. P. Groß, ed., *Die vergessene Front. Der Osten 1914/15. Ereignis, Wirkung, Nachwirkung* (Paderborn, Germany, 2006), 160. For the rest, see Dalecki and Mielnik, eds., "Oblężenia i okupacja Przemyśla," 185–186, and idem, "Dziennik Józefy Prochazka," 284 (entries for May 2 and 4, 1915).

28. The Orthodox services in the railway station are mentioned in "Bericht des Legationsrates Baron Andrian" (July 26, 1915), 23, in AVA Vienna: Min.d.Innern, Präs., 22/Galiz. (1914–1915): 2116: Doc. 19644; Szczupak, *Greckokatolicka diecezja Przemyska*, 133, discusses the guard posted in Bishop Czechowicz's palace. For the rumors and arrests of the Polish elite, see Jabłońska, *Dziennik*, 167–168 (diary entry for May 1, 1915), and Dalecki and Mielnik, eds., "Dziennik Józefy Prochazka," 282 (diary entry for April 21, 1915).

29. AP Przemyśl: 397 (Afisze, plakaty i druki ulotni): 501. The poster is undated, but the Russian order to Jews to leave is mentioned circulating on this date in Dalecki and Mielnik, eds., "Dziennik Józefy Prochazka," 283 (diary entry for April 28, 1915). This is the earliest date it appears in a contemporary source.

30. K.k. Bezirkshauptmannschaft in Przemyśl to k.k. galizische Statthalterei, June 10, 1915, reproduced in K.u.k. Ministerium des Äussern, *Sammlung von Nachweisen . . . II. Nachtrag*, 89. Ansky (*Enemy*, 123–124) gives the figure of 20,000 Jewish expellees and states that 13,000 arrived in Lwów. Others went to Dobromil, Mościska, and Sambor. For Przemyśl empty of Jews, see Dalecki and Mielnik, eds., "Dziennik Józefy Prochazka," 282 (diary entry for May 8, 1915), and for the crisis in Lwów, see S. Bromberg-Bytkowski, "Die Juden Lembergs unter der Russenherrschaft," *Jüdisches Archiv. Mitteilungen des Komitees "Jüdisches Kriegsarchiv,"* Lieferung 8–9 (January 1917): 37.

31. A search through TsDIAL Lviv: Collection 645, "Office of the Governor, Przemyśl," revealed no documentation at all about the expulsion of the city's and district's Jews. The paperwork must have been removed or destroyed. For Russian and local theft of Jews' property, see K.k. Bezirkshauptmannschaft in Przemyśl to k.k. galizische Statthalterei, June 10, 1915, reproduced in K.u.k. Ministerium des Äussern, *Sammlung von Nachweisen . . . II. Nachtrag*, 90, and K.k. Bezirkshauptmannschaft in Przemyśl, Polizeiabteilung, "Verhalten der Polen in Galizien gegenüber der jüdischen Bevölkerung," September 27, 1915, AVA Vienna: Min.d.Innern, Präs., (1916–1917): 22/Galiz.: 2117: Doc. 26250; Jabłońska, *Dziennik*, 190, 213 (entries for May 21 and June 22, 1915).

32. For the explanation that Jews could not reside in a Fortress, see Y. Altbauer, "Przemysl During the Time of the Siege During the First World War (1914–1915)," translated by J. Landau, in A. Menczer, ed., *Sefer Przemyśl*, Jewish Gen, www.jewishgen.org/Yizkor/przemysl/prz172.html. The rumors are recorded in Jabłońska, *Dziennik*, 168–169 (diary entry for May 1, 1915).

33. Stone, *Eastern Front*, 128–140. The most recent study is R. L. DiNardo, *Breakthrough: The Gorlice-Tarnow Campaign, 1915* (Santa Barbara, CA, 2010), esp. chaps. 3, 4, 5.

34. Jabłońska, *Dziennik*, 172, 179, 184–185, 188, 195 (entries of May 5, 12, 16, 17, 19, 21, and 24, 1915). See also Dalecki and Mielnik, eds., "Dziennik Józefy Prochazka," 286–287 (entries for May 17 and 19, 1915). Jabłońska (*Dziennik*, 185 [diary entry for May 19, 1915]) mentions the fire brigade's arrest. The municipal police had operated until April 21, on which day (forty-eight hours before the Tsar's visit) all had been summoned to police headquarters and arrested. After three days some were released. The rest were made to walk to Lwów and

imprisoned. See K.k. Bezirkshauptmannschaft in Przemyśl to k.k. galizische Statthalterei, June 10, 1915, reproduced in K.u.k. Ministerium des Äussern, *Sammlung von Nachweisen . . . II. Nachtrag*, 89.

35. Draft memorandum by Przemyśl's governor to the military governor-general of Galicia, June 24 (July 7), 1915, inventories, and other correspondence on Glushkievich's flight and Przemyśl's funds in TsDIAL Lviv: 645/1/148, esp. fos. 1, 21–22, 32. For the quotation comparing Prussians to Hungarians, see Jabłońska, *Dziennik*, 195 (diary entry for May 24, 1915). For the seizure of military-aged men and boys, see Dalecki and Mielnik, eds., "Dziennik Józefy Prochazka," 286 (diary entry for May 18, 1915). The order to "clean the city of harmful elements" is in the telegram of Przemyśl's district head to the Przemyśl governor, April 30 (May 13), 1915. TsDIAL Lviv: 645/1/148, fo. 1. For subsequent arrests and executions, see Jabłońska, *Dziennik*, 184 (diary entry for May 18, 1915). More generally, see 181–188 (entries for May 14–21, 1915).

36. Grand Duke Nikolai's decision is discussed in Forstner, *Przemyśl*, 269; Robinson, *Grand Duke*, 236–239. For the Central Powers' assault on the city, see Bundesministerium, *Österreich-Ungarns letzter Krieg*, 2:393, 433–434. See also Forstner, *Przemyśl*, 270–271.

37. For the shells, see Dalecki and Mielnik, eds., "Dziennik Józefy Prochazka," 289 (diary entry for June 2, 1915). The German attack is described in DiNardo, *Breakthrough*, 73–82.

38. J. Różański, "Przemyśl w latach drugiej wojny światowej," in Persowski et al., eds., *Tysiąc lat Przemyśla*, 2:356–363. The Hotel Royal, once a Przemyśl landmark, was destroyed by incendiary bombs in an air raid on September 8, 1939. See Forum Rozwoju Przemyśla, https://frp.com.pl/hotel-royal-na-przeciwko-dworca-glownego-pkp,a-47.html. For the murder of Przemyśl's Jewish elite, see A. B. Rossino, "Nazi Anti-Jewish Policy During the Polish Campaign: The Case of the Einsatzgruppe von Woyrsch," *German Studies Review* 24, no. 1 (February 2001): 41–44.

39. The Polish-Ukrainian struggle in Przemyśl of November 1918 is recounted in Z. Konieczny, *Walki polsko-ukraińskie w Przemyślu i okolicy listopad grudzień 1918* (Przemyśl, 1993), esp. (for the casualties) 67. For the wider context, see Watson, *Ring of Steel*, chaps. 11 and 12. For the Przemyśl pogrom, see W. Wierzbieniec, "Żydzi w Przemyślu w okresie I wojny światowej," in H. Węgrzynek, ed., *Żydzi i Polacy w okresie walk o niepodległość, 1914–1920: Materiały z sesji towarzyszacej wystawie "Żyd, Polak, legionista 1914–1920" w Muzeum Historii Żydów Polskich POLIN* (Warsaw, 2015), 77–78, 85–86. For the wave of pogroms in Poland at this time, see Hagen, *Anti-Jewish Violence*, esp. chaps. 3, 4, and 7–9.

40. A. J. Motyl, "Ukrainian Nationalist Political Violence in Inter-War Poland, 1921–1939," *East European Quarterly* 19, no. 1 (Spring 1985): 45–55; L. Kulińska, *Działalność terrorystyczna i sabotażowa nacjonalistycznych organizacji ukraińskich w Polsce w latach 1922–1939* (Cracow, 2009), 80, 169–171, 190–192.

41. See W. Wierzbieniec, *Społeczność żydowska Przemyśla w latach 1918–1939* (Rzeszów, Poland, 1996), 163–169, 272–283. W. W. Hagen, "Before the 'Final Solution': Toward a Comparative Analysis of Political Anti-Semitism in Interwar

Germany and Poland," *Journal of Modern History* 68, no. 2 (June 1996): 351–381 offers insightful analysis of Polish anti-Semitism, especially its modernizing concerns.

42. Różański, "Przemyśl w latach drugiej wojny światowej," 362–363. A vivid description of the invasion and panic is in M. Schattner, "From Outbreak of WWII until the Liberation," translated by J. Landau, in A. Menczer, ed., *Sefer Przemyśl*, at Jewish Gen, www.jewishgen.org/Yizkor/przemysl/prz371.html. For the partition of Poland in 1939, see R. Moorhouse, *The Devils' Alliance: Hitler's Pact with Stalin, 1939–1941* (London, 2014), esp. 36–39, 46. The Soviets' justification for their invasion to the Polish ambassador in Moscow on September 17, 1939, was telling. After claiming that "the Polish state no longer exists," it stated that the Soviet Union could not "remain indifferent at a time when brothers of the same blood, the Ukrainians and Byelorussians, residing on the Polish territory have been abandoned to their fate."

43. The figure comes from Snyder, *Bloodlands*, 410–411, and includes the Soviet genocide of 3.3 million Ukrainians through starvation in 1932–1933 and the murder of 300,000 other (non-Russian) Soviet citizens before the Second World War, but excludes the hundreds of thousands who perished through disease, malnutrition, and exhaustion in camps and through deportations. The Russian state's role in restricting its army's anti-Semitic violence from escalating to genocide in 1915 is discussed in P. Holquist, "Les violences de l'armée russe à l'encontre des Juifs en 1915: Causes et limites," in J. Horne, ed., *Vers la guerre totale: Le tournant de 1914–15* (Paris, 2010), 191–219.

44. J. T. Gross, *Revolution from Abroad: The Soviet Conquest of Poland's Western Ukraine and Western Belorussia*, expanded ed. (Princeton, NJ, 2002), esp. 65–66, 106–108, and, for Przemyśl specifically, E. Grin-Piszczek, "Polityka Sowietów wobec mieszkańców Przemyśla na tle sytuacji terenów okupowanych przez ZSRR w latach 1939–1941," *Archiwum Państwowe w Przemyślu: Rocznik Historyczno-Archiwalny* 18 (2004): 75, 83–92, 100–103.

45. For the victims of Soviet murder, see Gross, *Revolution*, 228–229. The numbers of deportees from occupied Poland given in the literature vary wildly, from 315,000 (Snyder) to 1.5 million (Davies). The differences are due both to the vagaries of the sources and nuances in the definition of "deportee." Grin-Piszczek, drawing on Polish historian Daniel Boćkowski's research, has a detailed breakdown indicating between 750,000 and 780,000 deportees. See ibid., chap. 6; Grin-Piszczek, "Polityka Sowietów," 96, 98–100; Snyder, *Bloodlands*, 151; N. Davies, *God's Playground: A History of Poland*, vol. 2, *1795 to the Present* 2 (Oxford, 2005), 331–334.

46. For the fighting in Przemyśl during the Nazi attack on the Soviet Union, see T. Zając, "Fall Barbarossa 22 czerwca 1941 roku—Walki na terenie 08. Przemyskiego Rejonu Umocnionego," *Rocznik Przemyski* 51 (2015): 136–146. The general's quotation appears in Snyder, *Bloodlands*, 121. The rest of the paragraph draws on M. Mazower, *Hitler's Empire: Nazi Rule in Occupied Europe* (London, 2009), chap. 4; Snyder, *Bloodlands*, 126, 146–148. For Przemyśl specifically, see Różański, "Przemyśl w latach drugiej wojny światowej," 406–416.

47. The importance of racism and imperialism in the east and radicalizing military mentalities in the First World War has been recognized, but are frequently presented as primarily German characteristics. In fact, all were much more extreme in the Tsar's army in 1914–1915. See, especially, V. G. Liulevičius, *War Land on the Eastern Front: Culture, National Identity, and German Occupation in World War I* (Cambridge, 2000); and I. V. Hull, *Absolute Destruction: Military Culture and the Practices of War in Imperial Germany* (Ithaca, NY, 2005). For Zasanie's prewar Jewish population, see Wierzbieniec, *Społeczność żydowska Przemyśla*, 18 (figure for 1921).

48. The literature on the Holocaust is legion, but the trajectory is well-described in Snyder, *Bloodlands*, esp. chap. 6. For Bełżec, ibid., 258–261. For the Holocaust in Przemyśl, see Dunagan, "Lost World," 393–401, and H. J. Hartman and J. Krochmal. eds., *Pamiętam każdy dzień . . . Losy Żydów Przemyskich podczas II Wojny Światowej* (Przemyśl, 2001).

49. Z. Konieczny, "Przemyśl w latach 1944–1948," in Persowski et al., eds., *Tysiąc lat Przemyśla*, 2:455–456, 487–488. For the forcing of Ukrainians from Poland, see, especially, K. Stadnik, "Ukrainian-Polish Population Transfers, 1944–46: Moving in Opposite Directions," in P. Gatrell and N. Baron, eds., *Warlands: Population Resettlement and State Reconstruction in the Soviet–East European Borderlands, 1945–50* (Basingstoke, 2009), 165–187; and O. Subtelny, "Expulsion, Resettlement, Civil Strife: The Fate of Poland's Ukrainians, 1944–1947," in P. Ther and A. Siljak, eds., *Redrawing Nations: Ethnic Cleansing in East-Central Europe, 1944–1948* (Lanham, MD, 2001), 155–172.

APPENDIX I: THE ORGANIZATION OF THE HABSBURG ARMY IN 1914

1. Rothenberg, *Army*, 74–78, 109, 165; Rauchensteiner, *First World War*, 52–53. For the General Staff, see S. W. Lackey, *The Rebirth of the Habsburg Army: Friedrich Beck and the Rise of the General Staff* (Westport, CT, 1995), esp. 88–97.

2. For the Habsburg army's adoption of Prussian-style conscription, see C. Hämmerle, "Die k. (u.) k. Armee als 'Schule des Volkes'? Zur Geschichte der Allgemeinen Wehrpflicht in der multinationalen Habsburgermonarchie (1866–1914/18)," in C. Jansen, ed., *Der Bürger als Soldat: Die Militarisierung europäischer Gesellschaften im langen 19. Jahrhundert: ein internationaler Vergleich* (Essen, 2004), 175–186. Baczkowski, *Pod czarno-żółtymi sztandarami*, 21–24, covers the conscription system comprehensively. For officers, see I. Deák, *Beyond Nationalism: A Social and Political History of the Habsburg Officer Corps, 1848–1918* (New York, 1990), 85.

3. Rothenberg, *Army*, 109–111; Hecht, "Heeresergänzung," 8–17.

4. Deák, *Beyond Nationalism*, 99, 194; Rauchensteiner, *First World War*, 52; Watson, *Ring of Steel*, 111; Sanborn, *Drafting the Russian Nation*, 21.

5. Watson, *Ring of Steel*, 73, 118–119; Hecht, "Heeresergänzung," 34.

6. Lackey, *Rebirth*, 131–135; Hecht, "Heeresergänzung," 16–17, 41–47. For equipment, see Stuckheil, "Ausrüstungszeit," 208–209; Reichsarchiv, *Weltkrieg*,

vol. 2, "Anlage 2." The 108th Landsturm Infantry Brigade, which served at Przemyśl, was exceptional in having only six (later five) battalions. The 93rd Landsturm Brigade operated with eight (after one regiment was detached), the 111th with eleven, and the Hungarian 97th with twelve.

7. Hecht, "Heeresergänzung," 38–40. See also Stuckheil, "Ausrüstungszeit," garrison order of battle chart.

8. Hecht, "Heeresergänzung," 37; Reichsarchiv, *Weltkrieg*, vol. 2, "Anlage 2"; Bundesministerium, *Österreich-Ungarns letzter Krieg*, 1:62–79; Rauchensteiner, *First World War*, 53.

APPENDIX II: THE ORGANIZATION OF THE RUSSIAN ARMY IN 1914

1. The extract from the Fundamental Laws is quoted in D. R. Jones, "Imperial Russia's Forces at War," in A. R. Millett and W. Murray, eds., *Military Effectiveness*, vol. 1, *The First World War* (Cambridge, 1988), 253. For the aristocratic Tsarist officer corps and its ideology, see A. K. Wildman, *The End of the Russian Imperial Army*, vol. 1, *The Old Army and the Soldiers' Revolt (March–April 1917)* (Princeton, NJ, 1980), 22; W. C. Fuller Jr., *Civil-Military Conflict in Imperial Russia, 1881–1914* (Princeton, NJ, 1985), 9–10; G. Vitarbo, "Nationality Policy and the Russian Imperial Officer Corps, 1905–1914," *Slavic Review* 66, no. 4 (Winter 2007): 682–701. For comparison, in the Habsburg army around 1900 two-thirds of the generals were of noble origin, and nobles made up around one-quarter of the entire professional officer corps. See Deak, *Beyond Nationalism*, 160–161.

2. For officer education, especially in military statistics, see Fuller, *Civil-Military Conflict*, 8–9; Holquist, "To Count, to Extract, to Exterminate," 113–115. The Russian army's adoption of conscription is discussed in Wildman, *End of the Russian Imperial Army*, 1:13–17, 25–26.

3. The quotation from the 1874 Conscription Law appears in N. N. Golovine, *The Russian Army in the World War* (New Haven, CT, 1931), 2. More generally on conscription and the Russian army's ambitions, see Sanborn, *Drafting the Russian Nation*. Kappeler, *Russian Empire*, 285, and Rothenberg, *Army*, 108, offer information on the Russian population and its lack of education. For the Russian military's organization across the Tsar's empire, see Stone, *Russian Army*, 36; War Office, General Staff [Great Britain], *Handbook of the Russian Army, 1914* (London, 1996), 11, 19.

4. M. von Hagen, "The Limits of Reform: The Multiethnic Imperial Army Confronts Nationalism, 1874–1917," in D. Schimmelpenninck van der Oye and B. W. Menning, eds., *Reforming the Tsar's Army: Military Innovation in Imperial Russia from Peter the Great to the Revolution* (Cambridge, 2004), 40–43; Stone, *Russian Army*, 35–36; War Office, General Staff [Great Britain], *Handbook of the Russian Army*, 11–13.

5. McNeal, *Tsar and Cossack*, 1–23, 37–41, 58–62.

6. For Russian military strength, see Stone, *Russian Army*, 55. For funding, see Jones, "Imperial Russia's Forces," 258–259. For artillery, see Pavlov, "Russian

Artillery," 257; and for the Russian army's weak "linkages," see Menning, *Bayonets Before Bullets*, esp. 270–271.

7. Reichsarchiv, *Weltkrieg*, vol. 2, "Anlage 2"; War Office, General Staff [Great Britain], *Handbook of the Russian Army*, 21, 31–33, 205–207, 264, 267; Jones, "Imperial Russia's Forces," 281.

8. War Office, General Staff [Great Britain], *Handbook of the Russian Army*, 49–50; Stone, *Eastern Front*, 55; Knox, *With the Russian Army*, xx–xxi, 268–269.

BIBLIOGRAPHY

ARCHIVAL SOURCES

Archiwum Główne Akt Dawnych, Warsaw, Poland (AGAD Warsaw)

Austriackie sądy wojskowe okręgu X Korpusu w Przemyślu [Austrian military courts in the X Corps region in Przemyśl] (417): 238, 281, 283, 290, 296, 297, 300, 370.

Archiwum Narodowe w Krakowie, Poland (AN Cracow)

Naczelny Komitet Narodowy: 279 (Mikrofilm: 100,477), 282 (Mikrofilm: 100,480), and 296 (Mikrofilm: 100,494).

Archiwum Państwowe w Przemyślu, Poland (AP Przemyśl)

129 (Akta Miasta Przemyśla)—1382, 1392, 1594, 1595.
397 (Afisze, plakaty i druki ulotni)—19, 20, 47, 49, 482, 483, 484, 501.

Biblioteka Jagiellońska w Krakowie, Poland

Klemens Bąkowski—rps 7283.

Hadtörténelmi Levéltár, Budapest, Hungary (HL Budapest)

AKVI 9510, 25931, 29769, 32935—Personnel files: Oberstleutnant Elek Molnár.
II. 169. M.kir. 23 Honvéd Gyaloghadosztály (HG), 2, 3, and 4 Doboz.
Tanulmánygyűjtemény (TGY) 18. István Bielek.

Muzeum Narodowe Ziemi Przemyskiej w Przemyślu, Poland (MNZP Przemyśl)

Archiwum Podpułkownika Eleka Molnara—DVD Introduction, 1–12.

Österreichisches Staatsarchiv, Vienna, Austria

ALLGEMEINES VERWALTUNGSARCHIV (AVA VIENNA)

Ministerium des Innern, Präsidiale (1914–1915): 22/Galiz. Karton 2116.
Ministerium des Innern, Präsidiale (1916–1917): 22/Galiz. Karton 2117.
Ministerium des Innern, Präsidiale (1918) 22/Galiz. Karton 2118.
Ministerium des Innern, Präsidiale (1918) 22/Galiz. Karton 2119.

KRIEGSARCHIV (KA VIENNA)

Luftfahrtarchiv (LA): Ms. 27: Nikolaus Wagner v. Florheim, "Als Flieger in Przemysl" (n.d.).
LA: Ms. 77: Roman Grutschnig, "Unser letzter Tag und Flug aus Przemysl" (1916).
Militärkanzlei Seiner Majestät des Kaisers (MKSM): 69–8/9 (1914); 69–11/1 (1914); 28–3/2 (1915).
Neue Feldakten (NFA): 30 ITD: Karton 1721, 1722.
NFA: 43 Sch.D: Karton 2180.
NFA: Festung Lemberg.
NFA: Festungskommando Przemysl: Karton 1321, 1322, 1323.
NFA: Gefechtsberichte 1914–1916 der 30 ITD: Karton 31.
Nachlaß (NL): B/486 Oberleutnant Felix Hölzer.
NL: B/497 Eduard Freunthaler.
NL: B/608 Oberleutnant Rudolf Biedermann.
NL: B/726/1 Robert Nowak.
NL: B/737 Major Ludwig Páger.
NL: 763(B,C) Major Ferdinand Ritter Reder von Schellmann.
NL: B/1017 Leutnant Reinhold Kollmayr.
NL: B/1137/4, 8, 11–15 Generaloberst Hermann Kusmanek von Burgneustädten.
10. Übers.—NO.: G. Korolkow, *Strategische Studie über den Weltkrieg, 1914–1918.—Periode vom 14. Sept. Bis 28. Nov. 1914.* Höherer Mil. Redaktionsrat, trans. Mjr. Th. Pibl (Moscow, 1923).
14. Übers.—NO.: P. Tscherkassow, *Der Sturm auf Przemysl, 7.X.1914. Stab der Roten Armee. Abteilung für die Erforschung u. Auswertung der Kriegserfahrungen,* trans. Mjr Th. Pibl. (Moscow: Ausgabe der Militärdruckerei der Aktenabteilung des Volkskomm. für Heer und Flotte u des Militär Revol. Rates, 1927).

The Central Archives for the History of the Jewish People, Jerusalem, Israel (CAHJP Jerusalem)

HM2-9177—Dr. Bernard Hausner's reports on Jewish communities under Russian occupation.

Tsentral'nyi derzhavnyi istorychnyi arkhiv Ukrainy u L'vovi, Ukraine (TsDIAL Lviv)

146/8/68—Materials on the Situation of Jews in the Kingdom of Poland and in Galicia, 1915.
645/1/3—Decrees of the Governor of Przemyśl Gubernium and General Governor of Galicia.
645/1/7—Materials on the Situation of Jewish Population Outside the Towns of Galicia.
645/1/16—Preparations for the Visit of the Tsar to Przemyśl.
645/1/148—Materials on the Transfer of Przemyśl Treasury to Kiev.

The National Archives, London, United Kingdom (TNA London)

WO 106/1122 and 1123—British Military Attaché to the Russian Army Captain Neilson's despatch on and photographs from Przemyśl after its capitulation (May 1915).

Private Collections

Stanisław Szopa, "Wspomnienia z dziecinnych lat" (Przemyśl, July 1976).

NEWSPAPERS

Echo Przemyskie
Fremden-Blatt
Kriegsnachrichten
Neue Freie Presse
Die Neue Zeitung
Neues Wiener Tagblatt
New York Times
Nowa Reforma
Oesterreichische Wehrzeitung
Pester Lloyd
Reichspost
Ziemia Przemyska

PRINTED PRIMARY SOURCES

Ansky, S. *The Enemy at His Pleasure: A Journey Through the Jewish Pale of Settlement During World War I*, ed. and trans. Joachim Neugroschel. New York: Metropolitan Books, 2002.

Archiwum Państwowe w Przemyślu. *Wojenna skrzynka pocztowa*. Przemyśl: Archiwum Państwowe w Przemyślu, 2014.

von Auffenberg-Komarów, Moritz. *Aus Österreichs Höhe und Niedergang: Eine Lebensschilderung*. Munich: Drei Masken Verlag, 1921.

Baedeker, Karl. *Austria-Hungary: Handbook for Travellers*. Leipzig: Karl Baedeker, 1911.

Bergmann, Siegfried, ed. *Galizien: Seine kulturelle und wirtschaftliche Entwicklung*. Vienna: Reise und Sport, 1912.

Bloch, Ivan [Jan] S. *Is War Now Impossible? Being an Abridgment of "The War of the Future in Its Technical, Economic and Political Relations,"* ed. W. T. Stead. London: Grant Richards, 1899.

Brändström, Elsa. *Unter Kriegsgefangenen in Rußland und Sibirien, 1914–1920*. Berlin: Deutsche Verlagsgesellschaft für Politik und Geschichte, 1922.

Bromberg-Bytkowski, S. "Die Juden Lembergs unter der Russenherrschaft." *Jüdisches Archiv. Mitteilungen des Komitees "Jüdisches Kriegsarchiv."* Lieferung 8–9 (January 1917): 1–38.

Broucek, Peter, ed. *Ein General im Zwielicht: Die Erinnerungen Edmund Glaises von Horstenau*. Vol. 1, *K.u.k. Generalstabsoffizier und Historiker.* Vienna: Böhlau, 1980.

———. *Theodor Ritter von Zeynek: Ein Offizier im Generalstabskorps erinnert sich*. Vienna: Böhlau, 2009.

Brussilov, A. A. *A Soldier's Note-Book, 1914–1918*. London: Macmillan, 1930.

Conrad von Hötzendorf, Franz. *Aus meiner Dienstzeit, 1906–1918*. Vol. 4, *24. Juni 1914 bis 30. September 1914. Die politischen und militärischen Vorgänge vom Fürstenmord in Sarajevo bis zum Abschluß der ersten und bis zum Beginn der zweiten Offensive gegen Serbien und Rußland*. Vienna: Rikola, 1923.

———. *Aus meiner Dienstzeit, 1906–1918*. Vol. 5, *Oktober–November–Dezember 1914. Die Kriegsereignisse und die politischen Vorgänge in dieser Zeit*. Vienna: Rikola, 1925.

Cross, Tim, ed. *The Lost Voices of World War I: An International Anthology of Writers, Poets and Playwrights*. London: Bloomsbury, 1998 [1988].

Dalecki, Maciej, and Andrzej Kazimierz Mielnik, eds. "Dziennik Józefy Prochazka z okresu oblężenia i okupacji rosyjskiej Przemyśla w 1915 roku jako źródło historyczne." *Archiwum Państwowe w Przemyślu: Rocznik Historyczno-Archiwalny* 17 (2003): 269–290.

———, eds. "Oblężenia i okupacja Przemyśla przez Rosjan w latach 1914–1915 według kroniki Szkoły Ludowej Czeroklasowej Męskiej Imienia Św. Jana Kantego. *Archiwum Państwowe w Przemyślu: Rocznik Historyczno-Archiwalny* 23 (2011–2012): 179–190.

————. "Wspomnienia przemyskich nauczycielek z okresu I wojny światowej." *Przemyskie Zapiski Historyczne* 18 (2010–2011): 143–169.

Ehrenstein, Leopold. *Der Fall der Festung Przemysl*, ed. Emil Portisch. Bratislava: Eigenverlag des Autors, 1937.

von Fabini, Ludwig. "Die Feuertaufe des Eisernen Korps: Der erste Tag der Schlacht von Złoczów am 26. August 1914." *Militärwissenschaftliche Mitteilungen* 61 (1930): 785–843.

Fleischer, Rudolf. "Rückzug nach Przemyśl im Herbst 1914. (Erinnerungen eines Truppenoffiziers)." *Militärwissenschaftliche und technische Mitteilungen* 55 (1924): 18–26, 120–129.

Gayczak, Stanisław. *Pamiętnik Oberleutnanta Stanisława Marcelego Gayczaka*, ed. Jan Gayczak. Przemyśl: Urząd Miejski w Przemyślu, n.d.

Geőcze, Bertalan. *A przemysli tragédia*. Budapest: Pesti Könyvnyomda Részvénytársaság, 1922.

von Guttry, Aleksander. *Galizien: Land und Leute*. Munich: Georg Müller, 1916.

Hašek, Jaroslav. *The Good Soldier Švejk and His Fortunes in the World War*, trans. Cecil Parrott. London: Penguin, 2000 [1973].

Hemberger, Andreas. *Der europäische Krieg und der Weltkrieg: Historische Darstellung der Kriegsereignisse von 1914/15*, 5 vols. Vienna: A. Hartleben, 1915.

Horne, Charles F., ed. *Source Records of the Great War: A Comprehensive and Readable Source Record of the World's Great War, Emphasizing the Most Important Events, and Presenting These as Complete Narratives in the Actual Words of the Chief Officials and Most Eminent Leaders*, vol. 3. N.p.: National Alumni, 1923.

Kalendarz pamiątkowy z czasów oblężenia Przemyśla w r. 1914 na rok pański 1915. Przemyśl: Jan Lazor, 1914.

K.k. Statistisches Zentralkommission, *Österreichische Statistik: Bewegung der Bevölkerung der im Reichsrate vertretenen Königreiche und Länder im Jahre 1910*. Vienna: K.k. Hof- und Staatsdruckerei, 1912.

Knox, Alfred. *With the Russian Army, 1914–1917: Being Chiefly Extracts from the Diary of a Military Attaché*. London: Hutchinson, 1921.

[Komadina, Constantin.] *Dziennik oficera Landsturmu*, trans. Marcin Wichrowski. Przemyśl: Tomasz Idzikowski Fort VIII, "Łętownia," 2004.

Kovács, Elisabeth, Pál Arato, Franz Pichorner, and Lotte Wewalka, eds. *Untergang oder Rettung der Donaumonarchie? Politische Dokuments zu Kaiser und König Karl I. (IV.) aus internationalen Archiven*, vol. 2. Vienna: Böhlau, 2004.

von Kozma, Miklós. *Mackensens ungarische Husaren: Tagebuch eines Frontoffiziers, 1914–1918*, trans. Mirza von Schüching. Berlin: Verlag für Kulturpolitik, 1933.

Krasicki, August. *Dziennik z kampanii rosyjskiej, 1914–1916*. Warsaw: Instytut Wydawniczy Pax, 1988.

Krauß, Alfred. *Die Ursachen unserer Niederlage: Erinnerungen und Urteile aus dem Weltkrieg*, 3rd ed. Munich: J. F. Lehmanns Verlag, 1923.

K.u.k. Kriegsministerium. *Schematismus für das k.u.k. Heer und für die k.u.k. Kriegsmarine für 1914: Amtliche Ausgabe*. Vienna: K.k. Hof- und Staatsdruckerei, 1914.

K.u.k. Ministerium des Äussern. *Sammlung von Nachweisen für die Verletzungen des Völkerrechts durch die mit Österreich-Ungarn Krieg führenden Staaten. Abgeschlossen mit 31. Jänner 1915*. Vienna: K.k. Hof- und Staatsdruckerei, 1915.

————. *Sammlung von Nachweisen für die Verletzungen des Völkerrechts durch die mit Österreich-Ungarn Krieg führenden Staaten. I. Nachtrag. Abgeschlossen mit 30. April 1915*. Vienna: K.k. Hof- und Staatsdruckerei, 1915.

————. *Sammlung von Nachweisen für die Verletzungen des Völkerrechts durch die mit Österreich-Ungarn Krieg führenden Staaten. II. Nachtrag. Abgeschlossen mit 30. November 1915*. Vienna: K.k. Hof- und Staatsdruckerei, 1916.

————. *Sammlung von Nachweisen für die Verletzungen des Völkerrechts durch die mit Österreich-Ungarn Krieg führenden Staaten. III. Nachtrag. Abgeschlossen mit 30. Juni 1916*. Vienna: K.k. Hof- und Staatsdruckerei, 1916.

Künigl-Ehrenburg, Ilka. *W oblężonym Przemyślu: Kartki dziennika z czasów Wielkiej Wojny (1914–1915)*, ed. Stanisław Stępień and trans. Edward Pietraszek and Anna Siciak. Przemyśl: Południowo Wschodni Instytut Naukowy, 2010.

Lagzi, István, ed. *Węgrzy w Twierdzy Przemyskiej w latach 1914–1915*. Warsaw: Węgierski Instytut Kultury and Muzeum Narodowe Ziemi Przemyskiej w Przemyślu, 1985.

Lenar, Jan. *Pamiętnik z walk o Twierdzę Przemyśl*. Przemyśl: Tomasz Idzikowski Fort VIII, "Łętownia," 2005.

Lévai, Jenő. *Éhség, árulás, Przemyśl*. Budapest: A "Magyar Hétfő" Kiadása, 1933.

Ludendorff, Erich. *My War Memories, 1914–1918*, 2 vols. London, 1919.

Magyar Kir, Központi Statisztikai Hivatal. *A magyar szent korona országainak 1910. évi népszámlálása. Első rész: A népesség főbb adatai községek és népesebb puszták, telepek szerint*. Budapest: Az athenaeum irodalmi és nyomdai r.-társulat nyomása, 1912.

Menczer, Arie, ed. *Sefer Przemyśl*. Tel Aviv: Irgun Yotzei, 1964. Available in English translation at Jewish Gen, www.jewishgen.org/yizkor/przemysl/przemysl.html.

von Michaelsburg, I. *Im belagerten Przemysl: Tagebuchblätter aus großer Zeit*. Leipzig: C. F. Amelangs Verlag, 1915.

Molnár, Ferenc. *Galicja, 1914–1915: Zapiski korespondenta wojennego*, trans. Ákos Engelmayer. Warsaw: Most, 2012.

Nerad, Viktor. *Przemysl: Erinnerungen des Genieoffiziers Viktor Nerad*. Salzburg: Österreichischer Milizverlag, 2015.

Nónay, Dezső. *A volt m. kir. szegedi 5. honvéd gyalogezred a világháborúban.* Budapest: Szerzői magánkiadás, 1931.

Odezwy i rozporządzenia z czasów okupacyi rosyjskiej Lwowa, 1914–1915. Lwów: Skład główny w księgarni p. f. H. Altenberg, G. Seyfarth, E. Wende i Spółka, 1916.

Orłowicz, Mieczysław. *Illustrierter Führer durch Przemyśl und Umgebung: Mit besonderer Berücksichtigung der Schlachtfelder und Kriegsgräber, 1914–15.* Lemberg: Verlag des Verbandes der Polnischen Vereine in Przemyśl, 1917.

Pares, Bernard. *Day by Day with the Russian Army, 1914–15.* London: Constable and Company, 1915.

Pethö, Albert, ed. *Belagerung und Gefangenschaft: Von Przemyśl bis Russische-Turkestan. Das Kriegstagebuch des Dr. Richard Ritter von Stenitzer, 1914–1917.* Graz: Ares, 2010.

Pirquet, Clemens, ed. *Volksgesundheit im Kriege*, 2 vols. Vienna: Hölder-Pichler-Tempsky; New Haven, CT: Yale University Press, 1926.

Pomykacz, Tomacz. "Jenő Lévai: Bój o fort I/1 'Łysiczka.'" *Nasz Przemyśl* 3 (March 2014): 9–11; 4 (April 1915): 14–15; 5 (May 2014): 9–11.

Redlich, Josef. *Schicksalsjahre Österreichs, 1908–1919: Das politische Tagebuch Josef Redlichs*, ed. Fritz Fellner, 2 vols. Graz: Hermann Böhlau, 1953.

Remarque, Erich Maria. *All Quiet on the Western Front*, trans. Brian Murdoch. London: Vintage Books, 1996.

Romer, Jan Edward. *Pamiętniki.* Warsaw: Muzeum Historii Polski and Bellona, 2011.

Sands, Bedwin, ed. *The Russians in Galicia.* New York: Ukrainian National Council, 1916.

Schwalb, Hans. "Improvisationen zur Bekämpfung von Luftfahrzeugen in der Festung Przemyśl, 1914/15." *Mitteilungen über Gegenstände des Artillerie- und Geniewesens* 59, Jahrgang, Heft 10 (1918): 1539–1545.

———. "Die Verteidigung von Przemyśl, 1914/15," Sonderabdruck aus den *Mitteilungen über Gegenstände des Artillerie- und Geniewesens* 59, Jahrgang, Heft 9 (1918): 1–20.

Schwarz, Engelbrecht, *Frauen in Przemysl: Sittenbilder aus der belagerten Festung, 1914/15.* Darmstadt: Ernst Hofmann, 1936.

z Seifertów Jabłońska, Helena. *Dziennik z oblężonego Przemyśla, 1914–1915*, ed. Hanna Imbs. Przemyśl: Południowo Wschodni Instytut Naukowy, 1994.

Stenographische Protokolle über die Sitzungen des Hauses der Abgeordneten des österreichischen Reichsrates im Jahre 1917. XXII. Session 1. (Eröffnungs–) bis 21. Sitzung. (S. 1 bis 1155), vol. 1. Vienna: k.k. Hof- und Staatsdruckerei, 1917.

Stepun, Fedor. *Wie war es möglich: Briefe eines russischen Offiziers.* Munich: Carl Hanser, 1929.

Stiefler, Georg. "Erfahrungen und Vorschläge über die militärarztliche Verwendung und Stellung des psychiatrisch geschulten Neurologen im Kriege, im besonderen bei der Armee im Felde." *Zeitschrift für die gesamte Neurologie und Psychiatrie* 59, no. 1 (December 1920): 287–293.

———. "Über Psychosen und Neurosen im Kriege (I.)." *Jahrbücher für Psychiatrie und Neurologie* 37 (1917): 374–488.

———. "Über Psychosen und Neurosen im Kriege (II.)." *Jahrbücher für Psychiatrie und Neurologie* 38 (1917): 159–183.

———. "Über Psychosen und Neurosen im Kriege (III.)." *Jahrbücher für Psychiatrie und Neurologie* 38 (1917): 381–430.

———. "Über Psychosen und Neurosen im Kriege (IV.)." *Jahrbücher für Psychiatrie und Neurologie* 39 (1919): 131–180.

———. "Über Psychosen und Neurosen im Kriege (V.)." *Jahrbücher für Psychiatrie und Neurologie* 39 (1919): 448–527.

Stock, Jan Jakub. *Notatnik z Twierdzy Przemyśl, 1914–1915*, ed. Janusz Bator. Przemyśl: ZUP MONTEL-BR, 2014.

Stolz, Otto. *Das Tiroler Landsturmregiment Nr. II im Kriege, 1914–15, in Galizien*. Innsbrück: Tiroler Landesmuseums Ferdinandeum, 1938.

Stuckheil, Franz. "Die Festung Przemyśl in der Ausrüstungszeit." *Militärwissenschaftliche und technische Mitteilungen* 55 (1924): 201–230.

———. "Die strategische Rolle Przemyśls auf dem östlichen Kriegsschauplatze." *Militärwissenschaftliche und technische Mitteilungen* 54 (1923): 60–78, 131–146.

———. "Die zweite Einschließung der Festung Przemyśl." *Militärwissenschaftliche und technische Mitteilungen* 55 (1924): 289–309, 395–417; 56 (1925): 1–21, 110–133, 222–236, 346–367; 57 (1926): 162–173, 286–296, 405–410, 530–535, 680–688.

Талергофскій альманахъ: Пропамятная книга австрійскихъ жестокостей, изуверствъ и насилий надъ карпато-русскимъ народомъ во время Всемірной войны 1914-1917 гг. Lviv: Изданіе «Талергофскаго Комитета», 1924.

Tăslăuanu, Octavian C. *With the Austrian Army in Galicia*. London: Skeffington and Son, n.d.

Veltzé, Alois, ed. *Die Geschichte des großen Weltkrieges unter besonderer Berücksichtigung Österreich–Ungarns*, 3 vols. Vienna: Verlag für Vaterländische Literatur, 1917.

Vit, Jan. *Wspomnienia z mojego pobytu w Przemyślu podczas rosyjskiego oblężenia, 1914–1915*, trans. L. Hofbauer and J. Husar. Przemyśl: Południowo Wschodni Instytut Naukowy, 1995.

Völker, Rudolf. *Przemysl: Sieg und Untergang der Festung am San*. Vienna: Tyrolia, 1927.

War Office, General Staff [Great Britain]. *Handbook of the Russian Army, 1914*. London: Imperial War Museum and Battery Press, 1996.

Washburn, Stanley. *On the Russian Front in World War I: Memoirs of an American War Correspondent*. New York: Robert Speller and Sons, 1982.

Wichrowski, Marcin, trans. *Dziennik oficera Landsturmu*. Przemyśl: Tomasz Idzikowski—Fort VIII "Łętownia," 2004.

Winkler, Wilhelm. *Die Totenverluste der öst.-ung. Monarchie nach Nationalitäten. Die Altersgliederung der Toten. Ausblicke in die Zukunft.* Vienna: L. W. Seidl and Sohn, 1919.

Welles, Eva Anna. *Der verblasste Krieg: Vom Feld der Ehre in die Dunkelheit. Geschichte einer Familie in der Zeit des Ersten Weltkriegs.* Mödling, Austria: CCU, 2014.

Wolfgang, Bruno. *Batjuschka: Ein Kriegsgefangenenschicksal.* Vienna: Wiener Verlagsgesellschaft, 1941.

———. *Przemysl: 1914–1915.* Vienna: Kommanditgesellschaft Payer, 1935.

Zakrzewska, Wanda. *Oblężenie Przemyśla rok, 1914–1915: Z przeżytych dni.* Lwów: Nakład Autorki, 1916.

Zombory-Moldován, Béla. *The Burning of the World. A Memoir of 1914*, trans. Peter Zombory-Moldovan. New York: New York Review Books, 2014.

Zubrycki, Myczajło. "Dziennik." In Andrzej A. Zięba and Adam Świątek, eds., *Monarchia, wojna, człowiek: Codzienne i niecodzienne życie mieszkańców Galicji w czasie pierwszej wojny światowej.* Cracow: Polska Akademia Umiejętności and Księgarnia Akademicka, 2014, 65–76.

SECONDARY SOURCES

Afflerbach, Holger, and David Stevenson, eds. *An Improbable War: The Outbreak of World War I and European Political Culture Before 1914.* New York: Berghahn, 2007.

Avrutin, Eugene M. "Racial Categories and the Politics of (Jewish) Difference in Late Imperial Russia." *Kritika: Explorations in Russian and Eurasian History* 8, no. 1 (Winter 2007): 13–40.

Bachmann, Klaus. *Ein Herd der Feindschaft gegen Rußland: Galizien als Krisenherd in den Beziehungen der Donaumonarchie mit Rußland (1907–1914).* Vienna: Verlag für Geschichte und Politik and R. Oldenbourg, 2001.

Baczkowski, Michał. *Pod czarno-żółtymi sztandarami: Galicja i jej mieszkańcy wobec austro-węgierskich struktur militarnych, 1868–1914.* Cracow: Towarzystwo Wydawnicze "Historia Iagellonica," 2003.

Bartov, Omer, and Eric D. Weitz. *Shatterzone of Empires: Coexistence and Violence in the German, Habsburg, Russian, and Ottoman Borderlands.* Bloomington: Indiana University Press, 2013.

Bator, Juliusz. *Wojna Galicyjska: Działania armii austro-węgierskiej na froncie północnym (galicyjskim) w latach 1914–1915.* Cracow: Libron, 2005.

Binder, Harold. *Galizien in Wien: Parteien, Wahlen, Fraktionen und Abgeordnete im Übergang zur Massenpolitik.* Vienna: Verlag der Österreichischen Akademie der Wissenschaften, 2005.

Bobusia, Bogosław, and Marek Gosztyła. *Plany Twierdzy Przemyśl: The Stronghold of Przemyśl—Plans*, 3 vols. Przemyśl: Archiwum Państwowe w Przemyślu, Przemyskie Towarzystwo Archiwistyczne "Archiwariusz" w Przemyślu and Stowarzyszenie Opieki nad Twierdzą Przemyśl i Dziedzictwem Kulturowym Ziemi Przemyskiej, 2004, 2006, and 2010.

Böhler, Jochen, Włodzimierz Borodziej, and Joachim von Puttkamer, eds. *Legacies of Violence: Eastern Europe's First World War*. Munich: Oldenbourg, 2014.

Bundesministerium für Heereswesen und Kriegsarchiv. *Österreich-Ungarns letzter Krieg*. Vol. 1, *Vom Kriegsausbruch bis zum Ausgang der Schlacht bei Limanowa–Łapanów*. Vienna: Verlag der Militärwissenschaftlichen Mitteilungen, 1931.

———. *Österreich-Ungarns letzter Krieg*. Vol. 2, *Vom Ausklang der Schlacht bei Limanowa–Łapanów bis zur Einnahme von Brest–Litowsk*. Vienna: Verlag der Militärwissenschaftlichen Mitteilungen, 1931.

Bushnell, John. "Peasants in Uniform: The Tsarist Army as a Peasant Society." *Journal of Social History* 13, no. 4 (Summer 1980): 565–576.

———. "The Tsarist Officer Corps, 1881–1914: Customs, Duties, Inefficiency." *American Historical Review* 86, no. 4 (October 1981): 753–780.

Clark, Christopher. *The Sleepwalkers: How Europe Went to War in 1914*. New York: Basic Books, 2013.

Cohen, Gary B. "Nationalist Politics and the Dynamics of State and Civil Society in the Habsburg Monarchy, 1867–1914." *Central European History* 40, no. 2 (June 2007): 241–278.

Cole, Laurence. *Military Culture and Popular Patriotism in Late Imperial Austria*. Oxford: Oxford University Press, 2014.

Cornwall, Mark. "Morale and Patriotism in the Austro-Hungarian Army, 1914–1918." In John Horne, ed., *State, Society and Mobilization in Europe During the First World War*. Cambridge: Cambridge University Press, 1997, 173–191.

Czernin von Chudenitz, Franz. *Das Postwesen in der öu: Festung Przemyśl während der beiden Belagerungen 1914/1915*. Vienna: The Author, 1985.

Dalecki, Maciej. "Rozbudowa urządzeń komunalnych Przemyśla w latach 1867–1914." *Rocznik Historyczno-Archiwalny* 6 (1989): 49–62.

Davies, Norman. *God's Playground: A History of Poland*. Vol. 2, *1795 to the Present* Oxford: Oxford University Press, 2005.

Deák, István. *Beyond Nationalism: A Social and Political History of the Habsburg Officer Corps, 1848–1918*. New York: Oxford University Press, 1990.

Deak, John. *Forging a Multinational State: State Making in Imperial Austria from the Enlightenment to the First World War*. Stanford, CA: Stanford University Press, 2015.

DiNardo, Richard L. *Breakthrough: The Gorlice-Tarnow Campaign, 1915*. Santa Barbara, CA: Praeger, 2010.

Dowling, Timothy C., ed. *Russia at War: From the Mongol Conquest to Afghanistan, Chechnya, and Beyond*. Vol. 1, *A–M*. Santa Barbara, CA: ABC-CLIO, 2015.

Duffy, Christopher. *Fire and Stone: The Science of Fortress Warfare, 1660–1860*. Newton Abbot, UK: David and Charles, 1975.

Fahey, John E. "Przemyśl, Galicia: A Garrison Town Before, During, Between and After War (1873–1953)." *Revista Universitaria de Historia Militar* 5, no. 9 (2016): 212–229.

———. "Undermining a Bulwark of the Monarchy: Civil-Military Relations in Fortress Przemyśl (1871–1914)." *Austrian History Yearbook* 48 (2017): 145–158.

Forstner, Franz. *Przemyśl: Österreich-Ungarns bedeutendste Festung*, 2nd ed. Vienna: ÖBV Pädagogischer Verlag, 1997 [1987].

Führ, Christoph. *Das k.u.k. Armeeoberkommando und die Innenpolitik in Österreich, 1914–1917*. Graz: Hermann Böhlaus Nachf., 1968.

Fuller, William C., Jr. *Civil-Military Conflict in Imperial Russia, 1881–1914*. Princeton, NJ: Princeton University Press, 1985.

Galántai, József. *Hungary in the First World War*. Budapest: Akadémiai Kiadó, 1989.

Gatrell, Peter. *A Whole Empire Walking: Refugees in Russia During World War I*. Bloomington: Indiana University Press, 1999.

Geinitz, Christian. "The First Air War Against Noncombatants: Strategic Bombing of German Cities in World War I." In Roger Chickering and Stig Förster, eds., *Great War, Total War: Combat and Mobilization on the Western Front, 1914–1918*. Cambridge: Cambridge University Press and The German Historical Institute, 2000, 207–226.

Gerwarth, Robert. *The Vanquished: Why the First World War Failed to End, 1917–1923*. London: Penguin, 2016.

Golczewski, Frank. *Polnische-jüdische Beziehungen, 1881–1922: Eine Studie zur Geschichte des Antisemitismus in Osteuropa*. Wiesbaden: Franz Steiner, 1981.

Golovine, Nicholas N. *The Russian Army in the World War*. New Haven, CT: Yale University Press, 1931.

Gray, Peter, and Owen Thetford. *German Aircraft of the First World War*. London: Putnam, 1962.

Grin-Piszczek, Ewa. "Polityka Sowietów wobec mieszkańców Przemyśla na tle sytuacji terenów okupowanych przez ZSRR w latach 1939–1941." *Archiwum Państwowe w Przemyślu: Rocznik Historyczno-Archiwalny* 18 (2004): 76–119.

Gross, Jan T. *Revolution from Abroad: The Soviet Conquest of Poland's Western Ukraine and Western Belorussia*, expanded ed. Princeton, NJ: Princeton University Press, 2002.

Gudmundsson, Bruce. "Introduction." In Sanders Marble, ed., *King of Battle: Artillery in World War I*. Leiden: Brill, 2015, 1–34.

Gumz, Jonathan E. *The Resurrection and Collapse of Empire in Habsburg Serbia, 1914–1918*. Cambridge: Cambridge University Press, 2009.

von Hagen, Mark. "The Limits of Reform: The Multiethnic Imperial Army Confronts Nationalism, 1874–1917." In David Schimmelpenninck van der Oye and Bruce W. Menning, eds., *Reforming the Tsar's Army: Military*

Innovation in Imperial Russia from Peter the Great to the Revolution. Cambridge: Woodrow Wilson Center Press with Cambridge University Press, 2004, 34–55.

———. *War in a European Borderland: Occupations and Occupation Plans in Galicia and Ukraine, 1914–1918.* Seattle: REECAS, University of Washington, 2007.

Hagen, William W. *Anti-Jewish Violence in Poland, 1914–1920.* Cambridge: Cambridge University Press, 2018.

———. "Before the 'Final Solution': Toward a Comparative Analysis of Political Anti-Semitism in Interwar Germany and Poland." *Journal of Modern History* 68, no. 2 (June 1996): 351–381.

Hall, Richard C., ed. *War in the Balkans: An Encyclopedic History from the Fall of the Ottoman Empire to the Breakup of Yugoslavia.* Santa Barbara, CA: ABC-Clio, 2014.

Hämmerle, Christa. "Die k. (u.) k. Armee als 'Schule des Volkes'? Zur Geschichte der Allgemeinen Wehrpflicht in der multinationalen Habsburgermonarchie (1866–1914/18)." In Christian Jansen, ed., *Der Bürger als Soldat: Die Militarisierung europäischer Gesellschaften im langen 19. Jahrhundert: ein internationaler Vergleich.* Essen: Klartext, 2004, 175–213.

———. "'. . . Dort wurden wir dressiert und sekiert und geschlagen . . .': Vom Drill, dem Disziplinarstrafrecht und Soldatenmisshandlungen im Heer (1868 bis 1914)." In Laurence Cole, Christa Hämmerle, and Martin Scheutz, eds., *Glanz—Gewalt—Gehorsam: Militär und Gesellschaft in der Habsburgermonarchie (1800 bis 1918).* Essen: Klartext, 2011, 31–54.

Hann, Chris. "Postsocialist Nationalism: Rediscovering the Past in Southeast Poland." *Slavic Review* 57, no. 4 (Winter 1998): 840–863.

Harmat, Ulrike. "Divorce and Remarriage in Austria-Hungary: The Second Marriage of Franz Conrad von Hötzendorf." *Austrian History Yearbook* 32 (January 2001): 69–103.

Harris, Jason, Regina C. LaRocque, Firdausi Qadri, Edward T. Ryan, and Stephen B. Calderwood. "Cholera." *The Lancet* 379 (2012): 2466–2476.

Hartman, John J., and Jacek Krochmal, eds. *Pamiętam każdy dzień . . . Losy Żydów Przemyskich podczas II Wojny Światowej.* Przemyśl: Towarzystwo Przyjaciół Nauk w Przemyślu, 2001.

Hauser, Leopold. *Monografia miasta Przemyśla.* Przemyśl: Południowo-Wschodni Instytut Naukowy w Przemyślu, 1991 [1883].

Heiden, Hermann. *Bollwerk am San: Schicksal der Festung Przemysl.* Oldenburg i.O.: Gerhard Stalling, 1940).

Herwig, Holger H. *The First World War: Germany and Austria-Hungary, 1914–1918.* London: Arnold, 1997.

———. *The Marne, 1914: The Opening of World War I and the Battle That Changed the World.* New York: Random House, 2009.

Hofer, Hans-Georg. *Nervenschwäche und Krieg: Modernitätskritik und Krisenbewältigung in der österreichischen Psychiatrie (1880–1920).* Vienna: Böhlau, 2004.

Hoffmann-Holter, Beatrix. *"Abreisendmachung": Jüdische Kriegsflüchtlinge in Wien 1914 bis 1923*. Cologne: Böhlau, 1995.

Holquist, Peter. "The Role of Personality in the First (1914–1915) Russian Occupation of Galicia and Bukovina." In Jonathan Dekel-Chen, David Gaunt, Natan M. Meir, and Israel Bartal, eds., *Anti-Jewish Violence: Rethinking the Pogrom in European History*. Bloomington: Indiana University Press, 2010, 52–73.

———. "To Count, to Extract, and to Exterminate: Population Statistics and Population Politics in Late Imperial and Soviet Russia." In Ronald Grigor Suny and Terry Martin, eds., *A State of Nations: Empire and Nation-Making in the Age of Lenin and Stalin*. Oxford: Oxford University Press, 2001, 111–144.

———. "Les violences de l'armée russe à l'encontre des Juifs en 1915: Causes et limites." In John Horne, ed., *Vers la guerre totale: Le tournant de 1914–15*. Paris: Tallandier, 2010, 191–219.

Holzer, Anton. *Das Lächeln der Henker: Der unbekannte Krieg gegen die Zivilbevölkerung, 1914–1918*. Darmstadt: Primus, 2008.

Hull, Isabel V. *Absolute Destruction: Military Culture and the Practices of War in Imperial Germany*. Ithaca, NY: Cornell University Press, 2005.

Idzikowski, Tomasz. *Fort I "Salis-Soglio."* Przemyśl: Tomasz Idzikowski Fort VIII "Łętownia," 2004.

———. *Fort XV "Borek."* Przemyśl: Tomasz Idzikowski Fort VIII "Łętownia," 2004.

———. "Fortyfikacje polowe Twierdzy Przemyśl—Problematyka ochrony reliktów pola bitwy 1914–1915." In Waldemar Brzoskwinia, ed., *Fortyfikacja austriacka—Twierdza Przemyśl. Materiały z konferencji naukowej Towarzystwa Przyjaciół Fortyfikacji Przemyśl 30 IX–2 X 1999 roku*. Warsaw: Towarzystwo Przyjaciół Fortyfikacji, 1999, 101–109.

———. "Grupa Siedliska." In Janusz Polaczek, ed., *Twierdza Przemyśl w Galicji: Materiały z konferencji naukowej, Przemyśl, 25–27 kwietnia 2002*. Przemyśl: Regionalny Ośrodek Kultury, Edukacji i Nauki w Przemyślu i Studenckie Koło Naukowe Historyków Uniwerstetu Jagiellońskiego, 2003, 83–107.

———. *Twierdza Przemyśl: Powstanie—Rozwój—Technologie*. Krosno, Poland: Arete, 2014.

———. "Uniwersalny fort pancerny Twierdzy Przemyśl—Fort IV 'Optyń' w świetle ostatnich badań terenowych i archiwalnych." In Waldemar Brzoskwinia, ed., *Fortyfikacja austriacka—Twierdza Przemyśl. Materiały z konferencji naukowej Towarzystwa Przyjaciół Fortyfikacji Przemyśl 30 IX–2 X 1999 roku*. Warsaw: Towarzystwo Przyjaciół Fortyfikacji, 1999, 79–90.

Jasiek, Marek. "Overcoming Ukrainian Resistance: The Deportation of Ukrainians Within Poland in 1947." In Philipp Ther and Ana Siljak, eds., *Redrawing Nations: Ethnic Cleansing in East-Central Europe, 1944–1948*. Lanham, MD: Rowman and Littlefield, 2001, 173–194.

Jeřábek, Rudolf. "The Eastern Front." In Mark Cornwall, ed., *The Last Years of Austria-Hungary: A Multi-National Experiment in Early Twentieth-Century Europe*, revised and expanded ed. Exeter: University of Exeter Press, 2002, 149–165.

Jones, David R. "Imperial Russia's Forces at War." In Allan R. Millett and William Murray, eds., *Military Effectiveness*. Vol. 1, *The First World War*. Cambridge: Cambridge University Press, 1988, 249–328.

Judson, Pieter M. *The Habsburg Empire: A New History*. Cambridge, MA: Belknap Press of Harvard University Press, 2016.

Kappeler, Andreas. *The Russian Empire: A Multiethnic History*. Harlow, UK: Routledge, 2001.

Kargol, Tomasz. *Odbudowa Galicji ze zniszczeń wojennych w latach 1914–1918*. Cracow: Historia Iagellonica, 2012.

Konieczny, Zdzisław. *Walki polsko-ukraińskie w Przemyślu i okolicy listopad grudzień 1918*. Przemyśl: Spółdzielna Invalidów "Praca," 1993.

Kramarz, Walerjan. *Ludność Przemyśla w latach 1521–1921*. Przemyśl: Jan Łazor, Wydano z zasiłku Ministerstwa Wznań Religijnych i Oświecenia Publicznego, 1930.

Kronenbitter, Günther. *"Krieg im Frieden": Die Führung der k.u.k. Armee und die Großmachtpolitik Österreich-Ungarns, 1906–1914*. Munich: R. Oldenbourg, 2003.

Kulińska, Lucyna. *Działalność terrorystyczna i sabotażowa nacjonalistycznych organizacji ukraińskich w Polsce w latach 1922–1939*. Cracow: Księgarnia Akademicka, 2009.

Lackey, Scott W., *The Rebirth of the Habsburg Army: Friedrich Beck and the Rise of the General Staff*. Westport, CT: Greenwood Press, 1995.

Lambroza, Shlomo. "The Pogroms of 1903–1906." In John D. Klier and Shlomo Lambroza, eds., *Pogroms: Anti-Jewish Violence in Modern Russian History*. Cambridge: Cambridge University Press, 1992, 195–247.

Levene, Mark. *The Crisis of Genocide*, 2 vols. Vol. 1, *Devastation: The European Rimlands, 1912–1938*, and vol. 2, *Annihilation: The European Rimlands, 1939–1953*. Oxford: Oxford University Press, 2013.

Lieven, Dominic. *Towards the Flame: Empire, War and the End of Tsarist Russia*. London: Allen Lane, 2015.

Lindemann, Albert S. *Esau's Tears: Modern Anti-Semitism and the Rise of the Jews*. Cambridge: Cambridge University Press, 1997.

Liulevičius, Vėjas Gabriel. *War Land on the Eastern Front: Culture, National Identity, and German Occupation in World War I*. Cambridge: Cambridge University Press, 2000.

Lohr, Eric. *Nationalizing the Russian Empire: The Campaign Against Enemy Aliens During World War I*. Cambridge, MA: Harvard University Press, 2003.

———. "1915 and the War Pogrom Paradigm in the Russian Empire." In Jonathan Dekel-Chen, David Gaunt, Natan M. Meir, and Israel Bartal, eds., *Anti-Jewish Violence: Rethinking the Pogrom in East European History*. Bloomington: Indiana University Press, 2010, 41–51.

Lucas, James. *Austro-Hungarian Infantry, 1914–1918*. London: Almark, 1973.

———. *Fighting Troops of the Austro-Hungarian Army, 1868–1914*. New York: Hippocrene Books; Tunbridge Wells, UK: Spellmount, 1987.

Macartney, C. A. *The Habsburg Empire, 1790–1918*. London: Weidenfeld and Nicolson, 1968.

Małecki, Jan M. "W dobie autonomii Galicyjskiej (1866–1918)." In Janina Bieniarzówna and Jan M. Małecki, eds., *Dzieje Krakowa*. Vol. 3, *Kraków w latach 1796–1918*. Kraków: Wydawnictwo Literackie, 1979, 225–394.

Marshall, Alex. "Russian Military Intelligence, 1905–1917: The Untold Story Behind Tsarist Russia in the First World War." *War in History* 11, no. 4 (November 2004): 393–423.

May, Arthur J. *The Passing of the Hapsburg Monarchy, 1914–1918*, 2 vols. Philadelphia: University of Pennsylvania Press, 1966.

Mazower, Mark. *Hitler's Empire: Nazi Rule in Occupied Europe*. London: Penguin, 2009.

McMeekin, Sean. *The Russian Origins of the First World War*. Cambridge, MA: Belknap Press of Harvard University Press, 2011.

McNeal, Robert H. *Tsar and Cossack, 1855–1914*. Basingstoke: Macmillan, in association with St. Antony's College, Oxford, 1987.

Menning, Bruce W. *Bayonets Before Bullets: The Imperial Russian Army, 1861–1914*. Bloomington: Indiana University Press, 1992.

Mick, Christoph. *Kriegserfahrungen in einer multiethnischen Stadt: Lemberg, 1914–1947*. Wiesbaden: Harrassowitz, 2010.

Moorhouse, Roger. *The Devils' Alliance: Hitler's Pact with Stalin, 1939–1941*. London: Bodley Head, 2014.

Mosse, George L. *Fallen Soldiers: Reshaping the Memory of the World Wars*. New York: Oxford University Press, 1990.

Motyl, Alexander J. "Ukrainian Nationalist Political Violence in Inter-War Poland, 1921–1939." *East European Quarterly* 19, no. 1 (Spring 1985): 45–55.

Nachtigal, Reinhard. "Privilegiensystem und Zwangsrekrutierung: Russische Nationalitätenpolitik gegenüber Kriegsgefangenen aus Österreich-Ungarn." In Jochen Oltmer, ed., *Kriegsgefangene im Europa des Ersten Weltkriegs*. Paderborn, Germany: Ferdinand Schöningh, 2006, 167–193.

———. *Rußland und seine österreichisch-ungarischen Kriegsgefangenen (1914–1918)*. Remshalden, Germany: Bernhard Albert Greiner, 2003.

———. "Zur Anzahl der Kriegsgefangenen im Ersten Weltkrieg." *Militärgeschichtliche Zeitschrift* 67, no. 2 (2008): 345–384.

Nierhaus, Andreas. "Austria as a 'Baroque Nation': Institutional and Media Constructions." *Journal of Art Historiography* 15 (2016): 1–22.

O'Rourke, Shane. "The Don Cossacks During the 1905 Revolution: The Revolt of Ust-Medveditskaia Stanitsa." *Russian Review* 57, no. 4 (October 1998): 583–598.

Pająk, Jerzy Z. *Od autonomii do niepodległości: Kształtowanie się postaw politycznych i narodowych społeczeństwa Galicji w warunkach Wielkiej Wojny, 1914–1918*. Kielce, Poland: Wydawnictwo Uniwersytetu Jana Kochanowskiego, 2012.

de Paula, Mörz. *Der österreichisch-ungarische Befestigungsbau, 1820–1914*. Vienna: Heide Stöhr, 1997.

Pavlov, Andrey. "Russian Artillery." In Sanders Marble, ed., *King of Battle: Artillery in World War I*. Leiden: Brill, 2015, 255–280.

Persowski, Franciszek, Antoni Kunysz, and Julian Olszak, eds. *Tysiąc lat Przemyśla: Zarys historyczny*, 2 vols. Rzeszów, Poland: Krajowa Agencja Wydawnicza and Państwowe Wydawnictwo Naukowe, 1974, 1976.

Pomykacz, Tomasz. "Kontrowersje wokół dowódcy obrony Fortu I/1 'Łysiczka.'" *Rocznik Przemyski* 51, no. 3 (2015): 135–148.

Prusin, Alexander V. *Nationalizing a Borderland: War, Ethnicity, and Anti-Jewish Violence in East Galicia, 1914–1920*. Tuscaloosa: University of Alabama Press, 2005.

Pudłocki, Tomasz. "Działalność inteligencji Przemyśla na tle życia mieszkańców miasta między sierpniem a listopadem 1914 r." In Janusz Polaczek, ed., *Twierdza Przemyśl w Galicji: Materiały z konferencji naukowej. Przemyśl, 25–27 kwietnia 2002*. Przemyśl: Regionalny Ośrodek Kultury, Edukacji i Nauki w Przemyślu i Studenckie Koło Naukowe Historyków Uniwerstetu Jagiellońskiego, 2003, 109–128.

———. "'Lolu, gdzie mój frak?' Prowincjonalne bale Galicji wschodniej w latach 1867–1914 jako przkład synkretyzmu estetyki życia codziennego." In Agata Seweryn and Monika Kulesza-Gierat, eds., *Powinowactwa sztuk w kulturze oświecenia i romantyzmu*. Lublin, Poland: KUL, 2012, 79–102.

Rachamimov, Alon [Iris]. *POWs and the Great War: Captivity on the Eastern Front*. Oxford: Berg, 2002.

Rauchensteiner, Manfried. *The First World War and the End of the Habsburg Monarchy*. Vienna: Böhlau, 2014.

Reichsarchiv. *Der Weltkrieg, 1914–1918*. Vol. 2, *Die Befreiung Ostpreußens*. Berlin: E. S. Mittler and Sohn, 1925.

———. *Der Weltkrieg, 1914–1918*. Vol. 5, *Der Herbst-Feldzug 1914: Im Westen bis zum Stellungskrieg; Im Osten bis zum Rückzug*. Berlin: E. S. Mittler and Sohn, 1929.

Renzi, William A. "Who Composed 'Sazonov's Thirteen Points'? A Reexamination of Russia's War Aims of 1914." *American Historical Review* 88, no. 2 (April 1983): 347–357.

Robinson, Paul. *Grand Duke Nikolai Nikolaevich: Supreme Commander of the Russian Army*. DeKalb: Northern Illinois University Press, 2014.

Rossino, Alexander B. "Nazi Anti-Jewish Policy During the Polish Campaign: The Case of the Einsatzgruppe von Woyrsch." *German Studies Review* 24, no. 1 (February 2001): 35–53.

Rothenberg, Gunther E. *The Army of Francis Joseph*. West Lafayette, IN: Purdue University Press, 1998 [1976].

Rozenblit, Marsha L. *Reconstructing a National Identity: The Jews of Habsburg Austria During World War I*. Oxford: Oxford University Press, 2001.

Rudnytsky, Ivan L. "The Ukrainians in Galicia Under Austrian Rule." In Andrei S. Markovits and Frank E. Sysyn, eds., *Nationbuilding and the Politics of Nationalism: Essays on Austrian Galicia*. Cambridge, MA: Harvard Ukrainian Research Institute, 1982, 23–67.

Sanborn, Joshua A. *Drafting the Russian Nation: Military Conscription, Total War, and Mass Politics, 1905–1925*. DeKalb: Northern Illinois University Press, 2002.

Scheer, Tamara. "K.u.k. Regimentssprachen: Institutionalisierung der Sprachenvielfalt in der Habsburgermonarchie in den Jahren 1867/8–1914." In Klaas-Hinrich Ehlers, Marek Nekula, Martina Niedhammer, and Hermann Scheuringer, eds., *Sprache, Gesellschaft und Nation in Ostmitteleuropa: Institutionalisierung und Alltagspraxis*. Göttingen, Germany: Vandenhoeck und Ruprecht, 2014, 75–92.

Schindler, John R. *Fall of the Double Eagle: The Battle for Galicia and the Demise of Austria-Hungary*. Lincoln, NE: Potomac Books, 2015.

Schmitz, Martin. *"Als ob die Welt aus den Fugen ginge": Kriegserfahrungen österreichisch-ungarischer Offiziere, 1914–18*. Paderborn, Germany: Ferdinand Schöningh, 2016.

Sheffield, Gary. *Leadership in the Trenches: Officer-Man Relations, Morale and Discipline in the British Army in the Era of the First World War*. Basingstoke: Macmillan, 2000.

Sierakowska, Katarzyna. *Śmierć—Wygnanie—Głód w dokumentach osobistych: Ziemie polskie w latach Wielkiej Wojny, 1914–1918*. Warsaw: Instytut Historii PAN, 2015.

Smith, Mark M. *The Smell of Battle, the Taste of Siege: A Sensory History of the Civil War*. Oxford: Oxford University Press, 2015.

Snyder, Timothy. *Bloodlands: Europe Between Hitler and Stalin*. New York: Basic Books, 2010.

———. *The Reconstruction of Nations: Poland, Ukraine, Lithuania, Belarus, 1569–1999*. New Haven, CT: Yale University Press, 2003.

Sondhaus, Lawrence. *Franz Conrad von Hötzendorf: Architect of the Apocalypse*. Boston: Humanities Press, 2000.

Stadnik, Kateryna. "Ukrainian-Polish Population Transfers, 1944–46: Moving in Opposite Directions." In Peter Gatrell and Nick Baron, eds., *Warlands: Population Resettlement and State Reconstruction in the Soviet–East European Borderlands, 1945–50*. Basingstoke: Palgrave Macmillan, 2009, 165–187.

Steinberg, John W. *All the Tsar's Men: Russia's General Staff and the Fate of the Empire, 1898–1914*. Washington, DC: Woodrow Wilson Center Press; Baltimore: Johns Hopkins University Press, 2010.

Stockdale, Melissa Kirschke. *Mobilizing the Russian Nation: Patriotism and Citizenship in the First World War*. Cambridge: Cambridge University Press, 2016.

Stone, David R. *The Russian Army in the Great War: The Eastern Front, 1914–1917*. Lawrence: University Press of Kansas, 2015.

Stone, Norman. "Army and Society in the Habsburg Monarchy, 1900–1914." *Past and Present* 33 (April 1966): 95–111.

———. *The Eastern Front, 1914–1917*. London: Penguin, 1998 [1975].

———. "Die Mobilmachung der österreichisch-ungarischen Armee 1914." *Militärgeschichtliche Mitteilungen* 16, no. 2 (1974): 67–95.

Strachan, Hew. *The First World War*. Vol. 1, *To Arms*. Oxford: Oxford University Press, 2001.

Subtelny, Orest. "Expulsion, Resettlement, Civil Strife: The Fate of Poland's Ukrainians, 1944–1947." In Philipp Ther and Ana Siljak, eds., *Redrawing Nations: Ethnic Cleansing in East-Central Europe, 1944–1948*. Lanham, MD: Rowman and Littlefield, 2001, 155–172.

Szczupak, Adam. *Greckokatolicka diecezja Przemyska w latach I wojny światowej*. Cracow: Towarzystwo Wydawnicze "Historia Iagellonica," 2015.

———. "Represje austro-węgierskie wobec duchowieństwa greckokatolickiego Łemkowszczyzny w latach I wojny światowej." In Tomasz Pudłocki and Arkadiusz S. Więch, eds., *Prowincja Galicyjska wokół I wojny światowej. Konteksty—Porównania—Przykłady*. Przemyśl: Wydawnictwo Naukowe Towarzystwa Przyjaciół Nauk w Przemyślu, 2014, 69–79.

———. "W pamiętnych dniach Przemyśla: Wojenne zapiski Bp. Konstantyna Czechowicza, Ks. Mirona Podolińskiego i Ks. Aleksandra Zubryckiego z lat 1914–1915." *Rocznik Przemyski* 51, no. 3 (2015): 177–194.

Szlanta, Piotr. "Der Erste Weltkrieg von 1914 bis 1915 als identitätsstiftender Faktor für die moderne polnische Nation." In G. P. Groß, ed., *Die vergessene Front: Der Osten 1914/15. Ereignis, Wirkung, Nachwirkung*. Paderborn, Germany: Ferdinand Schöningh, 2006, 153–164.

———. "The Lemkos' Great War: Wartime Experiences of the Lemko People, 1914–1918." *Acta Poloniae Historica* 113 (2016): 7–36.

———. "'Najgorsze bestie to są Honwedy': Ewolucja stosunku polskich mieszkańców Galicji do monarchii habsburskiej podczas I wojny światowej." In Urszula Jakubowska, ed., *Galicyjskie spotkania 2011*. N.p.: Instytut Badań Literackich PAN, 2011, 161–179.

Thompson, Mark. *The White War: Life and Death on the Italian Front, 1915–1919*. London: Faber and Faber, 2008.

Tunstall, Graydon A. *Blood on the Snow: The Carpathian Winter War of 1915*. Lawrence: University of Kansas Press, 2010.

———. *Written in Blood: The Battles for Fortress Przemyśl in WWI*. Bloomington: Indiana University Press, 2016.

Varga, Bálint. *The Monumental Nation: Magyar Nationalism and Symbolic Politics in Fin-de-siècle Hungary*. Oxford: Berghahn, 2016.

Vitarbo, Gregory. "Nationality Policy and the Russian Imperial Officer Corps, 1905–1914." *Slavic Review* 66, no. 4 (Winter 2007): 682–701.

Wagner, Walter. "Die k.(u.)k. Armee—Gliederung und Aufgabenstellung 1866 bis 1914." In Adam Wandruszka and Peter Urbanitsch, eds., *Die Habsburgermonarchie, 1848–1918*. Vol. 5, *Die Bewaffnete Macht*. Vienna: Verlag der Österreichische Akademie der Wissenschaften, 1987, 142–633.

Watson, Alexander. *Enduring the Great War: Combat, Morale and Collapse in the German and British Armies, 1914–1918*. Cambridge: Cambridge University Press, 2008.

———. "The Greek Catholic Church and the Problem of Ruthenian Desertion in Przemyśl, January 1915: Documents from the Kriegsarchiv, Vienna." *Rocznik Przemyski* 54 (2018): 287–301.

———. "Junior Officership in the German Army During the Great War, 1914–1918." *War in History* 14, no. 4 (November 2007): 429–453.

———. "Morale." In Jay Winter, ed., *The Cambridge History of the First World War*. Vol. 2, *The State*. Cambridge: Cambridge University Press, 2014, 174–195.

———. *Ring of Steel: Germany and Austria-Hungary in World War I*. New York: Basic Books, 2014.

———. "'Unheard of Brutality': Russian Atrocities Against Civilians in East Prussia, 1914–15." *Journal of Modern History* 86, no. 4 (December 2014): 780–825.

Wawro, Geoffrey. *A Mad Catastrophe: The Outbreak of World War I and the Collapse of the Habsburg Empire*. New York: Basic Books, 2014.

Weeks, Theodore R. "Between Rome and Tsargrad: The Uniate Church in Imperial Russia." In Robert P. Geraci and Michael Khodarkovsky, eds., *Of Religion and Empire: Missions, Conversion, and Tolerance in Tsarist Russia*. Ithaca, NY: Cornell University Press, 2001, 70–91.

Weinberg, Robert. "Look! Up There in the Sky: It's a Vulture, It's a Bat. . . . It's a Jew: Reflections on Antisemitism in Late Imperial Russia, 1906–1914." In Eugene M. Avrutin and Harriet Murav, eds., *Jews in the East European Borderlands: Essays in Honor of John D. Klier*. Boston: Academic Studies Press, 2012, 167–186.

Wendland, Anna Veronika. *Die Russophilen in Galizien: Ukrainische Konservative zwischen Österreich und Rußland, 1848–1915*. Vienna: Verlag der Österreichischen Akademie der Wissenschaften, 2001.

Wielgus, Krzysztof. "Lotniska Twierdzy Przemyśl." In Waldemar Brzoskwinia, ed., *Fortyfikacja austriacka—Twierdza Przemyśl. Materiały z konferencji naukowej Towarzystwa Przyjaciół Fortyfikacji Przemyśl, 30 IX–3 X 1999 roku. Część pierwsza*. Warsaw: Towarzystwo Przyjaciół Fortyfikacji, 1999, 111–150.

Wierzbieniec, Wacław. *Społeczność żydowska Przemyśla w latach 1918–1939*. Rzeszów, Poland: Wydawnictwo Wyższej Szkoły Pedagogicznej w Rzeszowie, 1996.

————. "Żydzi w Przemyślu w okresie I wojny światowej." In Hanna Węgrzynek, ed., *Żydzi i Polacy w okresie walk o niepodległość, 1914–1920: Materiały z sesji towarzyszącej wystawie "Żyd, Polak, legionista, 1914–1920" w Muzeum Historii Żydów Polskich POLIN.* Warsaw: Muzeum Historii Żydów Polskich POLIN, 2015, 77–88.

Wildman, Allan K. *The End of the Russian Imperial Army.* Vol. 1, *The Old Army and the Soldiers' Revolt (March–April 1917).* Princeton, NJ: Princeton University Press, 1980.

Wingfield, Nancy M. *The World of Prostitution in Late Imperial Austria.* Oxford: Oxford University Press, 2017.

Wohl, Robert, *The Generation of 1914.* Cambridge, MA: Harvard University Press, 1979.

Wolff, Larry. *The Idea of Galicia: History and Fantasy in Habsburg Political Culture.* Stanford, CA: Stanford University Press, 2010.

Wurzer, Georg. *Die Kriegsgefangenen der Mittelmächte in Russland im Ersten Weltkrieg.* Göttingen, Germany: V&R Unipress, 2005.

Zając, Tomasz. "Fall Barbarossa 22 czerwca 1941 roku—Walki na terenie 08. Przemyskiego Rejonu Umocnionego." *Rocznik Przemyski* 51 (2015): 127–158.

Zsuppán, F. Tibor. "The Hungarian Political Scene." In Mark Cornwall, ed., *The Last Years of Austria-Hungary: A Multi-National Experiment in Early Twentieth-Century Europe,* revised and expanded ed. Exeter: University of Exeter Press, 2002, 97–118.

UNPUBLISHED DISSERTATIONS

Dunagan, Curt. "The Lost World of Przemyśl: Interethnic Dynamics in a Galician Center, 1868 to 1921." PhD thesis, Brandeis University, 2009.

Dzugan, Franziska. "Chamäleons im Blätterwald: Die Wurzeln der ÖVP-ParteijouralistInnen in Austrofaschismus, Nationalsozialismus, Demokratie und Widerstand. Eine kollektivbiographische Analyse an den Beispielen 'Wiener Tageszeitung' und 'Linzer Volksblatt' 1945 bzw. 1947 bis 1955." PhD thesis, University of Vienna, 2011.

Fahey, John E. "Bulwark of Empire: Imperial and Local Government in Przemyśl, Galicia (1867–1939)." PhD thesis, Purdue University, 2017.

Hecht, Rudolf. "Fragen zur Heeresergänzung der gesamten bewaffneten Macht Österreich-Ungarns während des Ersten Weltkrieges." PhD thesis, University of Vienna, 1969.

Jeřábek, Rudolf. "Die Brussilowoffensive 1916: Ein Wendepunkt der Koalitionskriegführung der Mittelmächte," 2 vols. PhD thesis, University of Vienna, 1982.

Mentzel, Walter. "Kriegsflüchtlinge in Cisleithanien im Ersten Weltkrieg." PhD thesis, University of Vienna, 1997.

Suchorzebska, Ewelina. "Zur Geschichte der polnischen Militärsprache in der Habsburgermonarchie." Diplomarbeit, University of Vienna, 2009.

ILLUSTRATION CREDITS

INSERT ILLUSTRATIONS

1. Postcard, author's collection.
2. Postcard, author's collection.
3. Postcard, author's collection.
4. Photograph, Muzeum Narodowe Ziemi Przemyskiej.
5. Postcard, author's collection.
6. Postcard, author's collection.
7. Photograph, Kriegsarchiv Vienna: BS IWK Fronten Galizien: 7502.
8. Postcard, Marek Król collection.
9. Vojenský ústřední archive—Vojenský historický archiv Praha: 24 632 popravy.
10. Photograph, Kriegsarchiv Vienna: BS IWK Fronten Galizien: 7510.
11. Postcard, author's collection.
12. Postcard, author's collection.
13. Postcard, author's collection.
14. Postcard, author's collection.
15. Illustration by Theo Matejko in A. Hemberger, *Der europäische Krieg und der Weltkrieg: Historische Darstellung der Kriegsereignisse von 1914/15*, vol. 1 (Vienna: A. Hartleben, 1915), 501.
16. Postcard, author's collection.
17. Postcard, author's collection.
18. Photograph, Kriegsarchiv Vienna: BS IWK Fronten Galizien: 7481.
19. Postcard, author's collection.
20. Photograph, Kriegsarchiv Vienna: BS IWK Fronten Galizien: 7717.
21. Photograph, Kriegsarchiv Vienna: BS IWK Fronten Galizien: 7719.
22. Photograph, Kriegsarchiv Vienna: BS IWK Fronten Galizien: 7398.
23. Photograph, Kriegsarchiv Vienna: BS IWK Fronten Galizien: 7712.

24. Photograph in H. Heiden, *Bollwerk am San: Schicksal der Festung Przemysl* (Oldenburg i.O.: Gerhard Stalling, 1940), insert after p. 208.
25. Postcard, author's collection.
26. Postcard, author's collection.
27. Photograph from the Russian Propaganda Album *Przemyśl*, published in the spring or summer of 1915.
28. Photograph, Muzeum Narodowe Ziemi Przemyskiej.
29. Photograph from the Russian magazine *Letopis voiny*, no. 41 (May 30 [June 12], 1915): 650.
30. Postcard, author's collection.

TEXT ILLUSTRATIONS

63 Copyright Tomasz Idzikowski.
64 Copyright Tomasz Idzikowski.
100 Original held by Muzeum Narodowe Ziemi Przemyskiej. Online at Podkarpacka Biblioteka Cyfrowa (Podkarpacka Digital Library), www.pbc.rzeszow.pl/dlibra/show-content/publication/edition/11060 ?id=11060.
109 Copyright Tomasz Idzikowski.
114 Copyright Tomasz Idzikowski.
161 Original held by Muzeum Narodowe Ziemi Przemyskiej. Online at Podkarpacka Biblioteka Cyfrowa (Podkarpacka Digital Library), www.pbc.rzeszow.pl/dlibra/show-content/publication/edition/11063 ?id=11063.
187 Original held by Muzeum Narodowe Ziemi Przemyskiej. Online at Podkarpacka Biblioteka Cyfrowa (Podkarpacka Digital Library), www.pbc.rzeszow.pl/dlibra/show-content/publication/edition/11063 ?id=11063.
257 Archiwum Państwowe w Przemyślu: 397 (Afisze, plakaty i druki ulotni): 501.

MAPS

1. Cartography and copyright: Penguin Books.
2. Cartography and copyright: Penguin Books.
3. Cartography and copyright: Penguin Books.
4. Cartography: Neil Gower. Copyright: Penguin Books.

INDEX

Credit: Kevin Moran

Alexander Watson is professor of history at Goldsmiths, University of London. He is the author of *Ring of Steel: Germany and Austria-Hungary in World War I*, which won the Wolfson History Prize and the Guggenheim-Lehrman Prize in Military History, and *Enduring the Great War*, winner of the Fraenkel Prize.